The Quadrangle Series in
RUSSIAN HISTORY

Alfred J. Rieber, GENERAL EDITOR

THE FORMATION

OF THE

GREAT
RUSSIAN
STATE

THE FORMATION
OF THE
GREAT
RUSSIAN
STATE

A Study of Russian History in the
Thirteenth to Fifteenth Centuries

BY

A. E. Presniakov

TRANSLATED FROM THE RUSSIAN BY
A. E. Moorhouse

INTRODUCTION BY
Alfred J. Rieber

CHICAGO
QUADRANGLE BOOKS

The Quadrangle Series in RUSSIAN HISTORY
Alfred J. Rieber, GENERAL EDITOR

Library of Congress Catalog Card Number: 75-78314

Designed by Vincent Torre

General Introduction to the Series

This series has been undertaken in the conviction that translations of the great works of Russian history written in the late nineteenth and early twentieth centuries can still perform a valuable and unique service for those laymen, students, and scholars who seek to broaden their understanding of Russia's past. From the beginning of the last century to the 1920's, Russian historians occupied a prominent place in the intellectual life of their country. Although they never achieved the international fame of their literary compatriots, their best work easily stood comparison with the leading Continental scholars of their day. But due to a widespread unfamiliarity with the Russian language and a lack of good translations, only a very limited audience read them outside Russia. Consequently, their reputation suffered to the point where they were slighted even in the most thorough surveys of European historiography. Yet, ironically, their work retains much of its original importance.

Severe handicaps have prevented their successors both within the Soviet Union and abroad from matching their achievements. Stalin almost wrecked the historical profession. Even after Stalinism was publicly condemned, a single interpretive scheme, though increasingly flexible, continued to monopolize the writing of history in the U.S.S.R. Meanwhile, in the English-speaking world since the Second World War, scholarly monographs and surveys of Russian history have literally poured forth. But, not surprisingly, many of these studies were aimed largely at uncovering the antecedents of Soviet power, and the natural fascination with the revolutionary movement resulted in less attention toward other aspects of Russian history. Until very recently the impossibility of carrying on sustained research in the great Russian archival collections has further hampered foreign scholars. For these reasons, many of the classics of Russian history remain to this day, despite corrections of detail and emphasis, the standard interpretations of their subjects.

The purpose of this series is to present in English, either for the first time or in modern translation, a representative sampling of the most significant of these works. An introductory essay to each volume seeks to evaluate the contribution of the historian. When completed, the series will offer not only some of the best examples of Russian historical writing, but also a broad survey of Russian historiography over the past century.

This volume is an unabridged translation of A. E. Presniakov's *Obrazovanie velikorusskogo gosudarstva*, originally published in Petrograd in 1918. The extensive footnotes in the original have been omitted due to considerations of cost and space. The translator has supplied a map, genealogical table, and explanatory notes.

Note on Transliteration

The question of transliterating Russian proper names has never been resolved in a way to suit everyone's taste. In order to standardize spelling in the translations in this series, I have adopted, sometimes to the despair of the translator, a uniform system based upon the Library of Congress model. The modifications include the use of a single *i* at the end of given names (Vasili) and a *y* at the end of family names (Kliuchevsky). By and large I have retained the Russian forms of given names (Vasili instead of Basil), but have given English equivalents to the less familiar ones, such as Metropolitan Job (instead of Iov).

Common usage and the absence of exact equivalents in English have also determined the choice of Russian terms such as *Zemsky Sobor* (Assembly of the Land) instead of translating them wherever they occur. An attempt has been made to keep these to a minimum, even at the cost of employing rather unsatisfactory translations, such as "gentry" for *dvoriane*.

The system used by W. E. D. Allen in *The Ukraine* has been borrowed for Ukrainian and Russo-Lithuanian (e.g., Orthodox as opposed to Roman Catholic) names in order to distinguish them from Great Russian and Polish.

A.J.R.

Contents

Princes of Kiev - Chernigov

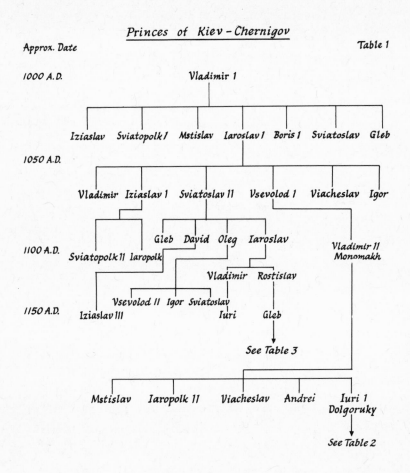

1000 A.D.   Vladimir 1

Iziaslav   Sviatopolk 1   Mstislav   Iaroslav 1   Boris 1   Sviatoslav   Gleb

1050 A.D.

Vladimir   Iziaslav 1   Sviatoslav 11   Vsevolod 1   Viacheslav   Igor

Gleb   David   Oleg   Iaroslav

1100 A.D.   Sviatopolk 11 Iaropolk   Vladimir 11
                          Vladimir   Rostislav   Monomakh

Vsevolod 11 Igor Sviatoslav

1150 A.D.   Iziaslav 111   Iuri   Gleb

See Table 3

Mstislav   Iaropolk 11   Viacheslav   Andrei   Iuri 1
                                            Dolgoruky

See Table 2

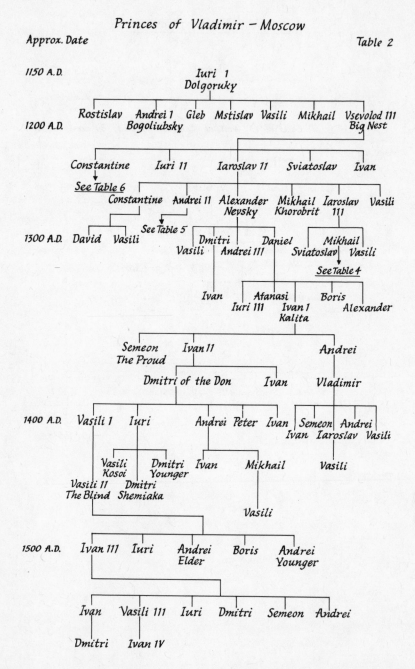

Princes of Vladimir – Moscow

Approx. Date

Table 2

Princes of Riazan

Table 3

Approx. Date

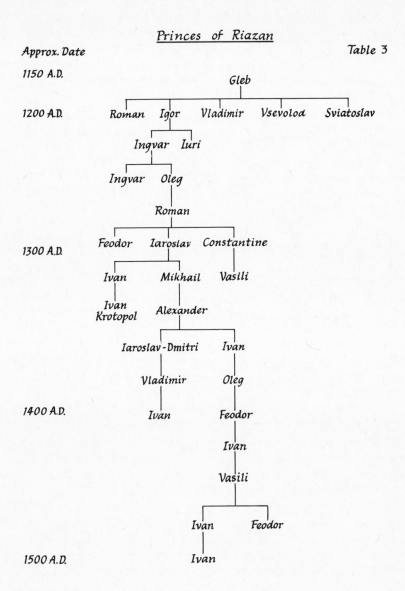

1150 A.D.

Gleb

1200 A.D.

Roman   Igor   Vladimir   Vsevolod   Sviatoslav

Ingvar   Iuri

Ingvar   Oleg

Roman

Feodor   Iaroslav   Constantine

1300 A.D.

Ivan   Mikhail   Vasili

Ivan
Krotopol   Alexander

Iaroslav - Dmitri   Ivan

Vladimir   Oleg

1400 A.D.

Ivan   Feodor

Ivan

Vasili

Ivan   Feodor

1500 A.D.

Ivan

Princes of Tver

Approx. Date

Table 4

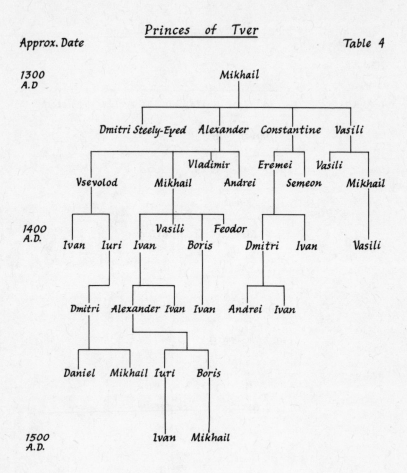

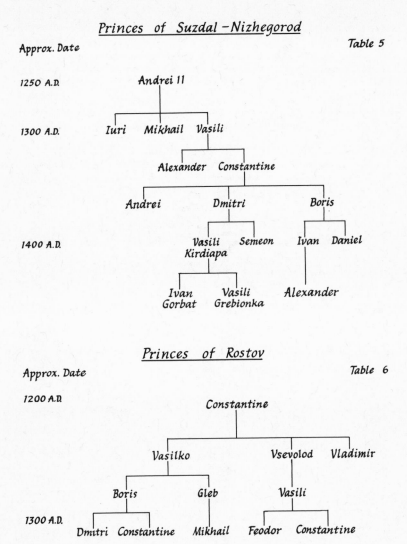

Princes of Suzdal − Nizhegorod

Approx. Date   Table 5

1250 A.D.   Andrei 11

1300 A.D.   Iuri   Mikhail   Vasili

                    Alexander   Constantine

         Andrei   Dmitri   Boris

1400 A.D.   Vasili   Semeon   Ivan   Daniel
                 Kirdiapa

            Ivan   Vasili   Alexander
            Gorbat   Grebionka

Princes of Rostov

Approx. Date   Table 6

1200 A.D.   Constantine

              Vasilko   Vsevolod   Vladimir

         Boris   Gleb   Vasili

1300 A.D.
      Dmitri Constantine   Mikhail   Feodor   Constantine

Central Russia

In The 13th – 15th Centuries

0   50   100   200

Miles

barbara long

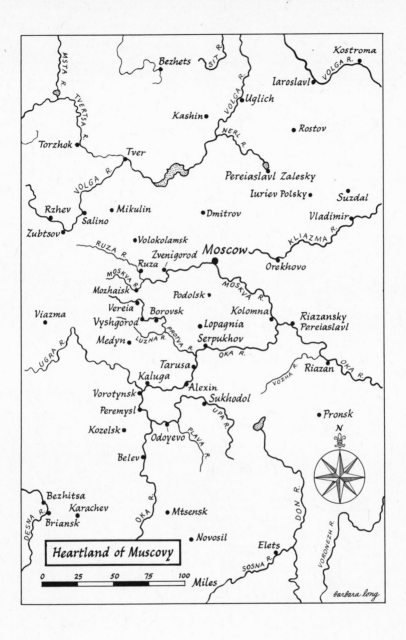

Heartland of Muscovy

Bezhets

Kostroma

VOLGA R.

Iaroslavl

Uglich

MSTA R.

STA R.

VOLGA R.

Kashin

NERL R.

Rostov

TVERTSA R.

Torzhok

Tver

Pereiaslavl Zalesky

Iuriev Polsky

Suzdal

VOLGA R.

Rzhev

Mikulin

Dmitrov

Vladimir

Salino

KLIAZMA R.

Zubtsov

Volokolamsk

Moscow

RUZA R.

Zvenigorod

Ruza

Orekhovo

MOSKVA R.

MOSKVA R.

Mozhaisk

Podolsk

Viazma

Vereia

Borovsk

Kolomna

Vyshgorod

Lopagnia

Riazansky
Pereiaslavl

UGRA R.

Medyn

LUZNA R.

PROVA R.

Serpukhov

OKA R.

Tarusa

VOZHA R.

Riazan

OKA R.

Kaluga

Alexin

Vorotynsk

Sukhodol

UPA R.

Pronsk

Peremysl

PLAVA R.

N

Kozelsk

Odoyevo

Belev

Bezhitsa

Karachev

Briansk

OKA R.

Mtsensk

DON R.

DESNA R.

Novosil

Elets

VORONEZH R.

SOSNA R.

Heartland of Muscovy

0   25   50   75   100   Miles

barbara long

Editor's Introduction

The life and works of Aleksandr Evgenevich Presniakov span the great divide of modern Russian historiography and reveal another aspect of the basic continuity underlying Russian social and intellectual history. Born in 1870 and already a well-established teacher and scholar before 1917, Presniakov continued to lecture during the turmoil of revolution, actively supported the Bolsheviks, and died in 1929 a highly respected and much-honored figure. His transitional role was symbolized by the publication in 1918 of his most important work, *The Formation of the Great Russian State*. A brilliant challenge to previously accepted interpretations of the rise of Moscow, it also represented a synthesis of the most exciting scholarship of the times. The skill with which Presniakov handled an extraordinary range of sources continues to command respect among historians who do not always share the same ideological assumptions. Presniakov's provocative and controversial conclusions still echo strongly in the work of specialists and generalists writing on the origins of the Muscovite state. The lasting influence of his work in the Soviet Union seems all the more remarkable because Presniakov never embraced Marxism-Leninism.

Like the "fellow-travelers" in literature, the tsarist officers in the Red Army, and the "bourgeois technicians" in industry, Presniakov joined that element of the prerevolutionary elite who accepted the Soviet regime on their own terms, helped stabilize it, and trained a new generation which then unceremoniously swept them aside. Within this element, mercenaries and opportunists were plentiful, but they offer little of interest to the historian.

Presniakov was not one of them. Rather he stood with those who came to regard the Revolution as the product of certain cultural and historical forces with deep roots in Russian history. The more sophisticated among them readily detected, in the wake of vast social changes, the great potential for both good and evil. Might they not tip the balance by throwing their weight onto the scales?

Traces of the intellectual process which led Presniakov to answer in the affirmative lie scattered throughout his early career. But he left behind so little evidence of his personal life that it is necessary in this case to adopt his own dictum as a guide: "The biography of a scholar is contained in his work." Having completed his secondary schooling in (Tiflis) Tbilisi, where his father, a transportation engineer, was stationed, he enrolled in the historical-philological faculty of St. Petersburg University. His association with this distinguished institution, which continued uninterruptedly to the end of his life, was the dominant influence in his intellectual development. While working for his advanced degrees, he began a teaching career which brought him at one time or another into close contact with every level in the Russian educational system from schools and gymnasia to the Pedagogical Institute and the University itself, where in 1907 he became a *privat-dotsent* (a lecturer receiving a small salary supplemented by students' fees). Whether by accident or design, his varied experience as a classroom teacher kindled an interest in mass education which served him well during the first decade of Soviet rule. On one occasion he admitted that his careful preparation of courses was partially responsible for his slow rate of publication in these early years.[1] But far from regretting the time spent in class, he attributed much of his success as a scholar to the high standards of historical accuracy demanded by his students.[2]

Presniakov also benefited from a long tradition, still very much alive in Leningrad, which discourages a sharp distinction between the activist historian-writer and the passive collector-archivist.

1. S. N. Valk, "Istoricheskaia nauka v Leningradskom universitete za 125 let," *Trudy iubileiskoi nauchnoi sessii, seksiia istoricheskikh nauk* (Leningrad, 1948), pp. 58–59, note 2.
2. A. E. Presniakov, "Rech pered zashchitoi dissertatsii pod zaglaviem 'Obrazovanie velikorusskogo gosudarstva,' " appendix, *Obrazovanie velikorusskogo gosudarstva* (Petrograd, 1920, 2nd ed.), p. 7.

Because of the close ties between Russian medieval history and archaeology, Presniakov found it natural to participate in the work of the Archaeographical Commission, where he helped to collect, edit, and publish source materials on the history of early Russia. Fluent in many Slavic languages, he was also widely read in Latin, Greek, French, and German, with a smattering of Swedish and English. Despite his heavy professional duties, Presniakov demonstrated a remarkable grasp of the latest developments in science, literature, politics, psychology, and philosophy. There were very few Russian academic figures, to say nothing of medievalists, who had read and absorbed Marx, Lenin, Martov, Trotsky, and Rosa Luxemburg.[3] In addition to being well informed, he possessed rare insight into the long-term significance of social movements that were just rising to the surface in his own day. For example, he regarded Russian Social Democracy as more than a small sect of extremists. A sharp mind and a gentle nature endeared him to his colleagues and students alike.[4]

The relationship between Presniakov's life and work is not always clear, and gaps in his biography have given rise to some confusing speculation. For example, in an appraisal written in 1950, the Soviet academician L. V. Cherepnin was critical of Presniakov for having ignored the student movements in the 1880's and 1890's, aligned himself with elements of the conservative wing of the teaching faculty at St. Petersburg University, and accepted without a murmur the Stolypin "reaction."[5] Cherepnin does not support his view with direct evidence, and makes no effort to provide any proof from Presniakov's work. Thus it became something of a problem for him to explain

3. See Presniakov's analysis of their views on revolution in "Obzory perezhitogo," *Dela i Dni*, 1920, No. 1, pp. 348–352.

4. The details of Presniakov's biography are drawn largely from the brief death notice written by his former teacher, the distinguished historian and academician S. F. Platonov, *Izvestiia Akademii Nauk SSSR, Otdelenie Gumanitarnykh nauk*, 1930, pp. 83–86. Curiously, none of Presniakov's colleagues or students have written a reminiscence about him. The Presniakov archive in the Academy of Sciences contains 175 letters used by Valk, "Istoricheskaia nauka," and N. L. Rubinshtein, *Russkaia Istoriografiia* (Moscow, 1941). I have not seen this collection.

5. L.V. Cherepnin, "Ob istoricheskikh vzgliadakh A. E. Presniakova," *Istoricheskie Zapiski*, XXXIII, 1950, 206, 212. It was unfair of Cherepnin to attempt to tar the entire faculty of St. Petersburg with the brush of reaction, especially by giving a foreshortened and misleading account of the

Presniakov's subsequent attitude toward the Bolshevik Revolution and his highly successful career in the first decade of Soviet
rule. Since Cherepnin published his authoritative article on Presniakov, neither he nor any other Soviet scholar has tried to clear
up this apparent contradiction. Instead, Presniakov's contribution
to Soviet education has been glossed over.[6]

Before attempting to throw some light on this perplexing matter, it is important to set the record straight. Shortly after the
end of the Civil War, Presniakov defended in print the guiding
role of the Communist party in raising the cultural level of the
masses. In a forthright way he paid his respects to Marx as a
brilliant analyst of nineteenth-century revolutions and praised the
main leaders of Russian Social Democracy, especially Lenin, for
their keen understanding of modern revolutions.[7] While continuing to serve as professor at Leningrad University, Presniakov
assumed additional teaching and administrative responsibilities as
professor and later as dean of the Archaeographical Institute and
director of the institute of history in RANION (Russian Association
of Scientific Institutes for Research in the Social Sciences), Leningrad Section. He lectured at the Pedagogical Institute and contributed to such semi-popular historical series as "The Images of
Mankind," designed for use in the professional schools.

On the eve of his nomination as academician, *Izvestiia* singled
him out for praise in a long article. Although he had become "in
the eyes of the broadest range of Soviet society one of the most
outstanding scholars of our time," he also demonstrated his sense

---

Semevsky incident. But he wrote this in the wake of the "Leningrad
affair," when the cultural institutions of that city were under sharp attacks
for cosmopolitanism, especially by their Moscow rivals. For a strongly contrasting view of the faculty, see Valk, "Istoricheskiia nauka," a good
example of the kind of "city patriotism" that lay at the heart of the entire
dispute.

6. See *Sovietskaia Istoricheskaia Entsiklopediia*, XI, 534.

7. Presniakov, "Obzory," pp. 346–347. Cherepnin cites the article briefly
but omits Presniakov's comments on Marxists and gives insufficient biblio-
graphical information to identify and locate the journal in which it was
published. He admits that Presniakov tried sincerely to serve the Soviet
regime, but concludes that his bourgeois background prevented him from
doing so. In all fairness it should be noted that Cherepnin has written a
more recent and more generous evaluation of Presniakov the scholar in
his major work *Obrazovanie russkogo tsentralizovannogo gosudarstva v
XIV-XV vekakh* (Moscow, 1960), pp. 92–95.

of civic responsibility by having taken up a "heavy load of teaching even at the expense of his research." [8] Within a year Presniakov was dead of cancer. His prestige was still high at the time of his death, but his future reputation was uncertain in the light of mounting attacks by communist historians against their "fellow-traveling" colleagues. Presniakov has had few defenders since that time, but the influence of his ideas upon the generation of Soviet scholars he helped to train cannot be denied.

Although Presniakov's interest in mass education and his institutional loyalties suggest some reasons for his decision to remain in the Soviet Union, a deeper understanding of his motives must be sought in his historical method and philosophical outlook. If he could not accommodate the Revolution to his intellectual life, then he could not accept it at any level. But it is not a simple matter to discover the sources of his thinking about history. The author of numerous historiographical essays on other historians, Presniakov never made explicit his own views. Nevertheless, by drawing upon the total corpus of his work, including monographs, lectures, articles, and reviews, a substantial, if still incomplete, outline of them can be reconstructed.

Presniakov came of age in a decade of great intellectual ferment. During the 1890's in Russia, as well as in Western Europe, thinkers strove to reconcile the warring but discredited schools of positivism and German idealism. In the Russian setting the controversy gave rise to theories which had no precise equivalent in the West. Such was the case with giants like Lenin and Vladimir Solovyev, and with historians like Presniakov who were sensitive to the main currents of Western thought, yet preoccupied with the formative period of their own nation's history. For Presniakov, as for the others, the overriding problem ultimately became how to explain the relationship between the peculiar historical evolution of the Russian people and the general course of European civilization. But his first concern as a student was more practical and immediate: to set down the guidelines and limitations of the historian's craft.

Early in his career Presniakov recognized that "we [historians] do not have a satisfactory methodology, not even an established

8. *Izvestiia*, October 14, 1928, No. 240.

definition of historical science." [9] As Presniakov saw it, the confused situation was the result of a general loss of faith in previous philosophical systems upon which historians had traditionally drawn for their theory-building. Post-Kantian idealism had crumbled under the attack of the empiricists, but positivism had proved barren of any practical significance for historiography. Lacking a firm organizing principle, historians confronted a mass of accidentally surviving data which threatened to overwhelm them. Presniakov identified two distinct approaches to this problem. One sought to recreate the past "objectively" in all its bewildering variety, with an end to establishing the wholeness of "historical reality." Another attempted, through a comparative study of the past, to uncover similar phenomena in different societies which might serve as the basis for a sociology of historical causation. Presniakov rejected both schools as unscientific, the first because it depended in the final analysis upon intuition or artistic flair, and the second because it represented nothing more than an accumulation of empirical evidence held together by superficial similarities of form. Neither revealed the basic modes of human behavior which to him represented the true objective of scientific investigation. He further questioned the artificial distinction often drawn between history as an accumulation of raw data and sociology as a formulation of laws of causation. If the historian merely provided the facts for the sociologist to systematize, he remarked, then they did not represent different disciplines but two related aspects of the same discipline.[10]

A more fruitful approach to historical method, in Presniakov's view, might be fashioned out of the connection between social change and discoveries in psychology about the nature of human needs. Accepting the then prevailing views of psychologists, Presniakov regarded the substitution (or displacement) of the drive to "sense life" as the underlying motive for the external acts recorded by the historian. He further recognized that up to the mid-1890's psychological theory had been able simply to

9. A. E. Presniakov, "Novyi trud po teorii istoricheskoi nauki," *Zhurnal Ministerstva Narodnogo Prosveshcheniia* (hereafter ZhMNP), V. 297, pt. 2 (January 1895), 188. This was a review article of P. Lacombe, *De l'histoire considérée comme science* (Paris, 1894). The greatest care has been taken to separate Presniakov's views from those of Lacombe.

10. *Ibid.*, p. 194.

show, in his words, "general motives for action without providing a real basis for the causal explanation of all events." He regretted that the present state of theoretical work in psychology did not meet the needs of historians; only when psychologists succeeded in breaking down this yearning for a greater intensity of life into specific logical forms of consciousness could historians in turn work out their own scientific methodology. Until that time, however, it was possible to gain insights into human motivations by studying them at their lowest common denominator, the group. The interaction within a group of individuals seeking satisfaction of their personal needs created a new level of demands which could only be met by collective action in the form of institutions. Institutional change resulted, in turn, from increasingly higher levels of expectations. Thus, in Presniakov's mind, the study of institutional change was a history of the collective consciousness of a people.

How could the historian make certain that his descriptions and analyses of this secondary level of human experience would be accurate and balanced if the columns of the ground floor had not yet been firmly set in place? This was the question to which Presniakov found no reassuring answer in the prescriptions of the past. Out of this doubt he began to fashion his own rigorous empirical method without, however, ever renouncing the hope that a scientific underpinning would be elaborated at some future time. For the sources of his method he selected judiciously from a rich variety of intellectual currents in the lively atmosphere of St. Petersburg at the end of the nineteenth century. By enrolling in the university there, Presniakov never came under the direct influence of Kliuchevsky, whose magnetic personality inspired a generation of students at Moscow University to emulate him. By temperament, Presniakov was attracted to the contrasting style of the so-called St. Petersburg school—less artistic but more precise, solid rather than flamboyant, deeply rooted in an exhaustive analysis of sources. The tradition found its earliest expression in the work of Professor M. S. Kutorga, the first real Russian specialist on ancient Greece, who taught at St. Petersburg in the 1830's. His constant reminder that "where there is no criticism, there is no history" became something of a motto for the historical-philological faculty. As early as the 1850's, marked differ-

ences of emphasis divided professors at Moscow University, who
stressed general history of social significance, from their Petersburg colleagues, who defended monographic studies of detached
scholarship.[11] Over the next century the rivalry flared up from
time to time, and Presniakov contributed as much as anyone to
keeping it alive.

His first contact with the St. Petersburg style came in the class
of K. N. Bestuzhev-Riumin, the grand old man of the faculty.
Although a former student of Solovyev in Moscow, Bestuzhev-
Riumin turned his back on the master, shied away from generalizations and systems, and concentrated on amassing great quanti-
ties of factual material with which he filled his course in Russian
history. Presniakov recalled Bestuzhev-Riumin's reluctance to
raise the large questions in seminar and his insistence that students
be trained thoroughly in textual analysis.[12]

Under S. F. Platonov, Bestuzhev-Riumin's successor, and V. G.
Vasilevsky, the well-known Byzantinist, the trend gathered momentum. Platonov, who was to supervise Presniakov's advanced
work, began his authoritative studies of the Time of Troubles
with a critical investigation of early seventeenth-century manu-
scripts. It became a model for the study of such literary-political
sources as chronicles and legendary tales (*skazanie*). Vasilevsky,
for his part, emphasized the analytic method to the point that
even in his lectures he rejected the traditional survey course in
Medieval Europe in favor of a systematic explanation of the
texts upon which the standard interpretations were based. Consequently, the full cycle of his course took four years instead of
one as was customary, causing, incidentally, much annoyance on
the part of some of his colleagues.[13] By incorporating advances

11. Valk, "Istoricheskaia nauka," pp. 6–7, 12–13. In the sharp polemic between T. Granovsky and M. M. Stasulievich, the latter insisted that "science
is always science, and its character is not defined by any location," a sentiment which Presniakov clearly shared.

12. Presniakov also noted that Bestuzhev-Riumin once defined his historical ideal as an attempt to show "the wholeness and unity of popular life"
by revealing the connections between its various aspects, but then never
pursued this ideal in his work. A. E. Presniakov, "K. N. Bestuzhev-Riumin,"
Dela i Dni, 1922, No. 3, pp. 169, 170, 172. Later Presniakov made this ideal
his own.

13. I. M. Grevs, "Vasili Grigorevich Vasilevsky, kak uchitel nauki;
nabrosok vospominanii i materialy dlia kharakteristiki," ZhMNP, V. 324,
pt. 5 (August 1899), p. 41.

in numismatics, diplomatics, philology, and archaeology into their research methods, historians at the end of the nineteenth century broadened the material base of their inquiry and shifted their attention more and more to identifying, verifying, and classifying concrete data. From Presniakov's own intellectual development it becomes clear that the implications of these techniques for larger interpretive problems were only gradually perceived.

In his student thesis on the origin and composition of the *Tsarstvennaia Kniga*, which won a gold medal and was published in 1893, Presniakov showed signs of having moved beyond a formal exercise in textual analysis by raising questions about the original political purpose of the documents. Another article, "The Moscow Historical Encyclopedia of the Sixteenth Century," provided valuable insights into the ideological motives of the anonymous compiler.[14] It was not, however, until 1900–1901, when A. A. Shakhmatov published the first of his brilliant philological-historical studies of the Russian chronicles, that Presniakov found the methodological master key to the rich source material which up to that time had resisted persistent attempts by historians to clarify often obscure language, unravel the intricate lines of inter-princely relations, and trace accurately the political unification of Great Russia. To Presniakov, Shakhmatov represented the third and most advanced stage in the study of the chronicles begun by A. L. Schlötzer and continued by Bestuzhev-Riumin. By placing a study of the chronicles against the historical background of the times in which they were compiled, and then subjecting them to a minute philological study in order to uncover the internal development of the text, Shakhmatov showed that each succeeding redaction of the chronicles was a reworking of a previous compilation, often with additions, sometimes with excerpts from several other compilations. A careful and skilled researcher could determine which were the original sections and thereby disclose in pure form a contemporary source of much earlier date than any of the surviving copies. Although the results were often speculative and questionable, as Shakhmatov was the first to admit, the importance of his discoveries for the history of early Russia can hardly be exaggerated.

14. *Izvestiia otdeleniia russkogo iazyka i slovestnosti*, V (1900), No. 3.

For Presniakov the method yielded a major conclusion for his subsequent work; "the existence of all-Russian metropolitan collections of chronicles following one another in succession from the first decade of the fourteenth century to the final compilation in 1423 of the Vladimirsky Polikhron . . ." testified to "a general Russian interest in the unity of the Russian land at a time when this idea was only beginning to emerge in the political dreams of the Moscow rulers." [15]

Turning from philology to law, Presniakov found a third source of inspiration in V. I. Sergeevich, another towering figure at St. Petersburg University, who first set Russian legal history upon a firm theoretical foundation and enthroned a study of law as the dominant element in early Russian history. What could be more natural than for his student to apply the new critical methods acquired from others to the very subject matter which Sergeevich argued must occupy a central place in the historical process? In the curious fashion by which scholars pay a debt to their masters, Presniakov refuted Sergeevich's first important work, *Veche and Prince* (1867), in his master's thesis, *Princely Law in Ancient Russia* (1909). Rejecting Sergeevich's idea that the princely administration in Kievan Rus was "an unstable superstructure" over the communal form of the people's life, Presniakov went on to demolish the interpretation of dual power. A thorough analysis of sources on the *veche* in the towns showed that no evidence existed (with the possible exception of Novgorod and Pskov) to support the tradition that ancient Russian cities could be described as self-governing communes. The prince's control of justice and administration rested upon complex familial and social relationships. Presniakov denied that the princely family accepted the seniority principle as a formal and fixed method of organizing its social life. Rather, he interpreted the principle as nothing more than a survival of the ancient family-kinship tradition. Just as there had been no firm order of inheritance by seniority, so there was no clear definition of the political or sovereign rights of seniority. The actual strength of

---

15. A. E. Presniakov "A. A. Shakhmatov v izuchenii russkikh letopisei," *Izvestiia otdeleniia russkogo iazyka i slovesnosti, Rossisiskaia Akademiia Nauk,* XXV (1920), 167–169.

the prince did not derive so much from his governing powers as from the social groups supporting him.[16]

As his master's thesis had grown organically from his previous studies of sources, so *Princely Law in Ancient Russia* served as the springboard to the most significant work of Presniakov's life. Thoroughly trained in history, law, and philology, and equipped with the most sophisticated research methods of his time, Presniakov now undertook the preparation of his doctor's dissertation, which in Russia was a major study written in a scholar's mature years. Historical syntheses are not spun off by youthful virtuosos. Published when Presniakov was forty-eight, *The Formation of the Great Russian State* remains to date the single most impressive and original contribution to an understanding of the long and complex process that led to the creation of the Muscovite autocracy. The result of twenty-five years of accumulated research, it challenged the dominant school in Russian historiography founded by S. M. Solovyev. Perhaps the last Russian doctoral dissertation whose methodology arose generically from historical sources, this work capped the end of a great tradition. Yet in both method and interpretation it served as a model for young historians in the transitional phase of the Soviet regime. In the face of attempts by Marxist vulgarizers, such as M. N. Pokrovsky, to scrap all previous historical training, Presniakov's work played an important role in conserving and transmitting the best in prerevolutionary historiography to the new generation.

In the defense of his dissertation Presniakov caught some of the larger significance of the study. He freely admitted, to be sure, his own intellectual debts, first to the master of them all: "following Solovyev all subsequent historical writing derived from him and returned to him." But he regarded as "unacceptable" Solovyev's attitude toward historical sources. Careful study of his early works convinced Presniakov that Solovyev's main purpose had been to uncover a constructive principle upon which to build a theory of historical process leading from a clan organization to a centralized state. Once the scaffolding had been

16. "Rech pered disputom pri zashchite magisterskoi dissertatsii 'Kniazhnoe pravo v drevnei Rusi,' 19 aprelia 1909," appendix 1, A. E. Presniakov, *Lektsii po russkoi istorii*, "Kievskaia Rus," I, 241–245.

erected, Solovyev "subjugated" to his design the great mass of
evidence he had marshaled in his monumental *History of Russia
from the Earliest Times*. In comparison with rival schools of
interpretation, such as the Slavophil "*obshchina* theory," F. I.
Leontovich's principle of association, or the contractual scheme
of B. N. Chicherin and Sergeevich, Solovyev's *History* substi-
tuted another philosophical doctrine. It was buttressed, to be
sure, with an unprecedented mass of detail, but it offered no significant innovation in methodology. As a result, Presniakov concluded, the source material available for a study of early Russian
history "has not been examined thoroughly and fully" in such a
way as to affect the traditional outlook. Even Kliuchevsky,
Solovyev's most distinguished student, while attempting to transform the system, could not break free of it. He permitted his
sense of aesthetic form to corrupt his handling of sources.[17]

As an alternative point of departure, Presniakov argued, "scientific realism demands that questions be posed which reflect the
peculiarities of the material being studied . . ." The sources themselves should become for the historian the subject rather than a
reservoir of illustrative examples, no matter what dramatic function they might fulfill. To reach this conclusion Presniakov con-
ceded that he had fought hard to resist "the undeniable charm
of Kliuchevsky." By attributing his victory to "the living communion with the younger generation of historians," Presniakov
paid tribute to the intensely critical and skeptical attitudes widely
prevalent among university students in the first two decades of
the twentieth century.

The logical outcome of his reasoning would have been a study
devoted simply to the collections of chronicles, but Presniakov
insisted that historians, in contrast to philologists, were bound to
place the sources in a wider context where additional evidence
drawn from treaties, church records, deeds, and wills could be
used to verify and enrich the historical narrative. Taken together
these sources yielded a "more complex texture of historical life,"
which forced a reevaluation of previous interpretations sketched
in much broader strokes.[18] For example, Presniakov's painstaking

17. A. E. Presniakov, "Rech pered zashchitoi dissertatsii . . . , appendix,
Obrazovanie, pp. 3–6.
18. *Ibid.*, pp. 7–8.

reconstruction of the *udel-votchina* appanage system completely undermined Kliuchevsky's elegant theory of colonization in the twelfth and thirteenth centuries. As Presniakov showed, the udel-votchina developed later than this, and colonization had its roots in an earlier period. So too, in contrast to Chicherin's static interpretation, Presniakov demonstrated how the main features of the udel-votchina changed in response to different socio-political conditions. What it retained as its essential characteristic, Presniakov maintained against Kliuchevsky's views, was the quality of family property as opposed to individual ownership. Thus it resembled more the peasant than the boyar form of landholding. Consequently, the political struggle in northeast Russia was not resolved by gathering lands but by gathering power, that is by enhancing the authority of the grand prince over the military forces, fiscal resources, and disposition of lands within the common patrimony. The break-up of the larger udel-votchina into ever smaller parcels did not precede the growth of the Muscovite state, as Kliuchevsky stated. Instead, the two closely related processes ran parallel to one another with the grand princely power draining strength from the steadily weakening minor princes. Although this dual process developed organically within society, the driving force behind it came from the outside. Presniakov pointed out how the sharp contradiction between the need for national unity against external enemies and the fragile socio-political structure was finally resolved by a violent civil war from which a strong, new form of government emerged— the hereditary Moscow autocracy.

Based on an unprecedented mastery of sources, these stimulating and original conclusions could not be dismissed lightly. But Presniakov's reputation rests mainly upon his ability to sift the sources with great sensitivity for nuances of meaning, and to reconstruct the sequences and interrelationships of political events without resort to the artificial linkages and speculative flights that often characterized both his predecessors and his successors. He came as close to the purely inductive method as the nature of his materials would allow.

Presniakov did not pretend, to be sure, that a study of history was possible without some sociological and historical assumptions. Nor did he deny that his work was held together by some-

thing more than the relation of one event to the next.[19] Because
he avoided stating those assumptions, however, the full range
and power of his scheme has remained largely unappreciated.
When *The Formation of the Great Russian State* is placed in the
more general context of his teaching and writing, it becomes
clear that Presniakov undertook an ambitious reinterpretation of
the origin and nature of the Russian nationality, defined in the
broadest way to include the three major groups—Great Russian,
Ukrainian, and Belorussian. For all the importance Presniakov attributed to the evolution of grand princely power, he fully recognized that its ultimate success depended upon the social forces
at its disposal. In the grand princely power he discovered the
conscious organizing element of society. Its institutional behavior
was susceptible of empirical analysis. But underlying this level
of experience he perceived deeper currents in the form of compelling but unorganized national aspirations.

In a great trio of works, *Kievan Rus, West Russia and the
Lithuanian State,* and *The Formation of the Great Russian State,*
Presniakov orchestrated the subtle and dynamic relationships between the growth of power and national consciousness into a
general synthesis of the historical development of the Russian
people, a process which he believed "had not yet been completed" in the early twentieth century. Setting aside the question
of the original unity of the Slavs and beginning with Kievan Rus,
Presniakov's basic assumptions become clear: "the state emerged
earlier than the people who inhabited its territory made themselves into a nation." In fact, the level of national consciousness
is directly proportional to the degree of political organization and
independence. On the other hand, nationality itself is a "cultural-
psychological" phenomenon, the real bearer of which is not the
people but "the individual personality." [20] Thus the unconscious,
subjective feelings for the "complex of factors" which create
nationality are heightened and focused by the conscious, objective power of the state.

The institutional change leading from the early elective organization of the veche to the emergence of the monarchical principle in the form of the prince grew out of the increasingly

19. *Ibid.,* pp. 5, 9.
20. Presniakov, *Lektsii,* I, 7–9.

complex functions of government (defense of territory against aggression from the steppe nomads, and creation of law flexible enough to regulate diversified socio-economic conditions). Princely power became "the necessary organ of ancient government for the satisfaction of innate social needs of the population —external defense and domestic order." [21] Rejecting the notion that inheritance by the eldest relative was the chief institutional obstacle to unification, Presniakov explained the failure of Kiev to unite the country in terms of the power struggle between rival princes (the sons and grandsons of Iaroslav the Wise) who believed they all had a stake in the common heritage. Since no one prince was able to secure firm control over all Rus, each one fought to secure at least a part of the patrimony where he carried out his administrative-judicial functions as sovereign ruler.

With the decline of Kiev as a political and commercial center in the twelfth century, the princes shifted to the West and North their efforts to build a power base around which to unify the country. They acknowledged the difficulty of defending Kiev by denying its traditional role as the political center. What emerges clearly from Presniakov's account is the outline of an all-Russian interpretation of the Kievan period. He sought to refute Ukrainian national historians, such as M. S. Hrushevsky, and champions of the Great Russian school, such as P. N. Miliukov, as well as the older scheme of Solovyev-Kliuchevsky. While the traditional view depicted a linear development of Russian unity in the equation Kiev-Vladimir-Moscow, the newer schools emphasized the discontinuities between Kiev and Muscovy. For Hrushevsky, Kievan history was the prologue to Ukrainian history, which gave his nation the longest political pedigree of all the Eastern Slavs. In Miliukov's eyes, Northwest Russia developed into a great state independently of all other regions, which he relegated to the position of underdeveloped areas, gradually absorbed by Muscovy. In the overheated atmosphere that followed the revolution of 1905, the controversy between these two interpretations resounded with ominous political overtones. When the revolution of March 1917 thrust Hrushevsky and Miliukov into political leadership in the Ukrainian Rada and the Provisional Government respectively, they applied practical lessons drawn

21. *Ibid.,* p. 174.

from their historical theories in a clash over Ukrainian autonomy.

Although Presniakov stood well outside the arena of active politics, his views also carried strong political implications. In contrast to his colleagues, he perceived a dynamic relationship between the three distinct but interconnected political and cultural centers of the Eastern Slavs, destined to be united into an all-Russian state. In the south, he agreed with the Ukrainian historians, the Mongol invasion had not completely swept away the old culture. Despite heavy emigration to the north and west, Kiev retained its commercial character into the second half of the thirteenth century. Even though the southern towns of Kiev, Chernigov, and Pereiaslavl remained on the periphery of the expanding new centers of Russian political life, the old social structure resting on the boyars still held the reins of local power.[22] Thus when the area was absorbed into the Polish-Lithuanian state, its social and cultural identity was intact.

Meanwhile, to the southwest the principality of Galich-Volyn (Galicia-Volhynia) enjoyed a brief but brilliant period of political leadership, which, however, long obscured a more lasting and significant development in West Russia. At the height of Kievan power, West Russian princes, especially in Polotsk, cut their ties with Kiev and were drawn gradually into the commercial and political world of their Western neighbors. In fact, the initial rapid expansion of the Lithuanians under Mindovg in the thirteenth century was due in no small measure to powerful support by West Russian boyars. When Gedymin and his successors laid the foundations of the great Lithuanian state in the fourteenth century, the West Russian principalities became an organic part of the state. By contrast, when the old Kievan lands in the south were conquered in the course of the fourteenth century, they were ruled as "annexed lands," retaining their distinctive local, social, and legal institutions. Consequently, despite a common ethnic character, the particularist sentiment which lingered on in both areas rested on a broader social and political base in the south. Returning again to the theme of state power and national consciousness, Presniakov showed how the Lithuanian state, lacking ethnic and cultural homogeneity, failed

22. Presniakov *Lektsii*, II, chapter 2, "Western Russia and the Russo-Lithuanian State."

to build up the centralized institutions necessary to instill the population with true national consciousness.[23] In South and West Russia, the latent national feelings could be awakened only by a centralized state organized and led by other Russians.

In Northwest Russia, the fierce power struggle among the princes for political leadership symbolized by the grand princi-pality of Vladimir produced the standard bearer for a unification of all Russians. Out of the three cultural regions which emerged from the wreckage of Kievan Rus, the princes in the Northwest had one concrete advantage over their rivals in the South and West. Their greatest external enemy, the Tatars, never tried to incorporate the Russian domains into an alien culture. Yet by remaining a formidable obstacle to independence and a constant threat to security, the Tatars aroused the dormant feeling of common purpose among those social groups like the boyars and the clergy who stood to benefit most from national unity. Once the grand prince of Moscow gathered sufficient power to chal-lenge Tatar sovereignty over the Northwest, national conscious-ness, rising on a parallel curve, crystallized in the Muscovite state. It was then only a matter of time before Great Russia restored the unity of all Russians at a higher political level than ever before by winning over the allegiance of West Russia and the Ukraine from the ramshackle Polish-Lithuanian state.

The product of a profound historical imagination, this entire process was held together by a dialectical scheme of great orig-inality and subtlety. From the precarious unity of the Kievan state to dispersal into three cultural-linguistic groups during the appanage period and final reunification in a centralized national state, the historic destinies of all Russians were linked together by deep-seated psychological needs which could only be satis-fied in a national context. Presniakov's message for his own time was the equal claim of each of the three groups to a share in the past glories of the great states of Eastern Europe, and, by implication, to a significant role in the Russian empire. But this appreciation of the contribution by each was tempered by the historic necessity for a single political leadership over all of them. With extraordinary perception, Presniakov understood, when he set down these thoughts on the eve of revolution, that a Russian

23. *Ibid.*, II, 166.

nationality had not yet been formed. Thus side by side with Presniakov the rigorous empiricist stands Presniakov the romantic nationalist. The two figures do not conflict but blend into a harmonious unity. Many influences seem to have converged in order to produce this result. Hegelian overtones and Pan-Slavist visions appear to mingle. Yet there is something novel about the mix. One has the sense that in Presniakov's hands historical events determine their own organization. No philosophical scheme has been superimposed upon them, and they in turn do not produce one. There is process, movement, even a kind of progress in the sense that people seek constantly to reorganize themselves in ways best suited to fulfill their own aspirations. But Presniakov offers no elaborate patterns; he does not impose stages or make escatological pronouncements. To him the structure has no meaning outside the events which compose it.

It should now be clear why Presniakov was able to accept the Bolshevik Revolution as another step in the ongoing process of national unification without endorsing its philosophy. First of all, Presniakov believed profoundly in universal laws of human behavior rooted in logical categories of the human consciousness. Although psychologists had not yet defined these forms, historians could discover their external expression through the application of "scientific realism," based upon a precise analysis of sources, to the history of institutions. To Presniakov the inner dynamic of Russian history was expressed in the powerful drive toward national unity under the leadership of a centralized state which continued to respond to its growing needs. Following the persuasive logic of his own history, Presniakov saw the triumph of the Bolsheviks in the civil war as the sole guarantee that the age-old and "as yet incomplete" process of national unification would continue. With keen perception, Presniakov defined the peculiar characteristic of the Russian Revolution as the irresistible subjugation of "the elemental play of the revolutionary forces" by the "conscious party leadership." Echoing Leninist rhetoric he proclaimed, "The overcoming of 'spontaneity' is the basic task of the revolutionary epoch." [24] Here lies the answer to the apparent contradiction between Presniakov's conservative social stand before the Revolution and his subsequent

24. Presniakov, "Obzory perezhitogo," p. 346.

endorsement of the Soviet regime. Platonov was wrong to hint at opportunism, simply because Platonov chose the alternative of aloof semi-retirement.[25] Presniakov's "conversion" has all the more ring of sincerity because it is not based on ideological congruity with Marxism-Leninism. He escapes the curse of idolatry but lends the Bolshevik Revolution a sense of historical legitimacy. One can hardly expect him to have gone much beyond this. To have embraced Marxism would have meant abandoning the very line of reasoning that had led him to endorse the Soviet power.

Despite his real services to the historical profession, Soviet historians today dismiss Presniakov as a bourgeois survival in a socialist era. Even more objectionable is their effort to discredit him further by tossing his name into that ill-defined catchall for independent thinkers called "neo-Kantianism." All those who do not accept Marxism-Leninism are lumped together as ambivalent intellectuals caught in irreconcilable contradictions between positive knowledge of the natural world and intuitive knowledge of the human world. Despite these symptoms of "crisis" in a doomed social order which can never possess real understanding of itself, they oppose the scientific theory of historical materialism.

In fact, among Russian historians of the prerevolutionary decades there was a widespread conviction that scientific history was both possible and desirable. The Moscow school, inspired by Kliuchevsky and including such diverse figures as Miliukov and M. N. Pokrovsky, sought the answers in sociological regularities. Presniakov, as a representative of the St. Petersburg school, favored a psychological base. Too much has been made of the influence of German idealism in Russian intellectual history. The powerful currents of Enlightenment thought in early twentieth-century Russia have been overlooked. Nowhere have the results been more damaging than in historiography. Presniakov, for example, made clear what he thought of neo-Kantianism on a number of occasions when he reviewed the life and work of A. S. Lappo-Danilevsky.

Despite Presniakov's respect for the range and depth of his former teacher's learning, he regarded Lappo-Danilevsky's search for an ideal ethical basis of historical judgments as an "obsession

25. Platonov, *Izvestiia*, p. 85.

. . . imbued with an almost tragic character." [26] Presniakov found Lappo-Danilevsky's ambitious *Methodology of History* (1913) strongly influenced by the German neo-Kantian philosopher Heinrich Rickert and the Russian Populist N. K. Mikhailovsky, and deeply imbued with a "metaphysical, essentially religious orientation." [27] An aloof aristocrat, the most European of Russian historians in Presniakov's eyes, Lappo-Danilevsky was "a bearer of the old culture." Even his death was symbolic of his own theories, which linked the identity of the individual with the world spirit, for at the moment of his passing the entire civilized world he cherished was passing through its own mortal crisis. Despite the medical bulletin, Presniakov concluded, Lappo-Danilevsky fell victim to the tragedy of "the Cherry Orchard of old Russian life." [28]

To a very large degree, Presniakov's adjustment to the new Russian life came easily because he never embraced the dualism of neo-Kantians. More specifically, he rejected the notion that historical method rested in the final analysis upon the absolute value system of the researcher. So strong was his attachment to a scientific "theory of the conscious" underlying institutional change that Freud had no visible influence upon him. Indeed, by leaving open the question as to whether psychological drives derived from more fundamental material needs rooted in class consciousness, Presniakov avoided a direct clash with the early Marxist historians. More important for his subsequent reputation, his ideas on group consciousness and national unification could be incorporated into the revival of patriotism by Soviet historians in the 1930's and 1940's.[29] How else can one explain the

26. A. E. Presniakov, *A. S. Lappo-Danilevsky* (Petrograd, 1922), p. 46.
27. A. E. Presniakov, "A. S. Lappo-Danilevsky kak uchenyi i myslitel," *Russkii Istoricheskii Zhurnal,* 1920, No. 6, pp. 91, 92.
28. *Ibid.,* p. 96. The term "neo-Kantianism" has been much abused by Soviet philosophers and historians, who use it to mean any form of post-Hegelian idealism. It is used in this essay in the more precise meaning as defined, for example, in H. Stuart Hughes, *Consciousness and Society* (New York, 1958), pp. 190–191. I would further argue, however, that Presniakov does not fit even the Soviet definition.
29. This debt was never acknowledged and occasionally denied. For example, Cherepnin tried, albeit in a very puzzling way, to discount Presniakov's influence upon ideas currently held by Soviet historians on the relationship between Kievan Rus and its successors. He began by citing a passage from the authoritative work of B. D. Grekov, *Kievan Rus:* "The

decision to publish Presniakov's lecture notebooks dating back to 1907–1908 and 1915–1916 at the height of the patriotic campaign in Soviet Russia just before the Second World War? In his post-1920 writing, Presniakov expanded upon his earlier themes in order to demonstrate how the Revolution erupted out of an organic contradiction between state power and the mass of the people. In three brief studies of Alexander I, Nicholas I, and Alexander II, he sketched the main outlines of his thesis, but he lacked time to bring them together into a major work. As a result a number of his fertile ideas did not mature in Soviet historiography, although signs of his influence may be detected among Western historians.

Presniakov attributed the collapse of autocracy to the fact that the forms of state authority had become emptied of social content. The external façade of decorative order masked an absence of purpose and direction.[30] Having created an all-Russian empire by unifying the nation and defending it against external enemies, the state failed to meet new levels of social and psychological needs engendered by the very conditions of security it had created. Political power became the instrument of its self-perpetuation.[31] This "impotent autocracy," unable to root out the causes of social disorder by repression and unwilling to share

history of the Kievan state is not the history of the Ukraine, nor of Belorussia, nor Great Russia. It is the history of a state which enabled the Ukraine and Belorussia and Great Russia to mature and develop. Herein lies the enormous significance of this period in the life of our country." Cherepnin then came to the astounding conclusion that "Such an approach to the study of Kievan Rus was foreign to A. E. Presniakov." Cherepnin, "Ob istoricheskikh vzgliadakh," p. 212. (Cherepnin uses the 4th edition, 1944. The passage may be found on p. 10 of the 1953 edition and on p. 12 of the English translation of 1959.) In fact, such an approach lay at the very heart of Presniakov's life work. To be sure, Grekov was critical, and often justifiably so, of Presniakov on other counts, as, for example, his exaggeration of the extent and importance of princely power in the early Kievan period (tenth century). Grekov, *Kievan Rus*, 1953, pp. 292ff. But he did not and indeed could not reject Presniakov's all-Russian scheme because he had made it his own. One can only wonder why Cherepnin attacked Presniakov on the very issue where his views accorded most closely with those of Soviet historians.

30. A. E. Presniakov, *Apogei samoderzhaviia: Nikolai I* (Leningrad, 1925), pp. 90–91.

31. *Ibid.*, p. 58; A. E. Presniakov, "Samoderzhavie Aleksandra II," *Russkoe Proshloe*, 1923, No. 4, pp. 4–5, 9.

or institutionalize its power, shaped the personalities of its rulers to fit its own premolded form. As individuals the tsars were shot through with the same contradictions that characterized their authority. Alternatively depressed and enraged by their helplessness to deal with the corruption, waste, and coarseness of Russian life, they all qualified for Countess Nesselrode's description of Nicholas I: "He ploughs his vast state but does not sow it with any fruitful seeds." [32] To Presniakov the decline of the autocracy in the nineteenth century appeared as a startling reversal of the very process which had created it in the fourteenth and fifteenth centuries.

To be sure, Presniakov's last works lack the massive documentation of his earlier ones, but even a longer life might not have enabled him to supply it. By the early 1930's it was not enough to have accepted the Revolution or even to be committed to the goals of scientific history based on a combination of rigorous empiricism and a search for fundamental laws. Was Presniakov prepared to accept an unparalleled effort by the Soviet state to organize and discipline the "elemental masses" into a new form of social order which reflected the "objective needs" and aspirations of the people? In the absence of sufficient evidence and also of a "scientific theory of psychological phenomena," we may pay a final tribute to A. E. Presniakov by leaving that question unanswered.

---

32. Presniakov, *Apogei*, p. 56.

THE FORMATION

OF THE

GREAT
RUSSIAN
STATE

Foreword

There is little that is new in the present work. It deals with a rather well-worn theme, on the basis of material published long ago and widely known. It is, however, an attempt to restore as far as possible the rights of the sources and established facts in the treatment of one of the most important events in Russian history: the rise of the Great Russian state. In our historical scholarship the study of the early history of northeastern Russia has been hampered by a theoretical approach to the materials under consideration, so that facts drawn from early sources have been transformed into a series of illustrations of some ready-made scheme not to be derived from the facts themselves. Many facts, when they did not fit into an established theory, were simply ignored by historians and did not enter into their conclusions. On the other hand, these conclusions could not be reconciled with the sequence of particular events in the historical process being studied, and indeed severed their inner connections. An effort has been made to take greater advantage of available source materials, with more attention being paid to the actual chronology of events, and this effort has altered the entire historical perspective of the epoch. Its characteristic features are now seen in new ways. The vigor of the "grand princely" tradition has been made more plain, the concepts of the *udel* [1] and the *votchina* [2] have been put in a new light, as well as the whole evolution of interprincely relationships. The sources are now approached in new ways. The princes' testaments and treaties reveal their true meaning only when each one is studied in the context of the circumstances that brought it into being. If they are taken outside this context and used to answer questions they themselves did not have in view, they will lead to precisely those false conclusions that have been fastened on them in the traditional historical schemes. If there is an indiscriminate use of the varied redactions of the chronicles, with a refusal to consider the different tendencies and points of view that determined these redactions, then the chronicles will not yield all they can, and—more important—the way is opened for the selection of a late and biased revision of the text in preference to the original and genuine historical witness. This has happened quite frequently, in fact. We may note how the Chronicle of Nikon and the history of Tatishchev, which depends on it, have been used to illustrate the conventional theory.

Our study will touch only the external history of the formation of the Great Russian state—the interrelations of its princes and the development of its grand princely policy. The task of organizing grand princely sovereignty [3] from within will not be considered. That is a separate and complex subject, and the nature of the materials available would indicate that its consideration

1. *Udel:* a prince's share in a family's common patrimony; the grant (in the form of land, attached persons, revenues, and ruling powers) made by a ruling prince to his sons, each son possessing his *udel* under the leadership of the eldest among them, or the one accounted eldest.—TRANS.

2. *Votchina:* the combination of all ruling powers and possessions in a given patrimony or domain, as viewed especially from the standpoint of the ruler of such a domain ("an inheritance that will pass to my sons"). —TRANS.

3. This is a translation of the Russian word *vlast*. In different contexts I have translated it variously as power, ruling power, rule, authority, dominion. The Russian word carries all these meanings.—TRANS.

belongs properly to a study of the structure of the Muscovite state in the sixteenth century, an epoch that begins where the present work ends. This book must be seen as the first part, therefore, of a larger project, which could be entitled *Princely Law in Old Russia*.[4]

---

4. I have translated the Russian name Rus as "Old Russia" in certain places for the sake of clarity.—TRANS.

Introduction

I. *SOME OBSERVATIONS ON RECENT HISTORICAL SCHOLARSHIP*

When the *Slavianskaia Entsiklopediia* was published by the Imperial Academy of Sciences in 1904, M. S. Hrushevsky announced in one of its articles his flat rejection of the conventional scheme of Russian history and tried to put the question of the historical rationale of eastern Slavism in a new way. By "conventional scheme of Russian history" Hrushevsky had in mind that scheme which had been accepted in textbooks of Russian history, setting forth the prehistory of eastern Europe and its non-Slavic peoples down through the settling of this territory by Slavic peoples; the formation of the Kievan state and its history to the second half of the twelfth century, leading to the grand principality of Vladimir and the history of the Muscovite state; and ending with the Russian Empire of the eighteenth and nineteenth centuries. The history of the south and west of Russia, i.e., of the Ukrainian and White Russian lands, remained outside the scope of this historical exposition. Certain elements of it were touched on, but only externally and as if by accident, such as the Galician state of Daniel, the formation of the Lithuanian grand principality and its union with Poland, the ecclesiastical Union of Florence, the Cossack wars, and the exploits of the hetman Khmelnitsky.

In the light of his ethnological theories, Hrushevsky has asserted that the aim of the "conventional" scheme—to produce a "comprehensive history of Russia"—was by nature impossible, since there was no such thing as a "Russian" people or nation. The historian's task was rather to develop a history of the Ukrainian people on the one hand, and a history of Great Russia on the other. To join in a single scheme the early history of the south Russian tribes (the history of Kiev) and the history of Vladimir and the Muscovite state in the twelfth to fourteenth centuries seemed to him completely unreasonable. Such an approach, he felt, had the effect of cutting off the early part of the history of southern Russia and fastening it artificially onto the history of the north. "The Kievan period," he insisted, "did not lead into the Vladimir-Moscow era, but led rather into the periods of Galician and Volhynian ascendancy in the thirteenth century and of Lithuanian and Polish prominence in the fourteenth to sixteenth centuries."

In Hrushevsky's opinion the northeastern part of Old Russia "was neither the heir nor the successor" of Kievan Russia, but "sprang from its own roots." Hrushevsky was prepared to compare the relationship of these two Russias with that of the Roman Empire and the Gallic provinces: "The Kievan rule passed on to the Great Russian lands its forms of social and political organization, its law, its culture, as these had developed in the life of Kiev—but nothing more." Hence the conclusion: "The history of the Great Russian nation remains in fact without a beginning. The history of the rise of the Great Russian nation remains obscure, since it is traced only from the middle of the twelfth century." Also not considered, of course, was the problem of "how the sociopolitical structures, law, and culture of Kiev were actually received and modified on Great Russian soil."

Hrushevsky's view may seem paradoxical to Great Russian readers, since it demolishes the accepted notion of a "single" history of a "single" Russian people. Yet it is not nearly so extraordinary as it might seem at first glance. It would scarcely be an exaggeration to say that it is in many respects actually typical of our Great Russian historical outlook. Influenced by the need to separate the whole history of the Ukrainian people from the history of Great Russia, Hrushevsky's view can find support in a number of conclusions and opinions developed and accepted in the literature of general Russian history.

Within the broad framework of Russian historical scholarship the fortunes of the conventional scheme criticized by Hrushevsky are most instructive. Hrushevsky agrees with P. N. Miliukov on the question of its origins: "This is a very old scheme," he writes, "with its origins in the historical outlook of the Muscovite bookmen. A genealogical idea lies at its basis—the genealogy of the old Muscovite dynasty."

We are indebted to Miliukov for a very valuable observation on the "historical outlook of the Muscovite bookmen" and its decisive influence on the presentation of Russian history by Russian writers in the eighteenth and nineteenth centuries. This influence was aptly described by Miliukov in the following words:

In the last century, when Russian historical scholarship began gradually to uncover its sources, these sources came into the hands of historians with their own ready-made view evolved over the centuries. It is not surprising that the ready-made ideology presented in sources led the student of history along well-worn paths, ordering historical facts for him as they were seen and understood by contemporary writers. The student imagined that he was discovering and giving meaning to history when in reality he was simply riding on the shoulders of fifteenth- and sixteenth-century philosophers.

Two facts have diminished the fruitfulness of this insight. Miliukov centered his study of the Muscovite historical theory on the question of "the origins of the historical scheme of Karamzin," and failed to distinguish all the elements that so profoundly affected the conclusions of nineteenth-century scholars regarding early Russian history. Also, it is unfortunate that Miliukov's work was never completed. If it had been, we would undoubtedly have been given a more complete evaluation of the effect of the historical outlook of the Muscovite bookmen not only on the works of the eighteenth-century historians and Karamzin, but also on the theories of S. M. Solovyev and his school.

Among the factors influencing early Russian historiography noted by Miliukov, the most important was the development, as a kind of "historical axiom," of "the idea of an identity and hereditary connection between the sovereign powers of Moscow and Kiev." This "axiom" was utilized by the ruling powers of Moscow in the time of Ivan III and his son Vasili as a foundation for Moscow's claim to be the sole heir of all land belonging to the princes of the Rurik dynasty. In their disputes with the grand princes of Lithuania, the Muscovite princes claimed through their envoys that "by the will of God and the tradition handed down from our forefathers, the whole Russian land is our votchina," and in this claim they included Kiev, Smolensk, Polotsk, and Vitebsk, as well as "other cities." In advancing these claims, "the Muscovite diplomats set up goals for Russian state policy which were not to be realized for another two and a half centuries." It was here, in these "political ideals of fifteenth-century Muscovite diplomats," in their attempts to define "the task of the future" so broadly that their program must have appeared almost fantastic to the people of that time, that Miliukov discerned the origin of the theory of a "hereditary connection" between the sovereign powers of Kiev and Moscow. I shall not dwell at this point on the extent to which the roots of this "historical axiom" of the fifteenth- and sixteenth-century bookmen reached back even further into the past—how its elaboration as a "genealogy" in the spirit of Muscovite patrimonial and dynastic pretensions and its application in diplomatic correspondence was only a continuation of a more ancient tradition. Let me simply take note of the historical theories that began to appear in Russian scholarly writing to meet the need to round out this scheme with real historical content and better to explain the period between the reigns of Vladimir Monomakh and the Muscovite state of Ivan III.

On this point historians of the eighteenth century, ending with Karamzin, were content to deplore the practical results of the breakdown of power, and here, as Miliukov has shown, they were simply following the view expressed in the documents of Ivan III regarding the defects of multiple centers of power.

M. P. Pogodin may be credited with the first really scientific hypothesis attempting to define the organic connection between north Russian history and the Kievan past. Among other things, his hypothesis had one great formal merit: its explanation of the relationship of these two historical periods was founded on the solid basis of the ethnological unity of the great masses of people who lived through these eras. This remarkable hypothesis was born under the shock of discoveries by linguists that "there were no traces of present Ukrainian usage" in the language of the literary memorials of Kievan Russia. Combining this discovery with the fact that *byliny* [5] of the Kievan cycle "are being sung among us on every side, in Archangel and Vladimir, in Kostroma and Siberia," yet not in the Ukraine, Pogodin came to the conclusion that "the Great Russian race" lived in Kiev from very ancient times, or at least that the Polianians who "settled Kiev and its environs" were "Great Russians," and that later these "Great Russians migrated to the north into the land of Suzdal under Iuri Dolgoruky [Long Arm] and Andrei Bogoliubsky." "The real Great Russian race," he wrote, "moved outward into this land, where it grew and multiplied."

Once accepted, Pogodin's hypothesis had many consequences for the whole course of historical study. It made it possible to take full advantage of facts derived from examination of the historical life of northeastern Russia in more recent times (in the fifteenth and sixteenth centuries) as a way of explaining the phenomena of Old Russian or Kievan life. We may note, for example, Pogodin's attempt to explain the genealogies of princely families by the records of court precedence, which took on such great significance in the theories of S. C. Solovyev, I. E. Zabelin, and V. O. Kliuchevsky.

Pogodin's concept of a massive migratory shift of population from Kiev to the north and east as the basic reason for the consolidation of the Rostov-Suzdal area under Iuri Dolgoruky and Andrei Bogoliubsky has prospered extraordinarily well in Russian historical study. His view has become an unquestioned premise in the presentation of the history of northern Russia, providing an externally satisfactory explanation for the transition from the Kiev to the Vladimir period.

Further research in the history of northeastern Russia, however, has concentrated on explaining not so much its connections as its

5. *Byliny:* ancient ballads or folk songs on epic themes.—TRANS.

dissimilarities and contrasts with the earlier Kievan state. It is as
if with this transition to a new territory, to new geographic and
ethnic conditions, Russian history made a completely fresh start.
This particular feature of our historical reconstructions can be
explained by the widely accepted view that northeastern Russia
in the twelfth century was a "harsh and virtually savage" land,
that here a new order of relationships grew up on "new and
virgin soil," from the time that Andrei Bogoliubsky broke the
tradition of a relationship between seniority in the Russian land
(the grand princely rule) and the golden throne of Kiev. "The
north began its historical life when its prince took this step
in the direction of a new order," wrote Solovyev. He saw northeastern Russia as a vast region "where only one city is mentioned
in the Chronicle as having risen before the coming of the Varangians." This was Rostov the Great, from which the whole region
received the name of the Rostov land. Under Iaroslav I, Rostov
was joined to the territory of southern Pereiaslavl, as the domain
of his son Vsevolod. Then, Solovyev continues, "quickly a number
of new cities began to rise around Rostov. Iuri, the son of Monomakh, distinguished himself particularly as a tireless builder. The
Rostov region was thus filled with younger cities, Rostov towering in their midst." The "younger" cities were "built and settled
by the princes, and having been brought into being by them,
each city was inevitably regarded as its prince's personal property." It was this last aspect of the younger cities of the northeast that Solovyev saw as the basic condition for the development of a "new order." He did not think it possible to call
this new order an udel system, since he envisioned Russia as
divided not into udels, but into a number of independent principalities, each with its own grand prince and its own udel princes.
He even felt it would be desirable to "eliminate the terms 'udel
period' and 'udel system' from the history of interprincely relations." This view was not generally accepted, however, since
Solovyev believed that an essential feature of the "new order"
rising in the north was the development of precisely that form
of princely domain which he himself regarded as an udel domain.
"In view of their origins, the new cities looked upon their princes
as absolute masters, and the princes looked upon their cities as
their own inalienable property." Here was an assertion of the

concept of property, of an inalienable right, of individual ownership passing from generation to generation according to the will
of the ruling prince. Here "property stood above family relationships, each prince seeing himself as the sole owner of a particular domain, and no longer as a member of a given family, a
particular dynasty." This new form of domain, no longer limited
by the law of kinship or family, and having developed "when
the concepts of individual ownership and the hereditary nature
of a domain had begun to take precedence over concepts of
family," Solovyev called an udel domain, thereby equating the
term "udel" with *oprichnina*.[6] "The term 'oprichnina,' " he wrote,
"is sometimes used in the sense of an udel that belongs to a prince
as a wholly separate and private domain." The udel is thus a
property of the prince which he can "dispose of at will," and in
particular by testament.

In spite of the fact that he felt a prince's domain could be
referred to in this way as an udel, Solovyev did not acknowledge
the existence of any special "udel period," since he saw the
decline of family relations as a process leading to the final triumph
of "relations of state." As "the sole owner of a given district,"
the prince stood at the head of his own individual state. Thus, in
a reference to the assembly of princes at Vladimir in 1296,
Solovyev wrote: "These assemblies of princes are not to be confused with earlier tribal assemblies. The princes do not now appear as brothers, but as rulers of separate and independent
domains." When Russia broke up into two parts, one to the
southwest and the other to the northeast, and when later, in
northern Russia, "Tver and Moscow became grand principalities,
and Riazan and Nizhni Novgorod followed their example, there
appeared a number of distinct princely clans, distinct states,
independent of and hostile to one another." "The family relationship of princes was replaced by a relationship as of a ruler
to subjects at a time when the land, the district, and the city
were bound to the prince by the closest ties of property and
ownership, and had become his own settled estate." A stubborn

6. *Oprichnina:* a lesser domain set aside within a votchina as the possession
of a widowed princess or a minor son; a special grant as distinct from an
udel grant. To be distinguished from the *Oprichnina* under Ivan the
Terrible, which was essentially an organization of secret police and Ivan's
chief weapon in subduing the boyar class.—TRANS.

struggle developed between these independent domains. "Every movement on the part of one prince was a threat to all the others, since every movement was a trespass on another's land." Now, however, in the Great Russian land of the north, the struggle was historically more interesting than the disputes of former times. "Now the issue was this: to be the sovereign of the whole Russian land, or to be the servant of such a sovereign."

On the one hand, Solovyev's scheme of Russian history served in its own way to legitimize the traditional presentation of a historical process beginning in Kiev and proceeding through Vladimir to Moscow. "At the end of the twelfth century the earliest center of Russian historical development, the remarkable water route from the Varangians to the Greeks, revealed its incapacity to develop any solid foundations for a single state. Following a definite path from the beginning, all the best elements of the land poured out of the southwest toward the northeast. Settlement moved in the same direction, and with it the course of history." Of course, Solovyev was aware that history did not simply abandon the south, and that it continued in its own way there too. "It would be unjust," he said, "indeed it would be scientifically unwarranted and one-sided, to lose sight of south-western Russia after its separation from the northeast, or to skim superficially over the events that took place there." But he also held that "it would be equally unjust and unwarranted to put the history of southwest Russia on a level with that of northeast Russia." It is precisely to Solovyev that we must be grateful for having planted in Russian historical study the view that the process he thought of as a transition from tribal to proprietary and ultimately to state relationships, having begun at Kiev in the south, was fully realized only in the land of Great Russia to the north. His description of this process was rather one-sided, however, since he remained dependent on local north Russian sources—a characteristic of north Russian historical scholarship. Solovyev knew that "the same concepts of property, of succession from father to son, and of testamentary law" were developing in southern Russia too during the decline of the Kievan state, but he did not make use of this information in his general historical and sociological conclusions because he regarded these elements in south Russian history as products of foreign influences, even as he recognized the significance of the "historical circumstances" that determined their "inevitable development."

Thus, on the other hand, Solovyev's scheme tended to destroy rather than to support the hypothesis of an organic historical connection between the history of northern Russia and that of Kiev. Transferred to the north, south Russian "tribal" principles were subjected to conditions in which they were bound, sooner or later, to dissolve and perish, being totally unadaptable to life on the fresh-plowed plains of this newly colonized and still half-savage land.

Solovyev's scheme led to a special way of posing the whole question of "the formation of the Muscovite state." Historians explaining how tribal relationships were displaced by state obligations moved quickly from Kiev to Moscow. Only one thing was important for any history of Russia "from the earliest times": the change in the principles on which its unity was based. In the Kievan epoch it was the "family relationship of the ruler of each region to the rulers of other regions and especially to the eldest among them that served as the link between the various parts of the state." Here, in the north, the Muscovite state was founded on the ruins of this old tribal system. The whole significance of the period lying between the history of Kievan ascendancy and the state of Ivan III lies in the breakdown of tribal relationships and the consolidation of the power of Moscow.

The break actually occurred in the reign of Andrei Bogoliubsky, who "disclaimed" the south and "began a new order of things" in the north. The younger princes

clearly understood that he wished to replace the old family relationships with the new bonds of state, to deal with them not as relatives having equal rights, but as subordinates, as commoners. A long struggle began, in which the younger princes were little by little obliged to accept these new relationships, were obliged to submit to the eldest among them as subjects to a king.

The historian's task is then to explain how Andrei developed the character and views of a child of the north, who was thus unfamiliar with southern traditions, and then to trace the conflict between the ties of family and the state concept down to its

resolution in the sixteenth century, when the latter finally prevailed. Andrei had to deal also with the boyars in his struggle for
sovereign power. According to Solovyev, he was clearly striving
not only for a monarchy, but also for absolute power in the
spirit of the autocracy of the sixteenth century, and he died in
the resulting clash with the forces of opposition. "The transition
from the grand prince's position as the eldest member of his
family (yet still depending on his brother princes) to the position
of sovereign grand prince" was achieved at the moment when
one of the grand princes gained "independence from his kinsmen"
and in addition acquired "the necessary material strength." The
first of these two conditions was created by that tradition of
princely relations on which Andrei Bogoliubsky had been brought
up in the north—"the primary importance of proprietary relationships and the consequent neglect of family considerations."
The second was created by the favorable circumstances leading to
the rise of Moscow. "The rise of Moscow" became the key to
the history of northern Russia in the fourteenth and fifteenth
centuries. The major task of the historian was to explain its
"causes."

Solovyev thus sanctioned the substitution of a partial question
dealing with "the causes of the rise of Moscow" for the basic
question concerning the rise of the Great Russian state, a simplifi-
cation that has been characteristic of all subsequent Russian historical scholarship, so that our histories of the Muscovite state
almost always begin with a summary of these causes. Solovyev
himself never took this fatal step, and offered rather a series of
broad general observations on the formation of the Russian state.
He regarded this growth as an organic process,

as it happens when states, coming into being as a result of various
tribal and above all geographical circumstances, emerge in almost the
exact areas in which they are destined subsequently to exist and
function. For every state there then begins the long, hard, and painful
process of inner growth and consolidation. At the beginning of this
process the state is usually quite clearly disunited. This disunity then
disappears gradually, giving place to unity, and at last the state is
formed.

When the Russian state first began to emerge,

the country was a vast wilderness. From time to time tribes would travel across it along its river routes. Taking advantage of these convenient water roads in all directions, the new state rapidly subdued the native tribes and marked out a huge territory for itself. But this territory was still an empty wilderness. It was necessary to settle the land. Everything had to be built; everything had to be created.

And so began the "long, hard, and painful period of inner growth and consolidation." Russia began to pass out of this period "when a strong center of state power was established"; in short, when northeastern Russia was unified around the city of Moscow.

Thus the broad goals of research were set forth in abstract terms, the outlines to be filled in later with concrete historical detail. The task was to explain the development that led to the formation of the wide-flung and inwardly united Russian state. It is important to note, perhaps, that although Solovyev defined the task in this way, the question that actually came to the fore in the study of the unification of northeastern Russia was in fact that of "the causes of the creation of this state around the center of Moscow." Attention was focused mainly on the opposition encountered and aid received by the Muscovite princes in their efforts to strengthen their position, subjugate other princes, beat off the Tatars and the forces of Lithuania, and increase their power over the people of the land.

Solovyev's main contribution to the task of historical study was precisely his overall scheme, but in it we may see one of the basic reasons why both for his critics and for his followers the formation of the Muscovite state has not seemed to fit into the view of the organic formation of states which he himself had described, but rather into his description of "inorganic development," as when states "are assembled by a process of external accumulation, by the external joining together of parts."

In 1834 an article by N. V. Stankevich appeared in *Uchenye zapiski Moskovskovo Universiteta* (Moscow University Studies), under the title "Factors Leading to the Gradual Rise of Moscow up to the Death of Ivan III." This article has been regarded as a presentation of the views of Professor Kachenovsky. Citing A. H. Heerin [7] and F. P. Guizot, Stankevich took as the starting

7. German historian, 1760–1842, known for his theories on the importance of the trade relations of ancient peoples for an understanding of political organization.

point for his study the significance of the process of centralization. He saw "the uniting of the land into a single indivisible
whole" as "the first period of political significance in the history
of this people," and "the dominant position of one city, one
region, one reigning prince" as the "first condition of internal
union and centralization." Hence the importance of the "gradual
rise of Moscow, so closely connected with Russia's movement
toward existence as a political power." Stankevich's work outlined
the usual "causes" of the rise of Moscow. "In all probability Moscow was founded by settlers moving in from the south, as was the
case in all the cities around it." Stankevich found proof of this
in the fact that "many of the cities and lands of northern Russia
bear southern names." It is said that "the rise of Moscow was not
dependent solely on the character of its princes. . . . Moscow was
not the product simply of their power, leading to a mechanical
joining together of hitherto separate regions." Moscow acquired
its lasting domination because a "more natural, organic" link
existed between it and other Russian lands, making Moscow "not
just the chief power but also the heart of Russia." Instead of an
analysis of this "organic link," however, we are given an inventory
of the "major conditions" for Moscow's success: its geographical
position (its central location in the system of northern principalities, the influx of settlers, its secure position in the face of enemies);
the invasion and domination of the Mongols (Moscow's separation from southern Russia, the devastation of the principality of
Vladimir, the patronage of the khans, its enrichment by tribute);
the residence of the metropolitan in Moscow (Moscow as a
spiritual center, and the support of Muscovite policy by the
spiritual power); the character of its princes, their policies and
foreign relations. This became the traditional manner of posing
the question, all the more so in that the elaboration of Solovyev's
scheme in the works of K. D. Kavelin and B. N. Chicherin simply
reinforced the theory of a complete disruption of the tradition
of political unity in northeastern Russia in the thirteenth and
fourteenth centuries, with the later revival of this tradition by
way of growth in the power and domains of the Muscovite
princes.

Solovyev rejected the scientific value of any distinction of an
udel period in the history of Old Russia because he accepted as
an essential element in this history the existence of only two

systems of political unification, one after the other: first the system of family relationships among the princes in Kievan Russia, which knew no "separate" domains; second, the system of state relationships between separate domains which the Muscovite princes used to mold northern Russia into a single political whole. The breakdown of Russia into two parts (northern and south-western), the division of the former into a number of independent grand principalities, the dividing up of its land into udels or lands ruled and occupied by princes as personal domains—all these seemed to be only external phenomena, useless in the construction of any major theory of the Russian historical process.

Historians of law looked at this question in a different light. Kavelin attached special significance to the period of "separate domains," acknowledging the votchina principle as a key element in the organization and administration of the princely domains and an essential feature of Russian political and legal life in the twelfth to fifteenth centuries, sufficiently well defined and wide-spread to play a decisive role in any classification of periods in the Russian historical process. Admitting, with Solovyev, that "all interests and indeed the whole life of old Russia were centered on the concept of statehood or political power," Kavelin found that the "history of our princes involved the completely natural rebirth of family life in a juridical, social form." The breakup of the system of family relationships among the princes —the most ancient form of Russian political life—led to the triumph of the votchina or hereditary principle, giving rise to the idea that the "prince's votchina was an inherited possession which he could, as sole owner, dispose of in any way he wished." Once this thought was established, "territorial and proprietary interests" took precedence over questions of blood or family re-lationship. The final victory was won with the abolition of udel lands and the unification of northern Russia in the Muscovite state. In opposition to Solovyev's view of the role played by colonization and the "new cities" in the destruction of the old system based on kinship, Kavelin asserted that "there were no violent ruptures in the formation of our nation. All changes in the political life of Russia occurred gradually, and developed organically out of the patriarchal, family way of life." In his remarkable articles Kavelin presented a coherent explanation of this organic development, although his logic was undermined somewhat by his admission of an exclusive significance for Andrei Bogoliubsky. As a result of special factors influencing Andrei's upbringing in the north, Kavelin saw "in this extraordinary historical figure a new type in the political life of old Russia—the type of a possessor of a votchina domain, a lord, an absolute ruler; a type to be seen even more clearly in his brother and successor, Vsevolod III (Big Nest), and developed finally in the grand princes of Moscow." For the personification of this type in its developed form, Kavelin looked to Ivan Kalita (Moneybag) and his successors, whose main task was "to multiply the number of their domains," using the title and power of grand prince as the "best means to this end." These men pursued their goal so successfully that "Russia was quickly turned into their hereditary votchina." Along the way the old blood ties were broken down. Family obligations replaced tribal obligations; obligations to one man replaced obligations to family, this one man being regarded as an absolute ruler who rejected all obligations in the name of one idea: the idea of the state.

Chicherin sought to answer the question "When did the Russian state come into being?" from this same viewpoint, that "the real significance of our history lies in the development of the state." He worked from the general proposition that "the indivisibility of a society, the identity of a territory with its supreme sovereign, or, in a word, monarchy, constitutes the first and major condition of the life of a state." Obviously, on these terms, we can speak of a Russian state only from the time that a monarchy was established in the Muscovite land. As for the "juridical form" of Russia prior to the fifteenth century, it must be regarded as a "social community" and not a state. All relationships were based on the principles not of state, but of private law—on ownership and private contract. The law of kinship, as the basis of the whole social organism, prevailed in Russia up to the coming of the Varangians; this way of life and indeed the very social significance of family relationships were destroyed by the establishment of the power of the Varangian princes, and in Kievan Russia all relationships were determined by the co-existence of two principles, two forms of private law: ownership and free contract. These two principles "existed side by side, neither one displacing the other, but constantly in conflict with one another since in the last analysis they were mutually contradictory." The movement of Old Russian history presented itself to Chicherin essentially along the following lines:

Southern Russia was incapable of resolving this inner contradiction in its life, and for this reason was condemned to impotence. The contradiction was resolved in the north, where the principles were separated and each one became the basis for a distinct form of civic life. The free community developed in Novgorod and Pskov; a strict votchina rule was adopted in the other regions of northern Russia. The free community disappeared without a trace, however, and the Russian state, like all other European empires, grew out of the votchina system, since the law of inheritance had far more strength than the law of free contract.

The epoch of life based on kinship, of the dominant influence of blood ties as the organizing force in society, was limited by Chicherin to the period before the princes, before the records of the chronicles. "The intermediate period" between that original mode of life and the formation of the Muscovite state "had its own principles, its own system of common life, founded on private law." But differences between Kievan and northeastern Russia, between the way of life of the ninth to eleventh centuries and that of the twelfth to fifteenth centuries, had no real significance. The votchina principle was established in Russian life from the time of the Varaingian conquest; hence the view that a prince's domain was the inherited personal property of the prince and that all the land within it belonged to him.

The main difference between the earlier and later periods was that as long as the concept of the unity of a princely family was maintained, the land was considered as belonging to the whole family, but later the family lines were separated, and each prince began to regard himself as the sole master and lord of his own inheritance. . . . To the degree that the concept of a common birth was obscured, the notion of the unity of the domain and the subordination of one prince to another was also lost.

The country was divided into a number of separate estates.

The princes of Moscow, Riazan, and Tver entered into contracts with each other as completely independent landholders. Each prince strove to increase his lot at the expense of the others, and he did this not with interests of state in mind, but with a view to increasing his own personal property and augmenting his own personal revenues.

On the basis of its landholdings, Moscow built up the edifice of monarchical rule over northern Russia, and its strength created the Russian state. Once the real significance of our history "is seen to lie in the development of the state," then of course such a history must begin with the rise of Moscow. Relying on the historical and sociological theories of Guizot, Chicherin held that "we must regard every element of social life in the middle ages as an expression of either weakness or power." In Russia "the first appearance of power is to be found among the votchina princes, whose disruptive ambitions were subsequently subordinated to the interests of a single center, gradually gathering round itself all the varied elements of life out of which the Russian state was to be formed."

In the works of V. I. Sergeevich we find a considerable and extremely important broadening of the historian's task and subject with regard to the formation of the Muscovite state. The question he raised was: How and out of what was the territory of the Muscovite state formed? His thesis was elaborated in a brilliant essay entitled "A History of the Rostov Volost." [8] In a somewhat abbreviated version this essay appeared also in his book *Drevnosti russkogo prava* (The Beginnings of Russian Law) in a section devoted to "The Territory of the State." The essay drew attention to the political role and aspirations of the north Russian boyars, anticipating the development of an idea later set forth in his master's thesis: "The Muscovite State as the Work of the Boyars and Free Servants." Sergeevich's observations on the role of the boyars in the political destinies of Great Russia carried the question of the conditions determining the formation of the Muscovite state beyond the confines of the traditional scheme, which had indeed reduced the study of this process to (a) a description of the efforts of the Muscovite princes to "build up" Moscow, and (b) an evaluation of the results of these efforts. Sergeevich dwelt especially on "the leading role played by the

8. *Volost:* a rural district within a votchina, usually attached to a city or town; also a district attached to a free city.—TRANS.

Rostov boyars" in the struggle that broke out immediately following the murder of Andrei Bogoliubsky. The boyars of the ancient cities of Rostov and Suzdal were trying to maintain "the unity of the Rostov Volost," which was in danger of being shattered "by the private interests of the princes." With the cautious note that he "had no intention of endowing Dobryn the Tall and his comrades with far-reaching political insight," Sergeevich went on to say that

it would be one-sided to explain the efforts of the leading men of Rostov to maintain the unity of their volost simply in terms of self-interest. The disadvantages of having many rival princes, with the inevitable consequence of interprincely war, were so obvious that the boyars could very well desire the unity of the volost simply for the good of the land.

Prince Constantine, placed in Rostov by his father, Vsevolod Big Nest, was deeply influenced by the convictions of the boyars. "He did not regard his father's domain as his own private property, which he could subdivide at will. He held the concept of an indivisible political whole." Thus, "the advantages of monarchy were recognized and vigorously promoted by the Rostov boyars" almost a hundred years before Ivan Kalita. Hence the tradition preserved among the Moscow boyars that "the majority among them must be composed of boyars of the grand principality of Rostov-Vladimir." The boyars were "natural supporters of the policy of unification." "They obviously retained the old idea of the unity of the Rostov-Vladimir volost, and they began now to restore the ancient boundaries of their volost, sometimes expelling unwanted hereditary princes, sometimes forcing them into a state of dependence on the Grand Prince."

Sergeevich did not connect these valuable observations with the tradition of seniority as it had developed in Kiev. To establish such a connection would have been to contradict his general thesis that the legal form of Old Russian political life was "the volost system of state administration"—the coexistence of a great many small states or volost principalities. In contrast to Chicherin, Sergeevich saw the interrelations of princes as a form not of private or civil law, but rather of international law. The assemblies of princes were assemblies of independent rulers, the agreements of princes were the treaties of sovereigns. He considered this volost system as having originated prior to the period dealt with by our oldest historical sources, and in his review of the Russian princes from Rurik to Dmitri of the Don, he insisted on the existence of "politically independent volosts." In this period, he continued, "up to the second half of the fourteenth century, none of the princes showed any sign of wanting to form a larger undivided state reaching beyond the boundaries of the volost structure." "The first unification" of the northeastern princely domains, one that was "purely external," occurred in their subordination to the power of the Tatar khan. "Contrary to their own interests, the Tatars appeared as initiators of the unification of the Russian land under the rule of the Grand Prince of Vladimir." "The first clear thought of forming a unified state out of several volosts arose, in fact, among the princes of Moscow, and even here it did not appear very early." Sergeevich saw the first glimmer of this idea in the Testament of Dmitri of the Don.

The Rostov boyars and their successors, the grand princely boyars of Vladimir and Moscow, emerge rather unexpectedly against this general background of Russian political history. In his attempt to explain what made them not just the "natural supporters" of the policy of unification, but also its defenders against the aims and policies of the princes, Sergeevich dwelt mainly on the boyars' "private interests" and their desire for "rich feedings" (distributions of land, goods, or money)—all the more easily extracted, of course, from the lesser princes in need of their help. Only in two places, where there is mention of the "unity" and "wholeness" of the Rostov land, is there a hint of a more substantial and likely explanation. In his review of Sergeevich's *Beginnings of Russian Law* T. V. Taranovsky rightly notes that "the author does not give a sufficient explanation why the tradition of unity in the old Rostov-Vladimir volost was transformed in the minds of the boyars into a desire to unify this and other lands under the rule of the newly formed principality of Moscow." According to Taranovsky, Sergeevich had not clarified the factors that "turned the interests of the boyars away from the independent volost tradition in the direction of a stronger political union," and which later "changed the boyars' policy of state unity into a need of the people as a whole." Sergeevich failed to explain where the "unifying" tendency of the north Russian boyars came from, yet without that it is impossible to define the historical significance of the "century-old experience and tradition" that (according to Sergeevich) molded the thought of Ivan III. As the organizer of the Muscovite state, Sergeevich wrote, Ivan relied on the "age-old custom of the grand princely boyars and his own ancestors, which was to become a family tradition in the eldest line descending from Dmitri of the Don." We can only regret that Sergeevich did not elaborate his extraordinarily valuable observations on the policy of the boyars, since in them he was pointing the way to a more accurate explanation of the factors leading to the formation of the Muscovite state.

On the basis of the position taken in *The Beginnings of Russian Law,* Sergeevich later returned to the distinction made by Solovyev of two general periods in the history of Russia before Peter the Great. Chicherin has noted that Sergeevich found the "distinctive feature of the first period to lie in the prevalence of private, personal freedom with a corresponding weakness in the principle of common welfare, the principle of the state." This period "had its fullest expression when Russia lived under the joint rule of its princes." This first period, he felt, began with the era of the *veche.*[9] "In contrast, the second period was characterized by the prevalence of the notion of the whole, a notion that was not and indeed could not be sufficiently recognized and valued in the first epoch." This latter period was "clearly revealed in Muscovite Russia." "The fourteenth and fifteenth centuries constitute the broad boundary between these two periods. This was the time when the characteristic features of the second period acquired such strength that the final triumph of its new principles could already be foreseen." In the light of all this, the section on "Sovereign Power" in Sergeevich's *Lektsii i issledovaniia* (Lectures and Essays) consisted of a definition of the power of the prince in the udel period, as he called it, and a treatise on "The Power of the Muscovite Sovereigns." But his description of the system of relationships between the princes in the fourteenth

9. *Veche:* a legislative assembly of boyars and townsmen in certain free cities of Old Russia.—TRANS.

and fifteenth centuries had been presented in *Beginnings of Russian Law* with no recognition that princely sovereignty in this period contained elements of vital importance for a scientific study of Russian law. Defining an udel as the possession by a prince of an independent volost (as a small but sovereign state), Sergeevich regarded the sons of Sviatoslav Igorevich as the first udel princes, and in opposition to Solovyev he saw no essential difference between udel domains and grand principalities in northern Russia. Disagreeing also with Chicherin, Sergeevich did not place the affairs of Russia in this interim period under the heading of "private law." He did not see the relations of the princes as a "system of private inheritance," and could find in them no basis for "the view that a prince's territory was his own private property." He regarded the Testament of Semeon the Proud (d. 1353) as the moment when "the notion of the existence of separate states disappeared in the principality of Moscow," and in his opinion the growth and development of the new state principle began with Dmitri of the Don.

The dogmatic historical generalizations of Chicherin and Sergeevich seemed to have abolished the distinction between a south Russian or Kievan and a north Russian or Vladimir-Moscow period in the history of Russia. Their historical and juridical arguments moved with a single historical scheme that began at Kiev and passed through Suzdal to Moscow. The interprincely relationships prevailing in northeastern Russia in the fourteenth and fifteenth centuries were transferred to Kievan Russia, and were regarded, especially in the works of Sergeevich, as fundamentally identical to those that determined the political life of southern Russia in that earlier period. In the general scheme of Russian history the fourteenth and fifteenth centuries were described as an era of transition, having no distinctive, characteristic features expressed in new juridical forms of princely power and social order. Sergeevich's views were thus unable to introduce much that was new to the general understanding of the conditions leading to the formation of the Muscovite state, apart from his observations on the role of the boyars noted earlier, which did not, however, influence his general concept of the juridical foundations of political life in this period.

Historians have moved in the footsteps of Solovyev and Kavelin, smoothing over the differences in the views of these two scholars in their own eclectic generalizations. Characteristic in this respect is the small work of P. V. Polezhaev, *Moskovskoe kniazhestvo v pervoi polovine XIV veka* (The Principality of Moscow in the First Half of the Fourteenth Century), published in 1878. In his general understanding of Old Russian political history, Polezhaev worked mainly under the influence of Chicherin and Sergeevich:

Before the fourteenth century [he wrote] the social life of the Slavonic, Varangian-Russian principalities was nothing more than a preservation of principles that lay at the very foundation of the principality as an independent political unit. In the meantime, by their very nature, these principles were neither designed nor had they the capacity to develop the forces required for the organic growth of elements characteristic of statehood. It was necessary to turn to a more vigorous principle, and this was accomplished in the development of Moscow.

Polezhaev viewed the fourteenth and fifteenth centuries as a special votchina period, characteristically attaching significance to it only insofar as it related to the "development of Moscow." Moscow was a votchina city that had grown out of a votchina village; with the formation of the Muscovite principality Polezhaev regarded the veche period as having been succeeded and replaced by a votchina or Moscow-votchina period, lasting up to the time of Ivan III. It was in the first half of the fourteenth century, when "none of the historical records that have come down to us reflect the slightest trace of the state principle," that "the hereditary (votchina) power of the prince was at last fully developed." Acknowledging Vladimir as a city organized on the old principle of the veche, Polezhaev saw the development of Moscow from a village settlement into a "votchina land" as an "exceptional circumstance," as a result of which "there appeared for the first time, in Moscow, the idea of an autocracy, as the hereditary (votchina) rule or sovereignty of its prince." The history of Moscow up to the death of Semeon the Proud shows how the principality was created, "developing within itself those vital forces that were to lead to the organization of the state." For Polezhaev, it was at this point—that is, in the first half of the

fourteenth century—that "the history of the Muscovite principality became the history of Russia." Thus the basic task of the
historian is to identify and explain the reasons for the rise of
Moscow; to answer the question: Why was it precisely Moscow
and not some other principality that had the good fortune to
become the focus for all the interests of the Russian land?

This manner of putting the question concerning the factors that
determined the formation of the Great Russian state became firmly
established in subsequent study as a kind of axiom in the sche-
matic treatment of Russian history. V. O. Kliuchevsky emerged
as a second creator of scientific theories already articulated in his
works *Boyarskaia Duma* (The Boyar Duma) and *Kurs russkoi
istorii* (A Course in Russian History). In his comments on the
political organization of Kievan Russia he adopted the scheme
established by Solovyev, endeavoring simply to give it a different
foundation. The concept of an orderly succession of princely
rule in Kievan Russia; the notion of the colonization of northern
Russia along the upper Volga as the basis of a new political order
that became established in this part of Russia, leading eventually
to the Muscovite state; the theory of udel domain and the
explanation of the rise of Moscow as the center of the Russian
state—in Kliuchevsky all this was only a development and restate-
ment of the conclusions of Solovyev and Chicherin. Kliuchevsky,
of course, was able to introduce into the accepted schematiza-
tions such new insight and substance that in his own interpretations the old familiar theories and facts acquired completely new
significance and were, so to speak, born again. The dry, abstract
outlines of the old schemes were filled in with living, earthly
content, interspersed with details concerning social relationships,
topography, economic arrangements, and psychological atmosphere, acquiring the dignity and concrete force of an artistic
reproduction of the era under study, presented in clear and
graphic images. The new material, however, was set in the
same old basic outlines, and adapted to them. The outlines themselves were not derived from his content. Actually, the characteristic features of the traditional scheme were revealed all the
more clearly and distinctly in Kliuchevsky's work, including its
inner contradiction—on the one hand the affirmation of a genuine
continuity between the historical life of the north and that of

Kiev in the south; on the other hand the description of the sharp contrasts between north and south and the independent roots of the north Russian historical process.

According to Kliuchevsky, the Rostov land was "a district that lay outside the old, original Russia. In the twelfth century it was more alien to Russia than any of her frontier lands. Three Finnish tribes lived here in the eleventh and twelfth centuries—the tribes of Murom, Meria, and Ves." The intermixing of these tribes with Russian settlers created the Great Russian race. When "the population of the central middle Dnieper region, which formed the basis of the original Russian people, broke down into opposing groups," there was a "breaking apart" of these original people, and in the course of the twelfth to the fourteenth centuries "a broad, slow, and spreading movement" carried large population masses out of the southwestern region of Russia into the northeastern sections. These "masses" of settlers from the south were presented by Kliuchevsky as the basic colonial stock that fed the growth of northeastern Russia. The general type and character of these people and their way of life were then modified, in their mixing with local inhabitants of different race and under the influence of new geographical and economic conditions, until they became a quite different people from what they had been formerly in the south. The first major turning point in this process of colonization came when "the settlers gathered together in the triangle between the Oka and the upper Volga." This was "the time of the rise of the land of Vladimir, of the first appearance of udels. It was a time also when the Vladimir district began to experience growing political successes." Here, then, a new people came into being, a new order of social and political relationships developed, a new historical life began. Its first political form was the princely udel (regarded by Kliuchevsky as an oprichnina, as the "designated nest" of a princely family). The udel actually does not appear until the fourteenth to fifteenth centuries, but in the formation of udels in this latter period "we may see a continuation or even fulfillment of a process whose beginning, although not very clear to us today, marked the first appearance of the udel in northern Russia." Characteristic of this new "udel system, as it was called," was a new type of ruler, the votchina prince, and also a new social type, the boyar, a landholder liable to service to the prince. The "prince's udel domain" itself took on the features of "a simple, private landhold," much like that of a boyar. In particular "the udel domains were now generally inherited by testament, were transferred in accordance with the personal wishes of the testator, and not according to any established order." The udel form of rule was "a rather exact copy of the Old Russian boyar's votchina." Moreover, both the Great Russian people (not formed "by the continuing development of old local ways," but rather created anew out of the virgin soil of the upper Volga region) and the udel system itself were formed under the influence of local geographical and ethnological conditions. Both represented an open break with all former traditions.

When we examine the various consequences of the Russian colonization of the upper Volga, "we are looking at the earliest and deepest roots of a form of state which will appear in a later period," i.e., in the Muscovite period. True, Kliuchevsky defined the "udel system as a transitional political form," but we will not understand him properly if we give this term the significance of an evolutionary phenomenon. "The national Russian state," according to Kliuchevsky,

developed out of the udel system of the fourteenth century, and not out of the earlier system; not, however, because the earlier system was further removed from the national state than the udel system of the fourteenth century; neither one, by itself, contained much that entered into the formation of the Muscovite state, least of all the latter of the two. Both had to be destroyed so that the new state could be created. The udel system was much easier to destroy than the earlier order, however, *and it is just for this reason* that one of the udel domains, the votchina of the Danilovichi,[10] became the kernel of the national Russian state.

In Kliuchevsky's hands the traditional scheme of Russian history fell to pieces. Historic periods seemed to lose all methodological relatedness. Each one acquired such inner finality and was so decisively marked off from the period following that it appeared to be connected with it by only the most tenuous evolutionary thread. There was in fact a decisive rupture be-

10. Heirs of Daniel (d. 1303), traditional founder of the Moscow dynasty.

tween Kievan Russia and udel Russia. I. E. Zabelin could well find grounds in Kliuchevsky for his thesis that the roots of the development of the history of the north lay in Suzdal and Moscow, while the roots of southern history lay in Kiev. Kliuchevsky did not speak even of "a modification of Kievan social and political forms, laws, and culture on Great Russian soil," as did Hrushevsky. Instead he referred simply to the breakdown "of political, economic, and ecclesiastical structures of the earlier period," and with amazing detail recounted how the new social and historical forms of life, new social types, and new relationships sprang up out of local conditions in the upper Volga country.

Almost equally decisive in Kliuchevsky's interpretation was the antithesis between the udel period and that of the Muscovite state. His general scheme of the early history of northern Russia was built up out of two opposing processes, one being "the breakup of northern Russia into princely votchinas held among the descendants of Vsevolod III (Big Nest)," the other being the efforts "of one branch of this line to gather these broken parts into a single whole, with Moscow as the center of the state thus formed."

Thus in Kliuchevsky also the analysis of the conditions that brought about the formation of the Muscovite state was reduced to a study of "the political and nationalistic successes of the Muscovite princes." The rapid growth of Moscow checked the process of the breakup of northeastern Russia and gathered "the crumbling parts into a single whole." The first question in any study of this second process, the question of the origins of Moscow's power to unify the land, is to be answered by referring to the two "primary conditions for the rapid growth of the Muscovite principality"—first, Moscow's favorable geographical position; second, the lineage of its princes. Kliuchevsky's scheme led to the necessity of finding in the city of Moscow itself and its surrounding territory the center and source of the powers that developed later in the extension of territory and subjugation of neighboring princes. The examination of the advantages of its geographical position delivered the historian from "the enigma of Moscow's early successes," since it "revealed the hidden forces that helped prepare the way for the successes of the Muscovite

principality from the very moment it came into being." In the
foreground are the "economic factors contributing to the growth
of the city: Moscow is the point of intersection of two crossing
movements—the migratory movement to the northeast, and the
trading and shipping movement to the southeast." From later
genealogical traditions in boyar families it may be concluded
that "the most eminent people of the free serving classes were
gathered into Moscow from all sides—from Murom, Nizhni
Novgorod, Rostov, Smolensk, Chernigov, and even from Kiev
and Volhynia, from about the end of the thirteenth century
onward." "These boyar traditions," according to Kliuchevsky,
"are a reflection of a general movement of population. The most
notable men migrated with the great popular masses, all these
forces moving into Moscow as a kind of central reservoir, coming
from all the frontiers of the Russian land as they were threatened
by attack from enemies without."

His analysis of external factors in the position of Great Russia
in the fourteenth century and his assertion that the massive
wave of migration from the south made Moscow its "ethnological
center" illuminated, for Kliuchevsky, one of the basic causes of
"the comparatively early and intensive settling of the Moscow
region." Here was one of the major factors in its early success.
The first wave of this flood of people toward Moscow was the
migratory movement out of the Dnieper region of Russia.
Colonists from the southwest, pouring over the Ugra River,
came first upon the region of Moscow, and "it was here, therefore, that they settled in the greatest numbers." This concentration of population brought substantial economic advantages to
the prince of Moscow, "the number of persons paying direct
tribute being greatly increased." On the other hand, this geographic position also contributed to the early commercial success
of Moscow. "The development of trade and shipping along the
Moscow River brought life to the industry of the area, drew it
into this trading movement, and enriched the treasury of the
local prince with receipts from customs duties on articles of
trade." The economic consequences of Moscow's key position
brought its grand prince very substantial material wealth, while
his lineage—he was a descendant of Vsevolod III—"showed him"
how he could best put this wealth to use. As a representative of

one of the youngest lines in the genealogy of Vsevolod, he "could entertain no hope of living long enough to acquire seniority and thus of occupying in his turn the throne of the senior grand prince." He stood as "the prince having the least rights to the throne in the whole family." A prince with no large domain, "deriving no support from the age-old customs and traditions," he developed "his own unique policies." "Earlier and more decisively than others, the Prince of Moscow departed from the established interprincely relationships, sought new ways, giving no thought to the old order, to old political customs and traditions."

It is along these lines that Kliuchevsky defined the basic reasons why Moscow and its princes became such a great force in history. Destroying the old traditions, Moscow's power operated against the disintegrating tendencies that prevailed in northern life, and began the "reverse process" of assembling the various parts of Russia in the upper Volga region into a new whole.

According to Kliuchevsky, this "new task" facing the princes of Moscow rested on no historical tradition, and therefore was able to acquire significance as a broad national and political movement only very gradually and slowly. Its first stage was the extension of the territory of the Muscovite domains—by buying up of other lands, by seizing them by force, sometimes by "diplomatic seizure, with the aid of the Tatar horde," by contracts of service entered into with other udel princes, and finally, by taking land through colonization, by migration out of the Muscovite estates into the land beyond the Volga. A model ruler and administrator, the Muscovite prince knew not only how to acquire land, but also how to preserve his acquisitions, and how to establish order within them. The second phase was the acquisition of the title and influence of grand prince. The strength of Moscow and its crafty diplomatic policies gave the Great Russian land a period of rest from external alarms, and by the time of Dmitri of the Don they had made the prince of Moscow a "national leader of northern Russia in the struggle against external enemies." This significance was only reinforced by the transfer to Moscow of the metropolitan see. This extremely important event came about, according to Kliuchevsky, rather by accident, once again in connection with Moscow's geographical location, on the route taken by the metropolitan on his way from Vladimir to the southwestern dioceses. Metropolitan Peter was frequently in the city, was a friend of Ivan Kalita, and also died in Moscow. This "accident" became a kind of legacy for later metropolitans. All this helped to determine the "territorial and national growth of the principality of Moscow," which "absorbed the disunited parts of the Russian land" and in this process transformed itself into a national Russian state.

Another process was developing parallel to the one just described: this was the "political elevation" of one of the princes of Moscow, who, as the eldest member of its princely family and as grand prince, reaped the greatest rewards from the external successes of the principality. A major factor in this "political elevation," which in the end turned the grand prince of Moscow into a monarchical Russian sovereign, was the gradual increase in his share of the patrimonial or votchina inheritance, which by tradition fell to the eldest son. "Thus by means of this inherited supremacy, which in itself had no political privileges or powers, the grand prince was transformed into a sovereign ruler not only of the common people, but also of the udel princes, his younger brothers." This happened because the "family ambitions of the Muscovite grand princes happened to coincide with the needs and aspirations of the people." The real motive for the activity of the Moscow princes was a "dynastic interest, in whose name both the external expansion of the principality and the internal concentration of power were carried forward." It was not until "about the middle of the fifteenth century, however, when a new national power (the Great Russian people) had appeared in the midst of the general political disintegration," that the successes of the princes of Moscow at last created a form for meeting the new and growing need of the masses "for a political centralization of their disunited forces, their need, in other words, for a strong state organization as a way out of the confusion of the udel system and the Tatar enslavement." It was then, in the reigns of Vasili the Blind and Ivan III, that the "hidden, dormant national and political aspirations of the Great Russian people, which had so long and so unsuccessfully sought some reliable focus, coincided with the dynastic struggle of the grand prince of Moscow and carried him to the lofty position of national sovereign of Great Russia." Such, for Kliuchevsky, were the "major phases in the political growth of the Moscow principality."

These "major phases" were sharply delineated and brilliantly characterized in Kliuchevsky's lectures. Their outlines were drawn so that they appeared as the juxtaposition of two contrasting elements or processes in the historical life of Great Russia. In order to appreciate the powerful, concrete quality of Kliuchevsky's presentation, which is such an attractive feature of his writing, one must regard the decline of the udel system in Great Russia as the primary historical element in this process, coming as a direct result of the colonization of northeastern Russia; one must see this colonization itself as a comparatively late phenomenon; and one must date the emergence of "the Great Russian people" about the middle of the fifteenth century, connecting this with the "coincidence" of the family quarrels and ambitions of Moscow's princes with the needs and aspirations of the common people. The form of the future Great Russian state was drawn up within the little world of inherited estates in Moscow; and in this same isolated world its future content was developed to meet the growing needs of a new nationalism. Kliuchevsky's brilliant dramatization of this historical scheme then finds its denouement in the appearance of a "national sovereign of Great Russia," who leads the way out of the disorder of the udel system and the Tatar yoke by creating a firmly established state structure.

In one of his earlier articles P. N. Miliukov characterized the work of this *coryphaeus* of Russian historical scholarship as an example of "the juridical school in Russian historiography." Certainly the description of "works dealing with the history of Russian law" which A. D. Gradovsky has set forth in reference to Sergeevich's *Veche i kniaz* (The Town Assembly and the Prince) is to a remarkable degree applicable to the work of Kliuchevsky. The task of such works, he writes, is to "discover the 'principles' whose emergence in the historical process is reflected in examples taken from Russian history. Historical material does not have its own independent significance; it is important only to the extent that it is possible to study in such material the manifestation of juridical principles"—of principles, it should be noted, defined and established quite outside any analysis of the given historical material.

The decisive influence of sociological dogmatism in the method of the "juridical school" explains the fact—so strange at first sight—that the very historical facts dealt with by our historians in their study of the question of the rise of the Great Russian state, although illumined from various points of view, remain in themselves essentially unexamined, while the sources from which these facts are drawn also remain insufficiently analyzed. This whole question, surely one of the most important for the scientific study of the history of Russia, has not once been subjected to scholarly consideration. The works of Stankevich, Veshniakov, and Polezhaev have only reflected, each in its own way, the general positions of the courses offered in our universities. It seems absolutely essential to this author, therefore, that an attempt be made to reexamine in greater detail the data contained in the historical material at our disposal, and to explain the conditions affecting the formation of the Great Russian state without any dependence on traditional historical and sociological theories and concepts. The fact is that any more or less careful and thorough survey of the genuine historical material given to us in our sources leads to this interesting and scientifically valuable conclusion: the domination of theoretical concepts in our historical scholarship has led to a one-sided selection of data, involving the omission from the theories developed of everything that does not serve to illustrate or confirm the premises of an established scheme. There has also been an insufficiently critical approach to the sources themselves. The most important of these sources—princes' testaments and treaties and the chronicles—still await careful study. We do not yet have a complete and scientifically accurate edition of the official documents. Their analysis is limited to one article by Chicherin, which fails in many respects to satisfy the demands of the historian. The study of the chronicles has only recently been taken up seriously in the works of A. A. Shakhmatov, and the conclusions drawn from this study have yet to be utilized in a review of the history of the fourteenth to sixteenth centuries.

II. NORTHEASTERN RUSSIA BEFORE THE TATAR INVASION: THE ROSTOV-SUZDAL LAND IN THE TWELFTH AND THIRTEENTH CENTURIES

The Rostov land occupies a unique place in the various presentations of Russian history. It breaks into the traditional historical treatment of the twelfth and thirteenth centuries as something freshly formed and quite unforeseen. Pursuing Solovyev's theory, Kliuchevsky spoke of it as a region "lying outside the old, original boundaries of Russia, and in the twelfth century more a foreign than a Russian land." He saw its first colonization by Russians as occurring when the "great mass of the Russian people moved northward in the face of overwhelming external pressure, away from the region of the Dnieper in the southwest toward the Oka and the upper Volga valley." Kliuchevsky found it possible, therefore, to study the "earliest and deepest roots of the later Muscovite state" in the early Russian colonization of the upper Volga. This fascinating task, that of tracing the formation of a new order of political and social life on virgin soil, produced perhaps the finest pages in Kliuchevsky's remarkable *Course in Russian History*. Against the background of primeval nature with its half-savage Finnish population there appears in bold outline the princely landholder, a colonizer and organizer of the land, building up a completely new culture on the strength of his own personal skill and energy. This historical type was created by Solovyev and effectively elaborated by Kliuchevsky. "Once the armed guardian and mobile ruler of the whole Russian land, the prince in the north becomes, from the thirteenth century on, the master of his town and lord of his own patrimonial estate." Iuri Dolgoruky is the Columbus of the Volga region. "Here in the north," we read in Solovyev, "in this vast, forbidding, and sparsely settled country, there was only one ancient city—Rostov the Great. Soon, however, new cities began to rise around Rostov. Iuri Dolgoruky is especially renowned as a tireless builder." Kliuchevsky adopted Solovyev's view here.

Beginning with Iuri Dolgoruky, who left many cities and towns in the Suzdal land to his sons, each prince, as he ruled this land or the part of it that had been willed to him, left his domain in a very different state than that in which he found it. The area came to life before his eyes—the dense forests were cleared, new arrivals from the south were settled on the fresh soil, industries were developed, new revenues were added to his treasury, new social classes came into being.

How did this concept of Iuri as a builder of cities arise? Our sources indicate that he built four towns: Ksniatin at the mouth of the Nerl, Iuriev-Polsky, Dmitrov, and Moscow. Yet Tatishchev credited Iuri with a broad program of city building, and Solovyev and Kliuchevsky have then cited Tatishchev as a source. Kliuchevsky explained this by saying that Tatishchev himself claimed to have "discovered a whole series of other new cities in northern Russia hitherto unknown . . . in sources now no longer accessible." In Tatishchev, however, we find something quite different. Clarifying his mention of Iuri as the builder of many new cities in "White Russia," Tatishchev says only that there were other cities "which the sources do not describe in this way, and although the names of all are not mentioned, nevertheless under various circumstances and on various occasions from this time onward the recently erected cities are mentioned in the chronicles one by one." Tatishchev thus considered those cities that were not previously mentioned in the chronicles but which were mentioned from this point on in the accounts of the activities of Iuri and his successors as in fact "recently erected cities." The construction of these new cities with old south Russian names was then ascribed to Iuri by Tatishchev on the strength of a passage in the Novgorod Chronicle, which he quoted as follows: "Recalling the older Russian cities that had once been his and had then been seized by Iziaslav, Iuri built Iuriev-Polsky and other cities with similar names." To which Tatishchev adds the comment: "We may understand this to mean: to which he gave the names of cities existing then in the vicinity of Kiev." Kliuchevsky was obviously relying not on Tatishchev's sources, but on Tatishchev's assumptions. Still more characteristic are other quotations from Tatishchev in Solovyev and Kliuchevsky. Solovyev referred to a passage on page 76 of the third volume of Tatishchev's work as evidence from the sources. Kliuchevsky then quoted this same passage from Solovyev, telling how "Andrei Bogoliubsky took pride in his colonizing activity," and how, in connection with his plan to establish Vladimir as a separate metropolitan see, it was he (and not Iuri) who said to the boyars: "I have settled the whole of White Russia with cities and towns and have made it populous." But there are no grounds whatever for referring either of these passages in Tatishchev to his "sources now no longer accessible." The text that misled Solovyev is actually an insertion by Tatishchev in his *Compilation of the Chronicles,* at the beginning of a chapter titled "The Division of the State into Two Grand Principalities," as can be seen from the author's own notes on pages 457–58 of the same work. Kliuchevsky's quotation, then, is clearly the fruit of the same reworking of the chronicle text.

The notion that an extremely elementary cultural level existed in the Rostov land in the twelfth century has no positive foundation whatever in the data that have come down to us. For the most part it is based on the lack of information in our sources concerning the inner life and general condition of this region. It is often difficult for historians to bear the test of the old truth the absence of information must never be taken as proof of the absence of "historical life." In the light of a close and unprejudiced examination of the vague outlines that in our sources do reflect something of the conditions of life in the Rostov region along the upper Volga before Iuri Dolgoruky, during his reign, and then under Andrei Bogoliubsky, it is possible to say they actually contradict the established view. The features of that culture are defined rather clearly, in fact, in the works of Sergeevich and N. P. Kondakov.

Surely the accepted view is already put in question when one realizes that the affirmation of a well-established hereditary princely rule in a given area must serve as a sign, for the historian, of substantial successes in previous colonization and in the organization of local life; or when one realizes that not only in Kievan Russia, but always and everywhere, society "antedates its prince." On the other hand, if Kliuchevsky had wished to apply to northern Russia his theory on the significance of foreign trade in the rapid development of complex social institutions and a distinct political order among the eastern Slavs, surely there is no lack of supporting evidence. The abundance of currency and products coming to the Slavs from the East in the eighth and ninth centuries; the knowledge among Arab peoples of a significant Russian trade with the Bulgars, with the Khazar kingdom, with merchants on the Caspian Sea and beyond; the rich finds of western currencies of the tenth and eleventh centuries; the information we have concerning the collection of tribute by Khazars from the people of Viatka in the form of *shchliagi*, i.e., western shillings, a fact that is, incidentally, extraordinarily difficult to explain; the early knowledge Scandinavian people had of distant northeastern Europe—all this gives us a picture of the significance of the trade route along the Volga, not only earlier but also more clearly defined than the picture we have of the route from the Varangians to the Greeks along the Dnieper; not to speak of the vast property holdings, the revenues from wilderness areas, and the general early interest of the princes of Kievan Russia in the distant Rostov country. The political organization of this frontier land under the sons and grandsons of Iaroslav is not quite clear. According to the narrative of the Kievan Chronicle, Boris ruled as prince in Rostov under Vladimir the Great, and Gleb in Murom. I see no convincing reason for taking a negative approach to this record in the old chronicle, as Shakhmatov has done. The use of sons to hold the frontier outposts of their domains was a constant feature of the policy of the Kievan princes. Under the sons of Iaroslav were the domains along the Dnieper, those of the right bank under Iziaslav and those of the left bank under Sviatoslav. Alongside these we see Rostov, Suzdal, and the Volga land, including southern Pereiaslavl, in the hands of Vsevolod. This geographical (and rather artificial) grouping of volosts created the special tradition of Vsevolod's *otchina* [11] and served as the basis for the pretensions of the northern princes to southern ("Russian") Pereiaslavl, these pretensions being reinforced by their desire to hold a "portion" of the Russian land in order not to lose influence on the center of the whole system of traditional interprincely relations. Although engaged in the war against the

---

11. *Otchina:* basically the same as votchina, but viewed from the standpoint of the recipient of the patrimonial domain ("an inheritance from my father").—TRANS.

Polovtsy and embroiled in southern political affairs, Vladimir Monomakh never let Rostov drop out of his sight. He traveled there from time to time on princely business; with the aid of his sons he vigorously defended this "his father's volost" against seizure by Oleg Sviatoslavich of Chernigov, and he built there, "in his own name," the city of Vladimir on the Kliazma. Before the reign of Monomakh and also under his rule, Rostov was apparently governed at times by *posadniks* [12] appointed by the prince. Monomakh sent his *tysiatsky* [13], Georgi the Varangian, to govern Rostov, placing his son Iuri "in Georgi's hands." Iuri later became prince of Rostov and ruled over this northern volost without interruption for a period of forty years. The basic characteristics of this country began to appear more clearly in his reign, and as soon as we are able to find more or less precise descriptions in the chronicles of the structure of political relationships in the Rostov land, the emerging features of internal order at once bear witness to the breadth and complexity of the historical process through which it must have passed in earlier times.

According to the latest compilation of chronicles that has come down to us, there were two great city centers in this region: Rostov and Suzdal. We do not know when the city of Suzdal was founded, but politically it was younger than Rostov, although from the time of Iuri it stands on a level with it, and in our chronicles there is more mention of "the Suzdal land" than of "the land of Rostov." Almost certainly the same process that we shall observe later as "the rise of Vladimir" in the reign of Andrei Bogoliubsky was seen as "the rise of Suzdal" in the Rostov region under Iuri Dolgoruky. To my knowledge only Sergeevich has appreciated the significance of this process for a proper understanding of the early history of northeastern Russia. For Andrei Bogoliubsky the "throne of his father" was in Rostov, but, as Sergeevich has noted, "Iuri lived more often in Suzdal than in Rostov"; it was from Suzdal that he set out on his cam-

12. *Posadnik:* the mayor of a free city elected by its veche; or the administrative head of any city, town, suburb, or district in Old Russia. —TRANS.

13. *Tysiatsky:* a commander of militia; a senior administrative official, having control over the police and military personnel of a city or town. —TRANS.

paigns and to Suzdal that he returned; in Kiev he was surrounded
not with men of Rostov, but with men of Suzdal; and it was
to the latter that he distributed the homes and villages of
Iziaslav's *druzhina*.[14] Although Sergeevich speaks of "the growing predominance" of Suzdal, Suzdal did not completely over-
shadow Rostov. The terminology of the Laurentian Chronicle *
in its description of the reign of Andrei Bogoliubsky and of the
events following his death definitely places Rostov and the men
of Rostov in the foreground, to the disadvantage of Suzdal. Nor
is that all. Its text bears the clear marks of being a reworking of
a different account, in which Rostov alone stood as the center of
northeastern Russia, Suzdal being added by the compiler of a
new and later edition of the text. Thus, for example, in the celebrated words of the chronicler on the relationship between the
old cities and their dependent towns, we read: "and here the
ancient city [singular] of Rostov and Suzdal and all the boyars
wished to do what was right in their own eyes, and not what
was right in the eyes of God." These lines prompted Sergeevich
to write: "It would seem from this that Rostov and Suzdal
formed a single city." Sergeevich explained the rise of Suzdal
by analogy with the subsequent rise of Vladimir:

In old Rostov there were not a few strong men or boyars who
naturally strove to control all the affairs of the volost. It was to get
away from these boyars, we must conclude, that Iuri went to Suzdal.
In all probability the boyars managed to stir up conflict in Suzdal
also, however, and so Iuri's son Andrei moved to Vladimir.

Thus already in the reign of Iuri Dolgoruky a powerful boyar
class had appeared in the Rostov land. It is hardly possible to
regard this view of the importance of the boyars as pure con-
jecture. It is supported by all the narratives of the chronicles
dealing with Iuri, Andrei, and their descendants.

The main goal of Iuri's policy was to preserve the Rostov
votchina for his own family and at the same time to consolidate
its domination over the rest of Russia. Iuri decided to place his
eldest sons (from his first marriage, with the daughter of the

---

14. *Druzhina:* a prince's following or bodyguard; the basic and most
reliable unit of a prince's army.—TRANS.

* The fourteenth-century redaction of the Russian Primary Chronicle.

Polovtsian khan Aepa) in the cities of Kievan Russia in the south, and he appointed them to rule under him in "Russian" Pereiaslavl, Turov, Peresopnits, Vyshgorod, and Kanev. He kept the sons of his second marriage (with a princess of Byzantium) in the north —Mstislav as prince of Novgorod, Vasilko, Mikhalko, and Vsevolod in Rostov and Suzdal. According to the Vladimir Chronicle, "the men of Rostov, Suzdal, and Pereiaslavl Zalesky and the whole druzhina" kissed the cross to Iuri "in the name of the younger sons, Mikhalko and his brother." When he had to go and consolidate his position in Kiev, he left the youngest (Mikhalko and Vsevolod) in Suzdal under the tutelage of their mother and his tysiatsky, Georgi the Varangian. Thus we are confronted with the growing significance of the votchina of Iuri's sons in the Rostov-Suzdal land (his youngest son by a second marriage), which obviously had the support of the most influential forces there. Iuri's eldest son, Andrei, upset his father's plans by leaving Vyshgorod and moving north "into his volost of Vladimir." There is some truth, perhaps, to the hint contained in Karamzin's quotation of a connection between Andrei and a special party of boyars. The Kuchko family "rose against" his willful entry into Suzdal. This was the very family with which he was to enter into mortal conflict in later years. This hint of an influential participation of the boyars in the events that took place in Suzdal in the time of Iuri and Andrei is confirmed by the subsequent course of events. Twenty years later Andrei was the ruler of Suzdal, but he achieved this goal only by wiping out his adversaries with the support of friendly boyars.

We read in the chronicles that on the death of Iuri "the men of Rostov and Suzdal, having considered all things, called Andrei, his eldest son, and placed him on his father's throne in Rostov and Suzdal." Three years later Andrei drove his rival brother princes with their supporting boyars—"formerly his father's men"—out of Suzdal.

In all these events the interaction of the pretensions and quarrels of the princes with the struggle and strategy of the boyar parties is obvious. In my book *Kniazhoe pravo v drevnei Rusi* (Princely Law in Old Russia) there is a detailed analysis of the chronicle text which tells of the events in Suzdal surrounding the murder of Andrei Bogoliubsky. This study has led me to the conclusion that the frequent mention of actions taken by "the men of Rostov and Suzdal" must be regarded as references not to "veche assemblies" in these cities, but to the same activity on the part of the Rostov-Suzdal boyars as we see in the secret agreement to murder Prince Andrei made by the boyar Kuchko's son Iakim and his son-in-law Peter. Sergeevich has rightly explained the power of Rostov right next to the principality of Suzdal by pointing to the significance of the Rostov boyars. The unique twofold "seniority" of Rostov and Suzdal in the upper Volga region cannot be explained otherwise than as the result of the common action of "the boyars and the whole druzhina," even though this class was organized around two centers. "Rostov, Suzdal, and all the boyars" . . . "the men of Rostov and Suzdal and Pereiaslavl and the whole druzhina" . . . such are the formulae used in the chronicles. Even if we were to hold to the usual theory that these phrases point to the active role of "the old veche assemblies," this would not change very much our conclusion concerning the leading political role of the powerful boyars, who stood at the head of "the whole druzhina" and determined the destinies of the entire land. This boyar class in Suzdal was the same as everywhere in old Russia—it was the "senior druzhina," wielding power not only by its administrative influence, but also by reason of its social position and its great landholdings. There are no grounds for considering this class as something that emerged for the first time in the reign of Andrei Bogoliubsky or Iuri Dolgoruky. The wealth of the powerful rural class forces us to the conclusion that Iuri and Andrei, as the first princes of the Rostov-Suzdal land, built their political and territorial dominion not on freshly settled and unstable ground, but on the basis of a firmly established way of life characterized by very complex internal relationships, and in the context of the same general situation that we find at that time in Kiev, Volhynia, Galicia, and Chernigov. All over Russia the twelfth century was a time of marked increase in boyar landholdings, influence, and privileges.

For the Suzdal region the reigns of Iuri and Andrei represented an epoch of increased organization of the princes' administrative system and physical power, with an accompanying consolidation of the possession of this land as the votchina of a single princely line. This development of princely power was reflected not only in building programs, but also in colonization and local political activity, in the same concerns of the princely heir for his land as we shall observe somewhat later in the activities of the ancient line of Monomakh in southwest Russia, in the lands of Volhynia and Galicia.

Of course it was necessary for the princes to build cities, either in new places of strategic importance or as a means of strengthening existing settlements. But the clearest and most characteristic feature of the building activity of the northern princes was their construction of churches. Vladimir Monomakh built the Church of the Holy Saviour in Vladimir. Iuri Dolgoruky is credited with building the Church of the Saviour in Pereiaslavl Zalesky, the Cathedral of Iuriev-Polsky, the Monastery of the Holy Saviour of Evfimevsky in Suzdal, the Churches of St. Boris and St. Gelb on the Nerl, and the Church of the Mother of God in Rostov (decorated with mural painting in 1187). Andrei Bogoliubsky was the builder of the Cathedral of the Assumption in Vladimir, and the Churches of St. Joachim, St. Anna, and the Golden Gate in Vladimir. His brother Vsevolod continued this building, erecting in Vladimir the Dmitrovsky Cathedral and the Church of the Nativity of the Holy Virgin; he also repaired the Cathedrals of Vladimir and Suzdal. Vsevolod's son Constantine built a new Cathedral of the Assumption in Rostov, when the church built by Iuri was destroyed by fire in 1211, and in Iaroslavl he built the Churches of the Assumption and the Transfiguration. All this church building represents an important and fascinating page in the history not only of Russian art, but of art in general. The favorite material for this building was white stone transported up the Volga from the lands of the Bulgars on the Kama River. Among these churches there are examples of outstanding craftsmanship and a well-developed and original architectural style. These architectural monuments have prompted N. P. Kondakov to say that "Russian art is an original artistic style, a great historical development, growing out of the work of the Great Russian race in cooperation with other foreign and Eastern peoples."

Such a striking increase in the construction of stone churches, and even more important, the elaboration of an original and artistically interesting style, are possible only in a country with a developed city life, rich in material resources, in local trades and crafts, and in the general level of its culture. Kondakov justly points to the decoration of the exteriors of the Suzdal churches with symbolic and instructive sculptured figures as a sign of a cultured urban life. Obviously this sculpture could count on capturing the attention of and being comprehended by the people thronging the squares around the churches. By itself this ecclesiastical architecture is sufficient cause to reject the notion that northeastern Russia in the twelfth century was a dark and primitive country where the general level of culture, wealth, and urban life stood far below that of Kiev in the south.

The original creative style of Suzdal art in the twelfth century is one of the outstanding features of this particular section of Russia. But it would be wrong to exaggerate its uniqueness and ignore its ties with trends in the south and the west. There is ample evidence in our chronicle sources to show how much the princes of northeastern Russia valued these ties. In the meantime, a fascination with the "family theory" has left a deep mark on our historical scholarship, in the sense that the policy of Iuri Dolgoruky has been thought of as a struggle for the abstract principle of seniority in the Russian land, involving also the question of possession of "Kiev's Golden Throne," but without sufficient attention being paid to its real motives. What is quite evident from the facts of his life as they are presented in our chronicles is that Iuri was striving to preserve and strengthen his hold in southern Russia and to pursue at the same time his local Suzdal interests. His struggle for Kiev must not be separated from his characteristic efforts to secure the votchina of Vsevolod Iaroslavich and Vladimir Monomakh—southern Pereiaslavl and also Russian Gorodets, Posemye, and Kursk—by a line connecting Suzdal with the south. From this viewpoint the activities of Andrei Bogoliubsky and Vsevolod Big Nest are not such a violent departure from their father's policies. They rejected the concept of Kiev as the necessary center of all Russian influence, but it should be noted that there were other reasons for this besides their desire to retain a powerful influence over the destinies of the south. Over and above the political motive—which was to hold in their own hands the traditional center of the entire system of relationships between the princes and thereby prevent their rivals, the older sons of Monomakh, from gaining influence that would threaten Suzdal in its relations with Novgorod, Smolensk, and Chernigov—their policy must be explained also by certain commercial and cultural interests. The commercial and cultural connections between Suzdal and Chernigov, Galician Russia, Smolensk, and Novgorod were broad and of vital importance. They have not yet been sufficiently investigated. If they are not taken into account, however, then not only the art and architecture of Suzdal, but also the development of literary creativity in northeastern Russia are rendered historically inexplicable. Valuable commodities came from the south, and also from the west. German merchants and other European artisans were known in Suzdal; through Suzdal passed the trade between East and West—Bulgar wax, for example, and German woolen goods. The great Volga River route, marked out in the eighth and ninth centuries, was still in active use in succeeding centuries. The Rostov-Suzdal land was located on the path of this ancient route, and it is this, together with the other factors, that explains the appearance of a highly developed historical life in the northeast of Russia at a very early time.

Even under Iuri Dolgoruky a particular set of interests had already become central in the general policy of Suzdal, and this set of controlling interests was to remain in large part basic and typical in the history of Great Russia in the centuries that followed. The celebrated struggle for Kiev did not by any means occupy the whole of Iuri's attention and energies. During the life of his father and of his older brother, Mstislav, and then later during the eight-year reign of Vsevolod Olgovich on the princely throne of Kiev, he was engrossed in local concerns, primarily the desire to secure full control over the waterway from Novgorod down the Volga. The first information we have about Iuri in the north concerns his campaign against the Kama Bulgars in 1120. An attack on Novgorod was a characteristic feature of his strategy. More than once he placed his sons on the throne of Novgorod; twice he seized Novi Torg, closing off the main artery of trade from Novgorod to the east. Iuri's ambitions went further: he launched an attack on the *Zavolot-*

sky [15] domains of Novgorod, thereby cutting off Novgorod's sources of tribute and its trade routes to the north. The struggle between Iuri and Mstislav's son Iziaslav was engaged here on the soil of Novgorod, Iziaslav launching an attack because "Georgi of Rostov had given offense to his city of Novgorod, had taken away its tribute, and was breathing insults against it along its routes of trade." This clash drew Iuri into a struggle with Iziaslav for Kiev, and his victory destroyed the hostile forces of the southern princes at their very center.

The Suzdal orientation in the policy of Iuri Dolgoruky also molded the activities of Andrei Bogoliubsky. Andrei's energies were also directed mainly against Novgorod. He installed obedient princes in Novgorod by force—sometimes his sons, sometimes his nephews, once the son of Rostislav, the vassal prince of Smolensk—subduing the people of Novgorod by stopping the transport of grain into the city from the Volga. The famous campaign against Kiev in 1169, which led to the destruction of "the Mother of Russian cities," came as a result of the struggle for control of Novgorod between Andrei and Iziaslav's son Mstislav. Andrei was also concerned about his relations with the Bulgars, and made two campaigns down the Volga in 1164 and 1172.

Vsevolod Big Nest pursued the same policy, on the same two fronts. Besides a great campaign against the Bulgars in 1184, when he stood for ten days before the walls of their capital city, Veliki Gorod, Vsevolod sent his troops to war against the Bulgar land in 1186. As with Andrei, however, his main concern was for his relations with Novgorod. These relations became more and more complicated as the Novgorod forces sought aid against the pressure from Suzdal among the princely rivals of this growing northern power. Kiev had fallen. The other branch of the line of Monomakh had become occupied with the affairs of Volhynia and Galicia. Novgorod tried now to meet the pressure from the princes of Suzdal and Vladimir by turning first to the princes of Smolensk, then even to the princes of Chernigov.

15. *Zavolotsky:* from *Zavolochie,* the "land beyond the portages," i.e., the Novgorod hinterland, extending hundreds of miles north and east of the city itself.—TRANS.

Novgorod could not do without the aid of a powerful prince. It was bound to princely power, however, by something more than just the need for protection of its trade routes or its interests in its dependent lands and in the votchinas established as the basic property of its princely families. The twelfth century and the beginning of the thirteenth century was a time of trouble in the life of Great Novgorod. Its trade was taking on a western orientation, and its campaign against the western and eastern Finns was being broadened as a source of fur tribute and as a way of gaining control over important industrial districts. A stubborn struggle with Swedes, Lithuanians, and Germans was begun for control of the Baltic trade routes and dominion over the Finns. Such a commercial city could not exist without a prince experienced in military leadership who would not only organize its campaigns and self-defense, but also carry out these activities with his own military forces. The princes of Suzdal were stronger than others, and their interests were closer to the purposes of Novgorod. In them Novgorod was to find the most effective support in its struggle with the Finns and its western enemies. But precisely for this reason the Suzdal princes were a threat to Novgorod's independence, which had not yet been fully consolidated. From the time of Iuri and Andrei onward the princes of Vladimir-Suzdal strove vigorously and constantly to bring Novgorod into subjection even as they defended and supported it against others.

It was Vsevolod Big Nest who laid the solid foundations for "the grand principality of Vladimir and Great Novgorod," the name usually given to this political formation in the later chronicles of the Suzdal land. After several decisive clashes, Vsevolod brought the men of Novgorod to such a point that they petitioned him to send them a prince, and Vsevolod, the first to be given the title of "grand prince" in the chronicles, then sent his nephews or sons to rule as princes in that city. The aggressive policy of the Grand Prince of Vladimir made it necessary for him to have the largest possible military force at his disposal. The desire of the north Russian grand princes to bring other Russian princes under their rule (in order to paralyze the opposition to their extension of power and to utilize the forces of vanquished princes in their own undertakings) was determined by the very real demands of Suzdal's general policy. This appears with special clarity in the relations of Andrei Bogoliubsky and Vsevolod Big Nest to the princes of Murom-Riazan and Smolensk. The princes of Vladimir sent them out on campaigns with their own troops, reducing them to the position of vassals. They sought to justify their command of these forces by appeal to the traditional idea of seniority among the princes, although Andrei had "detached" seniority from the throne of Kiev and Vsevolod had attached it specifically to "the grand princely throne of Vladimir." The real meaning of "seniority among the whole brotherhood of Russian princes" had been essentially distorted in this process. The earlier Kievan seniority was not only justified but also sustained by the common interests of all elements of Kievan Russia, above all by the essential task of doing battle with the Polovtsy. In contrast to this, the seniority of the Suzdal prince became a force compelling "the brotherhood" to serve policies and goals that were either unrelated or in fact opposed to the interests of the lesser princes. It was only under duress that the sons of Rostislav of Smolensk served under Andrei and Vsevolod in their campaigns against Novgorod and the princes of Chernigov. Or again, in the Murom-Riazan country, especially after its breakup into two princely votchinas (Murom going to the descendants of Sviatoslav and Riazan to the descendants of Rostislav), internal unrest gave the princes of Suzdal an opportunity to establish real dominion over these lands on the basis of an alleged "seniority." Iuri Dolgoruky had been the first to interfere arbitrarily and without challenge in the affairs of Murom-Riazan. His son Vsevolod, after attempts to "bring order among the brothers" of Murom and Riazan in 1180, commanded that the quarreling princes be expelled, and sent his own son Iaroslav to reign as prince in Riazan. An attempt to block this action was harshly put down with the destruction of the city of Riazan, the removal of a great number of people to Suzdal, and Murom being given over to the prince of Pronsk.

Having subjugated the princes of Murom and Riazan, Grand Prince Vsevolod then assumed the defense of the Murom-Riazan frontiers. In 1183 we find him going on a campaign against the Volga Bulgars with the princes of Riazan and Murom. In 1199 he marches with his son Constantine against the Polovtsy, advancing as far south as their winter headquarters on the Don. The struggle against the steppe nomads and the neighboring Mordva (Finns) kept the forces of Riazan and Murom in a state of constant alert, and it was absolutely necessary for them to rely on the rest of Great Russia for military support. In fact, therefore, the development of Vladimir's "seniority" tended to serve the local political interests of Suzdal, and the southern poet was right in reproaching Vsevolod: "Your thoughts did not fly far afield, your father's throne their chief concern." Southern Russia drew no benefit from Vsevolod's organizing abilities. His occasional arbitrary interference in southern affairs only hastened and made more acute the political disintegration of Kievan Russia, and his actions were determined primarily by his relations with Smolensk and Chernigov.

Even the riots and civil disorders that shook Rostov-Suzdal on the death of Vsevolod in 1212 failed to destroy the unity of the land. The grand principality of Vladimir remained intact. After the unstable agreements of 1212 and 1213, the rivalry of Vsevolod's sons Constantine and Iuri ended in 1217 in compromise: "Constantine sat on the throne in Vladimir, and Iuri in Suzdal, and there was great joy in the land of Suzdal, and the devil alone bewailed his loss." A situation had developed in Suzdal reminiscent of the joint rule of the elder sons of Iaroslav the Wise in Kievan Russia. As in the earlier agreement of 1213, when the seniority was given to Iuri, so also in 1217, when it was transferred to Constantine, the positions of the younger princes were determined by the "ordering" (*poriad*) of the two elder brothers. Thus in 1213 Iuri had removed his brother Vladimir from Moscow and sent him to "his otchina in Russian Pereiaslavl." Now when Vladimir returned to his brothers in Suzdal from imprisonment among the Polovtsy they "gave him Starodub and its domain." Iuri II became established on the grand princely throne following the death of Constantine in 1219, and firmly retained his position of seniority over the younger princes, sending his brothers, sons, and nephews off on numerous campaigns. In 1229

Iaroslav began to suspect his brother Iuri, who was giving ear to a party of flatterers, and he drew Constantine's three sons, Vasilko, Vsevolod, and Vladimir, away from Iuri, thinking to oppose his elder brother; but God did not allow this evil, and the wise Prince Iuri summoned them to appear before him in Suzdal, and all enmity that had come between them was settled, and all the princes bowed down to Iuri, accepting him as their father and master.

Even stronger were the common interests of the whole Rostov-Suzdal land. The sphere of Suzdal political activity was still too broad and its pressures were still too clearly felt to permit the tendency toward the disintegration of princely domains into separate votchinas to offset the process of the internal organization of the land. The connection between the grand principality of Vladimir and the city of Novgorod was strengthened as a result of the energetic activity of Vsevolod's third son, Iaroslav. Even during his father's lifetime Iaroslav was a supporter of Suzdal influence beyond its borders—in southern Pereiaslavl and Riazan. From 1215 onward, in his dealings with Novgorod, Iaroslav appeared in what for the residents of that city must have seemed a very ambiguous role: that of a vigorous proponent of the power of the prince versus Novgorod's independence, but also of a great leader in Novgorod's struggle against its western enemies and in the subjugation of the Finnish tribes. From the standpoint of the prince of Suzdal, of course, there was no ambiguity here whatever. He was pursuing his own ends and not those of Novgorod. There is no basis for regarding this policy of Iaroslav in Novgorod as an effort to set up his own separate domain or oprichnina. Grand Prince Iuri II and the whole brotherhood of Suzdal princes stood solidly behind him. Iuri's son Vsevolod did replace him on the throne of Novgorod for a time in 1221 and again in 1224, but not for long. Grand Prince Iuri sent his son to Novgorod, and then (again at the request of Novgorod) Iaroslav. Again, in 1224, he gave them his brother-in-law Mikhail of Chernigov, after forcing the men of Novgorod to pay a large tribute under threat of attack. Armed forces from Suzdal marched to the relief of Novgorod and Pskov in the wars these two cities were carrying on with German and Lithuanian forces. They also reinforced Novgorod troops in their advance against the Chud, Iam, and Karelian tribes of Finland. Novgorod and Pskov were grateful for this help, but also felt the pressure of the prince's own independent policies on the western frontier, since Iaroslav did not always take local factors and interests into consideration.

To the east, with the aid of his sons and nephews, Iuri II was engaged in a war with the Mordva, at this time not just a defensive operation, but a full-scale offensive. He was involved also in warfare with the Kama Bulgars. To help in the conduct of these wars he had built a new supply post at Nizhni Novgorod. Nor had other aspects of the general policy of Suzdal been forgotten. Iuri was working to keep southern Pereiaslavl in a position of dependence on Suzdal. He was also increasing his influence in the land of Chernigov, taking advantage of his relationship with Prince Mikhail. Iuri released the princes of Riazan who had been made prisoner by his son Vsevolod, letting them return to their estates. Following the cruel murder of their six brother princes by Gleb and Constantine of Riazan, he helped Ingvar, the son of Igor, overthrow the murderers and establish himself on the throne of that city.

Under Iuri II the general policies of Suzdal moved in the path already laid out by his father, Vsevolod III. Internal disorders and the multiplicity of princely domains threatened the unity of Suzdal, but its unity was far from being destroyed. From the evidence of our sources it is impossible to establish any instance of a division of the Rostov-Suzdal land into votchina or oprichnina domains of separate princes in the period before the Tatar invasion. In the changing generations of princes we do find, of course, as we do also in Kievan Russia, the votchina ties and claims of certain lines of princes to particular cities and volosts, but there are still no indications of a breakdown into separate votchinas of the Rostov-Suzdal land as a whole. The history of interprincely relations in northeastern Russia takes on vital interest only after the death of Vsevolod III in 1212. Before that date there is no evidence for the existence of votchina principalities in the Suzdal region.

Vsevolod's arrangements for the future of his domain are known to us only through accounts of contemporary chroniclers, which bear clear traces of the disorders that occurred at the time of his death and are obviously colored by their compilers' views. Grand Prince Vsevolod Big Nest ruled just as despotically as Andrei Bogoliubsky before him, keeping the younger princes in

the position of vassals and agents of his will. In the passages dealing with him in the chronicles a new political terminology is
developed: the title "grand prince" means consistently "the position of seniority" among the Russian princes; and for the first
time we encounter in these passages a form used by the princes
when they addressed the Grand Prince. He is referred to as
"master" (*gospodin*). But how did Vsevolod provide for a succession of power after his death? A passage that gives at least
a partial answer to this question is found in the compilation of
chronicles made by the monk Laurentius. This passage apparently entered the Laurentian Chronicle from a Rostov source,
since it is obviously composed by a supporter of Vsevolod's son
Constantine. The author's eager desire to establish Constantine's
right to the seniority on his father's death reveals the polemical
mood created by the struggle that developed between Constantine and his brother Iuri. In telling how Vsevolod sent his son
Constantine to the princely throne of Great Novgorod in 1206,
the narrator puts the following speech in the mouth of the Grand
Prince:

O my son Constantine, upon you first has God laid the seniority
among all your brothers, and Great Novgorod has the seniority in
the princely rule over all the Russian land; let your honor be then
in accordance with your name: God has laid on you the position of
seniority not only among your brothers, but also in the whole
Russian land, and I bestow this seniority upon you. Depart now into
your city.

Here, in a rather pompous and rhetorical style, is an account of
the manner in which Constantine was installed on the throne of
Novgorod by his father, the Grand Prince. Vsevolod bestowed
"the cross of honor and the sword" on his son—a solemn in-
vestiture representing the charge to "save his people from their
enemies." "All his brothers" accompanied him to the city; also
all his father's boyars and all the merchants (all "his father's men,"
and "all the people"); and, finally, "all his brothers' envoys." The
confusion of certain elements in this passage—for example, the
inconsistency of the personal presence of Constantine's brothers
alongside their "envoys"—prevents us from accepting the entire
narrative as a late rhetorical invention, but it also suggests that

in this passage there has been some distortion of an earlier and
more accurate text, which in all probability described the actual
event. According to the chronicle, the men of Novgorod, "from
the least to the greatest," accompanied by their bishop, Mitrofan,
solemnly greeted Constantine and led him in a procession of
crosses into the Church of St. Sofia, where the ceremony of
installation on the princely throne was performed.

It is extremely likely that as a partisan of Constantine, the
author used a simple narrative description of his departure for
Novgorod and his experiences along the way, inserting into this
basic account a series of impressive details designed to create a
scene rivaling in political significance the account of Vsevolod's
earlier bestowal of the seniority on Iuri. What is essential here
is not the factual accuracy of the scene portrayed, but the outlook reflected in it. We have here something new and alien to
Kievan Russia, alien even to earlier Novgorod chronicles: an
attempt to connect Constantine's right to the grand princely
throne (i.e., the position of seniority not only among his brother
princes, but also in the whole Russian land) both with the fact of
his princely rule in Great Novgorod and with the notion that
"Great Novgorod has the seniority in the princely rule over all
the Russian land." A new historical concept of the sovereignty
of the grand prince appears, which, on the one hand, will live
on in the northeastern chronicles' designation of the grand principality as that "of Vladimir and Great Novgorod," and, on
the other, will give special significance to the Novgorod tradition
of Rurik as the first of the Russian princes. As we shall soon see,
this concept was to gain strength from the real meaning that
actual possession of Great Novgorod came to have for the grand
princes.

But even in this particular question of Constantine's claim to
the seniority our author could not really have departed so
very far from historical fact in his rather polemical description
of Vsevolod's dealings with his son. Constantine's position during
his father's reign had in fact always been unique. After placing
his other grown sons on princely thrones outside Suzdal (in
Novgorod, Riazan, and southern Pereiaslavl), Vsevolod recalled
Constantine from Novgorod in 1207 and "set him beside himself," having given him "Rostov and five other cities, and placing

him in Rostov." Later events, incidentally, show that this was not a grant to Constantine of a votchina or udel.

It is typical of the Laurentian Chronicle that it does not preserve an account of the conflict between Vsevolod and his son Constantine over the question of the future destiny of the grand prince's rule. Information of this conflict has come to us only by way of later compilations, the most complete report being that of the Voskresensky Chronicle, which under the year 1211 says:

Grand Prince Vsevolod sent for his son Constantine in Rostov, giving him Vladimir for his living and giving Rostov to Iuri; but he did not go to his father in Vladimir, wishing rather to add Vladimir to Rostov. Vsevolod then sent for him again, calling him a second time, and once more he did not go to his father, wishing to join Vladimir to Rostov.

In the Chronicle of Nikon this text is already being expounded in such a way as to raise the question of rivalry between Rostov and Vladimir. It is rewritten in this later text as a speech by Prince Constantine addressed to his father:

Inasmuch as you have shown great favor to me and have regarded me as your eldest son and have wished to establish me in the seniority, so then give me the old and primal city of Rostov, and give Vladimir to Iuri; or if your pride of honor does not wish it so, then give me Vladimir, and give him Rostov.

It is very probable that it was at this time that Pereiaslavl was given to Iaroslav and Iuriev-Polsky to Vladimir.

Vsevolod definitely connected the position of seniority among his sons with the princely throne of Vladimir, and his disagreement with Constantine lay in the latter's desire to keep both Rostov and Vladimir in his own hands. Vsevolod did not take Rostov away from Constantine; instead, he gave to Iuri both Vladimir and the grand princely seniority connected with it.

Grand Prince Vsevolod summoned all his boyars from the cities and their volosts, and also Bishop Ioann [Ivan], with the abbots, priests, merchants, court servants, and all the people, and gave Vladimir to his son Iuri as his own city, and led all to the cross, and all kissed the cross [in fealty] to Iuri; he commanded all the princes to kiss the cross to him also.

We may suppose that in other respects the *riad* [16] established by Vsevolod remained the same. The Chronicle of Suzdal-Pereiaslavl adds to this text an exhortation by Vsevolod to his sons on the need to preserve unity: "nor must you separate one from another, but if any other prince shall rise against you, you shall all unite against him, and Christ and the Holy Mother of God will be your succor, and also the prayers of your grandfather Iuri and your great-grandfather Vladimir, and I too shall bless you." This notion of the testaments of Vladimir Monomakh, Iuri Dolgoruky, and Vsevolod Big Nest as guides that their descendants must follow is typical of the chronicles. It will live on for a long time both in the written tradition and in the thought of Great Russia. In time another chronicler will recall this idea as he notes the increasing power of the grand prince after Ivan Kalita, and will write that Ivan received "the grand princely rule over the whole Russian land, as did his forefather Grand Prince Vsevolod-Dmitri the son of Iuri."

Great changes occurred in the organization of the Rostov-Suzdal land about the time of the death of Vsevolod Big Nest. Suzdal quite clearly receded into the background after a short-lived rivalry with Rostov. Alongside the grand principality of Vladimir stood Rostov, on which Constantine counted just as heavily for support of his claim to the seniority as he did on Vladimir. His chronicler and supporter, whose view of the matter has clearly influenced the Laurentian text, completely left out any mention of the transfer of the seniority to Iuri and of the distribution of principalities to Iaroslav and Vladimir, just as if Vsevolod's riad spoke only of a succession in the position of grand prince. Quite obviously this chronicler was expressing a Rostov viewpoint, the desires of the Rostov boyars. But the social forces with which princely power had to reckon in the Rostov-Suzdal land were not limited to the boyars of a single city. Once again let us recall how on the death of Andrei Bogoliubsky the fate of the land was determined at an assembly in Vladimir "of the men of Rostov and Suzdal and Pereiaslavl and the whole druzhina, from the least to the greatest." One chronicler has

---

16. *Riad:* the testamentary disposition of a prince's votchina to his sons and widowed princess, including a definition of their ruling relationships. —TRANS.

called this assembly of boyars and princes a "council of the druzhina." It was not just boyars who were acting here, but also "the whole druzhina"—i.e., "the boyars, the junior princes, and the sons related by marriage." But the boyars decided the fate of the land. It was they who summoned the sons of Rostislav —the nephews of Vsevolod—to the prince's throne, they were the ones whom the Vladimir Chronicle blamed for the "heavy burden" laid on the land by the policies of the Rostislavichi, and it was in them that the princes found their real support. Vsevolod consolidated his power in the Rostov-Suzdal land only by opposing these boyars and relying on his own personal druzhina, on the men of Vladimir, and on "those boyars who remained with him."

Among the older boyars who opposed Vsevolod, one group, including Dobryn the Tall, Matvei Shibutovich, and Ivan Stepanovich, stands out especially clearly. Vsevolod's victory on the plain of Iuriev signaled the destruction of this boyar party. Some perished in the battle, others were imprisoned, with the victors seizing their villages, horses, and cattle. Vsevolod then ruled "without fear of the powerful boyars, who were offending the weak, exploiting the orphaned, and doing great violence." And yet he too was surrounded by "powerful boyars." The same boyars who had stirred up dissension among the princes and thereby wrecked their attempt to reach peaceful agreement by a division of the Rostov-Suzdal land into separate domains now made peace with Vsevolod as grand prince over the whole land, in the face of his great military and economic strength. The events of the year 1211 show clearly that this was not just a matter of rivalry between the two cities, but also an issue involving basic features in the organization of the Rostov-Suzdal land. It was in that year, in a new dispute between Constantine of Rostov and Iuri of Vladimir, that Vsevolod ratified his riad at a great assembly, which Zabelin has called the "first *zemsky sobor*." [17] The list of the various social groups represented at this assembly is suspect, since the text has come down to us in the form of a late redaction. But the general significance of the event is scarcely in doubt. We are confronted here with something very much like the assembly that took place in Vladimir after

17. *Zemsky Sobor*: Assembly of the Land.—TRANS.

the murder of Andrei Bogoliubsy, or at the time of the summons of Constantine to the princely throne of Novgorod in
1206. Vsevolod needed this assembly to get the popular backing
that would secure his riad. In the Rostov-Suzdal land, however,
this backing came not from a veche of the capital city, but from
the entire land through an assembly of "all the boyars from the
cities and their volosts," of the clergy with the bishops at their
head, of the whole druzhina, and finally also of the townsmen,
the merchants, and "all the people."

The assignment of specific principalities to individual sons did
not contradict, as it once did, the notion of the unity of the
land under the rule of the senior prince. Replacing the older
concept of seniority, the title of grand prince was now established in Rostov-Suzdal, and its political significance was reinforced by the ceremony of the kissing of the cross by "all the
boyars" and the whole druzhina—not just those of the capital
city. We have seen how Iuri II, having established himself in
the role of grand prince on Constantine's death, proceeded to
carry out a truly grand princely policy, controlling all the forces
of the Rostov-Suzdal land. Only the information we have of his
growing conflict in 1229 with his brother Iaroslav and his
nephews, the sons of Constantine, gives us any indication of the
instability of this princely solidarity. The first signs of a votchina
division of the Rostov-Suzdal land had now developed into a
prominent feature of local political life. But neither these first
signs of votchina disintegration in the north nor the preservation
of political unity in the face of the multiplicity of princes nor
the conflict of the princes with the boyars makes it possible to
draw a sharp contrast between south and north in the twelfth
and early thirteenth centuries, especially in any explanation of
the way a breakdown of political power into udels or votchinas
began. The unity of the land as a whole was more stable and
firm in the northeast than in any other region of Russia, and the
support of this territorial unity on the part of the boyars (and
other social elements associated with them) stands out more
clearly here than anywhere else. "The powerful Suzdal land"
lived by its own local interests, both political and commercial,
more and more drawing its princes away from involvement in
the wider sphere of "all-Russian" concerns. The southern poet—

the author of *The Song of the Host of Igor*—was right when he reproached not only Vsevolod III, but also Iaroslav the Sharp-Witted of Galicia, the descendants of Monomakh in Volhynia, and the princes of Smolensk and Polotsk for having forgotten the earlier traditions of "the Russian land." The disunity of political interests in different regions is a general feature of Russian history in the twelfth century. Suzdal became the special family domain of a single princely line, following the pattern of the older lands of Polotsk, Galicia, and Chernigov, and at the same time as the regions of Smolensk and Volhynia. Everywhere this individualization of regional interests was connected with a decline in the political significance of the citizens' assembly or veche and with a rise in the power of the prince. Also, we see everywhere an increase in the influence of the boyars on both the internal and external affairs of princely lands, and the continuing struggle of the boyars against the princes as the latter developed gradually into absolute sovereigns. This struggle was more successful for the princes in the north and produced more permanent results there, but it would be wrong to speak of a decline in the political influence of the leading classes of local society. Finally, it should be noted that in their desire to make the younger princes vassals of the eldest prince or sovereign, Andrei Bogoliubsky and Vsevolod Big Nest were only following in the footsteps of Vladimir Monomakh and Mstislav I as they put into practice the age-old concept of the senior prince ruling in his father's place. The princes of northeastern Russia preserved the unity of their grand principality—built as it was on traditional foundations—right up to the terrible time of the Tatar invasion; and indeed it survived this storm.

Chapter

I

The Grand Principality of Vladimir and the Votchina Principalities of the Thirteenth Century

In his study of the "relative positions of power among the descendants of Vsevolod," written from the point of view established earlier by Solovyev, Kliuchevsky found it possible to "forget for a moment that before the first generation of Vsevolod's sons had passed, Russia was conquered by the Tatars." In his opinion, "what we observe in the Suzdal land after this devastation grew consistently and without interruption out of factors already at work in the twelfth century, before the Tatar onslaught."

This opinion reflected a straight-line concept of "organic" development, which was characteristic not so much of Kliuchev-

sky as of the "juridical school." Its extraordinary sociological
dogmatism led to the study of the evolution of forms and
principles of political organization without regard to the general
conditions of political life. In the meantime, however, the general conditions of northern Russia were so profoundly altered
following the Tatar onslaught and the establishment of the domination of the Golden Horde that this change could not fail to
have a powerful influence on the ordering of Great Russian
internal and external affairs, and thus not only on the activity
of Russia's ruling powers, but also on their structure and relative positions within the Great Russian milieu. Let us recall certain well-known facts.

The formation of the kingdom of the Golden Horde severed
the relations between Suzdal and the Bulgars, and if it did not
completely paralyze the conditions for trade along the Volga, it
certainly sharply altered them for the worse. The eastward military advance and colonial expansion of Great Russia were halted,
not to be resumed for many years. A striking sign of the im-
poverishment of Suzdal in the thirteenth century is the fate of
its church construction, which died out so completely that the
architectural traditions of Vladimir-Suzdal were long forgotten
when efforts were made in Moscow at a later time to revive
them. The ties with trade centers on the Dnieper were cut, although relations with southwestern Russia were maintained.
Southern Pereiaslavl passed from the historical scene. Engulfed
in the same swift process of decay, the Chernigov land stood for
a long while beyond the radius of Suzdal's concerns. A general
narrowing of horizons and restriction of activity must be taken
as basic facts in any study of the political decay and widespread
degeneration of local life in northeastern Russia in this period.
Under such conditions, which of course prevented the setting up
of any broad tasks or goals, the significance of the grand principality of Vladimir declined and the ability of the grand princes
to centralize and focus the political life of Suzdal was weakened.
To the west the independence of Novgorod became more and
more firmly established, despite the efforts of the "downstream"
princes to retain their power over that city. For a while the
advance of the Suzdal princes to the north and northeast came to
a standstill, and the constant harassment of Novgorod's routes

and the infringement of its tribute ceased. The time of Grand Prince Iaroslav II and his sons and nephews appears as a complex period of deterioration in the power of the grand principality of Vladimir. The old form of grand princely sovereignty was dying. Its death was hastened not only by the decline in common concerns which had for so long sustained the sense of necessary unity, but also by the pressure of Tatar power and the increasing independence of Great Novgorod. These factors undermined the efforts of the grand princes of Vladimir to increase their power over the younger princes and to justify a broad policy that would be viewed as the task of the whole of northern Russia and upheld by the common interests of all Great Russian peoples.

We are almost wholly unable to assess the actual consequences of Batu's massacre. His blows were aimed for the most part at the cities, but when the rural population failed to vanish into the forests, it too was taken captive or was slaughtered. There were losses of cattle and possessions, and homesteads were burned to the ground. According to the chronicles, "there were practically no areas nor villages nor towns where the Suzdal land had not been ravaged" by the Tatar oppressors. The destruction was staggering. A single blow, even if severe, could have been absorbed and overcome rather quickly; the tremendous power of the Horde, however, pressed heavily and constantly on Great Russia from about 1240 onward. Our sources are deeply colored by the painful memory of this disaster. We may even guess that this alien power was more keenly felt and more harmful to Great Russian life at first than we have been accustomed to believe. Tatar *baskaks* [18] with military forces were stationed in every capital city to keep the princes and people in subjection and to guarantee the collection of tribute. In the land of the Horde the Russian principalities were dealt with through *darugs*,[19] whose excursions to Russia with other "envoys" of the Khan were both destructive and humiliating. The oppressive despotism of a strange and alien power hung over the whole of northeastern Russia. Attempts to resist the oppressors in the fifties and sixties provoked new invasions and ever more cruel repressions. Russia was compelled to humble herself before the Khan's power and

18. *Baskak:* a Tatar tax gatherer.—TRANS.
19. *Darug:* a Tatar tax commissioner; any official.—TRANS.

adapt herself to new ways. These new conditions helped to determine the fate of Iaroslav II and are clearly reflected in the achievements of Alexander Nevsky.

No sooner had the Tatar forces withdrawn to the south than Iaroslav assumed the grand princely rule in the place of his brother Iuri II, who had perished in a battle with the Tatars on the Sit River. Iaroslav set out to pursue the goals of earlier grand princely policy. In 1239 he defended Smolensk against the Lithuanians and placed a local prince, Vsevolod the son of Mstislav, on its throne. He put the defense of the western borders in the hands of his son Alexander. In the same year Alexander and a force from Novgorod established a town on the river Shelon; a year later Alexander's forces successfully turned away an attack by a Swedish army; in 1242 they beat off an attack by the German knights on the city of Pskov. Like the earlier activity of Iaroslav when he was prince of Novgorod, Alexander's western campaigns were a part of the policy of the grand princes of Vladimir. Recognizing the value of this help from the "downstream" princes, the men of Novgorod also felt the effects of their inevitably increased dependence on the Grand Prince's power. There was no other course open to them, however, in these difficult times. In 1241, after he had "come to terms with the men of Novgorod," Alexander left the city "with all his court" and went to Pereiaslavl Zalesky. Novgorod immediately sent to Iaroslav begging him to send another son to rule on its throne. The Grand Prince "gave them his son Prince Andrei," but it was not long before they forwarded a new petition asking that Alexander be returned, in the face of threatened attacks by the Lithuanians, the Germans, and the Chud. "And Grand Prince Iaroslav once again gave them his son Alexander." The latter then marched to the defense of Pskov, "taking with him his brother and all his men." Again in 1245, when Lithuania made an attack on the Torzhok and Bezhets region, it was not only the troops of Novi Torzhok and Novgorod who came out against them, but also detachments from "downstream," including men from Tver and Dmitrov. Alexander was victorious, and appointed the Novgorod host "to act as his court."

In the autumn of 1242 a new power broke into the history of Great Russia—the Tatars. Khan Batu's envoy demanded that

Iaroslav pay homage to the Khan in the land of the Golden Horde, "and he went accordingly." Our chronicles tell us that the Khan acknowledged his seniority over all the princes of the Russian land. Iaroslav traveled to the land of the Horde with his son Constantine. The latter was ordered by the Khan to go to distant Mongolia to pay homage to the Great Khan himself. When Constantine returned from this visit in 1245, Iaroslav was forced to travel to Batu, and then to Mongolia, where he "was afflicted by great exhaustion" and on the return trip died "as a result of his tribulations."

As a new fundamental element in princely law, the Khan's conferral of the right to the throne did not affect the principality of Vladimir alone. On Iaroslav's return from the land of the Horde in 1242, and probably in response to orders brought from the Khan, the princes of the house of Constantine (Iaroslav's elder brother)—Constantine's son Vladimir; Vasilko's two sons, Boris and Gleb; and Vsevolod's son Vasili—journeyed to the land of the Horde "for their otchina." Batu confirmed their rights and allowed them to return "once he had decided how each should enter into his otchina." Iaroslav set out on his second trip to the land of the Horde "with his brothers and sons," and with their own sons his two brothers Sviatoslav and Ivan returned "from the Tatars into their otchina." Iaroslav, of course, was then sent by Batu to Mongolia, on the trip that was to cost him his life.

Batu had ratified the internal order of territorial possession among the Russian princes. The descendants of Constantine received as their otchina the domains of their father, who before his death (in 1219) had given Rostov to his son Vasilko and Iaroslavl to his son Vsevolod. There is no mention in our sources of any assignment to the youngest son, Vladimir. Later, however, we see Vladimir ruling as prince of Uglich. Under Iuri II the three hereditary princes of Rostov acted "as one." Vasilko and Vsevolod perished in the fight against the Tatars, leaving minor sons—Vasilko's sons Boris and Gleb and Vsevold's son Vasili. As we have noted, these young princes traveled to the land of the Horde "for their otchina" with their uncle Vladimir in 1244, and Batu, in the typical language of the chronicles, "decided how each should enter into his otchina." We should not attach too much significance to this particular expression. In the light of the chronicle text, which tells us that "Boris and Gleb the sons of Vasilko sat on the throne of Rostov" even before Iaroslav's first journey to the land of the Horde, we should regard the Khan's "decision" as simply a ratifying of the status quo. We have no knowledge of any dispute over the rights of Boris and Gleb to Rostov. Their votchina right was simply accepted, just as the right to Polotsk was acknowledged by tradition to "the grandsons of Rogvolozh," or Chernigov to the descendants of Oleg. Vsevolod's son Vasili remained in his own city, Iaroslavl. Further on we shall have occasion to touch on the fate of Iaroslavl after Vasili's death in 1249. Although Boris' and Gleb's uncle Vladimir could have laid claim to the seniority among them, he was evidently satisfied with the modest throne of Uglich. This branch of the princely line of Rostov disappeared with Vladimir's sons, and Uglich continued as an integral part of the Rostov otchina. If we discount the loss of Iaroslavl, the Rostov otchina was to remain intact until it broke up under pressure from the city of Moscow.

Before his death, Grand Prince Vsevolod Big Nest had placed his younger sons, Sviatoslav and Ivan, in the care of their brother Iuri. In 1212 Iuri gave Iuriev-Polsky to Sviatoslav; as for Ivan, we have only the mention, under the year 1238, that Grand Prince Iaroslav gave him the city of Starodub. The principalities of Iuriev-Polsky and Starodub then became the votchinas of these two princely lines.

All other volosts in the grand principality of Vladimir were in the hands of Iaroslav. He also held control over all the princely forces at the disposal of the Grand Prince; the division of land into separately ruled domains did not yet signify a political disintegration. The seeds of such disintegration lay in the depths of the grand principality of Vladimir, just as they did in Kievan Russia under the sons and grandsons of Prince Iaroslav I, but the power of the Grand Prince outweighed that of the younger princes no less (if not more) than in the time of Monomakh and Mstislav the Great. Grand Prince Iaroslav comes before Khan Batu as the senior "of all the princes of Russia," surrounded by his "brothers and sons." The ratification of the individual princely votchinas by the Khan's conferral of rights simply confirmed what was already acknowledged in the customs of the princely families. In future, however, this ratification was to become a factor in the political decline of the grand principality of Vladimir and an occasion for the Khan to interfere directly in Russian affairs.

The throne of the Vladimir principality, connected since the time of Vsevolod III with the grand princely seniority, occupied a unique position among the principalities of northern Russia, similar to that of the "Golden Throne" of Kiev in ancient times. The rights to seniority among the Russian princes inevitably came into conflict with the votchina concept in the pressing of claims to this throne. This ambiguity in the princely tradition greatly affected the interrelations of the princes on the death of Iaroslav II. The principality of Pereiaslavl was the only undisputed votchina of his sons. Iaroslav had received Pereiaslavl from his father even during the latter's lifetime, and then again according to the terms of Vsevold's riad, made just before his death. Under the year 1213 the Chronicle of Pereiaslavl-Suzdal has an account of Iaroslav's coming to Pereiaslavl so that his father might "deliver" the men of that city to him. It speaks of how Vsevolod "gave him into their hands," and of how in turn the people of Pereiaslavl kissed the cross to Iaroslavl. It happened that Iaroslav later reigned also in Novgorod and Riazan, but Pereiaslavl always remained "his" city. This close tie was preserved even during the time of his rule as grand prince. His eldest son, Alexander, reigned in Pereiaslavl, and the city remained the votchina domain of Alexander's descendants, precisely the descendants of the senior line, passing first to Alexander's son Dmitri and then to his grandson Ivan. As we shall see, the close and prolonged association of Pereiaslavl with the throne of the grand prince had definitely affected the attitude of the princes toward this city and had given it a special significance. With the assignment of Rostov as the otchina of the descendants of Constantine, another important city, Suzdal, became associated in a special way with the grand princely throne. Although Iaroslav later gave Suzdal to his brother Sviatoslav, it did not become the votchina of the descendants of Sviatoslav, like the domain of Iuriev-Polsky. Sviatoslav evidently lost Suzdal when he lost the grand princely rule. The original transfer of Suzdal to Sviatoslav, then, might have been part of an arrangement between the brothers regarding the future destiny of the grand princely throne.

On Iaroslav's death, "Prince Sviatoslav the son of Vsevolod sat in Vladimir on the throne of his father, and placed his nephews in the other cities in the order that their father, Iaroslav, had established." The sons of Iaroslav, however, did not become reconciled to the transfer to their uncle Sviatoslav of Vladimir and the whole grand princely rule. In the same year (1247) both Andrei and Alexander traveled to Khan Batu. Batu then sent them on to Mongolia "to appear before the Khan's sons," i.e., the Great Khan's heirs and successors. Sviatoslav did not hold the grand princely rule for long. He "sat for one year" and then, before Alexander and Andrei had time to return, Mikhail Khorobrit (Iaroslav's third son) drove him from the throne.

Owing to the fragmentary nature of the records we have of this period, it is impossible to resolve the question of the immediate motives for this act of sedition: whether, for example, it had some connection with the suspicious death of Iaroslav II. Such a connection does seem probable. But the recognition of this possibility does not really help us much unless we know something about the increasing intrigue in the land of the Horde and the two negotiations between Iaroslav and Khan Batu. The conduct of Iaroslav's sons is enough to make us think that, having established relations with the Golden Horde, their father then made an attempt to settle the succession to the throne of Vladimir on his own direct line, without regard to the claims of others. Such attempts had been made before. Even if we reject this possibility in the case of Iaroslav, we have examples of similar intrigues in the conduct of Vladimir Monomakh, of his eldest son, Mstislav, and indeed of the whole ancient line of Vladimir II.

However that may be, the sons of Iaroslav did make their claim to the throne. And they were successful, although in a somewhat unexpected way (perhaps more unexpected for us than for them). If we are to judge by the literal text of the Laurentian Chronicle, the affair was settled not in the land of the Golden Horde, but at the court of the Great Khan in distant Mongolia. The "Khan's sons," we are told, "decreed Kiev and the whole Russian land to Alexander, while Andrei sat on the throne of Vladimir." Just how this division was understood is difficult to say. We know only that Novgorod was placed under the rule of Alexander, while Pereiaslavl was transferred out of his hands and placed under Andrei. Sviatoslav's journey to the Horde, if its purpose was the acquisition of the grand princely throne, led to nothing. He was destined to live out his days on the throne of Iuriev-Polsky. Such was the state of affairs in Russia in 1249. In the following year Metropolitan Kyril of Kiev visited the Suzdal land and solemnized the marriage of Andrei and the daughter of Prince Daniel Romanovich of Galicia. After the wedding the Metropolitan traveled to visit Alexander in Novgorod. It was at this time that Daniel "was maintaining an army at war with Khoresm." At the beginning of the 1250's we observe a drawing together of southern and northern Russia which must certainly have been connected with Daniel's strategy in his fight against the Tatars. In the words of the chronicle under the year 1252, when Batu sent an army under Nevriui against Prince Andrei, the latter "determined, with his boyars, to fly rather than serve the khans." At this same time "Alexander, prince of Novgorod, journeyed to the Tatars and they let him go in honor, giving him the seniority among all his brothers." Alexander had not associated himself with his brother's policies, but had hastened to the Horde in order to forestall the destruction of his own power and a further degradation of the Russian land. Pursued by the Tatars, Andrei fled first to Novgorod, and then went into hiding for a time in Sweden. Alexander had become the grand prince of Vladimir.

The disturbances did not come to an end with Andrei's flight abroad. Reading between the lines in the fragmentary entries in the chronicles, we can feel the intense alarm and will to resist with which Russia met the first stages in the organization of the Tatar domination. It is with such emotions and not with any considerations of rivalry among the princes that we should associate the fact that at the beginning of 1254 Prince Iaroslav of Tver "left his otchina" and journeyed "with his boyars" to Lake Ladoga and Pskov. The men of Novgorod summoned him from Pskov, after driving out Alexander's son Vasili. Vasili withdrew to Torzhok pending the arrival of Grand Prince Alexander, at which time Novgorod was humbled and compelled to receive him back as its prince. One feature of this disturbance—the fact that it was Novgorod boyars who supported Vasili and the common people who opposed him—will serve to connect it with later events when the Tatar *chislenniks* appeared in Russia. First to be placed by them in the Tatar *chislo* [20] were the lands of Suzdal, Riazan, and Murom, in which the Tatars "established *desiatniks, sotniks, tysiashchniks*, and *temniks*." [21] Next in turn for census and the levy of recruits was the land of Novgorod. On first hearing of this, "the people of Novgorod were in revolt for a whole year." When Grand Prince Alexander appeared in the city with Tatar envoys, his son Vasili fled to Pskov. Alexander recalled him from Pskov, sent him "back to ´the lands downstream," and severely punished the men "who had led Prince Vasili into this evil." The men of Novgorod, however, still did not permit the collection of "the *desiatina* and *tamga*." [22] "They did not will this to be," although they gave gifts to the Khan and let his envoys go in peace. Only after a year had elapsed did the fear of a new Tatar invasion of Russia bring the people of Novgorod to a bitter submission, and even then "there was great unrest in the city . . . the people were divided, and created an uproar. The majority demanded that the minority submit to the chislo, but the latter did not wish it so." It was necessary for Grand Prince Alexander to have guards set to protect the envoys from the Horde, but in the end the affair was settled. The "godless ones" departed "after taking the chislo," and Alexander placed his son Dmitri on Novgorod's throne. Soon resistance developed against the "pagan violence" in the "downstream" cities. Popular revolts expelled the *besermen* [23] from Vladimir and Suzdal, from Iaroslavl and Pereiaslavl. Alexander made haste to visit the Khan in the land of the Golden Horde, "to speak for the people and avert reprisals." The energy

20. *Chislennik, chislo:* from *ischislenie*, census, enumeration. These words all have to do with the taking of the Tatar census in Russia, and the subsequent levy of conscripts and tribute and taxes based on this census. *Chislo:* the actual quota of conscripts; the actual amount of the Tatar tribute; the Tatar tax list. *Chislennik:* Tatar tax assessor or census taker.—TRANS.

21. *Temnik:* the commander of a large Tatar force; a deputy khan. The other terms here refer to other ranks in Tatar military and administrative officialdom, with *desiatnik* being the junior grade.—TRANS.

22. *Tamga:* a Tatar sales tax or customs duty.—TRANS.

23. *Besermen:* the holder of a lease on the collection of Tatar tribute in a given area; a Tatar tax gatherer.—TRANS.

and power of the Grand Prince kept the Russian people from wasting their forces in sporadic outbursts of revolt against the Tatar yoke. To do this he had to overcome not only the rumbling dissatisfaction of the people, but also sharp disagreements in the ranks of the princes and boyars. Alexander pursued his own policy with the Horde—and indeed in Russia's relations with the Khan he was the grand prince of all northern Russia.

Thus we see Alexander as the chief bearer of grand princely power in both the internal and external affairs of northern Russia. In 1253 his son Vasili repulsed an attack by Lithuania against the domains of Novgorod. In 1256, on news from Novgorod that the Swedes were placing fortifications on the river Narva, Alexander advanced "in full force with the men of Novgorod and Suzdal," and "conquered the whole coastal land." In the difficult years of resistance against the Tatars, Alexander journeyed repeatedly to the land of the Horde. He also sent his brother Iaroslav and his son Dmitri "with all their troops" to Iuriev to make war against the Germans, alongside the men of Novgorod and their Lithuanian allies. The inescapable burden of war against external foes and the impossibility of carrying this war forward on two fronts stongly influence Alexander's policy with regard to the Tatars.

There were no signs yet of political disintegration within the grand principality of Vladimir. Vasilko's sons in the line of Constantine "sat on the princely throne in Rostov" following their father's death. The youngest, Gleb, had reigned in Beloozero from 1251, but this did not break the unity of the Rostov otchina. Prince Gleb took part in all the affairs of Rostov in full partnership with his brother, and only after Boris' death (on the throne of Rostov) did the principality of Beloozero begin to break away from Rostov and become the special otchina of the line of Gleb; not without a struggle on the part of Boris' sons, however, who upheld the unity of their father's land. During the reign of Grand Prince Alexander, Vasilko's sons in Rostov were his loyal vassals. They evidently identified themselves with his policies from the start. Prince Boris was in the land of the Horde when the tragic affair of Mikhail of Chernigov came to a head, and with the support of his boyars he urged Mikhail "to do the will of the Khan." There is evidence of an especially close relationship between Alexander and Vasilko's two sons. It was by way of Boris that he sent gifts to the favorite of Khan Berke, and it was to Rostov that he went from Novgorod after he had quelled the disturbance there, to share his success with Metropolitan Kyril and the Rostov princes.

The Grand Prince played a central role in the ecclesiastical affairs of the Rostov diocese. The Rostov principality was an integral part of the grand principality of Vladimir.

Iaroslavl was a domain within the Rostov otchina of Constantine's line, and had fallen to the lot of his son Vsevolod. After the latter's death in a battle against the Tatars, Iaroslavl was transferred to his son Vasili. The fate of Iaroslavl was greatly complicated at the time of Vasili's death, when Andrei II was reigning on the throne of Vladimir. Vasili died in Vladimir in 1249, leaving a widow and a daughter, his death occurring when Grand Prince Alexander and the Rostov princes were in the city visiting Prince Andrei. It was evidently decided, at this meeting of the princes, to leave Iaroslavl and its volosts to the widowed Princess Xenia and her daughter, Maria. It is possible that the family was anticipating the betrothal of the young princess to Feodor the son of Rostislav, prince of Mozhaisk, and that it was in view of this proposed marriage that "Iaroslavl was given to him." In any case, this transfer permanently separated this domain from the Rostov otchina. During the reign of Grand Prince Alexander and for a long time after, however, there was to be no local princely power in Iaroslavl that could play a distinctive, independent role. There is really no basis, therefore, for speaking of a complete removal of Iaroslavl from the influence of the Grand Prince at this time.

As princes of the third rank, the sons of Vladimir reigned in Uglich, and with their deaths this line of Rostov princes expired.

The relative positions of power occupied by Alexander and his brothers had been determined by the riad drawn up by their father shortly before his death. When their uncle Sviatoslav assumed the grand princely throne, he had "placed his nephews in the other cities in the order that their father, Iaroslav, had established." We do not know the exact nature of Iaroslav's disposition, but we may suppose that it coincided with the division of domains among his sons during his reign, and that

later Alexander, as grand prince, preserved his votchina relationship with Pereiaslavl, which he then passed to his eldest son, who
reigned in Pereiaslavl even during Alexander's lifetime. There is
reason to believe that Gorodets-on-the-Volga and Nizhni Novgorod were assigned to Andrei in Iaroslav's riad. Andrei returned
here in 1256 "as into his own otchina," and in the following
year he received the Khan's sanction of his rule, which cost
Grand Prince Alexander no small amount in gifts to the Khan's
favorite and to the Khan himself, although the agreement with
his brother added Suzdal to Alexander's domains. Prince Andrei
did not play a strong independent role during his brother's
reign. He journeyed with Alexander to the land of the Horde
and to Novgorod, but did not stand out in the circle surrounding
the Grand Prince. He outlived his brother by only a few
months. The third son, Iaroslav, occupied a similar position.
After the turbulent events at the beginning of the fifties, the
younger Iaroslav reigned peacefully in Tver, traveled with
Alexander to the land of the Horde in 1258, and in 1262 led a
campaign against the Germans for his elder brother. Iaroslav's
fourth son, Vasili, reigned in Kostroma, and was only twenty-
two years old at the time of Alexander's death. Constantine died
on the throne of Galich (beyond the Volga) in 1255, after
his journey, on behalf of his father, Iaroslav, to the Great Khan
in Mongolia. He was succeeded by his son David, about whom
all we know is that he died in 1280, and that the chronicle calls
him prince of Galich and Dmitrov.

The existence of these various princely domains still did not
indicate any real political disintegration of the grand principality
of Vladimir. In the period of Alexander Nevsky the Grand
Prince of Vladimir was the sole and undisputed spokesman for
the whole of northern Russia before the power of the Horde,
the defender of all its territories against the attacks of its western
neighbors, the organizer of all its military forces. At the same
time, however, there were local princes "reigning over and holding possession of" separate volosts within the grand principality,
their possession of these domains being independent of the will
of the Grand Prince and determined rather by that "family-
votchina" right which from ancient times had formed the basis
of "the princely law of Old Russia." This was a votchina or

hereditary right, acquired in principle by birth; it was also a family right, since its essence lay in the right of all the sons of the ruling prince to the domain left by their father—to the otchina shared by all his sons. This right was exercised either according to the father's riad, which defined exactly which share of the father's domain each son should receive, or, especially for sons not yet of age at the time of their father's death, through a division of volosts according to the wishes of an uncle or elder brother to whom these younger princes had been "committed" or "given in hand" by the father. The shares of the inheriting princes in their father's otchina were later to be called udels (this term was not yet known in the thirteenth century), and the time will come when the princes will begin to speak of their shares as "udels of their votchina." In the period we are now studying, however, there is nothing either in the terminology or in the nature of the relative positions of power among the princes that is essentially new in comparison with the basic elements of "princely law" in Kievan Russia. The votchina tendency in the rule of the princes was still too clearly subject to the influence of Great Russian political unity, which itself rested on the power of the Grand Prince of Vladimir, for any other system of relationships to develop clearly on the same ground. The period of Grand Prince Alexander reminds us, however, of that moment in the history of Kievan Russia when Vladimir Monomakh and his son Mstislav stood at the head of the land. Even under the great unifying power of the Grand Prince the foundations were already being laid in the internal organization of the land for the individualization of fully developed local votchina principalities. The Rostov domains of Constantine's descendants were regarded as a special hereditary and politically independent unit; votchina domains had been defined for all the princes, for all the sons of Iaroslav and their descendants. Alexander himself was the votchina (hereditary) prince of Pereiaslavl Zalesky, and this territory alone was his sons' otchina, in the strict sense of the term. The grand princely power did not yet have the necessary territorial base, its power was purely political, and herein lay the seeds of its weakness and decline. The internal forces of the country were organized without any direct exercise of grand princely power in each of the local principalities, and instead of supporting the general policy of the north Russian princes under the leadership of the grand prince of Vladimir, they could easily become, in the event of internal discord, a factor in the destruction of this leadership and of all attempts at unification. The history of the grand principality of Vladimir will proceed precisely along this ruinous course after the death of Alexander Nevsky. The oppressive influence of Tatar domination, established during his rule at the cost of tremendous strain on Russia's internal relationships, undoubtedly played a major role in hastening the decline of the grand prince's power.

II.

The Tatar domination of northern Russia was only just establishing itself in the reigns of Iaroslav II and Alexander Nevsky. The setting up of definite structures of dependency caused deep political discord both among the princes and among the common people. Our sources have preserved only a few references to this discord, only a few fleeting and often obscure hints, but even from these we can see how sharp and painful these disagreements must have been. Alexander succeeded in overcoming it and finding support for his policy from among the princes, the clergy, and the boyars. But it is hardly an exaggeration to say that the authority of the grand prince at the end of his reign was badly shaken. Alexander had retained it not only by his own personal energy and influence, but also by the fear of Tatar reprisals and by direct reliance on Tatar power. Over and above the authority of the grand prince a new authority had come into being, strange and alien, but formally accepted and wielding a real and terrible power. Tatar power became a constant factor in the internal political relations of Great Russia, so independent of and isolated from the deep-rooted elements of traditional Russian political organization that it could be utilized in the struggle of Russian political forces either to support or to oppose the authority of the grand prince.

The same can be said of the other major factor that had given support to the grand princes of Vladimir: the possession of Great Novgorod. The possession of this principality was an essential part of their policy: from the time of Iuri Dolgoruky the grand princes' rule had been intimately bound up with the struggle for Great Novgorod. The chroniclers who recorded the following entry were right: "Following his brother Grand Prince Alexander, Grand Prince Iaroslav III sat on the grand princely throne of Vladimir, and he was grand prince of Vladimir and Novgorod." Alexander apparently had established this connection between Great Novgorod and the grand principality of Vladimir on solid foundations, had won the permanent acceptance of his authority over Novgorod, and held it through his sons, defending the Novgorod and Pskov volosts with forces from "downstream" lands, combining the foreign policies of these two lands with the broad tasks of the grand princely power. His control of Novgorod gave a firm foundation to the tradition that the throne of the principality of Novgorod was an otchina for the princes of the "downstream" land, but it also opened up the possibility of ambiguity in this tradition: the sons of Alexander Nevsky could come forward as the hereditary possessors of the throne of Novgorod, but then each occupant of the grand prince's throne could also claim the right to this throne; indeed, in view of his own vital interests, he could not fail to make this claim. The possession of the princely power in Great Novgorod became a separate factor in the struggle for and against the grand princely rule, opening up broad opportunities for the master of Novgorod not only to influence this struggle, but also in the course of events to develop his own "democracy" there by increasing the concessions that the princes were compelled to make to secure Novgorod's support.

The main significance of the grand prince's authority—general control over the political destiny of Great Russia and above all over its self-defense against external enemies—began to decline under the pressure of a new political situation, when Tatar domination almost paralyzed the energies of Great Russia in its advance to the south and east, and turned the self-defense of Great Russia on these borders into a new and extremely costly form of minor frontier warfare. A certain lack of relatedness begins to appear now between the various goals of Great Russian policy, which will lead to a breakdown in the general participation of Great Russian forces in the achievement of these goals, as well as to confusion in the control of Russia's forces. The func-

tions of grand princely power become separated and pass little
by little into the hands of one or other of the local princes while
questions concerning all the representatives of princely power are
settled now only by a general agreement of the princes, in
which the bearers of the grand princely rule no longer always
play the leading role (all the more so in that the interference
of the power of the Horde seems again and again to be quite
inescapable), or by way of armed conflict and open civil strife.
All these elements in the political decline of the grand principality of Vladimir developed with increasing force in the closing
decades of the thirteenth century.

In our review of these events our attention is drawn above
all to the position of the princely families in relation to succession to the grand prince's throne. This is no longer a succession
in the family descended from Vsevolod Big Nest, son of Iuri,
the original ancestral lord of the whole Rostov-Suzdal land. It is
now a succession only in the line of Iaroslav—the sons and
grandsons of Grand Prince Iaroslav II. Disputes over seniority
and power arise only between these princes, as if the grand
principality inherited from their father and grandfather passed
only to them. This reduction of the circle of possible claimants
to the ancient throne was not new in the interrelations of the
princes in old Russia. Even earlier, in Kiev, the desire to limit
the circle to a single family arose each time a strong and active
prince appeared on the senior throne. But now the matter became even more complicated: the vast and obvious power of
Alexander Nevsky threatened to erase from the minds of later
generations the concept of succession through Iaroslav, and gave
rise to a new tendency, to new claims on behalf of an exclusive
succession through Alexander and his descendants, without regard to the other lines of the house of Iaroslav.

These claims on the part of the descendants of Alexander
Nevsky could not, however, be presented with full force and
clarity immediately following his death. Alexander's eldest son,
the disgraced Vasili, disappeared from the scene after the catastrophe of 1257, which proved to be his downfall; we know
nothing of his fate thereafter. Dmitri, the second son, was still
a boy at the time of his father's death and was unable to remain
in Novgorod, where he was living as the nominal representative

of the grand princely power. At the first news of Alexander's death the men of Novgorod banished his son from the city.

The circumstances of the transfer of the grand princely rule to Iaroslav III are extremely difficult to unravel in the texts of our chronicles. But if we consider certain dates that can be fixed quite precisely, we can say that shortly after Alexander's death, "the men of Novgorod, having taken counsel with the posadnik Mikhail, drove Prince Dmitri out of Novgorod," and "sent for Prince Iaroslav," and on January 27, 1263, "set him on the throne." The first treaty between Great Novgorod and Prince Iaroslav III has been assigned to this date. The men of Novgorod took advantage of this opportunity to ratify, by means of a written treaty, those "ancient rights and tolls" that had suffered so much, according to the language of the treaty, from the "violence" that Alexander had "committed" against Novgorod, and which Iaroslav must henceforth "abjure." The men of Novgorod secured the firmest guarantees possible for their political freedom, which was founded on the city's constantly developing "democracy" and on the growing connection between the exercise of princely power and control of Novgorod's "ancient rights and tolls." On the other hand, in its closing section the treaty reveals the significance of trading interests, prompting the men of Novgorod to seek not a weakening but a strengthening of the ties between Great Novgorod and the grand principality.

This strategic move on the part of Novgorod was made possible by the enthronement of Prince Iaroslav in Novgorod before he became grand prince. His whole conduct shows that he stood in need of Novgorod's support, and lost no time in securing the throne of Novgorod for himself in connection with his aspirations to the grand princely rule. Whether the reason for this action was the rival ambition of his elder brother Andrei, which Tatishchev assumed to be the case, or the threat of claims by the descendants of Alexander, which is suggested by the chronicles' association of Novgorod's summons of Iaroslav with its banishment of Dmitri, we must admit that support from Novgorod guaranteed Iaroslav's success in the land of the Horde, as happened more than once in later times with claimants to the grand prince's throne.

The equivocal attitude of Great Novgorod toward the grand princely power was very clearly reflected in the actions of Grand Prince Iaroslav. The separation of Novgorod and Pskov as independent political powers was becoming more and more evident in this period. Each had its own policy in relation to its western neighbors, and the grand princes were increasingly required to take these policies into consideration, even compelled at times to subordinate their own undertakings to them.

The stormy events of 1263 and the years immediately following in the borderlands between Russia and Lithuania tended to increase the independence of Pskov as well as its special significance in Russia's relations with western territories. In 1265 the Lithuanian prince Domont appeared as a fugitive in Pskov "with all his family." He became the organizer of Pskov's military forces, a leader in their struggle with Lithuania, and the molder of Pskov's local policy. The establishment of a Lithuanian prince in Pskov came as a shock to Grand Prince Iaroslav. He hastened to Novgorod "with much strength from the 'downstream' lands . . . intending to march against Pskov and Domont its prince." But the men of Novgorod "restrained him, saying: Ho, prince, you must discuss this matter with us before marching against Pskov." Domont's successful military campaigns had impressed the men of Novgorod. They had longed for some energetic, aggressive action without recourse to the Grand Prince, and evidently had won over some of the lesser princes to their plan, above all Alexander's son Dmitri, whose lot it was to continue his father's exploits in the west. After a year of unrest, and without the aid of the Grand Prince, Novgorod had organized a major campaign of Russian princes, under the leadership of Prince Dmitri of Pereiaslavl, against the German city of Rakovor on the Baltic coast. The battle at Rakovor turned out to be a costly victory, with heavy losses and nothing gained but trouble for Novgorod's neighbors. The Germans were not long in answering with an attack on Pskov, but military energies were exhausted on the Russian side and the princes dispersed without concluding a peace, just as they had done in 1228. Again "nothing good" had been accomplished. A situation had been created in which there was no escape without turning to the Grand Prince for help. So now after much argument and debate the men of Novgorod were persuaded by Iaroslav to put the matter into his hands. Iaroslav succeeded in replacing several rebellious city officials and in selecting his own candidate as tysiatsky; only then did he summon his "downstream" troops and Tatar reinforcements, and with this combined force he was able to compel the Germans to return all prisoners and "draw back from the entire Narva region."

The reestablishment of the Grand Prince's decisive role in Novgorod's external affairs was a part of Iaroslav's effort to restore his power over its internal administration also. He began to conduct himself in Novgorod as its votchina ruler, paying no attention either to Novgorod's "rights and tolls" or to the city's trade relations. Iaroslav spent much of his time personally in Novgorod, in the prince's fortress of Gorodishche, but in 1269–70 there was a "rebellion," and the men of Novgorod "wished to drive Iaroslav out of the city." Iaroslav's supporters were beaten and their homes plundered, and the rebels sent a petition to the Prince, "putting his whole offense in writing," with the demand that he leave Novgorod at once, "so that they might choose a prince for themselves." In spite of the fact that Iaroslav sent word to the Novgorod veche, through his son Sviatoslav and the boyar Andrei Vorotislavich, of his readiness (in the words of the chronicle) to be "deprived" of all his unlawful seizures and to kiss the cross "in deference to the will of all Novgorod," the city still insisted on his departure from Gorodishche. Novgorod had its own candidate for its princely throne: Dmitri of Pereiaslavl Zalesky. The latter, however, declined to enter into rivalry with his uncle, and when Iaroslav "began to bring up his troops" and summoned Tatar forces to his aid, Dmitri bowed to the Grand Prince and led his own men of Pereiaslavl also against the beleaguered city. Iaroslav's second son, Vasili, stood fast on the side of Novgorod. He journeyed to the Horde with Novgorod's envoys and succeeded in "recalling the Tatar host," assuring the Khan that "the people of Novgorod were in the right before Iaroslav." The Grand Prince was unable to subdue Novgorod by force and was compelled to seek peace with the city on its own terms, with his performance of the treaty provisions to be guaranteed by the whole brotherhood of Russian princes. All the dependent towns and rural volosts of Novgorod rose to the defense of their central city. Metropolitan Kyril had to send an epistle of admonition and pledge of Iaroslav's conduct before the people of Novgorod were finally persuaded to make peace with the Grand Prince.

These actions on the part of Novgorod during the reign of Iaroslav III deserve detailed study as signs of the decline of the Grand Prince's power. The aid that he sought from the Horde turned out to be a two-edged sword. Acting as a supreme court for all Russian affairs, the Khan had ruled that the people of Novgorod were justified in their dispute with Iaroslav, thus agreeing with the petition brought to the Horde by Prince Vasili and the Novgorod envoys. The fact that "the grand principality of Vladimir and Novgorod" desperately needed possession of Great Novgorod had inevitably increased that city's significance in Russian affairs at large. Also, the broad development of Novgorod trade in this period brought substantial material wealth to the leading classes of the city. These classes acquired a special influence both with the Horde and among the princes in Russia. At the same time the independent and even determining significance of Novgorod and Pskov interests in the question of Great Russia's western policy was also increasing. In short, the Grand Prince's dependence on the authority of the Horde and the power of Novgorod weakened his position among the other princes, who could and did seek to make their own arrangements with one side or the other to their own advantage and in support of their own growing ambitions.

These characteristic features of the political situation in Great Russia in the closing decades of the thirteenth century created very favorable conditions for the development of separate and independent princely domains at the expense of any general unification of the land under the Grand Prince of Vladimir. Strictly speaking, we do not have sufficient grounds for saying that Grand Prince Iaroslav III found less support in the grand principality as a whole than in his otchina domain of Tver. Among those who acted as his "vassals" we find Prince Iuri of Suzdal and Prince Gleb of Smolensk; quite probably others also—for example, the princes of Rostov and Iaroslavl—were present in his "downstream host." His brother Vasili of Kostroma

and his nephew Dmitri, however, carried out their own individual policies, undermining the authority of the Grand Prince
not only with the Horde, but also in Great Novgorod and
within their own princely circles. Vasili halted Iaroslav's advance
on Novgorod by appearing in the land of the Horde and speaking on behalf of its people before the Khan. Dmitri's circumspect
behavior in this case may be explained, perhaps, by the fact
that Iaroslav had obtained the Khan's permission to subdue
Novgorod. But another motive is also possible. There are indications that Grand Prince Iaroslav wished to be reconciled with
the house of Alexander and to have it on his side. We have
seen how in 1265 he "left Alexander's son Dmitri in Novgorod,"
where the latter had ruled during his father's time, and then
had been driven out when Iaroslav was summoned to its throne.
We know too that Iaroslav later sent his troops to Dmitri's aid
in a campaign against Novgorod planned secretly against his
will. Finally Andrei, Alexander's younger son, reigned as prince
in Volga Gorodets and Nizhni Novgorod, and this could have
happened only with the Grand Prince's consent.

All of Iaroslav's actions were designed to preserve the power
of the grand prince. We see nothing here that can be defined
as the activity of a "votchina ruler" of the Tver land, although
Iaroslav was the prince of Tver and retained it as his own
personal domain even when he occupied the grand princely
throne, and after his death (in 1271) left it to the rule of his
sons Sviatoslav and Mikhail. The only thing in Iaroslav's biography that can be defined as "Tver oriented" was his burial
there in the Church of Saints Kozma and Damian. Iaroslav died
as he was returning from the Horde, and his body was brought
back for burial in Tver rather than in Vladimir. In speaking of
Iaroslav's death, the chroniclers used the ancient formula: "In
the same year Prince Vasili of Kostroma the son of Iaroslav
sat on the throne in Vladimir and was the grand prince of
Vladimir and Novgorod." In fact, things did not turn out
precisely in this way. Vasili had evidently obtained the *yarlik* [24]
to the grand princely throne immediately following his brother's
death, and moved quickly to occupy the throne and the capital

24. *Yarlik:* a Tatar document issued by the khan, granting or approving a
claimant's right to a princely throne in Russia.—TRANS.

city of Vladimir. At this point, however, he learned of Dmitri's negotiations with the city of Novgorod. He sent his envoys there, and when the men of Novgorod "sent for Prince Dmitri" he apparently made an attempt to seize the latter on his way to the city. The attempt failed, and Prince Dmitri "sat on the throne" in Novgorod. Vasili then took Torzhok, established his deputies there, returned to Vladimir, and prepared a new campaign against Novgorod, to be mounted simultaneously from Vladimir, from which Vasili himself set out accompanied by the "Grand Baskak" of Vladimir and "many Tatar princes," and from Tver, where his brother Sviatoslav marched forth (also with "Tatar princes") against the Novgorod volosts. Once again the Novgorod land was laid waste. Grand Prince Vasili returned to Vladimir and made arrangements to seize all the Novgorod traders with their goods in the cities of Vladimir, Tver, and Kostroma. As was usual during disputes with the Grand Prince, bread became scarce in Novgorod. Dmitri made an attempt to organize "the whole Novgorod land" for a counterattack, but his host got only as far as Torzhok, where the Grand Prince's deputies were in control. A veche was held, and it was decided that Dmitri should be "disowned" and the Grand Prince called to Novgorod's throne. Dmitri withdrew to Pereiaslavl, and Vasili "was placed on the throne" in Novgorod.

Apart from his dealings with Novgorod, Vasili's brief reign is an uneventful page in the chronicle tradition. He died in 1276.

III.

With the death of Grand Prince Vasili the older generation of princes passed from the scene. In Solovyev's schematization this was a crucial moment. "We have arrived here at a time when the old concept of the right of seniority was vanishing," he wrote.

The grand princes were showing clearly that what they sought was not the seniority, but power. Each prince of Vladimir tried to increase his possessions at the expense of the other princes. Now that complete acceptance of the idea of the private ownership and separate identity of a domain had led the grand princes into concern only for

their own interests, the other princes could no longer trust the bonds
of family relationship and were themselves obliged to look to their
own interests and try in every way possible to increase their own
power. They faced a single choice: either to become victims of
another prince's power or to make the others victims of their own.
This is why we see now a revolt of the lesser princes against the
Grand Prince, and a flagrant disregard of all ancient rights and family
relationships.

The basic cause of princely quarrels was "their distrust of the
Grand Prince, their unwavering hostility toward any prince who
attached the region of Vladimir to his own udel."

Solovyev's keen perception helped him to distinguish a major
characteristic of the events that took place at the end of the
thirteenth and the beginning of the fourteenth centuries—the
alliances made by the younger princes, among themselves and
also with Great Novgorod, against those who bore the title of
grand prince or made claims to it. But then his preconceived
theory of the relations between the princes led to an explanation
of these facts which is not justified by the facts themselves, as
we have them from our sources, and does not correspond to the
historic realities under consideration.

We must continue our review of the events that were then
shaking the whole political life of Great Russia. On Vasili's
death Dmitri of Pereiaslavl, nephew and onetime rival of both
Vasili and Iaroslav, was free to occupy the thrones of both
Vladimir and Novgorod. He proceeded to "sit on the throne"
in Vladimir first, then in Great Novgorod. In the spirit of his
earlier activities he at once began to take energetic action along
the northwestern frontier. In the very first winter of his reign
he led "the men of Novgorod and of the whole 'downstream
land'" on a campaign against the Karelians. In the following year
he established a new fort in the west, the town of Koporye,
which in the space of another year he had "walled around with
stones." As before in the time of Alexander, the vigorous
military activity of the Grand Prince in the traditional territory
of Novgorod soon gave rise to conflict between Dmitri and the
men of the city, who objected to his infringement of Novgorod's
"ancient rights and tolls" and also to his despotic rule. In 1280
Archbishop Clement of Novgorod journeyed as an envoy to the

Grand Prince in Vladimir "on a mission of peace." Dmitri marched on Novgorod nevertheless, with an army that included "all his brothers," and it was only "after he had waged war in many of the Novgorod volosts" that he concluded peace.

Trouble began when Dmitri's brother Andrei "obtained the grand princely rule from the Khan in place of his elder brother" and "brought back with him a Tatar host." From the chronicles we can deduce only one motive for Andrei's behavior: an intrigue on the part of "his boyar Semeon Tonglievich and other men of substance." Solovyev follows Karamzin in identifying this Semeon with the boyar Semeon of Kostroma, a commander under Iaroslav III who played a prominent role in his prince's conflict with Dmitri. If this is true, and it must be accepted as highly probable, it establishes a connection between Dmitri's difficulties with his uncle Vasili and the revolt led by his brother Andrei. It is not the personal motives of the princes but the outlook and ambitions of the boyars that help to give us a clear understanding of these events. The chronicles were concerned only with the princes, and so they give us only incidental (but for this reason all the more valuable) hints concerning the influence of the boyars on the princes' relationships and on the policies of those bearing the grand princely power.

The arrival of Prince Andrei with the Khan's yarlik and a Tatar army drew all the Russian princes around him. "With a small druzhina" Dmitri fled from Pereiaslavl to Great Novgorod. Here, however, he was not only not received, but met "with all force," in a move designed to prevent him from taking his seat in Koporye, where his deputies were waiting with a garrison of troops. Dmitri had to give up this plan and go where the men of Novgorod "showed him the way"—in all probability to Pskov. In the same winter Prince Andrei arrived in Novgorod and "sat on its throne." He was still in Novgorod when Dmitri slipped through his lines and made his way to Pereiaslavl to prepare a new attack. Under this threat Andrei returned to Vladimir with a detachment from Novgorod and pressed on to Volga Gorodets. After seeing to Andrei's safe return from Novgorod, the posadnik Semeon Mikhailovich occupied the "stronghold" of Torzhok, thereby preventing its seizure by Dmitri's men. Novgorod guaranteed to keep him supplied in case of a failure to defend this outpost. As it happened, however, there were already signs of a change in Dmitri's fortunes. He succeeded in gathering sufficient forces to engage his enemies near Dmitrov. An army that included a detachment from Tver under Prince Sviatoslav, a troop from Moscow under Alexander's third son, Daniel, and a host from Novgorod was forced by Dmitri to sue for peace. The new Tatar forces that Andrei had brought up against him devastated the land but did not really strengthen Andrei's hold on the grand principality. In the meantime Dmitri went to the Horde and appeared before the temnik Nogai, probably to secure the aid of the Nogai Tatars against Andrei's allies among the Golden Horde. In spite of Novgorod's continued opposition, Dmitri subdued his brothers on his return. The Russian princes came over to his side. Dmitri then defeated Andrei's Tatar allies, forced Andrei to yield both the grand princely rule and the throne of Great Novgorod, and also dealt with Andrei's boyars—Semeon Tonglievich was condemned to death, the others he "sent away."

He did not succeed, however, in really consolidating his success or restoring the authority of the grand princely power. This authority had been shattered by the bitter and violent civil war dividing the country, and, even more important, it had been disgraced under the Tatar regime by the princes' constant solicitations and appeals to the Khan and his favorites, to his baskaks and envoys. The young prince Mikhail of Tver "did not wish to bow to Grand Prince Dmitri and he began to muster an army." Mikhail met Dmitri's host near Kashin, where Dmitri came against him accompanied not only by his two brothers, but also by the prince of Rostov and a troop from Novgorod. Peace was concluded without a battle, but the strained relations between the princes and the hostility toward Grand Prince Dmitri were not eased by this pact, and the continuing internal struggle for power among the Horde created a fertile soil for the princes' intrigues and plots. In 1293 Prince Andrei traveled to the Horde with complaints against his older brother, and other princes supported him. Khan Tokhta supplied Andrei with an army under his brother Diuden, and a new expedition against Dmitri was mounted. Once again "the whole Suzdal land was in revolt." Grand Prince Dmitri fled to Pskov. The Tatars

installed the new grand prince, at the same time plundering
Vladimir and fourteen other cities in the area. Great Novgorod
persuaded them not to devastate their volosts or make a campaign
against Pskov only by a presentation of gifts. Prince Andrei
occupied the princely throne in Novgorod, while Feodor (the
son of Rostislav) became prince of Pereiaslavl. The exiled Dmitri
found support this time in Tver. He moved to Tver from Pskov,
and it was from Tver that he conducted his negotiations with his
brother Andrei. These negotiations ended in a peace whose conditions we do not know precisely, although Dmitri's son Ivan
received Kostroma and Feodor gave up Pereiaslavl, after destroying it by fire. Prince Dmitri was on his way from Tver to
Pereiaslavl in 1294 when he died as a result of illness.

Andrei then assumed the grand prince's throne a second time.
His reign was full of strife, arising mainly out of a quarrel over
the possession of Pereiaslavl. The real powers in this period were
Tver and Moscow. The emergence of these "younger" cities
as independent political powers reveals the importance of the
inner changes that had been developing in the life of Great
Russia under cover of the old organization of the grand principality of Vladimir, now torn apart by discord.

The hereditary (votchina) claims of the elder line of Alexander
Nevsky to Pereiaslavl seemed indisputable. But there were two
other features of the tradition of "princely law" on which these
claims were founded which play a very important part in the
destinies of this city. Pereiaslavl was the patrimonial (otchina)
city of all of Alexander's sons, and one could argue whether
it belonged to Dmitri "as his votchina" or because he was the
eldest of Alexander's sons. But this of course created a connection between Pereiaslavl and the grand princely rule, a connection that was reinforced by the other and even more important
desire of Alexander's line to defend their exclusive claim to the
grand princely throne of Vladimir itself as their otchina.

By the Khan's favor and with his armed support, Andrei had
taken both the grand princely throne and Great Novgorod away
from his brother Dmitri; he had taken also Pereiaslavl, and had
tried to transfer it arbitrarily to his ally Feodor. From the
standpoint of tradition everything in his actions reflected arbi-
trariness, violence, and intrigue, since it was his own elder

brother whom he was "driving out of the land"; and yet, taken as a whole, his goals and ambitions never really violated accepted views concerning grand princely power.

On his brother's death Prince Andrei sat once more on the grand princely throne. Dmitri's death had of course nullified the agreement made between them, and, journeying to the Horde, the new grand prince again raised the question of Pereiaslavl, and again "there was enmity among the Russian princes." This time we see an attempt to resolve the "enmity" at a meeting, or what one of our chronicles aptly calls a "disputation," of the princes. On one side stood Grand Prince Andrei with Feodor and Constantine (of Rostov), on the other stood the votchina prince of Pereiaslavl, Dmitri's son Ivan, together with Daniel of Moscow and Mikhail of Tver, and also the people of Pereiaslavl to a man." The princes' stormy "disputation" in the presence of the Khan's envoys ended in an agreement, through the mediation of Bishops Semeon of Vladimir and Ishmael of Sarai, and the princes parted "each his own way." But Grand Prince Andrei did not accept the settlement, and began to gather troops for a campaign against Pereiaslavl. Ivan then hurried back to the Horde to get his right to his otchina ratified by authority of the Khan's decree, entrusting the defense of his domain to Mikhail of Tver and Daniel of Moscow. They stood with their armies near Iuriev, and forcing Andrei to "humble himself before them," they refused to let him pass through their lines to Pereiaslavl. In spite of this joint action by the princes of Tver and Moscow in the defense of Pereiaslavl against possible seizure by Andrei, it is very probable that occasions of intense rivalry had already risen between them, soon to break out in a stubborn struggle for rule over all Russia. At an assembly in Dmitrov in 1301 the princes "made peace among themselves," although "Mikhail and Ivan did not make any mutual settlement." Evidently the future of Pereiaslavl had been raised here and the question had led to a disagreement between the former allies. Prince Ivan died in the spring of 1302. Andrei moved quickly to place his deputies in the city, but Prince Daniel "had sent his deputies to Pereiaslavl, and Prince Andrei's men fled." Daniel's occupation of Pereiaslavl had been anticipated and in a way determined by Ivan's actions before his death.

These actions must be studied carefully if we are to distinguish the basic elements of the "princely law" in this period.

The formula of the Chronicle of the Trinity Monastery must be accepted as the earliest record of this transfer of power: Prince Ivan "gave his consent to Prince Daniel to rule in his place." By virtue of this consent, "Daniel sat in Pereiaslavl" and there established his deputies. Daniel was now prince of the city. In the reference we have to the presence of "the people of Pereiaslavl to a man" at the meeting in Dmitrov in 1301, and also in the passage telling now, after Daniel's death in 1303, "the men of Pereiaslavl sought his son Iuri and did not even allow him to go to his father's burial," we can see the participation of the men of Pereiaslavl not only in the ceremonies of their prince's enthronement, but also in the actual ratification of his claims to this princely throne.

Daniel's claims to Pereiaslavl had been created by Ivan's "consent" to have Daniel "rule in his place." Here is an example of the so-called nomination of a successor by his predecessor (with its analogy in the consent given by metropolitans, in agreement with the grand prince, to those candidates whom they wished to occupy the metropolitan see after them), a procedure that was a custom also in Kievan Russia.

This did not, however, exhaust all the legal steps necessary to confirm Daniel on Pereiaslavl's throne. Also needed was the Grand Prince's approval, and that of the other princes, as well as the sanction of the Khan. Prince Daniel did not succeed in obtaining this confirmation. In 1303, when Andrei returned from the land of the Horde with the Khan's envoys, there was an assembly in Pereiaslavl attended by the Khan's "royal envoys," Grand Prince Andrei, Metropolitan Maxim, Daniel's sons Iuri and Ivan, and "all the princes." "Here the Khan's official letters and yarlik were read," and the assembly came to the conclusion that "Prince Iuri had won favor, and he took Pereiaslavl for himself." Every aspect of this affair would have been in substance completely understandable to a south Russian prince of the twelfth century, and was carried out within the accepted, traditional forms of interprincely relations.

Only on the death of Grand Prince Andrei (in the summer of 1304) did events occur that may be said to represent a real break in Great Russia's political history. The period of struggle for power among the brothers of Alexander Nevsky may be described as historically quite insignificant. The brothers' personal conflict and behind it the struggle of boyar factions were only the symptoms of breakdown and decline in the old grand princely power of the Vladimir princes. Dmitri and Andrei were fighting for possession of this old grand princely power, built as it was on the possession of the princely thrones in Vladimir and Great Novgorod and on the primacy of the grand prince among the other princes of northern Russia. Insofar as the activity of these princes was not a reflection of civil strife, plots and intrigues in the land of the Horde, or secret arrangements and quarrels with one another, it represented a more or less direct continuation of the grand princely activity of Alexander Nevsky and the elder sons of Iaroslav, although with less force and less impressive results. Even during the lifetime of his uncle Iaroslav III, Dmitri was trying to follow in the footsteps of his father. We have seen him on a campaign against the Karelians "with men from the 'downstream lands' and Novgorod," and as the builder of the fort at Koporye, important enough in the defense of the Novgorod frontier to be valued later even by the lords of Moscow. His commanders also marched to the aid of the Novgorod forces. In an epoch of internal disorder and Tatar oppression, the weakening in the Grand Prince's defense of the Novgorod frontier was inevitable, and more and more it opened up broad opportunities for Swedish attacks on disputed territory. Increasingly Novgorod felt itself thrown back on its own forces. But this was only a circumstantial change; neither the leaders of Novgorod nor the grand princes lost sight of the "all-Russian" character of this western struggle, and Grand Prince Andrei took part in it to the limit of his strength and opportunity, now organizing a campaign with a Novgorod regiment to aid Prince Roman of Briansk, now organizing a counterattack against a Swedish fort on the Neva. There is nothing in any of the military or political activities of either Dmitri or Andrei to indicate that "having acquired the region of Vladimir, they then tried to increase their own possessions at the expense of other principalities." During their reigns as grand princes, Dmitri was no more Dmitri of Pereiaslavl, and

Andrei was no more prince of Gorodets, than Iaroslav had been prince of Tver or Vasili of Kostroma in the time of their grand princely rules, and the texts of the chronicles do not support Solovyev's assertion that Andrei "lived in Gorodets even when he was grand prince of Vladimir, just as Iaroslav had lived in Tver, Vasili in Kostroma, and Dmitri in Pereiaslavl."

In spite of all the vitality of the "grand princely tradition," the grand prince's power in the period of Alexander Nevsky's brothers and sons was in a state of accelerating decline. The pretensions to grand princely rule of Alexander's older sons were inconsistent both with their actual strength and with their real significance in the general political life of Great Russia. This "vitality of the grand princely tradition" is indeed illustrated by a number of rather minor facts, by the few attempts of those bearing the title of grand prince to act in the old manner, in the spirit of Alexander Nevsky, but these attempts were not only rather unimportant aspects of these princes' troubled and restless enterprises; they were also no longer expressions of a consistent and sustained policy. It was not just because the circle of tasks envisioned by their general policy had been reduced, or because its goals were less impressive, or because their policy had been narrowed down to that of maintaining the feeblest sort of defense on the (almost exclusively western) frontiers of Great Russia; more decisive in the historical destiny of grand princely power associated with the throne of Vladimir was its loss of leadership even in those activities that were essential for the defense of its central lands. Novgorod and Pskov, which had once grumbled at the fact that their relations with their western neighbors were almost wholly dependent on the selfish military and political interests of the grand princes of Vladimir, now took this western policy more and more into their own hands, constantly developing the "state" character of their local "democracies." Pskov almost completely escaped from the influence of grand princely power, entering more and more deeply into a sphere of relationships separated from Great Russian life and concerned instead with western Russia, Lithuania, and Germany. Great Novgorod was more closely bound with economic and political ties to Great Russia; but even it had its own policies with regard to the Swedes, the Danes, and the Baltic German states, to Lithuania and Pskov, to the Horde and to other Russian princes, who needed Novgorod as a rich and influential ally no less (if not more) than Novgorod itself stood in need of their military experience and their "downstream regiments." There was also a corresponding growth in the political freedom of "Lord Novgorod the Great"—in the influence it exercised in the resolution of conflicts over possession of the grand princely rule, and in the way it could determine the grand prince's relations with local ruling powers. The very development of these internal conflicts among Great Russian princes bears witness to the radical decline in the grand princely power, to its loss of significance as an essential and indispensable political focus of all the general interests of northern Russia. These conflicts rapidly multiplied in the struggle for the succession in Vladimir, in which Tver and Moscow were to become the major determining powers. But what precisely was this "succession in Vladimir," and what was it these new powers were fighting for?

Up to the death of Grand Prince Andrei, the weakened and deeply shaken grand principality of Vladimir still preserved its old political form and the basic features of its old internal structure, as they had been defined from the time of Vsevolod Big Nest, and as they were established even more securely from the time that his son Sviatoslav "placed his nephews in the other cities in the order that their father, Iaroslav, had established."

In Solovyev's words, "Sviatoslav confirmed his nephews, the sons of Iaroslav, in the udels given to them by the deceased grand prince," adding: "We feel that here for the first time we have the right to use this word, 'udel,' referring to a separate, allotted possession remaining permanently in the hands of a single princely line, since the earlier princely volosts were not udels and the ancient chroniclers had no knowledge of this word." But neither the chronicle texts from the thirteenth century nor any other literary memorial of the time knew of this term, and the truth is that we can fit a whole series of examples of princely possession of land in Kievan Russia into the concept of a "separate, allotted possession remaining permanently in the hands of a single princely line," beginning with the principality of Polotsk, allotted by Vladimir the Great to his son Iziaslav and remaining as the otchina of "the grandsons of Rogvolozh."

What does not fit into this concept, however, is precisely that
form of princely domain which in the fourteenth century both
the chronicles and official documents of the time will call an udel.
But let us return to the facts.

In Constantine's line Vasilko's sons, Boris and Gleb, sat on the
princely throne of Rostov after losing their father in the Tatar
onslaught, just as Vasilko, Vsevolod, and Vladimir had reigned
there before them as representatives of the older generation of
princes in the Rostov otchina. In the provisions for the princely
possession of Rostov we have the first clear example of the rule of
an otchina in the form of udels. Rostov had been assigned by
Constantine to his eldest son, Vasilko, with Iaroslavl being allotted
to his second son, Vsevolod. The third son, Vladimir, perhaps also
according to the father's riad, had been made prince of Uglich.
But this assignment to each prince of an udel within the common otchina did not make them "princely owners" of wholly
isolated possessions. Constantine's three sons were all princes of
Rostov and all three together were representatives of the princely
rule in the Rostov land. Their udels were hereditary, however,
and their transfer to succeeding generations inevitably created
the possibility (as family ties were weakened) of a destruction
of the unity of the common otchina. Its possession in the form
of udels could easily lead to the individualization of its parts
as the votchinas of the three separate princely lines. Thus it was
that Iaroslavl became detached from the Rostov otchina after
Vasili's death; in a very unusual way, as we have seen, since in
accordance with the decision of Vasili's surviving relatives it not
only was left to his widowed princess and her daughter, but
was permitted to pass then to the younger princess' husband,
Feodor (the son of Rostislav), and remained until 1299 the
special otchina of Feodor's sons. After the deaths of the elder
brothers, Vasilko and Vsevolod, the udel of Uglich remained in
Vladimir's hands, while Rostov was settled on his nephews
Boris and Gleb. The connection of Uglich with the Rostov
otchina was not broken, however. When Vladimir's line came
to an end after the death of his second son, Roman, in 1285,
Uglich was again made a part of the domain of the Rostov
princes.

Strictly speaking, the Rostov principality remained in the

hands of Vasilko's two sons, Boris and Gleb, but within it a distinct udel had been set apart for Gleb. An entry in the chronicle under the year 1251 reads: "Gleb journeyed to his otchina in Beloozero." It is possible that this meant Gleb's transfer from Rostov to the princely throne of Beloozero. It did not mean, however, that he then ceased to be a prince of Rostov, as he had been up to that moment alongside his brother Boris, and it is quite possible that Beloozero had been regarded as his udel even before he moved there. Certainly before this Gleb had taken part with his brother in all of Rostov's affairs. Boris died in the land of the Horde in 1277, when all the Russian princes were summoned with their armed troops to take part in a Tatar campaign against the Ias (Alans). Gleb then returned to the princely throne of Rostov alone. He died the following year, and "two princes sat after him in Rostov, his brother's sons Dmitri and Constantine."

A critical moment had arrived in the history of the Rostov principality. The udel of Beloozero was on the point of being detached and made the special otchina principality of Gleb's son Mikhail and his descendants. Only the Nikon Chronicle tells us that Prince Mikhail "sat in his votchina at Beloozero" after his father's death. The other chronicles simply pass directly to descriptions of the discord in Rostov. The disorder began when "Boris' son Dmitri seized Mikhail's volosts sinfully and with great injustice." For a year there was "enmity and sedition" between the Rostov princes. Constantine went over to Grand Prince Dmitri in Vladimir, and his brother Dmitri "began to assemble an army in Rostov to defend himself against his brothers." The Grand Prince reconciled the brothers, but only for a short time. Again in 1285 a new compromise was arranged. The principality of Uglich had returned to the Rostov princes when the princely line of Uglich expired. The house of Constantine now "divided up their otchina" in the light of these new and broader boundaries. Dmitri took the princely throne of Uglich, while Constantine ruled at Rostov. It is likely that Mikhail received the throne of Beloozero. Dmitri could hardly have been satisfied with this division. He began to establish close relations with Grand Prince Dmitri, giving his daughter in marriage to the latter's son Ivan, entering into all the Grand

Prince's plans, and taking part in his campaign against Tver. These actions help to explain the fact that he subsequently resumed the throne of Rostov "and began to take charge of the whole of his otchina," evidently supported in this move by both the Grand Prince and the Tatars. Constantine had to submit, and was apparently compelled to remain without a possession of his own as the second prince of Rostov under his brother. After his brother Dmitri's death in 1294, Constantine finally occupied the throne of the Rostov principality, and placed his son Alexander in Uglich.

Iuri occupied the throne of the Suzdal principality after the death of his father, Andrei (the son of Iaroslav III), but as far as we know, his activity was entirely confined to the area of Great Novgorod, where he served as a vassal of the Grand Prince. He died in 1279, having apparently spent only the last years of his life in Suzdal, since we hear nothing of his participation in any of the affairs of Suzdal during this period. Iuri was buried in one of Suzdal's cathedrals, and the princely throne passed to his brothers, first to Mikhail and then to Vasili, from whom the later princes of Suzdal are traced.

Besides these hereditary (votchina) principalities we must mention also the lands of Galicia, Starodub, and Iuriev. After the death of Prince Constantine (the eldest son of Iaroslav II) in 1255, Galich was ruled by his sons David (d. 1280) and Vasili (mentioned under the year 1310 in the chronicles). They are referred to only incidentally in the texts that have come down to us. Starodub was ruled by the descendants of Vsevolod's youngest son, Ivan, and we have such meager information about this line that its very genealogy remains in doubt. After the death of Prince Sviatoslav in 1253, Iuriev-Polsky was ruled by his son Dmitri, and after the latter's death in 1269 there is no mention of a prince of Iuriev except the reference to an Ivan Iaroslavich (probably Dmitri's grandson) under the year 1340.

Such were the votchina principalities within the territory of the grand principality of Vladimir, apart from Moscow and Tver, on the eve of the monumental struggle for grand princely power in which these two centers were soon to be engaged.

The stormy history of the Rostov principality is quite typical.

It shows how unfavorable the conditions were in the internal life of the Vladimir grand principality in the thirteenth century for the establishment of strong, permanent princely domains as separate votchina principalities turned in on themselves and isolated from the political life going on around them. Within the Rostov land itself the tendency toward disintegration into votchinas met with sharp opposition on the part of Prince Dmitri, who set himself against his brother and cousin in his attempt to "take charge over all his otchina." His plan was no whim. His activity was a deliberate attempt to acquire greater significance as prince of the land, and he might well be called a lesser Andrei Bogoliubsky. But Dmitri's ambitious goals were unattainable without involvement in the common affairs of the grand principality, in which the Rostov princes, together with Feodor of Iaroslavl and Iuri of Suzdal, played major roles. The common life of the grand principality still took precedence over the particular concerns of the local princes. The latter were very much dependent on the former, and governed by its demands. The princes of the entire Vladimir-Suzdal land were grouped around the Grand Prince; they took part in his campaigns, either under his military command or in obedience to his orders; they journeyed back and forth with him to the land of the Horde; and they were summoned by him to periodic assemblies for the settling of disputed questions. The texts of the chronicles take note also of a certain homely aspect of this interrelationship between the princes of the "downstream land," listing them as being present at every wedding and funeral of any one of the Russian princes. In the troubled times of the sons of Alexander Nevsky there were still no "private" wars among the individual votchina principalities; Moscow's seizures of Mozhaisk and Kolomna may be regarded as the first instances of this type of war. The civil disorders of the thirteenth century were genuine civil wars within the politically undivided grand principality of Vladimir. Local disputes were still insoluble without the aid of the Grand Prince, the common guardian of the peace and upholder of the princely law. The significance of the civil disorders of the thirteenth century lay in the fact that they were struggles for grand princely power, and the parties to these disorders were always united around some one pretender to the grand princely throne. It was with this type of civil disorder that "the whole Suzdal land was in turmoil."

Solovyev has noted the characteristic feature of this "time of trouble"—the revolt of lesser princes against the Grand Prince. The struggle was carried on sometimes for possession of the grand princely power itself, sometimes for Pereiaslavl, as a principality bound up with the far-reaching concept of an inheritance originating with Alexander Nevsky. Two groups of princes engaged in this struggle: some stood on the side of the existing bearer of the grand princely title, while the chief opponents of Grand Prince Dmitri (and after him Andrei III) were the princes of Tver and Moscow, who often sought alliance with Great Novgorod. For them this struggle was the path to the power, authority, and influence of the grand princely throne.

The "Vladimir inheritance" was above all the grand princely power, its supremacy over all Great Russia, its alleged right of disposing of all its military forces, and its claim to leadership in Russia's relations with the Horde and other neighboring peoples. Also connected by ancient tradition to the grand princely throne was the claim to the princely throne of Great Novgorod, which the grand princes regarded as the basis for broader political influence and as a possible source of material wealth. This claim extended also to Pskov as a result of its ties with Novgorod, although Pskov was becoming more and more independent in its relations with the west. Up to the end of the thirteenth century the grand princes of Vladimir retained some influence also over Smolensk and the decaying principality of northern Chernigov. The princes of Smolensk and Briansk took part in the activities dictated by the western policy of the grand princes in the time of Dmitri and Andrei III, and were subject to their call and "command." The principalities of Murom and Riazan were also closely associated with the grand principality of Vladimir. Before Batu's invasion and also afterward, throughout the thirteenth century, the princes of Murom and Riazan "could not really be considered independent, since the grand princes of Vladimir made use of them at will," in the words of A. V. Eksempliarsky. In their struggle with the Mordva and the Polovtsy, the princes of Riazan and Murom naturally sought support in the grand prince of Vladimir and took part equally with other lesser princes in his campaigns. The Tatar devastation and the domination of the Horde weakened this defensive alliance for a while. The Tatar rule lay especially heavily on these two lands. Our compilations of chronicles say almost nothing about them, but certainly the one prominent feature of life in Murom and Riazan all through the thirteenth century and into the fourteenth was the Tatar raid with its ensuing havoc. The grand princes were not strong enough to give any real protection to these frontiers of Great Russia, so constantly distressed by the hopeless difficulties of their position on the edge of the dangerous steppe. Until some new power developed at the center of Great Russia and assumed this task, it was up to local forces on the Russian frontier to organize their own defense. Their tendency to look to the center, however, and to try to find there some support, constantly sustained their weakened ties with it, in spite of their increasing resentment.

Chapter
II

The Struggle Between Tver and Moscow for the Grand Princely Rule over "All Russia"

On the threshold of the fourteenth century, at the moment of greatest decline in the grand princely power, the weakened yet still living traditions of grand princely policy found new support in the ambitions of the boyar class and the church, whose leaders had become alarmed by the threat of Great Russia's complete disintegration in the princes' strife.

Grand Prince Andrei III died in Vladimir in the summer of 1304. The account of the martyrdom of Iaroslav's son Mikhail (of Tver) states that before dying, Prince Andrei "had given consent to Mikhail to occupy his throne and the grand princely rule." In any case, both Metropolitan Maxim, who had moved his residence from ruined Kiev to Vladimir in the spring of 1300, and the boyars of the Vladimir principality immediately acknowledged Mikhail as grand prince. The boyars moved to Tver, while Mikhail journeyed as quickly as possible to the land of the Horde to secure the Khan's yarlik. In his absence the boyars, in all likelihood led by the influential and energetic Akinf, took steps to consolidate the grand princely power in Mikhail's name.

Prince Iuri (the eldest son of Daniel of Moscow) also journeyed to the land of the Horde seeking the grand princely rule. Metropolitan Maxim's attempt to forestall the princes' growing conflict failed, as did also the attempt of the boyars supporting Mikhail to intercept Iuri on his way to the Horde. Before his departure Iuri had managed to occupy Kostroma and had left it in the hands of his brother Boris, but the latter was seized by Mikhail's men and taken prisoner to Tver. The city was occupied by some of the Tver boyars, but the people of Kostroma rose against them in a veche and two of the Tver boyars were killed. Mikhail's boyars also tried to seize Great Novgorod, but this too failed. The men of Novgorod refused to accept Mikhail's deputies, and agreed only to a truce awaiting the return of the Grand Prince.

These actions on the part of Mikhail's boyars must be seen as directly connected with the events that occurred in Nizhni Novgorod, where the "common people" rose against the boyars and where Mikhail, on his return from the land of the Horde, "slaughtered the leaders of the veche." Finally, Mikhail's forces also made an attempt to seize Pereiaslavl, but Iuri's brother Ivan had succeeded in getting to Pereiaslavl first and preparing its defense. The boyar Akinf attacked the city with an army from Tver, and was beaten back with heavy losses. Akinf himself fell in the battle.

We come now to an important moment in the history of the grand principality of Vladimir, and we can only regret that the chronicles have preserved such a fragmentary and confused account of this period. Even in the light of this very inadequate information, however, it is clear that the struggle between Mikhail and Iuri was a struggle for goals of high importance —for power over all of Great Russia, and consequently for the restoration of the unity of its political forces and political supremacy over these forces. The attempts made by Mikhail and his boyars to seize such points as Great Novgorod, Pereiaslavl, Kostroma, and Nizhni Novgorod cannot be explained as a movement to "strengthen Tver" or to "extend the Tver udel." Obviously much broader political aspirations were involved: a struggle had been engaged for the grand princely inheritance of Alexander Nevsky and Iaroslav III.

Mikhail returned from the Horde with the Khan's yarlik granting him the grand princely rule. Metropolitan Maxim took part in the ceremony of "placing him on the throne" in Vladimir. Grand Prince Mikhail's first act was a campaign "against Prince Iuri and his brother," ending with the submission of these Muscovite princes. They were forced to acknowledge Mikhail as grand prince, and thus the first stage in the struggle between Moscow and Tver came to an end.

This phase was characterized not only by the active participation of the Grand Prince's boyars in Mikhail's attempt to seize the grand princely rule and restore its power, but also by the initiative they took in this strategy. In fact, however, the attempt failed, in spite of Mikhail's formal confirmation on the grand princely throne. There was to be a long and stubborn contest before his formal title to power could be confirmed with its actuality. But the significance of this power can only be measured in connection with the great literary enterprise that began to take form about this time in Vladimir in the court of the Metropolitan. We are speaking here of the first "complete" collection of Russian chronicles, to be dated about the beginning of the fourteenth century, as A. A. Shakhmatov has rather convincingly demonstrated.

Shakhmatov's painstaking comparison of the various collections of chronicles that have come down to us led him to the conclusion that their compilers had relied on one common compilation of chronicles having an "all-Russian" orientation and in its first redaction tracing Russia's history down to the year 1305. Its abundant information concerning events in northeastern Russia suggested to Shakhmatov an origin in Vladimir. The rich mass of information on events (frequently of only local significance) taking place in all sections of the Vladimir-Suzdal land, in the regions of Riazan, Chernigov, Novgorod, and Pskov as well as in the southern and western regions of Great

Russia, bears witness to such broad horizons, such large-scale concerns, and such a wealth of knowledge and sources as could have existed only in the court of a Russian metropolitan. His position alone, as head of the Russian church, gave the metropolitan and his clergy a broader perspective than any other center of power; in his court were men concerned with the destinies not of any one particular land, but of all Great Russia and western Russia as well. In addition, only the metropolitan had the men and resources necessary to carry out such a task. To his court local chronicle records and compilations could be gathered from all the diocesan offices and greater monasteries; here alone information was available concerning every major event in every corner of the Russian land. Most important, from the historical viewpoint, was the very thought of using these sources to compile a "complete" collection of Russian chronicles. This idea, anticipated by the old Russian tradition of the *Kievo-Pechersky Vremennik* (The Kiev Cave Monastery Chronograph) and the *Povest Vremennykh Let* (Book of Annals), evolved naturally in the grand princely city of Vladimir, in the court of the metropolitan, as a reflection of a definite political outlook. Once settled in Vladimir, the metropolitan had become a key factor in north Russian political life. In the broad sense, the church's concerns led him to support the quelling of all disorder and civil strife, and also to promote the creation of more stable relations with a real and not just titular grand princely power. Thus these collections of "all-Russian" chronicles give us a valuable insight into the political activity of the Russian metropolitans in the fourteenth and fifteenth centuries.

It was no accident that the first attempt to compile a complete collection of Russian chronicles coincided with the appearance of the Great Russian boyars as energetic proponents of the restoration of the much deteriorated grand princely power. The boyar class could not fail to be distressed by the weakness and degradation of their old political center, to which all their interests had been tied. The establishment in Vladimir of the metropolitan see, with its interests in Russia as a whole and with its old tradition of supporting internal peace under the guardianship of a single secular ruling power, was bound to emphasize the need for some way out of the painful situation that had been created.

And there was another coincidence. The year of Metropolitan Maxim's death was also the last recorded year entered in what was probably the first complete collection of Russian chronicles. This led Shakhmatov to say that the compiler of this collection was "most probably Metropolitan Peter, Maxim's successor." However, the fact that there is no record in the Laurentian Chronicle of Metropolitan Maxim's death (he died in December, 1304) suggests that the work on this collection was completed before this date, and thus under Maxim's direction. The very notion of compiling a "complete collection of Russian chronicles" and the fact that such a project was carried out in the metropolitan court may be connected with some other aspects of Maxim's career. He was the first leader of the Russian church to bear the title "metropolitan of all Russia," and the development of this title must be regarded as a symptom of a growing tendency in ecclesiastical circles to set the unity of ecclesiastical authority in the Russian church over against the accelerating decline of the one secular power. At a later time the patriarch of Constantinople would defend the unity of the Russian metropolitan see against efforts to divide it with the political argument that "the Great Russian land is divided into many different secular principalities" living in conflict and civil strife, and that "in view of the impossibility of unifying the secular powers," the church's duty "to teach all people about love, peace, mutual unity, and concord not in word only, but also in deed," was to be fulfilled in Russia only by preserving the unity of the metropolitan see in all Russia, with "the one metropolitan for all" acting as "a kind of bond, uniting in himself and with each other" all the diverse political forces of Russia. It will be seen that this argument, relating ecclesiastical unity with the dream of unifying the secular power, was already visible in Metropolitan Maxim's new title and in his activities in northern Russia. He supported the boyars in their efforts both to secure the grand princely throne for Prince Mikhail and to increase the latter's power by seizing the most important city centers in Great Russia.

There is no reason, of course, to believe that the Metropolitan took direct part in planning the hasty acts of violence with which the boyars tried to realize their plans, but we can see from the account of Mikhail's murder that Maxim did try to use his influence and powers of mediation in an effort to end the rivalry between Mikhail and Iuri. Taking all these observations into account, we have reason to suppose that Metropolitan Maxim, having noted how the grand princely boyars were drawn to Mikhail, saw in him that strength which could "unify the secular powers." This alliance of the metropolitan see with Mikhail's aspirations to the grand princely throne was very significantly expressed in the fact that Mikhail was the first Russian prince to be addressed in the patriarch's official documents as "Grand Prince of All Russia."

If Mikhail found support for his vaulting ambitions among the boyars and in the church, it is only natural to raise the question: Why was it precisely the prince of Tver who became the center of their political plans and hopes? In reply we may say that the general situation in Great Russia and the particular position of the Tver principality were pointing in that direction.

The decline in grand princely power in northern Russia at the turn of the fourteenth century was but one of the symptoms of profound disorder in Russian life. The grievous consequences of Tatar domination had become evident only gradually during the course of the second half of the thirteenth century. By the end of the 1250's an organized exploitation of the Russian land had been imposed by the Tatar power. This evoked a series of rebellions among the people in the early sixties, which of course did not pass without loss to the land, in spite of the princes' energetic mediation with the Horde. At the end of the sixties, however, under Khan Mangu-Timur, "the Russian land had become weakened by the Tatar oppression." A kind of *modus vivendi* had become established between Russia and the Khan's power, its main feature being the very frequent journeys of both grand princes and the younger princes to the land of the Horde to receive the Khan's "sanction" of the grand princely rule or of their otchinas, and for the purpose of settling various other matters and questions touching on Russian-Tatar relations. Our sources give 1273 as the date of the second Tatar census of the Russian *ulus*,[25] but we do not know how it differed from the first, or whether it was simply a "renewal" of the original chislo. During the seventies and eighties the Russian lands again suffered rather heavily from Tatar "appearances," when the Russian princes made a habit of bringing up "Tatar tsars" to help them in their civil wars. In their descriptions of these Tatar "appearances" ("The whole land was emptied"; "They departed, having wrought much evil and with many men taken prisoner") the epic language of the chronicles prevents us from forming any clear, precise picture of the losses suffered. We are left with the impression, however, that the havoc was very extensive indeed. We find the same lack of concrete information in the accounts of the burden of the Tatar tribute. We only know that it was constantly increased by the extortions of the Khan's envoys and baskaks, by the extra "surcharges" laid on by the Tatar authorities, and by the expenses involved in dealings with the Horde; it was always necessary to buy off the Khan's displeasure and buy his favor.

Under the successors of Mangu-Timur the kingdom of the Golden Horde underwent a period of internal disorganization, unrest, and outright conflict. Without lessening the burden of the Tatar domination, this weakening of the Khan's power and the internal ferment of the Tatar world only increased the danger of living adjacent to it. The closing decades of the thirteenth century are marked by Tatar raids along the Riazan and Murom frontiers. The principality of Riazan, left to rely on its own forces, became more and more isolated as it took the brunt of the Tatar attack. The relationships of the Riazan princes with the Horde were usually settled without reference to the grand princes. The southern frontier of Great Russia was not clearly marked off from the Tatar steppe, and Russian colonization gradually moved southward, down the Voronezh River to the Khoper and the Great Vorona, in spite of the constant threat of Tatar attack. This southern region developed and consolidated its own local Riazan interests, and built up its own organization of local political power under the "grand principal-

25. *Ulus:* a large district or provincial territory within the Mongol Empire, subject to the rule of a khan or his deputy.—TRANS.

ity" of Riazan without interference from the center of Great Russia, toward which it even developed a natural antagonism.

The relations of Great Russia with neighboring lands to the northeast also took on a new coloring. There is no further mention of campaigns by Russian princes against the Mordva or in the Kama valley. The eastern Finnish tribes were completely under the power of the Tatars. To a large extent the paths of colonization and war were cut off in this direction also. The political collapse of the eastern regions of Great Russia was the natural result of an absence of any real policy for its eastern borders. The decline of grand princely power left these regions without a definite political center. In the fourteenth century an organization of local forces developed here around the princely throne of Nizhni Novogord, but only very gradually. We find quite a different situation in the western part of Great Russia.

The twofold aspect of Alexander Nevsky's policies—his military defense of the western borders and his helpless submission on the east—had a prolonged and decisive influence on the political life of Great Russia and was a consequence of overwhelming external conditions. The disintegration and collapse of grand princely power was reflected in the west in a decentralization of military strength and leadership. We have seen how local Novgorod policy became more and more independent, and how Pskov became increasingly wrapped up in its own local interests and affairs. The principality of Tver could not avoid active participation in this western struggle, however, since it was immediately affected by it. The increased strength of its western enemies was reflected in attacks on the Tver volosts, and economic interests had for a long time connected Tver with Novgorod. It is very likely that Tver owed its original settlement to Novgorod trade, as a result of the ties between the outpost of Tver, at the mouth of the Tvertsa River, with Torzhok, on its upper reaches. From the time of Vsevolod III, Tver was in the hands of the prince of Vladimir, and was the key to the Torzhok and Novgorod regions. The Lithuanian raids of 1245 and 1248 closely affected the Tver region. The second of these raids was repulsed by the combined forces of the "downstream" land at the very gates of Zubtsov, and only after Mikhail Khorobrit had died in battle. In view of these connections with the west, both in the realm of trade and in the area of military activities, Tver's western orientation was only natural, and indeed was characteristic of this principality throughout its history.

At the end of the thirteenth century the Prince of Tver emerged as the one representative of princely power in a position to take leadership in the political affairs of western Great Russia, as heir to the crumbling grand principality of Vladimir. The principality of Tver was sufficiently well established to serve as a basis for the broadening political ambitions of its patrimonial (otchina) prince. He became a major independent political force in the struggle between Alexander's elder sons for the grand princely rule. At first Prince Sviatoslav of Tver (son of Iaroslav III) joined the men of Novgorod and Daniel of Moscow in supporting Prince Andrei against Grand Prince Dmitri. Later Sviatoslav was reconciled with Dmitri, shortly before Andrei's second return to Russia with Tatar troops. The transfer of power in Tver from Sviatoslav to Mikhail was marked by conflict between Mikhail and Grand Prince Dmitri, but Mikhail did not join Dmitri's adversaries. The Tver boyars organized a campaign against the Tatar forces that Andrei had brought up against his brother Dmitri. Tver became a sanctuary for those fleeing other regions in the face of the Tatar onslaught, and not only the Tatar forces but also Prince Andrei's plans were smashed by Tver's opposition. Dmitri found support and aid in this western principality, and Andrei occupied the grand princely throne only after his brother's death.

The Prince of Tver played an influential role also in the disputes over possession of Pereiaslavl Zalesky, even though these disputes apparently were not resolved as he would have wished. His alliance with Novgorod in 1296 and his participation in the assemblies at Pereiaslavl and Dmitrov reveal him as an independent and powerful political figure in the general affairs of the grand principality of Vladimir. Thus all of Mikhail's earlier activities were a preparation for his association with Metropolitan Maxim and the grand princely boyars. The position of the Tver principality on the western borders of Great Russia provided its prince with wider political horizons than had hitherto been open to any Russian prince in the thirteenth century.

At the very beginning of Mikhail's reign as independent prince of Tver, something happened that vividly displayed the necessary connection between local Tver interests and the unity of the whole grand principality of Vladimir. In 1285

Lithuania waged war on Oleshna and other volosts of the ruler of Tver; and there were gathered against them the men of Tver, Moscow, Volok, Novi Torzhok, Zubtsov, and Rzhev, and they drove them off into the forests on the eve of Christmas, and killed them, and pursued their prince Domant, and seized much of Lithuania, slaughtering some, while others fled, and they took away all the prisoners, and returned to their own land.

Such a success would have been beyond the reach of the Tver forces alone. The increasingly hazardous clashes with Lithuania, the trade and political ties with Great Novgorod, Pskov, and Smolensk, whose relationships with the west were becoming greatly complicated by their relentless struggle with their hostile neighbors—all this made Tver a key city in Great Russia's western policy, and drew its princes outside the confines of purely local interests into a wider historical arena. On the other hand, implementation of the tasks defined in this policy—the policy not only of Tver, but also of Great Russia as a whole —demanded the unification of considerable forces at a time when the impotence of Vladimir was becoming increasingly plain. For those dissatisfied with the decline in the Grand Prince's power, for those who dreamed of a grand principality in the style of Vsevolod Big Nest or Alexander Nevsky, the Prince of Tver, an active, capable, and ambitious leader, seemed to be the natural heir of the old and now badly shaken traditions, and the restorer of these traditions in the future. Mikhail actually obtained the grand princely power, relying both on his position as prince of Tver and on the cooperation of the grand princely boyars and the Metropolitan, but in his first conflict with Moscow the issue was not just the throne of the grand prince in Vladimir. The question posed was at once broader and more immediate: as grand prince he must possess genuine political power and rule over all the major points in the Great Russian politico-geographical area, from Nizhni Novgorod to Great Novgorod. His first attempt to fulfill these demands was made immediately and forcefully, but it foundered on the opposition of certain local social forces in Great Novgorod, Kostroma, and Nizhni Novgorod, and on the resistance of a dangerous rival: the prince of Moscow.

II.

In his careful study of the emergence of Tver and Moscow as the two most powerful centers of Great Russian life, M. K. Liubavsky has looked closely into this rise of two of Great Russia's "younger" cities (younger not only in historical significance, but also in political influence), and has noted evidence of popular support of their power in the wave of immigration moving then into the western regions of the old Rostov-Suzdal land. Liubavsky has advanced the theory that this westward population movement was caused by a "noticeable weakening" of the central and eastern sections of the "downstream land" under the heavy blows of Tatar attacks after Batu's massacre and the consolidation of the Tatar domination. "If we carefully weigh the chronicles' account of Batu's massacre and what came after," says Liubavsky, "it would seem that these massacres struck mainly at the most heavily settled parts of the Suzdal land." He considers it likely that after the first massacre, part of the population never returned to their burned-out homesteads, but moved on toward the north and west. "Repeated Tatar appearances pushed the population of the Suzdal land in this same direction all through the second half of the thirteenth century."

Liubavsky's theory was based mainly on the events of 1293, when the "Tatar tsars" allied with Prince Andrei ravaged the eastern and central regions of northern Russia. They decided not to advance on Tver only because here they encountered a defensive fortification, and because they found that "a great many people had fled into Tver from other principalities." These facts do illustrate his theory even if they do not give it solid foundation. Liubavsky's observation must be accepted as a fruitful hypothesis that helps to shed light on the development of colonization within Great Russia and the increase in landholding on the part of the boyars and the monasteries. It clarifies certain elements in the internal life of central Great Russia (especially in the lands of Moscow and Tver) which have so far been open to study only through later documents, i.e., from the second half of the fourteenth century and from the fifteenth century. Liubavsky's theory is an intelligent attempt to see further into one historical process by referring to facts from a different order which nevertheless touch on Great Russia's political development. The political powers of Great Russia moved westward at the beginning of the fourteenth century, seeking a firmer and more powerful base of operations than the weakened city of Vladimir. The period of struggle between Tver and Moscow was a crucial moment in Great Russia's search for a new focus of power. It was at this time that Moscow's ultimately successful opposition to Tver's brilliant, promising, but short-lived ascendancy was determined.

The present work represents an attempt to distinguish various historical turning points as clearly as possible, and so a summary of the celebrated "reasons for the rise of Moscow" would be rather out of place here. I shall dwell briefly, however, on one of these reasons, using as the starting point for my study an appraisal of the city's geographical position in an article entitled "On the Beginnings of Moscow" by S. F. Platonov. Reflecting on the references to Moscow in the chronicles, Platonov notes that the city lay at the intersection of several routes: one to the north, in the direction of Rostov; one to the northeast, in the direction of Vladimir; one to the south, in the direction of Chernigov; one to Riazan through Kolomna; one to Smolensk through Mozhaisk. Moscow therefore had strategic importance, looking out as it did toward all the major military frontiers. This significance was made plain even before the Tatar period, when Moscow served as a frontier outpost of the grand principality of Vladimir.

We may assume that it was precisely for this reason that Moscow remained so long a town within the grand principality of Vladimir, rather than becoming an independent center of princely power. A similar military significance, not so much of a frontier outpost as of a genuine headquarters, determined Moscow's role in the later development of this area. In the period of the Tatar yoke it became the center of a new organization of

Great Russia's divided military forces, which were to recover their lost unity in the warfare on Russia's eastern, southern, and western borders. Fully occupied by its dealings with the west, Tver was not destined to be the unifier of power over the Great Russian land. Moscow, however, was involved not only in these western matters, in its relations with Great Novgorod and Tver and in their unceasing conflict as well as economic and cultural ties with the Baltic countries and Lithuania, but also in its relations with the south and east—in dealings with the Tatar world, and in the tasks of the commercial, colonial, and agricultural development of the Volga valley and the land south of the Oka. As an attempt to describe Moscow's earliest beginnings, of course, there is nothing more than a sweeping view of the overall situation, a kind of preview of events *ex post facto*. These geographical considerations do point, however, to a direct link between several characteristic elements in Moscow's early history and its subsequent development, and they can serve as very helpful guideposts in any study of this period.

Other information will perhaps help to explain the emergence of Moscow's princes with their insistent claim to the throne of the grand principality and a leading role in the political destinies of Great Russia. Their claim can scarcely have been as poorly grounded in the princely tradition as it seemed to Kliuchevsky, who was simply following Solovyev. After the deaths of his two elder brothers, Daniel was left the sole representative of the line of Alexander Nevsky. Even during the grand princely reign of his brother Andrei, and in opposition to him, he had been able to consolidate his position on the throne of Pereiaslavl. This principality was the basic otchina of the sons of Alexander Nevsky, and its close tie with "the grand principality of Vladimir and Novgorod" prompted their claim to a direct succession from their father in all aspects of his power and princely rule. From Moscow's viewpoint, the struggle with Tver was a struggle to confine the sons of Iaroslav and his later descendants within their Tver otchina and to preserve the position of leadership and the hereditary seniority in the grand principality of Vladimir for the descendants of Alexander only; just as the princes of Tver were fighting for their otchina rights to the grand prince's throne by force of arms and the Khan's yarlik.

The fact that the princes of Moscow were consolidated on the throne of Pereiaslavl automatically put them in the position of being pretenders to the grand princely rule, if for no other reason than that their very desire to secure possession of Pereiaslavl demanded it. Those who bore the title and power of grand prince —Andrei, and now Iaroslav's son Mikhail—regarded Pereiaslavl as an integral part of the territory of the grand principality, and they were not prepared to let it pass into Moscow's hands. It was not by chance that Pereiaslavl had never entered into the composition of the Muscovite votchina—until, of course, the grand principality itself was merged with this votchina to form a single "Muscovite state." Thus both by virtue of its close connection with the grand principality and by virtue of its significance as the otchina of Alexander's line, the princely throne of Pereiaslavl brought its princes into the arena of struggle for the grand princely rule. Alexander's youngest son, Daniel, the first ruling prince of Moscow, had acquired the "capital city" of Pereiaslavl in addition to his own votchina on the death of his next elder brother, Andrei. His son Iuri had difficulty defending and securing his hold on the Pereiaslavl principality. It may be that Iuri's attack on Mozhaisk had something to do with the struggle for Pereiaslavl. At Mozhaisk he captured Prince Sviatoslav, the son of Gleb and nephew of Feodor Rostislavich, whom we last saw on the side of Grand Prince Andrei and among the opponents of the Prince of Moscow. The last information we have of Sviatoslav is that he was imprisoned in Moscow, while Mozhaisk was merged with the Muscovite votchina. By way of inheritance from Prince Daniel, Iuri became involved in another matter that was to lead to a further and equally important broadening and strengthening of this votchina. In 1301 Daniel had marched with a host against Riazan, and although Prince Constantine of Riazan had come out against him with strong Tatar reinforcements, Daniel had defeated him near southern Pereiaslavl, and had taken him prisoner to Moscow. Iuri's first act after his peace with Grand Prince Mikhail was to execute his father's prisoner. The result of all this was the addition of Kolomna to the Muscovite domains. The roles that were to be played later by Mozhaisk and Kolomna, as staging areas for Muscovite campaigns against Smolensk, on the one hand, and for its expeditions along the Volga and the Oka, on the other, show the great value of these acquisitions. They increased and confirmed Moscow's significance as the political and strategic center of Great Russia.

It was from this position of strength that Iuri could come forward as a powerful rival of Mikhail, in spite of Moscow's internal disorder arising out of Iuri's dispute with his brothers. His cause was certainly helped also by Mikhail's own faults and blunders.

III.

The early years of the reign of Grand Prince Mikhail were taken up with the question of Novgorod and relations between the Grand Prince and the Metropolitan. Both the Novgorod and the church questions were dealt with in such a way that the Prince of Moscow acquired new and powerful allies who helped to secure his advantage over Tver. A boyar attempt to place Mikhail's deputies in control of Great Novgorod was defeated by the people of Novgorod and left to be resolved "when the prince should come." Both the political and the commercial interests of Novgorod led it to accept as its prince one who could guarantee the support of the "downstream" troops and could promise trade throughout the Suzdal land "without border restrictions." Grand Prince Mikhail's return from the Horde and his enthronement as grand prince in the fall of 1304 were the *terminus post quem* for his negotiations with Novgorod. He arrived in Great Novgorod and was enthroned as its prince on July 16, 1307. The people of Novgorod accepted the Grand Prince's deputies, submitted to the rule of Mikail's "men" and to trial by Mikhail's "courts," but stubbornly insisted on the subordination of all such juridical and legislative administration to Novgorod's "ancient custom," which in disputed questions was formulated in the articles of their treaties, and they required the abolition of those actions by the Prince or his agents that had hitherto infringed on their "ancient rights."

Relations remained strained, and it is very likely that the men of Novgorod looked in the direction of Moscow, Tver's rival, although we have no information about contacts between them and the Prince of Moscow during these years. Only an incidental entry in an ecclesiastical document gives us a hint of a connection between the affairs of Novgorod and Grand Prince Mikhail's attack on Moscow in August of 1307. A situation had developed that was bound to give rise to a new contest between Tver and Moscow, with the active participation of Great Novgorod. This set of circumstances marked a moment of crisis in the political history of northern Russia which was not unrelated to the destiny of the metropolitan see following the death of Metropolitan Maxim.

IV.

Metropolitan Maxim died in December, 1304, and Mikhail lost an influential supporter of his political ambitions. It is natural to suspect an attempt on the part of the Grand Prince to influence the choice of Maxim's successor. It is in this sense that V. S. Borzakovsky and E. E. Golubinsky have explained the story of the Abbot Geronti, of whom it is said in both the biographies of Metropolitan Peter that he journeyed to Constantinople to seek consecration to the Russian metropolitan see, taking with him certain officials of the metropolitan court, the metropolitan's sacred vestments, and many ikons from the Cathedral of the Assumption in Vladimir. Peter's biographies tell us nothing of Geronti's activity on Mikhail's behalf, but the hint in Cyprian's "Life of St. Peter" of a permission granted by the secular power ("no one prevented him") and of a timely knowledge on the part of Prince Iuri of Galich (who was married to Mikhail's sister) of Geronti's journey permit us, quite apart from Golubinsky's general observations, to regard Geronti as the Grand Prince's candidate. Prince Iuri "did not favor the most learned Geronti," and began to negotiate for the consecration of a special metropolitan for southern Russia, sending his own Abbot Peter to Constantinople as the candidate for the metropolitan see of Galicia. Patriarch Athanasius resolved the matter in his own way. He made Peter metropolitan of all Russia (in June, 1307). A year passed before Peter was able to travel from Kiev to Vladimir. "The enemy of mankind stirred up certain people to oppose his coming" was Cyprian's rhetorical explanation of this delay. Later these adversaries of the Metropolitan "were ashamed of themselves, and received the holy man." Golubinsky sees an "element of caution in Cyprian's discourse," suggesting opposition to the Metropolitan on the part of Grand Prince Mikhail.

The metropolitan appointed by the Patriarch had to be accepted, but the clergy close to the Grand Prince, with Bishop Andrei of Tver at their head, immediately began proceedings to have him removed. "A weighty charge" against Peter was sent to the Patriarch. The accusations were sufficiently serious for the Patriarch to send one of his own clergy to Russia to investigate the matter on the spot. The investigation was carried on not at the metropolitan city of Vladimir, nor in the grand princely city of Tver, but in the cathedral at Pereiaslavl, where Bishop Semeon of Rostov and Andrei of Tver were assembled with the "best" of the clergy, both priests and monks, under the presidency of the Patriarch's representative. The Grand Prince himself was not present, but his sons and "a rather large number of other princes" were there with their boyars. The stormy disputes ended with the exoneration of Metropolitan Peter. His opponents, however, did not simply fold their hands in submission. The Bishop of Tver sent a monk, Akindin, to the Patriarch carrying evidence of the Metropolitan's unjust actions; Mikhail addressed a letter to the Patriarch on the same theme. The latter replied by summoning Metropolitan Peter to trial in Constantinople, ordering the Grand Prince to send him "by force" if he did not wish to go freely, together with his accusers and witnesses. Our documents do not tell us whether such a trial was actually held or how the whole affair was finally resolved. In fact, however, Peter emerged as the victor. Both the bishops who took part in the examination in Pereiaslavl later vacated their sees, Semeon of Rostov in 1311, Andrei of Tver in 1315, yielding their positions to bishops selected by Metropolitan Peter.

This break with the Metropolitan cost Mikhail dearly. The meager information we have about the ecclesiastical trial in Pereiaslavl does not indicate that Daniel's sons took part in it, but the council was held in their city, undoubtedly with their permission, and since it touched on fundamental relationships within the grand principality, they could not fail to gain from these circumstances. What happened thereafter serves to justify these remarks: Metropolitan Peter became a staunch ally of Moscow.

Tver's grand designs were not dropped at once, but as each year passed, some new setback occurred to foreshadow its eventual defeat. After its first failure to seize power by force, Tver experienced an uninterrupted series of reverses in its relations with Novgorod, and complete defeat in its conflict with the Metropolitan. In all of Tver's difficulties and failures there was a sense of the threatening rivalry of Moscow. Soon after the council in Pereiaslavl, Grand Prince Mikhail and his counselors ventured a new and hopefully decisive blow. In 1311 Mikhail's army was dispatched under his son Dmitri "against Nizhni Novgorod and Prince Iuri." Dmitri arrived at Vladimir, where the Grand Prince's forces were to assemble, but "Metropolitan Peter did not give him his blessing." This refusal of the Metropolitan to bless the campaign upset the entire undertaking. Dmitri stayed for three weeks in Vladimir, then dismissed his army and returned to his father.

These failures undermined not only the authority but also the actual strength of the Grand Prince, and they were soon reflected in an increase in opposition from Novgorod. We do not know the exact reasons for the break, but in 1312 Mikhail withdrew his deputies from that city, seized Torzhok and the Bezhetsk volost, and cut off the flow of "abundance" into Novgorod. The people of the city submitted and sent their leading boyar, David, to Tver, promising to pay the Prince one and a half thousand *grivnas*.[26] This "settlement" turned out to be nothing more than a truce. Prince Mikhail had struck Novgorod before it could prepare for the fight. Now the city began to seek allies against its grand princely oppressor. In 1313 Mikhail and Metropolitan Peter traveled to the land of the Horde to visit the new khan, Uzbek. The Metropolitan was permitted to return to Russia "forthwith," but the Grand Prince was detained there for more than a year. During his absence the men of Novgorod rebelled against the Grand Prince's deputies and appealed to Moscow for help. Prince Iuri sent Feodor of Rzhev to their aid. The latter seized Mikhail's deputies, and then marched with a Novgorod host against a Tver army under Mikhail's son Dmitri. The two

26. *Grivna:* the basic monetary unit in Old Russia, a silver bar weighing about one pound.—TRANS.

forces met on the Volga near Gorodets (in the Tver principality),
faced each other from opposite sides of the river for six weeks,
until the first ice formed, and then separated without a battle,
having concluded a peace "according to the whole will of Novgorod." This treaty evidently freed Novgorod from the Grand
Prince's deputies, since the men of Novgorod sent for Prince
Iuri in Moscow at once "from that place"—i.e., from the Volga
—and in the same winter Iuri arrived in Novgorod with his
brother Afanasi and "sat on its throne."

While in Novgorod, Iuri received an unexpected summons
from the Khan, probably as a result of a complaint made against
him by Mikhail. Iuri set out with the Novgorod envoys, but
again Mikhail had gained an advantage through his negotiations
with the Khan. In 1315 he appeared in Russia with a Tatar army,
defeated the men of Novgorod near Torzhok, and demanded
that they hand over Afanasi of Moscow and Feodor of Rzhev.
Novgorod delivered Feodor to Mikhail, and was obliged to pay
a heavy toll. Brought into complete submission, it was compelled
to accept once more the Grand Prince's deputies and to surrender
all its armor, weapons, and horses. Grand Prince Mikhail had
broken down all resistance, and on occupying Novgorod he instituted a harsh repression. He refused to recognize the elected
posadnik and took the office "out of his hands." He defined his
power in Novgorod and his demands upon it in a new treaty,
which established a tribute of 12,000 grivnas, to be paid in in-
stallments. He also exiled Prince Afanasi and the Novgorod
boyars to Tver as a "pledge" until the whole sum should be
paid.

This harsh pacification threatened to crush Novgorod's independence in spite of the guarantee of its "ancient rights and
tolls," as specified in the earlier treaty of 1307. Novgorod's
suppressed hostility sought some new release. Its attempt to
lodge a charge against Mikhail in the land of the Horde was
unsuccessful, its envoys being ambushed on the way by the men
of Tver. In the following year (1316), however, the men of
Novgorod rebelled again with new and better prepared forces,
expelled the Grand Prince's deputies, and so defended themselves
against Mikhail's forces that his campaign against Novgorod was
a complete failure.

Novgorod had escaped from the hands of Grand Prince

Mikhail and now opened its arms to Iuri of Moscow. Mikhail did manage, however, to make it sign a treaty specifying its neutrality in the approaching conflict. Prince Iuri was in the land of the Horde when all this was happening. He had spent approximately two years there, and had accomplished much during his stay. He had won the Khan's favor, married his sister, obtained the Khan's yarlik granting him the grand princely rule, and was allowed to return with the Khan's envoys, some of the princes of the Horde, and an armed troop in order to be installed officially on the throne of the Russian land.

But the material forces of the grand principality were still in Mikhail's hands. He set out with his vassal princes to meet Iuri, who was proceeding with the Khan's envoys not to Vladimir or to Moscow, but up the Volga to Kostroma. Here the two rivals came together. Iuri's possession of the Khan's yarlik completely undermined Mikhail's position. Finding no support among the younger princes, and threatened from the rear by the unreliable forces of Novgorod, Mikhail retreated to Tver and began to fortify his otchina. The enemy attacked under the Tatar commander Kavgadi "with great force," but was defeated near the village of Bortenev. Kavgadi grudgingly humbled himself before Mikhail, while Iuri escaped to Novgorod to gather a new host there and in the city of Pskov. Once again the two adversaries came together on the Volga, this time deciding (without a battle) to go to the land of the Horde and appeal their case to the Khan.

Prince Iuri traveled as the grand prince, surrounded by all the princes of the Vladimir-Suzdal land and a retinue of boyars from Great Novgorod and "the smaller towns." Because of Iuri's hurried departure, Prince Mikhail decided to send his son Constantine on ahead, accompanied by the boyars of Tver, while he and his elder sons remained in Vladimir, where the Khan's envoys found him when they came to summon him to the land of the Horde. This was Mikhail's downfall. Kavgadi accused him of flouting the Khan's authority and of refusing to go to the land of the Horde despite his agreement to submit his quarrel with Iuri to the Khan's judgment. Mikhail was found guilty by a court of princes of the Horde and died a martyr's death. This marked the end of the second act of this stubborn conflict.

Prince Iuri had won a complete victory over the Tver princes.

Not only Mikhail's son Constantine, but also the boyars and servants who were accompanying Mikhail to the land of the Horde, and even his mutilated body, were now in Iuri's hands. Mikhail's son Alexander arrived in Vladimir under the surety of Bishop Prokhor of Rostov, and at the cost of a "settlement" with the Grand Prince he obtained the release of his father's body for burial in Tver and freed the Tver boyars held prisoner. Having consolidated his position as grand prince, Iuri sent his brother Afanasi to Novgorod "in his place."

Iuri's position was extremely difficult and complicated. Much time and energy were spent on the management of Novgorod affairs. The years 1322–24, following Afanasi's death, were marked by a series of military expeditions made necessary by affairs at Novgorod and involving the personal participation of the Grand Prince. Iuri found it necessary to sit on the throne in Great Novgorod, leaving the administration of Moscow and the management of its dealings with the Horde to his brother Ivan. In 1322 Iuri made a campaign against Vyborg with Novgorod forces. In the following year he established a town at the mouth of the Neva, on the island of Oreshek, and concluded here a "perpetual peace" with envoys from the king of Sweden. In 1324 he marched with Novgorod forces against Ustiug and the North Dvina country, forcing the Ustiug princes to "a settlement of peace on the terms of the ancient toll."

Iuri's energetic work in Novgorod could well have had a special political significance for him, as the necessary condition for his control of Novgorod and its support in his strained and perilous relations with the Horde and Tver.

Moscow's struggle with Tver laid "a heavy burden on the Russian land." The princes had to draw on its resources to pay the increased sums of the Tatar "outlay," or tribute, and purchase costly gifts for the rulers of the Horde. The methods of handling this tribute, which in the thirteenth century the Tatars had tried to establish on the basis of their census, were now completely corrupted. Tax collection had taken on the character of a business farmed out to the highest bidder, or had become the occasion for simple extortion. The princes' rivalry only encouraged this process of corruption. What damaged Prince Mikhail more than anything else in relation to the Horde was his inability to fulfill the heavy financial obligations he had been compelled to assume at the hands of its capitalists and creditors. Prince Iuri's payments and obligations to the Horde must also have been very great. For the Grand Prince of Great Russia, the collection of tribute for the Tatar outlay was one of the chief means of meeting these obligations, and the promise of a "large outlay" was apparently one of the major arguments used to obtain the Khan's yarlik. Conflicts over who should collect the tribute to be used for this outlay gave rise to a new and bloody episode in the struggle between the Tver and Moscow princes.

As Mikhail's successor on the ancient throne of Tver, his son Dmitri did not humble himself before Moscow's prince for long. We do not know of any treaty between them, but the account of their break indicates that Iuri wanted to end Tver's direct relations with the Horde. There is mention of the arrival in Kashin of a Tatar envoy accompanied by a Jewish creditor or moneylender, indicating that the Tver principality was still accounting directly to officials of the Horde after the death of Grand Prince Mikhail. At this point Grand Prince Iuri prepared to march against Kashin "with all the forces of the 'downstream land.'" Mikhail's sons came out against him with all their forces, but a battle was never actually engaged. A "settlement" was made which provided that Iuri should "take the tribute silver from the sons of Mikhail," and that Prince Dmitri should not seek the grand princely rule. The conjunction of these two provisions suggests that the later desire of the grand princes to abolish (by way of treaty agreements) the right of the younger princes to "know the Horde" on their own initiative was only the ratification of a norm that had developed over many years, and that it stemmed from a view of the Grand Prince as the political representative of "all Russia." The subsequent course of events would also indicate that Dmitri's opposition to the concentration of arrangements for payment of the Tatar outlay in the Grand Prince's hands was not a sign of Tver separatism, but a way of fighting for the grand princely rule. He succeeded in taking advantage of the fact that in this particular case Iuri was opposing not only Tver's independent relations with the Horde, but also the official action of the Horde's envoy. Grand Prince Iuri avoided any confrontation with the Khan's envoy, regarding it as his right to pay the outlay himself in the land of the Horde, and he left for Novgorod, undoubtedly to raise the rest of the necessary tribute silver.

Detained in Novgorod territory by the campaign against Vyborg, Iuri gave his rival time and opportunity to strike a dangerous blow against him. Dmitri journeyed to the Horde with a denunciation that was confirmed by the Khan's envoy, and he received the yarlik to the grand princely throne. In the meantime, having settled his business in Novgorod, Iuri set out for the land of the Horde with the tribute silver, but Prince Alexander intercepted him en route and relieved him of his treasury. Prince Dmitri then occupied the throne of the grand principality, while Iuri fled to Pskov, and conducted negotiations from there with the men of Novgorod. He persuaded the latter to summon him to Novgorod's throne and kiss the cross in his name, and after completing a campaign with them against the "Ustiug princes," he set out for the land of the Horde by a roundabout route, through the Zavolochie and down the Kama River. Here the rivals met on November 21, 1324, and Prince Dmitri avenged his father's blood by killing Iuri. Shortly afterward Dmitri himself was executed at the Khan's command for thus disposing of justice "without the Khan's word." The grand princely throne then passed to Alexander of Tver, Dmitri's next younger brother.

Chapter

III

The Development of
Grand Princely Policy
Under Ivan Kalita

The rather brief period from 1326 to 1332 now became a complicated and crucial stage in Great Russia's political history. It may be regarded as the most difficult moment in what Solovyev has defined as the struggle of each prince to become "either the sovereign ruler of the whole Russian land, or his servant." This struggle was complicated by the acute crisis in the relations between Russia and the Horde and in the whole system of internal political relationships in Great Russia.

The loss of the grand princely rule on the part of the Prince of Moscow coincided with another reverse. Metropolitan Peter died in December, 1325. As ruling prince of Moscow at this time, Daniel's son Ivan Kalita (Moneybag) was prepared for this eventuality. As early as August in 1325 the cornerstone of the Cathedral of the Assumption had been laid, and in December the remains of the saintly metropolitan were laid in the tomb that had been prepared. Even after his death Metropolitan Peter was to remain Moscow's friend and protector. Peter's place of honor in the city's memory (he was canonized under his successor in 1339) soon made him the patron saint of Moscow. Before his death, according to the oldest account of his life, Peter "named Archimandrite Feodor as his successor to the metropolitan see," but the Muscovite candidate never assumed the office. There could be no thought of sending him to the Patriarch in the situation that had developed following the death of Prince Iuri in the land of the Horde and the transfer of the grand princely rule to Alexander of Tver. A Greek prelate, Theognost, was made metropolitan of all Russia. A series of important events took place shortly before the new metropolitan's arrival in northern Great Russia in 1328, and the situation was sufficiently settled by that time for him to enter at once into the developing political traditions of the local metropolitan court.

We have only a very general outline of the events of 1326–28 in our collections of chronicles, and this outline is by no means completely reliable. The struggle of the Russian princes for the grand princely rule, and especially for control of the Tatar out-lay, with the complete elimination of all interference by the Horde in the collection of tribute from the individual districts of the Russian ulus, was apparently alarming the rulers of the Golden Horde. The affair of Iuri and Dmitri the Steely-Eyed had evidently undermined the solid foundations of the Khan's power. Only this assumption can help to explain the Khan's sub-sequent actions. The Prince of Moscow did not obtain the yarlik to the grand princely rule. Dmitri, on the other hand, was de-tained by the Horde for almost a year after his bloody coup, and then executed. The grand princely rule was transferred to his brother Alexander, but the Horde's angry suspicion was re-flected in its decision to send to Russia Prince Shchelkan-Diuden-evich (Chol Khan), a second cousin of Khan Uzbek. The dispatch of such an important person with a large armed force can scarcely be explained, as one historian has argued, as an expedition made "to receive the Horde's outlay and perhaps also to summon Alexander to the Horde on some business." It would be more reasonable to suppose that Shchelkan's arrival was designed to terrorize the Russian ulus and restore the menace of the Khan's power. The chronicles reflect certain legends—which are familiar to us also in folk songs—of the Tatars' fantastic purposes: to destroy Christianity, to slaughter the princes, to establish the direct rule of the Tatars over all Russia. The description we have in the chronicles of how Shchelkan arrived in Tver "and drove the Grand Prince out of his court, and with great pride occupied the court of the Grand Prince, and began a great persecution of all Christians, with violence, plundering, beatings, and abuse," is very likely the basis of fact that gave rise to the folk tales and also, of course, to the unrest of the people. The men of Tver did not submit quietly to this Tatar violence. They rose up in battle, and killed Shchelkan with many of his men. The rest of Shchelkan's troops fled to Moscow and from there to the land of the Horde. We do not know whether these events in Tver were part of a general movement against the Tatars, involving other regions besides Tver, but not long after this Prince Ivan of Riazan was killed in the land of the Horde.

Prince Ivan of Moscow quickly traveled to the land of the Horde. He was able to turn away the Khan's anger from the Russian land, where apparently a general massacre was fearfully expected, and limited the reprisals to the region of Tver. Ivan and Prince Alexander of Suzdal received the Khan's commission to march against Tver with the Tatar commanders Feodorchuk and Turalyk and their hosts. This punitive expedition devastated the Tver land. Prince Alexander of Tver and his brother Constantine fled to Pskov. The people of Novgorod bought off the Tatar envoys "with many gifts" and a payment of 2,000 rubles of silver. Ivan reconciled Constantine (who had married one of Ivan's nieces) with the Tatars, Alexander remained in Pskov, and thus the storm was calmed.

The Khan's suspicion of the Russian princes was reflected again, however, in his refusal to restore the grand principality of Vladimir and Great Novgorod as a unified whole. "And with the host of Turalyk," we read in a supplement to the First Novgorod Chronicle, "the princes journeyed to the land of the Horde, and Uzbek divided the principality between them: Novgorod and Kostroma—half the principality—were given to Prince Ivan. To Prince Alexander of Suzdal he gave Vladimir and the Volga lands." Our collections of chronicles pass over this division of the grand principality in silence, noting only that Ivan "sat on the grand princely throne." Accepting the accuracy of the text quoted, we must also acknowledge the possibility that in 1328 Ivan received the yarlik to the grand princely rule and seniority among all the princes of the Russian land. The same passage in the supplement to the Novgorod Chronicle then goes on to say that Alexander of Suzdal reigned "for three and a half years," and "on his death Grand Prince Ivan journeyed to the land of the Horde, and the Khan granted and bestowed upon him the grand princely rule over all the Russian land, as it had been held by his forefather the great Vsevolod-Dmitri son of Iuri; and he committed to him the principality of Albug (that is, Vladimir and the Volga lands); and henceforth all the Russian princes held this rule."

According to this source, then, it was only on the death of Alexander of Suzdal in 1332 that the unity of the grand princely rule over "the whole Russian land" was restored, this restoration prompting the chronicler to mention the reign of Vsevolod Big Nest and also note the significance of the present restoration with the words "and henceforth all the Russian princes held this rule." Certainly the careful and precise nature of the chronicler's statements suggests that he was well informed and that his account is reliable. In addition he gives valuable information concerning Alexander of Suzdal that helps to shed light on the formation of the grand principality of Nizhegorod.[27] Prince Alexander received the city of Vladimir (with its volosts) and the mid-Volga valley. He strove to secure these possessions, and according to our source he removed the veche bell from Vladimir to Suzdal. On Alexander's death, however, Vladimir recovered its position as the capital city. What was done with the mid-Volga region at the time of Alexander's death is not quite clear, but under his brother Constantine it was built up into the powerful grand principality of Nizhegorod. In any case, this unusual division of the Great Russian grand principality did not influence Ivan's position as grand prince. In the eyes of the Horde and also of Russia, he stood at the head of Great Russia's political life. As grand prince of all Russia he entered into the affairs of Pskov and also Great Novgorod, and his ambition to exercise the grand princely rule "as did his forefather the great Vsevolod-Dmitri

27. *Nizhegorod:* the territory under the rule of the grand prince of Nizhni Novgorod.—TRANS.

son of Iuri" finds an echo in the statement that from this time "much violence broke out, which is to say that the grand principality fell into the hands of Grand Prince Ivan the son of Daniel."

II.

The growth of Pskov's political independence and its separation from the grand principality of Vladimir and Novgorod in the preceding decade had made Pskov a sanctuary for princes who' had suffered reverses in their struggle for the grand princely rule.

Alexander of Tver had fled there, and the people of Pskov received him. Ties with Lithuania and the desire to resist the power of Moscow and Novgorod drew them close to the princes of Tver. Prince Alexander's private affair became a matter of concern for Pskov itself; his arrival was a turning point in the city's history.

Khan Uzbek made peace with the Russian princes and commanded them to "go in search of Prince Alexander." Ivan arrived in Novgorod with Alexander of Suzdal, the other Alexander's brothers, Constantine and Vasili of Tver, and "many other Russian princes," and from there his envoys and those of Novgorod pleaded with the fugitive to go to the land of the Horde, "that these Christian lands be not destroyed by pagans." Metropolitan Theognost, who was in Novgorod at the time, laid an excommunication on both Pskov and Alexander. The only way the latter could avoid capture was to withdraw farther, into Lithuania. This he did, leaving his princess and court in Pskov. About a year and a half later he returned, "and the people of Pskov received him with honor and set him on the princely throne of that city." According to the Pskov Chronicle, Alexander reigned as their prince for about ten years, maintaining no ties with the grand principality of Vladimir, but very close relations with the grand principality of Lithuania. The body of law for the city of Pskov dates from Alexander's time, of which the earliest written memorial is the Charter of Grand Prince Alexander, which lies at the basis of the Pskov Charter. At the same time an attempt was made to withdraw Pskov from its position within the ecclesiastical jurisdiction of Great Novgorod by the creation of a separate episcopal jurisdiction. Envoys were sent by

Pskov, by Alexander himself, by Grand Prince Gedymin of Lithuania, and by all the Lithuanian princes to appear before Metropolitan Theognost in Volhynia, with the request that their candidate Arseni be made the ecclesiastical head of the Pskov jurisdiction, but the Metropolitan flatly rejected their petition.

The formation of the grand principality of Lithuania under Gedymin put severe pressures on Pskov, Novgorod, and the principality of Tver, not to mention also the principalities of Smolensk and northern Chernigov. At the time of the petition for a bishop of Pskov there was another equally significant development. Gedymin "peacefully" seized the Novgorod boyars as they made their way to Theognost in Volhynia with Vasili, their candidate for the episcopal see of Novgorod, and released them only after securing their guarantee to give Novgorod's dependent towns of Ladoga, Orekhovo, Karel (with all its lands), and half of Koporye to his son Narimont "as his votchina and a patrimony for his sons." The record of this treaty as preserved in our chronicles stresses the fact that the Novgorod boyars gave this "right" to Narimont only because they found themselves "in such distress." Other information that we have about Novgorod's relations with Narimont would suggest, rather, the emergence of a "Lithuanian party" in Novgorod, looking more toward a west Russian, Lithuanian center of political influence that would promise freedom from the Tatar power and its hateful outlay.

Ivan's position as grand prince of Vladimir and Novgorod was greatly complicated by these negotiations with Lithuania. This drawing of the western regions of Great Russia into the political orbit of the Lithuanian grand principality was largely a result of the role played by the Russian Grand Prince, who served as the representative of the Horde's power and its demands.

For Ivan this role was an unavoidable political necessity. Only with difficulty did he manage to avert the threat of reprisals on the part of the Golden Horde, and he built his position as head of the Great Russian political world on obedience to the Khan's power. The growing pressure of Lithuanian power only strengthened Great Russia's ties with the Horde, since the Khan was not eager to lose control of his Russian ulus.

The heavy pressure of dependence on the Horde which marked all of Ivan's policies appears with special clarity in his relations with Novgorod. In 1328 he sent his deputies to Novgorod. In 1329 he sat on the throne of the Novgorod principality. From 1332 on, when all the forces of grand princely power were in his hands and he bore the increasingly heavy responsibilities of dealings with the Horde, there was an increase in his demands on Great Novgorod and in his attacks upon its freedom. When he returned from the land of the Horde in 1332 as grand prince of all Russia, Ivan "visited his wrath on Novgorod, requiring that it pay him the silver tribute for the land beyond the Kama." Novgorod's refusal renewed its old struggle with the "down-stream" princes for control of the "Novgorod tribute." The Grand Prince gathered together the military power of the whole "downstream land," occupied Torzhok and Bezhetsk, and, rejecting its offer to conclude a peace, "laid waste the Novgorod land." This breach of peace only increased Novgorod's desire to find support in Lithuania. The city made a treaty with Gedymin and accepted his son Narimont-Gleb as prince of its dependent towns, binding him by the ceremonial kissing of the cross to stand "as one" with them in the face of their enemies. Novgorod also sought a rapprochement with Pskov and Prince Alexander. All these relationships, however, were extremely un-stable. It is very likely that dissatisfaction with the high price paid for Narimont's doubtful help and fear of the grand princely power of Vladimir with its support from the Horde forced Novgorod once again to ask for and obtain a reconciliation with Ivan. He arrived in Novgorod in February of 1335, and his reconciliation with Novgorod naturally marked a break between it and the principalities of Pskov and Lithuania. Ivan was deter-mined to make a campaign against Pskov "with the men of Novgorod and the whole 'downstream land,'" but the Novgorod boyars dissuaded him, even though they recognized Pskov as an enemy. As Ivan was returning from Novgorod through Torzhok, the Novi Torzhok volost was raided by Lithuanian forces. Ivan answered this attack by laying waste a number of Lithuanian dependent towns.

Obviously the situation on the western frontier of Great Russia in 1335 was nothing more than a stalemate, which neither Grand Prince Ivan nor the city of Novgorod had the power to bring to any decisive conclusion. The Grand Prince was bound by his relations with Lithuania and the Horde; Novgorod was unable to end its wavering between the two grand princes, and its indecision was complicated by party strife within the land itself. We do not know the content of the treaty between Ivan and Novgorod, but references to it in the chronicles indicate that the men of Novgorod insisted on a rather detailed riad, and required the Grand Prince "to kiss the cross to Novgorod in acceptance of its ancient rights and tolls and in accordance with the decrees of Iaroslav." But Ivan had no sooner returned from another trip to the land of the Horde in 1336 than he made a new thrust into the profitable Novgorod volosts. This was an unsuccessful expedition on the North Dvina River, beyond Volok. Ivan "did not remember his kissing of the cross," and constantly sought to extend his grand princely rights in Great Novgorod, spurred on largely by the need to satisfy the heavy demands of the Horde. It is interesting to note that his clashes with Novgorod occurred each time he returned from the Khan. This happened again in 1339, when the Horde's demands took on new force in the princes' quarrels and antagonisms. Grand Prince Ivan exacted the usual outlay from Novgorod, but then demanded "another outlay" for "the surcharge that the Khan had laid upon him." Novgorod appealed to its "ancient rights and tolls" and the treaty confirmed by the kissing of the cross, but Ivan answered its refusal to pay the surcharge by recalling his deputies and ending the peace.

In Ivan's relations with Novgorod we can see clear examples of that "violence" which so angered the opponents of his grand princely activity. As of old, Great Novgorod was an essential foundation of the Grand Prince's power and one of his main concerns. Possession of Novgorod's throne was required also by the ancient tradition that his was the grand principality of Vladimir and Great Novgorod. The formation of the grand principality of Lithuania and its growing power created a new and dangerous threat on the western border. Pskov had temporarily broken its political ties with Great Russia; in Novgorod and also in Tver there was an increasing western, Lithuanian influence. Smolensk also was virtually lost to the west. Khan Uzbek (hardly on his own initiative) sent a host under the command of Tovlubi and Prince Ivan Krotopol of Riazan against

Smolensk in 1340. The Grand Prince too was ordered to send his host in this campaign, but the whole expedition came to nothing.

A struggle for the unity of the grand principality with inadequate strength to maintain such unity—this was the characteristic feature of Great Russian political life in the first half of the fourteenth century. The struggle called for an increase in the Grand Prince's power and a concentration in his hands of the men and resources of the "downstream land." In his negotiations with Novgorod and also in his campaigns, Ivan appears to have been surrounded "by all his princes"—the princes of Suzdal, Rostov, Iaroslavl, Riazan, and Tver—but because of the fragmentary and meager information available in the chronicles, it is virtually impossible to define their exact interrelationships.

The facts that the compilers of the chronicles in the sixteenth century had at their disposal were by then already confused and incomplete. This is understandable, since the "all-Russian" collections of chronicles made under the supervision of the metropolitans (the main source of our chronicles) made practically no mention of the lesser princes, noting only incidentally their participation in campaigns or journeys to the land of the Horde or the events of domestic life—their marriages and deaths. The Rostov princes had become very insignficant by the time of Ivan Kalita. Their influence was a thing of the past and the Rostov otchina was breaking apart. The Beloozero udel had become the separate votchina of the descendants of Gleb's son Mikhail. Under Ivan Kalita the throne of Beloozero was occupied by Prince Roman, who is mentioned by the chronicles in only one place where we read that Prince "Romanchuk" of Beloozera journeyed to the land of the Horde. The last ties between Uglich and the Rostov otchina had also been broken. The heart of the old Rostov domain was passing through a period of rapid decline. The genealogy of the minor Rostov princes indicates that the division of Rostov into two parts was a result of the marriage of Vasili's younger son, Constantine, to Princess Maria, daughter of Ivan Kalita, and of the latter's establishment on the grand princely throne. This division may have been designed to protect the younger brother's ruling position vis-à-vis his older brother, Feodor. The division was undoubtedly accomplished as a result of Ivan's interference on his son-in-law's behalf, since during his reign Rostov was completely dependent on the Grand Prince's power. Epifani, the disciple and biographer of St. Sergius of Radonezh, has described Rostov's position in these words:

At this time there was a great Tatar host, led by Feodorchuk and Turalyk, and when a year had passed in this way and much violence had come upon the land—that is, when Ivan of Moscow acquired the grand princely rule—the Rostov principality was joined to Moscow, alas, alas; then the city of Rostov; and then also its princes; and they were deprived of power and of their princely rule, of their domains, and honor, and glory, and everything was attached to Moscow. And then from Moscow there came a decree of Grand Prince Ivan, and a certain commander was sent from Moscow to Rostov, one of the leading men of the city, by name Vasili the son of Kochev, and with him an official named Min, and when they were come to the city of Rostov, they laid great demands on the city and on all who lived therein, and a great persecution arose.

Epifani goes on to tell how the people of Rostov had to give their volosts to the men of Moscow "under duress" or, "saving this," were subject to beatings and abuse. Behind the author's bookish rhetoric we can see something more than simply an indictment of the abuses of the military commanders. What he had in mind was in fact the reduction of the power of the patrimonial (otchina) princes of Rostov, the meddling of Muscovite boyars in Rostov's domestic affairs as if they were its rulers, and the harsh measures taken to collect tribute. This account of Ivan's activity in Rostov suggests that the author was also thinking about those "royal surcharges" and severe measures for the collection of silver payments to the Horde of which we have already spoken. Epifani's story reflects the deep sense of wrong felt by the people of Rostov. This apparently led to an attempted revolt. Epifani tells us how the Muscovite boyars tortured the aged Rostov boyar Averki, and of the horror this produced among all the inhabitants of the Rostov land.

Oppressed by Moscow, the Rostov princes had now entered a period of decline in their "power and princely rule," and were being steadily reduced to the position of minor vassals of the Grand Prince or, as they would be called later, hereditary service princes. Their loss of all independent political significance inevitably led to the breakdown of the old Rostov principality into a number of minor votchinas and the degeneration of its ruling princes into little princely landowners. This process of deterioration proceeded gradually through the fourteenth and fifteenth centuries, but Epifani's hagiography is correct in placing the turning point in the history of the Rostov princes in the reign of Grand Prince Ivan Kalita. The princes of Beloozero, Starodub, Iuriev, Galich, Dmitrov, and Iaroslavl all faced a similar fate. The center of Great Russia was being gathered together under the Grand Prince's power, and this power was more and more concentrated in the hands of the Prince of Moscow. The first great foundation stone was being laid for the structure of the Vladimir-Moscow grand principality, which was soon to develop into the "Muscovite state," as defined in the narrow sense of this term as it was to be used in the political language of the sixteenth century.

III.

Ivan Kalita's "purchases" are essential to an explanation of this turning point in the destiny of Great Russia. In his testament Dmitri of the Don will speak of Galich, Beloozero, and Uglich as "his grandfather's purchases." This evidence from an extremely authoritative source has greatly perplexed historians, so much so that some of them have even denied its historical accuracy. On the one hand their perplexity has been caused by the fact that Ivan Kalita and his sons made no mention of such "purchases" in their testaments, and on the other hand by the evidence we have of princes in Galich and Beloozero in the time of Dmitri of the Don. Various historical theories have tried to account for these two circumstances. N. M. Karamzin concluded that "before Dmitri's time these lands were regarded as udels of the grand principality and not of Moscow, and for this reason were not mentioned in the testaments of Ivan's sons." Solovyev rejected this explanation, believing that Ivan could not have "bought additional land" for the grand principality, which "was in no sense a part of the personal property holdings of his family," but could pass after his death to the prince of Tver or the prince of Nizhegorod. In his opinion, "Ivan bought these cities from their princes, but let them retain certain ruling rights, subject, of course, to the sovereignty of the Grand Prince of Moscow. Later, under Dmitri of the Don, they were deprived of these rights."

V. I. Sergeevich admitted that "the territorial acquisitions ascribed to Ivan Kalita were not clearly explained," and that his "purchases" required further investigation. He accepted Solovyev's objection to Karamzin's theory, but noted that even after Solovyev's explanation, "the silence of the testaments is still incomprehensible and the questions thus raised cannot be ignored." These questions remain even if we hold the traditional theory that Ivan's activity was aimed at "assembling a mosaic of estates," and that the territory of the Muscovite state was "the fruit of a century and a half of close-fisted trading on the part of Moscow's princes in their effort to gather in surrounding lands" (Kliuchevsky). It was not land that the Muscovite princes were collecting, according to Sergeevich, but power. They were not extending the territory of the Moscow votchina, but building up the rule of the grand prince, and slowly but surely turning his principality into a "state."

If we fail to look beyond Ivan as the ancestral lord of the Muscovite domains and see him also as the grand prince of all Russia, not only will many of his actions be incomprehensible, but many of the passages in our sources as well. In particular it will be impossible to understand his "purchases." The fact that they were connected with the grand princely rule, as Karamzin has pointed out, explains why there is no mention of Galich, Uglich, or Beloozero in Ivan's testament, any more than there is mention of Pereiaslavl Zalesky or Kostroma or any other volost belonging to the grand principality; indeed, the grand principality itself is not mentioned. On the other hand, the exact provisions of the different parts of Dmitri's testament must be studied carefully if there is to be any understanding of the "purchases." After the opening section, which defines the boundaries of the udels of Dmitri's four princely sons within their Muscovite otchina, including the oprichnina set aside for the minor prince Ivan, a special section follows in which we find the bestowal of the grand princely rule ("as his otchina") on the eldest son, Vasili, with the "purchases" of his grandfather—Galich, Beloozero, and Uglich—granted to the three younger princes. This same distinction between the domains of Moscow and the domains of the grand principality appears in the next section of the testament, in the definition of the domains granted during her lifetime to Dmitri's widow. Two volosts from the grand principality are assigned to her, one from Pereiaslavl and one from Kostroma; then certain towns are assigned to her from Prince Iuri's domains of Galich, from Prince Andrei's domains of Beloozero, and also two from the grand principality: one from Vladimir and one from Pereiaslavl. The testament also mentions volosts given to the Princess from the udels of all the princes (excluding the minor son, Ivan).

Two points remain unclear and are difficult to resolve because of our lack of information: (a) the exact nature of those transactions that in Dmitri's testament are called "purchases"; and (b) what happened to Galich, Beloozero, and Uglich before they were merged with the votchina domains of the Moscow princes. An answer to these questions must begin with Solovyev's theory that Ivan "bought these cities (obviously we are speaking here not of cities but of principalities) from the princes," and then left these princes with certain ruling rights which they later lost under Dmitri of the Don. The transfer of princely domains to the grand prince with a preservation of the ruling prince's right to "supervise" his estates during his lifetime will be encountered later in Muscovite practice. The theory that Ivan's purchases were like these later transactions is weakened, however, by two facts: first, we do not know when or with what princes Ivan could have made such a riad for the purchase of Galich, Beloozero, and Uglich; second, if we are to understand Dmitri's "dismissal" of its ruling prince as a violation of his grandfather's riad, this is mentioned only in the case of the prince of Galich and then the prince of Starodub, whose votchina is not even mentioned in the list of lands "purchased" by Ivan. There is evidence, it might be noted, that the Beloozero princes were "dismissed" later, in the 1380's. The matter may have been still more complicated, with the riads of purchase being a part of the familiar twofold subjection of minor hereditary princes to the grand princely power, and made as a result of the new conflict that faced Ivan Kalita when Alexander returned to the throne of Tver. The fate of Galich and Beloozero may also have had some connection with the rivalry between Moscow and Nizhni Novgorod.

IV.

We have noted that Grand Prince Ivan planned a campaign against Pskov at the beginning of 1335 but abandoned this plan on the insistence of the men of Novgorod. This was a sign of his awkward position in the face of Lithuanian power in the western part of Great Russia. Lithuanian influence was especially dangerous because of its connection with the growing reaction of local princely powers against the Muscovite "violence," with the widespread hostility among princes and boyars as well as among other social classes toward Moscow and the power of the Horde. Prince Alexander's return to Tver once more upset all the delicate relationships within Great Russia.

While Alexander reigned as prince in Pskov, his brother Constantine had ruled the Tver principality "quietly and peacefully," as the "head of his otchina, confirmed in this rule by all the people." Related by marriage to Grand Prince Ivan, he was obedient to him and acted as one of his "younger" princes. But soon after Ivan's attempt to organize a campaign against Pskov, Alexander sent his son Feodor to the Horde, and the latter returned to Tver with the Khan's envoy Abdullah. These dealings with the Horde were obviously carried on without reference to Ivan, but Alexander had acted in concert with Metropolitan Theognost, having first sent his boyars to obtain the Metropolitan's approval. Prince Alexander made the journey from Pskov to Tver and evidently made some settlement with Constantine regarding his return, and also arranged with the Khan's envoy for an early journey to the land of the Horde.

The following year he went to the Khan with an explanation of his actions and returned with Tatar envoys, "having been confirmed in the rule of his Tver otchina." Alexander's return to the throne of Tver was certainly a political defeat for Grand Prince Ivan. Alexander would not stand in the same subservient relationship to him as Constantine. The Nikon Chronicle emphasizes that Alexander made contacts with the Horde prior to any peaceful settlement between himself and Ivan. A force uncontrolled by the Prince of Moscow and prepared for a new struggle for power had appeared on Great Russian soil. Alexander's ties with Lithuania and Ivan's own strained relations with Novgorod now threatened the Grand Prince with serious difficulties, all the more so in that the Tver princes had obviously made independent connections with the Golden Horde. There is evidence that Alexander's "hostility" toward Ivan was shared also by the younger princes, dissatisfied with Moscow's harsh measures. Prince Vasili of Iaroslavl and Roman of Beloozero were on the side of Tver. We may assume that the princes of Rostov and Suzdal must also have aroused suspicion and uneasiness in Moscow. In all these events, and in the fragmentary accounts of the chronicles, we can sense a rising dissatisfaction with Moscow's heavy hand. The resolution of the princes' conflict depended on the Khan, and the drama was to be played out in the land of the Horde. As he carried on his business with the Horde, however, Ivan could not lose sight of his affairs in Russia. When he journeyed to the land of the Horde on the heels of Alexander's son Feodor, he sent his own son Andrei to Novgorod, and at the last moment, when Alexander's application for the yarlik to Tver was granted, he sent his sons to the Horde and remained himself in Russia.

Grand Prince Ivan succeeded in defeating his rival and winning the upper hand. The chronicle collections hint more than they describe what happened in the land of the Horde, but there can be little doubt about the meaning of these hints. Alexander's negotiations with the Horde—he had again sent his son Feodor to the Khan, with the envoy Abdullah—forced Ivan to travel to the land of the Horde himself. While both Ivan and Feodor were present in the Khan's court, "many evil charges were brought before Khan Uzbek against Prince Alexander of Tver, and the Khan's ears were filled with many grievous tales." The cautious language of the Moscow collection of chronicles fails to conceal Moscow's strategy. The Khan summoned Alexander to the land of the Horde "in accordance with Ivan's wishes," but "with gentleness and mildness," not as if to some trial or investigation, but rather with promises of "the grand principality and great honors." Our sources give us no definite

information about the nature of the charges brought against
the Prince of Tver, and we do not know to what extent Alexander's "flight" to Pskov and his Lithuanian ties provided material for these accusations, but these things must certainly have
colored all his negotiations with the Horde. The chronicle tradition puts considerable emphasis on the cunning used to lure
Alexander to the land of the Horde, making it appear that the
Tatar rulers were afraid to let him slip out of their hands.
Prince Alexander could have found refuge in Lithuania; or he
could have risked an uprising in Tver, similar to the one during
the reign of his elder brother Dmitri the Steely-Eyed, only that
now he could count on Lithuanian aid. There is an obscure
statement in the chronicles referring roughly to the period of
these events, which tells us that "the Tatars made war on
Lithuania." Not long after this the Tatar host under Tovlubi
marched against Smolensk with Russian detachments. It was not
difficult for the head of the "Russian ulus" to represent Alexander as a threat to Tatar power in Russia. Neither gifts to the
Horde's rulers nor the patronage of powerful men close to the
Khan were able to save the Prince of Tver. On October 28, 1338,
he and his son Feodor were killed at the Khan's command.

Ivan had won a complete victory, and he proceeded quickly
with actions designed to reveal it was a victory of the grand
princely power over the independence of Tver. Ivan "removed
the bell from the Church of the Saviour in Tver and took it to
Moscow." The genealogical traditions used by the compiler of
the Nikon Chronicle place the transfer of many Tver boyars to
Ivan in Moscow in this period of struggle between the two
cities. The compiler has placed his account of this movement at
the beginning of his description of the final conflict between
Ivan and Alexander, but this does not help us much in dating
this movement. The chronicler was probably guided by the fact
that in his genealogical sources the movement of Tver boyars
was regarded as having been caused not by the overthrow of
Tver in its struggle with Moscow, but by the dissatisfaction of
the Tver boyars over Alexander's policy of "replacing" them by
new favorites recently brought in from foreign lands. This explanation does more to undermine the credibility of his report
of the transfer than help us grasp its meaning. If there really was

a removal of boyars from Tver to Moscow, it would seem more reasonable to connect it with the overthrow of Tver following Alexander's death, and with the very significant removal of the Spaso-Preobrazhensky bell to Moscow. Mikhail's son Constantine reoccupied the throne of Tver on the death of his brother Alexander, and the dependence of Tver on Moscow must be regarded as having increased substantially during this period.

It was in the land of the Horde that Grand Prince Ivan had won final victory over his rival from Tver, and he paid for it with heavy financial obligations. After this we begin to hear about his clashes with Great Novgorod over the "Khan's surcharges," and it is more than likely that the oppression of Rostov, so clearly described by Epifani the Wise, also began at this time. At the end of his life and princely reign Ivan was the true bearer of grand princely power, walking in the footsteps of his "forefather the great Prince Vsevolod-Dmitri son of Iuri." In the Smolensk campaign the "host" he sent in response to the Khan's order included the princes of Suzdal, Rostov, Iuriev, Druts, and Fomin, along with the men from Moscow. Even Riazan and Tver princes not directly involved in the clash between Ivan Kalita and Alexander marched in this campaign in response to the Grand Prince's summons. Ivan had laid a solid foundation for the restoration of the grand prince's shaken power. At the time of his death, however, the general political position of Great Russia was still very complex and strained. Great Russia was exposed to the pressure of external forces and to the weaknesses of its own internal organization, which had not yet developed a precise form for the grand prince's sovereignty.

Chapter
IV

The Moscow Votchina Under the Successors of Ivan Kalita

Ivan died on the last day of March in 1341. This was an important year in the history of eastern Europe. Gedymin, the true founder of the grand principality of Lithuania, died in the same year. Under Gedymin, Vilna had emerged as the center of this new Russo-Lithuanian state, and its influence was strongly felt in Pskov, Great Novgorod, and Tver. All through this century we can observe the crucial role played by Smolensk as the focus of conflict between Lithuania and Moscow. Lithuania became so powerful that as its control extended over these Russian lands, it was able to tear them away from their dependency on the Tatar empire. Under Olgerd the seizure of Russian lands was accompanied by many clashes with the Golden Horde, and we know that even in Gedymin's time the Tatars had waged war against Lithuania and sent their host against the city of Smolensk with the Russian princes. In 1341 Olgerd attacked Mozhaisk and burned its residential areas, but did not take the city. This constantly increasing pressure from

Lithuania forced Moscow to look to the defense of its own possessions, quite apart from any grand princely policy. Lithuanian influence extended far beyond the area in which it exercised direct power, and in the relationships developing within Great Russia itself the grand princes had more and more to reckon with Lithuania.

As far as we can tell from the very fragmentary information of our chronicles, the question of succession to the grand princely throne on the death of Ivan Kalita was decided without conflict in the land of the Golden Horde, the choice being determined by the supremacy Ivan had won for Moscow in his final victory over Tver. At a general meeting of the Russian princes in the land of the Horde, the Khan acknowledged Ivan's eldest son, Semeon, as grand prince, "and all the Russian princes were given into his hand." The ceremony of installing him on the throne of the grand principality took place in Vladimir on October 1, 1341, and soon after there was an assembly of all the Russian princes in Moscow. Apart from one obscure reference, no information about this meeting has been preserved in the chronicles. It was, however, another turning point. The Grand Prince's relationship with the other princes had to be defined, and Semeon apparently entered into some kind of agreement with his brothers and cousins which was sworn to "on his father's tomb." Would it be too bold to say that at this Moscow assembly Semeon made treaties also with the princes of Tver, Riazan, Suzdal, Rostov, Iaroslavl, etc.? It would be difficult to defend such a theory, of course, since there is no documentary evidence. A more important and an easier task for the historian would be to describe to what extent and in what way the princely interrelations in Great Russia entered a new phase during Semeon's reign. As the real basis for the grand princely policy of the Muscovite princes in Daniel's line, the Moscow votchina now stood face to face with at least three other local grand principalities: Tver, Riazan, and Nizhegorod. The interrelations of these four territorial-political units determined the future course of the history of Great Russia, and a study of this period must begin with a description of their internal organization, as it first developed in more or less clear outline about the middle of the fourteenth century.

II.

The Moscow votchina of the house of Daniel took on its basic shape with the seizure of Mozhaisk and Kolomna. Daniel's sons —according to the chronicle there were five—ruled over their family domain jointly, with no distribution of separate udels to the princes individually. At least we know nothing of any such distribution, although the account of the departure of Princes Alexander and Boris to Tver suggests that these two may have made some agreement with their elder brother to "rule in separate volosts." In any case, the starting point for our history of princely rule in the Moscow votchina is the testament of Ivan Kalita, who outlived all his brothers and was free once again to "give a riad to his sons."

On the basis of the dating of the *Collection of Official State Documents and Treaties*, the two testaments of Ivan that have come down to us are usually said to have been made in 1328, although Eksempliarsky has clearly demonstrated the impossibility of this dating. The formula used in both testaments, "And to you, my son Semeon, I commit your younger brothers, and also my princess with her little children, and under God's guidance you shall be their benefactor," obviously cannot refer to Semeon's widowed mother. John was speaking here of his second wife, Semeon's stepmother, correctly identified by Eksempliarsky as the Princess Uliana mentioned in the testament of Grand Prince Ivan II. Kalita's first wife, Elena, died in March, 1332, and the first of these two testaments could only have been written well after his first wife had died and enough time had elapsed for him to have married again and given Princess Uliana her "little children."

The purpose of a prince's testament was to set forth the riad that the father wished to make for his sons and widowed princess in the event that "God should bring his life to a conclusion." It is probably incorrect to define the old term riad by the newer word *zaveshchanie*, which in our usage has the meaning of "will" or "bequest." Ivan's testament was not concerned with the actual identification of heirs; its main purpose was to set forth the way in which he wished to arrange and define the rule of his votchina by his family in case he, the head of the family and maker of the testament, should die. His testament performed the age-old function of patriarchal authority defined in *Russkaia Pravda:* [28] "If one who dies divides his house among his children, let this division stand." In this case, however, the composition of the "house" was extremely complicated. The manner in which it was disposed of was complicated also. The entire family—Semeon's younger brothers, Ivan and Andrei, and the Princess Uliana with her daughters—was "enjoined" to Semeon. He was to be their "benefactor," the elder of the family in his father's place. Ivan committed "his otchina of Moscow" to his three sons, leaving it up to them to share among themselves the revenues from the cities ("the tamga and revenues from the other volosts and their towns"), with a portion of the *osmnichy* [29] set aside for Princess Uliana. The city of Moscow itself was excluded from division ("I enjoin my otchina of Moscow to my sons, and have established it to them as their portion"), as were also all the enumerated people of the Moscow principality (". . . and the enumerated people, these my sons shall have charge of jointly, and they shall supervise them as one man"). These "enumerated" people have usually been understood as "indited" or "bonded" persons. All such terms were replaced later by the term *tiaglye liudi,* i.e., "persons subject to taxation." From the standpoint of the prince's administrative authority, this class was made up of persons obliged to pay tribute, with the main part of this tribute being used to pay the Tatar outlay. The joint "charge" of these people and their supervision "as one man" by all three princely brothers (under Semeon, of course, as the one holding the seniority) was made secure by the unity of financial power in the Moscow principality, a unity of vital importance in the struggle to bring the payment of the outlay from the "Russian ulus" solely into the hands of the Grand Prince. Ivan's testament must evidently be understood as a handing over of the rule of Moscow to all three brothers "as one man," with a division among them of the revenues from "the other volosts and their towns." This disposi-

28. *Russkaia Pravda:* the Russian law code.—TRANS.

29. *Osmnichy, vosmnichy:* a sum of money taken as a commission or tariff on the sale or exchange of property—TRANS.

tion of the votchina must certainly have introduced an element of vagueness into its administration, and in fact it did cause grave problems for the three brothers.

All these features of Ivan's riad give evidence of the unity of the Muscovite principality and its ruling family. This unity was not impaired by Ivan's division of certain possessions within it to each son and to his widowed princess and her daughters. In accordance with this division, the eldest son, Semeon, received Mozhaisk and Kolomna—the two pivots of Moscow's military policies, one at the source and the other at the mouth of the Moscow River—and a number of substantial volosts along the course of the Moscow River below the "city district" (*uezd*) of Moscow, and also the "suburb" (*stan*) of Goretov, lying along the river above Moscow and stretching north to the upper reaches of the river Kliazma. Ivan, the second son, received Zvenigorod and the volosts along the Ruza River down to its juncture with the Moscow River and southward beyond it. The third son, Andrei, received the southern volosts of the Moscow principality from Peremysl to Serpukhov (including the latter), so that his domain extended to the Oka River. Princess Uliana and her daughters received volosts in the northern part of the Moscow otchina, along the Kliazma River. The term udel came to be used somewhat later to describe the share of individual princes in their family's common otchina. Ivan Kalita does not yet use this term, but speaks rather of the volosts assigned to his sons, and of each one's "city district" (uezd). Ivan's sons will call these shares udels, but will also refer to them as the "section [*uchastok*] bestowed on me by my father," or the "city district of my father." This division of the common votchina into sections or city districts was not regarded as final or irrevocable. It was not an assignment "in perpetuity," which of course would have destroyed the concept of a single votchina. Ivan's testament foresaw the possibility of changes in the general composition of the Muscovite domains, and thus also of a partial redistribution within the family: "and if for my sins the Tatars seek to possess anyone's volosts, and take them away, then you my sons and princess must again divide these volosts, each according to his rank." Ivan's riad was based on the concept of the family domain as a common otchina divided partially into sections or udels, but also ruled conjointly. It did not break up the votchina into several oprichninas seen as the private property of their respective rulers. There are no grounds whatever for suggesting here a right granted to separate the shares or udels as hereditary domains, which would become the inalienable possessions of their ruling princes.

III.

Ivan's riad left a great many things unclear in the relationships it was intended to define. His three sons confirmed this riad by a treaty, which they sealed by the kissing of the cross "on their father's tomb." Almost certainly there were some misunderstandings between the brothers before the kissing of the cross. At least this is suggested in the treaty document by the mention of boyars who had begun to "seduce" the princes, and by the admonition that the princes ought not to "harbor malice" as a result of this conflict, but should now "make amends" and "punish the guilty one as he deserves." At the end of the document there is a reference to some sedition on the part of the boyar Alexei Petrovich against Grand Prince Semeon, in which Semeon's brothers agree to renounce Alexei and give no further aid to him or his family. We can add to these facts Semeon's exhortation to his brothers (in his own testament) to "live as one" and not to listen to "the ravings of those who would seduce them," but give ear rather to Metropolitan Alexei, and to the old boyars who were well disposed to their father, Grand Prince Ivan, as well as to his princely sons. We might also note that under Grand Prince Ivan II we shall find the boyar Alexei Petrovich holding the post of tysiatsky of Moscow and later being killed in a Moscow square, the victim of a plot that led to the removal of Moscow's "great boyars" to Riazan.

Ivan's testament reflected a clear desire to preserve the unity of the princely family and keep the powers of the principality in the hands of Grand Prince Semeon, as the possessor of the Muscovite "seniority." This desire was developed still further in the treaty made by his sons. We find here a definition of the "solidarity" of the princes and a clarification of their relations to the one holding the seniority.

Let us be as one in matters of life and death, and let us accept and honor our eldest brother in our father's place; and it is for our brother to deal with us as brothers, giving no offense in any thing. Let anyone who is an enemy of our eldest brother be accounted an enemy of ours. Also, any friend of our eldest brother is a friend of ours.

This formula quite definitely establishes the leading position of the eldest brother. "And when I shall mount my horse," he says to his younger brothers in this treaty, "you will ride with me; and when it is not for me to ride, but rather to send you in my place, you will ride without disobedience." There is an element of sovereignty in Semeon's seniority. Accepting and honoring him "in their father's place," the younger brothers are also to obey him. But they are not yet simply vassals or subject princes: Semeon's seniority is combined with the provision for the autonomy of the younger princes on the principle of "brotherhood." This is reflected in several parts of the treaty. The Grand Prince is bound to act in agreement with his younger brothers: "And it is not for you, as our master the Grand Prince, to enter into any final settlement with anyone without us," they say to him, "and you are not to conclude any matter without us, your younger brothers." Furthermore, any notion of their responsibility to the Grand Prince for blunders committed in the area of military defense is carefully set aside: ". . . and in the event of any failure in measures of defense on our part or yours, or on the part of our tysiatskys or deputies, we are not to be held accountable, or to bear malice." Finally there is provision for complete reciprocity in the rights of boyars to move from one volost to another: ". . . and our boyars and servants have complete freedom, if any goes from us to you, the Grand Prince, or from you to us, no malice is to be borne." This right extended even to the princes' free or voluntary servants, to "anyone who has been maintained by or is under contract to our father or us."

Semeon's treaty with his brothers was a guarantee of the unity of the military forces of the Moscow principality. It would seem (although this part of the treaty text has been badly corrupted) that it also developed and completed the measures specified in Ivan's testament for the preservation of the unity of Moscow's financial resources, with its prohibition of any purchase of land from enumerated persons and of any conscription of such persons into another prince's service.

Both the grand princely seniority and the brotherly equality of all the princes were reflected in this treaty's further elaboration of the provisions of Ivan's "division." The younger brothers not only "yielded" the greater part of the Moscow tamga to Semeon "by right of seniority" (half of it, in fact, dividing the other half between them), but also accepted this division of revenues as a norm for the future: ". . . and thus whoever will be accounted the eldest, that one by right of his seniority will receive half the Moscow tamga, and half will go to the two younger princes; and it will henceforth be shared in this way." A number of other court revenues were also yielded to the elder brother by right of seniority: commission fees from the court falconer, from the master of the stables, the master of the hunt, the keeper of the gardens, the supplier of horses, and so on. The princes' treaty thus established the following basic features of an "udel domain": (1) its inviolability—"as our father has divided our portions, let them be guarded by us, and not violated," with the application of a similar guarantee in regard to future acquisitions: "or if any of us brothers should acquire or purchase land, or if any should purchase from us or add another's land to his own volosts, that also should be guarded by us and not violated"; (2) its heredi-tary nature—"God has called each of us to provide for his princess and children both in life and in death, and not to offend them, nor to take anything from a prince's wife or children of that which our father has bestowed on him as his portion"; (3) its independent administration by each prince—boyars and volun-tary servants are given the right to serve whichever prince they wish, and on the death of any one of them the right to serve his princess or children, with the assurance that the Grand Prince will not "bear any malice for this, nor lay hands on him unlaw-fully, but protect him as one of his own." Their treaty also estab-lished local courts to try cases between the boyars and servants of the Grand Prince and those of the udel princes. The princes were forbidden to send their agents into another prince's udel. Also the Grand Prince and his boyars and servants were for-bidden to buy up villages in the udels of the other princes, just as they were prohibited from doing this in his.

This treaty made between Semeon and his brothers Ivan and Andrei was an extremely complex document, combining two different systems of relationships. On the one hand it represented a grand prince's riad with his younger ruling princes; on the other hand it was a riad between brother princes defining the conditions under which they would rule their common otchina in the form of udels.

Let us consider for a moment the subsequent fate of the latter system. Semeon's testament, made some ten or twelve years later, gives us a valuable commentary on the provisions of his treaty with his brothers. Semeon lost his sons in the terrible plague of 1353, and a month later died himself, leaving a testament or riad addressed to his princess, Maria Alexandrovna. His riad was clearly based on the earlier treaty: "I have laid it upon you and my brothers, before God," Semeon wrote, "that you keep the agreements made in the settlement that we sealed by the kissing of the cross at our father's tomb." He then gave all that his father had bestowed on him to his wife—Kolomna with all its volosts, and Mozhaisk with its lands; in short, his entire udel, together with his share of the Moscow tamga, and also the towns that had come to him in his father's riad and in the supplementary agreement made by the three brothers, as well as his own acquisitions and purchases, and all his valuables. This provision for the direct inheritance of his udel in his own line created a serious threat to the power and unity of the Moscow principality. The transfer of such important Moscow domains as Mozhaisk and Kolomna into his wife's hands, indeed into the hands of a childless widow and daughter of the princely house of Tver, was politically intolerable. Nor was it ever put into effect. Unfortunately, our sources give no information as to what actually took place. What we do know, from the later testament of Ivan II, is that both cities had by that time come into his hands together with their volosts, although parts of these volosts remained under Maria's rule during her lifetime. Her immediate administration of these areas ended long before her death, however, perhaps because of her entry into a convent. In view of its extraordinary political and geographical significance, the udel of Kolomna became from this time onward an inalienable possession of the grand prince, and is described as such in the testament of Dmitri of the Don: ". . . and if for my sins God should take away my son Prince Vasili, whoever will be my eldest son after him, to that one shall be assigned Prince Vasili's udel." Thus in the very first stages of the history of the princely family of Moscow, in its second and third generations, the fact that the head of the family was also grand prince left its mark on the development of udel rule, subordinating this form of domain to an obvious political necessity.

IV.

In other respects, however, the assignment of udels continued to develop in a way contrary to the fundamental political interests of the Moscow principality, gradually weakening those foundations of unity that Ivan Kalita had tried to secure in his testament and which Semeon had later sought to reinforce in his treaty with his brothers.

Prince Andrei also died in the summer of 1353, not long after Semeon. His princely inheritance passed to his sons: Prince Ivan, who survived his father by only five years and died while still a child, and Prince Vladimir, who was born forty days after his father's death. The testament of Ivan II and the treaties of Dmitri of the Don with Andrei's son Vladimir show how this new branching out of the family increased the separation of udel possessions within the Moscow otchina. Ivan II allowed his nephew to retain the share of his father, Andrei: ". . . in the rule of Moscow a third; in the tamga, duties, and tolls from the towns a third; and a third of the rents." Ivan even yielded the privileges due to him "by right of seniority" and as established in Semeon's riad with Ivan and Andrei, since there is no mention here of the assignment of a full half of the tamga to himself, and the revenues from the master of the stables and the "supplier of horses for the camp and the road" are divided into thirds. Moscow, however, was granted as the sole possession of his two sons, Dmitri and Ivan. The Mozhaisk-Kolomna udel was assigned to Dmitri; Ivan received Zvenigorod. Prince Vladimir was to "oversee his own father's city district." This district had undergone some reduction in size since the time of Semeon's riad; Lopastna had been joined to Riazan, but Vladimir received in exchange Novi Gorodok, at the mouth of the Porotla. Other "Riazan places" had been joined to Moscow and were shared "in halves" between the Grand Prince's two sons. "All three princes shall oversee the enumerated people jointly, as one man." But on the death of Princess Uliana her volosts, villages, and income from the osmnichy were to be "divided into four parts," with the setting aside of the volost of Surozhik and the village of Luchinsk to her daughters, and portioned to the Grand Prince's two sons, Dmitri and Ivan, to his own widowed princess, and to Prince Vladimir.

And according to their sins these will have to go to the Horde in search of Kolomna, the place of Lopastna, or the separated places of Riazan, and according to their sins my sons Prince Dmitri and Prince Ivan and Prince Vladimir [of Serpukhov] will have whatever places they acquire, each in his own place, and the places of my princess will be distributed among them as inalienable possessions.

The votchina (family) group still stands on its old established foundations. Vladimir is still in all respects an udel prince of the Moscow votchina. Any signs of the setting apart of this member of the princely family are still insignificant. But they will become more and more evident in the subsequent development of the princes' interrelations.

On the death of Ivan II in November, 1358, three youthful princes were left in possession of the princely rule in Moscow: Ivan's two sons, Dmitri of the Don and Ivan, and Andrei's son Vladimir of Serpukhov. Their first treaty defined the relationship of the elder brother, Dmitri, with the "younger brother" Vladimir, and established the concept of two otchinas within the Moscow principality: ". . . it is for you to have charge of your otchina, and for me to have charge of mine." Serpukhov is now no longer an udel of the common votchina, but a separate otchina. Although this document continued to use the term udel in reference to Vladimir's domain, the significant formula specifying two otchinas pointed the way to the future development of their relations.

Dmitri's brother, Ivan, died in October, 1363, and his udel passed into Dmitri's hands. This took place at the time of Dmitri's final decisive struggle for the grand princely rule, which ended with his victory over Constantine's son Dmitri of Suzdal and his allies. Grand Prince Dmitri also brought the prince of Rostov under his control at this time, and drove the princes of Galich and Starodub from their thrones. By the end of 1364 Dmitri of Suzdal was completely subdued, and when the son of Dmitri in Moscow "brought the grand princely rule to his father from the Horde" in the company of the Khan's envoy, the Suzdal prince was forced to "yield the grand principality to Grand Prince Dmitri of Moscow," and in January, 1366, he gave his daughter Evdokia to the latter in marriage.

Not long after this, Grand Prince Dmitri of the Don made his second treaty with Vladimir. In spite of the difficulties of dating and our fragmentary and undoubtedly corrupt text, we can still draw scraps of information from our records of this treaty which are important to the history of the relations between the princes of Moscow.

The treaty was made in connection with Grand Prince Dmitri's "grant" of Galich and Dmitrov "with their volosts and villages" to Prince Vladimir, and with the creation of new conditions affecting both the scope and the nature of their relations. Changes in the composition of Vladimir's domains had altered his position of power. Dmitri was now "granting" him Galich and Dmitrov with their lands "as his udel." In the treaty Vladimir calls these acquisitions "my udel, which my master has conferred on me," contrasting them with his own inherited domains. In speaking of his possessions as a whole, Vladimir uses such expressions as "in my votchina and udel . . ."; "and it is not for you, my master, to send your toll collectors and overseers into my votchina or into my udel." The concept of two votchinas within the Moscow principality is growing stronger and becoming more clearly defined—on the one hand the votchina of the descendants of Ivan II, on the other the votchina of the descendants of his brother Andrei. And while ruling his own votchina, Prince Vladimir now received a share or udel in the newly acquired lands of the Grand Prince, a precedent that was to be long remembered by the younger members of the princely house of Moscow. Grand Prince Dmitri ruled not only over the whole grand principality, but also over his own Muscovite votchina and udel, the latter term being used in this document to signify the share of new acquisitions that remained in Dmitri's hands after the grant of the other udel to Vladimir. Thus while ruling their own votchinas, the two princes divided the newly acquired lands in the form of udels, or, more accurately, Dmitri made this division on his own initiative but "with the consent" of Prince Vladimir, ratifying this allocation by treaty in the form of a "grant." The treaty defined the relations not only between these two princes, but also between the two princely houses, since it contained a guarantee of hereditary possession in each line.

Here, then, in the second generation after Ivan Kalita, there was a further development of that separate character of udel domain which had been introduced earlier in the treaty between Semeon and his brothers. The individualization of Vladimir's votchina was also graphically expressed in the everyday life of the princes. The urban centers of the udels of the older generation—Mozhaisk, Kolomna, Zvenigorod, Serpukhov—had never been princely residences. Now, however, Vladimir had become the local ruling prince of Serpukhov, which he made his capital city. His treaty with Grand Prince Dmitri was evidently only one point in the development of their changing relationship, about which we have very little specific knowledge. Our evidence would indicate that Vladimir took possession of Galich and Dmitrov for only a short time, and perhaps not at all. If we take account of a third treaty made between then, Vladimir received Luzha and Borovsk from Dmitri (sometime during Alexei's reign as metropolitan and as a result of his mediation) as well as an increase in his domains following the death of Princess Uliana, and never did receive Galich and Dmitrov.

Thanks to a better preserved text, this third treaty (made in the 1380's with the approval of Metropolitan Pimen) gives a much more precise definition of the Grand Prince's votchina, and presents it as lying quite beyond the reach of any claim on the part of Vladimir. The votchina bestowed on Dmitri by his father, Grand Prince Ivan II, consisted of two shares in the city of Moscow and in its dependent districts with their revenues, with the addition of Kolomna, Mozhaisk, and Zvenigorod, with all the rights and privileges pertaining to them. Prince Vladimir's domains consisted of those things that he had inherited from his father—a third share in the city of Moscow and its dependent districts with their revenues, and the udel of Serpukhov, with the addition of certain new acquisitions, such as Novi Gorodok (received by Vladimir in exchange for Lopastna, which had been joined to Riazan), Luzha, Borovsk, and some volosts from the former udel of Princess Uliana.

In the 1370's Prince Vladimir emerged as the votchina prince of Serpukhov, the builder of his own capital city and principality. In 1372 he married a daughter of the Lithuanian Grand Prince Olgerd, and in 1374

Prince Vladimir built up the city of Serpukhov in his otchina, commanding that trees be felled and a house be put up there for his use; to those who lived there and to those who arrived there from elsewhere and wished to make it their home he gave much freedom and many privileges; as deputy in the city he appointed a certain Iakov Iurievich the Strong, one of his druzhina.

With the support of St. Sergius of Radonezh he then built a church there in honor of the Conception of the Holy Virgin, and also established a monastery. The Cathedral Church of the Holy Trinity was also built in the 1370's, and we read of its consecration in the year 1380. Serpukhov had thus become the capital city of a distinct votchina principality.

V.

Udel domain, as the shared rule and possession of a common votchina by a number of patrimonial (otchina) princes, was an extremely unstable and precarious basis for preserving the unity of rule within a family and maintaining its principality as a single votchina. The tendency toward the breakdown of such a principality into separate and distinct votchinas, with the weakening and ultimate collapse of shared rule over the parts of a single whole, must be regarded as a characteristic feature of this type of domain. This tendency is to be seen in the third generation of the descendants of Daniel in Moscow. Other forces—which might be called political motives, in contrast to the hunger for power displayed by the princes—were working against this tendency toward disintegration and preventing its full realization. We have already drawn attention to the passages in Ivan's testament and the treaty between Semeon and his brothers aimed at preserving the unity of the military and financial power of the Moscow principality. Even in those documents, however, we could see an increase in the separateness of the princes' domains which threatened to pass from possession of shares into an outright individualization of distinct votchinas. The treaties between Grand Prince Dmitri of the Don and Prince Vladimir give us an interesting glimpse of the struggle to preserve the unity of the Moscow principality under Dmitri's seniority, but they also served to sanction its breakdown into two udel-votchinas in this same realm of political relationships.

In principle Dmitri's treaties are on the same ground as Semeon's treaty with his brothers, Ivan and Andrei. In Dmitri's first treaty the princes agree "that it is for us to live as our fathers lived with their eldest brother, our uncle Grand Prince Semeon." The same formula is found in Dmitri's third treaty with Vladimir, and undoubtedly we would have found it also in the second if its opening section had been preserved. On the other hand, the brotherly equality and independence of the younger prince are expressed in a number of places much more distinctly and positively. The older formula was: "And when I shall mount my horse, you will ride with me without disobedience, and when it is not for me to ride, but rather to send you in my place, you will ride without disobedience." In the very first treaty between Dmitri and Vladimir this concept was put in question. While upholding the obligation of a younger prince to send his captains, boyars, and servants "without disobedience" on campaigns with the armies of the Grand Prince, Dmitri's treaty speaks of the younger prince's "obedient service" on behalf of the elder brother as being with his consent— "insofar as it is mutually acceptable both to me and to you my younger brother," we read in the chronicle—and it expects his personal participation in a campaign only in the event of the personal presence of the Grand Prince: ". . . so that you and I may ride side by side." In fact, however, Prince Vladimir went on campaigns at the command of the Grand Prince on several occasions, and the treaty of 1389 (their third) will return to the formula of the first treaty between Semeon and his brothers.

The guarantees of independent territorial sovereignty and of the princes' power over their own servants and men were developed in detail in the treaties between Dmitri and Vladimir. The completely independent exercise of power over dependent persons was constantly defeated, however, by the movement of the boyars and servants of one prince into the domain of the other, on the principle of their ancient right of freedom of removal. Dmitri's treaties stipulated that boyars and free servants were subject to the local princely power for the payment of tribute and the performance of military service, their obligations being determined by their place of residence and the amount of land held and founded on the principle of full reciprocity. These treaties thus served to strengthen the independence of each territorial power. These relationships were complicated, of course, by the special significance of Moscow, where each udel prince had his own court, his own boyars and servants, his own rights to a share in the revenues. The treaty between Grand Prince Semeon and his brothers protected the rights of the udel princes against the absolute power of the eldest brother and his deputies, and this same provision was made, in a somewhat more elaborate form, in the treaties between Dmitri and Vladimir. The Grand Prince or his deputy was to preside over the law courts of Moscow, but he could not send his officers in pursuit of another prince's boyar; the summons of a boyar to trial was a matter for the prince served by that boyar; and the deputy of the other udel prince was to be present at such a trial to assure its fairness and watch over the juridical rights of his prince.

Still more complicated were the relationships involved in the collection of tribute. Within his own votchina Vladimir held independent financial power, but he paid "the Horde's burden and expense" to the Grand Prince "out of his own udel, according to the ancient agreements." Such was the provision of Dmitri's first treaty with Vladimir. The treaty of 1389, however, established a share in the "Horde's burden and expense" to be paid not only out of his own udel, but also from the third of Princess Uliana's domain that had come to him, in the amount of 320 rubles, "and if this increases or decreases, then the share shall vary in proportion." In addition he was obliged to assume a "similarly proportionate" share of the debts owed to the merchants in the land of the Horde and to the Byzantine capitalists.

The treaties foresaw situations in which exceptional collections of tribute would be required—the type of tribute that in the deeds of grant was called "forced tribute." Whenever the Grand Prince exacted this tribute from his boyars, the udel princes were obliged to take it from their boyars also, and to deposit it in the treasury of the Grand Prince.

There is no sign in the treaties made between Dmitri and Vladimir of a proviso that will be encountered later on, when an udel prince will address the Grand Prince with the words: "but if God will change the will of the Horde and you do not have to give to the Tatars, and if you shall undertake to collect tribute from your own otchina and from the grand principality for yourself, then I too shall receive a tribute from my udel." Despite this, the notion that only the "Horde's burden" binds the udel prince to the collection and payment of tribute into the Grand Prince's treasury is quite obviously a basic feature of their relationship. This is reflected in the treaty definitions of the revenues that the princes shall still "supervise" jointly. The collection of Moscow's city tributes—in the city itself as well as in its suburban districts and outlying sectors—was carried out by the tribute collectors of both princes, even though all that they collected went into the Grand Prince's treasury, to be used by him to pay the Tatar outlay. If the size of the outlay diminished, a division of the surplus tribute was envisioned: "and in the event that God delivers and frees us from the Horde, then I shall have a two-thirds share in the tribute, and you one third," the Grand Prince said to the Prince of Serpukhov in the treaty of 1389.

The traditional view required a categorical distinction between ruling power over a votchina and possession of a common otchina in the form of an udel, all the more so as a result of the transformation of the old udels or portions into individualized votchina principalities.

In the riad he made before his death, Ivan Kalita had set up an important obstacle to the tendency toward a breakdown into separate votchinas: this was the limitation of the independent power of the udel princes by the traditional principle of the solidarity of all the princes under the seniority of the eldest brother among the Moscow princes. The power and meaning of the position of seniority were modified and complicated in Moscow by its combination in one person with grand princely sovereignty. The treaties of Moscow's princes—as grand princes and at the same time eldest among the princes of Moscow—with the younger princes of udels within the Muscovite otchina all reflect the search for a compromise between these two opposing tendencies.

The treaties made between Dmitri and Vladimir repeated the provision forbidding the princes and their boyars to buy villages and conscript free servants on another prince's land, but the practice of voluntary service inevitably created many instances of landhold of this type, and led to the compromise signified by the term *bliudenie* (safeguarding), by which free servants were subject to military conscription and payment of tribute not according to their personal allegiance to a given prince, but according to the location of their landholding. At the same time the very right of free choice of place of residence underwent a certain reduction in the first treaty between Dmitri and Vladimir, as compared with the treaty between Semeon and his brothers. "And if a boyar shall leave your protection and come to me, or shall leave mine and go to you," we read in Dmitri's treaty, "without having completed his service, such boyar shall receive the protection that is still due to him and shall be required to complete any service he still owes."

The departure of a person under obligation was further complicated by the requirement of a formal dismissal and accounting. This greatly emphasized the separation of legal and administrative structures within each princely udel. But it was more difficult to establish this kind of autonomy in the control of military forces. The udel prince was still under obligation to send his boyars and servants on campaigns "without disobedience." It was not left to him, therefore, to decide whether certain of his boyars and servants should or should not be released from the requirement to go on a campaign. This could be done only if it were brought to the attention of the Grand Prince, and "with the consent" of both princes; while those who refused and were disobedient were to be punished by the Grand Prince with the cooperation of the prince of the udel. These, then, were the conditions of the first treaty between Dmitri of the Don and Vladimir. Their treaty of 1389 did not repeat them, which could perhaps be taken as a sign of the reduction in this type of grand princely control over the military forces of the udel.

We can observe similar confusion and compromise in the realm of financial administration. The provision for separate collection of tribute within each territorial possession stood alongside the agreement that "we shall have safeguards over the enrolled people jointly, as one man," and was inconsistent with the cooperation of the princes in the collection of a whole series of other revenues. As far as we can tell from the treaty of 1389, the agreement to safeguard the enrolled people jointly was connected with the protection of their property against seizure not only by the princes, but also by the boyars and monasteries. As measures taken to protect the property and lands of servants attached to a particular prince, these provisions appear less as definitions of the interrelationships of the princes and limitations of their votchina power than as cooperative measures taken by the princes in the administration of the resources of the principality. Placed alongside the other provisions in this treaty for the control of military forces and the payment of tribute into the Grand Prince's treasury, they are clear evidence of the urgent need for unity in the general administration of the Moscow principality.

Grand Prince Dmitri's efforts were aimed at supporting and strengthening this unity, and it is hardly possible to view his activities outside the context of the struggle for a consolidation of the grand prince's power. His efforts to gain control of the principality of Moscow were not an isolated activity, but one aspect of his fight to win the grand princely power over all of Great Russia. The princes of Moscow were eventually to become the grand princes of Moscow, Vladimir, and all Russia.

A comparison of Dmitri's treaty relationships within the principality of Moscow with those established with Tver and Riazan
will give clear evidence of this fact.

Dmitri's treaties with Vladimir bear witness to his desire to
increase the power of the grand prince and at the same time
modify—on Muscovite soil—the concept and actual significance
of the ancient position of seniority. There was an increase in the
subordination of the younger princes to the sovereign power
of the eldest among them. This subordination was reflected in
the earlier treaty of Semeon; now in Dmitri's treaties it finds
further development. Vladimir's first treaty with Dmitri contains this formula: "and it is for you, my younger brother Prince
Vladimir, to be subject to me and to regard my grand princely
rule as something to be honored and held in awe, and to wish
me good in all things." Here was a formula defining not so
much the relation of a younger prince to his elder brother in
the principality of Moscow as his relation to the grand prince
of all Russia. The formula of obedient solidarity (he who is
a friend or enemy of the elder prince is also a friend or enemy
of the younger) was expanded to include a definition of fidelity
usually found in agreements between a prince and a boyar:

And whatever you have heard about me, whether it be from the
lips of a peasant or a pagan, concerning my goodness or my cunning,
or about our otchina and any of its peasants, you are to disclose it to
me in all honesty and without any dissimulation, according to the
kissing of the cross.

It is true that the treaty document makes a very careful proviso
whenever such a formula is used, designed to protect the distinction between simple service under the Grand Prince and a
brotherly, even if submissive, solidarity with him. Besides the
general statement, "It is for me as grand prince to hold you
my brother in brotherly love, without giving offense in any
thing," the Grand Prince admits his obligation not to conclude
a treaty or conduct negotiations with anyone without the
younger prince, and to communicate to him, in his turn, whatever he hears of his "goodness or cunning."

These provisos, however, did nothing to reduce the dominating position of the Grand Prince or to diminish the subordination of his "younger brothers." Their mutual relations were scarcely different from those of a prince and a boyar under voluntary service where such service was combined with the obligation to give good counsel and the obligation was seen not only as a necessity, but also as the boyar's right. "Obedient service" rendered to the Grand Prince by a younger prince could be reconciled only in a very conditional way, and not without some straining of words, with the descriptions of it in the treaty documents, in which the Grand Prince requires the younger brother to serve him "without disobedience and with common consent, so that what is agreeable to me is agreeable also to you, my younger brother," and in which at the same time he promises "to maintain" the younger prince "in return for his service."

The second treaty was concluded by Dmitri in a moment of alarm and in the face of such threatening circumstances that he felt compelled to make a number of concessions to Vladimir. These were revoked almost at once, however, and the treaty of 1389 defined Vladimir's dependence on the Grand Prince more clearly than ever. In place of the earlier formula, which required simply that he "hold his eldest brother, Grand Prince Dmitri, in his father's place," we find here that he must look to the Grand Prince as his father and to his eldest son as his eldest brother, and to his second son as his brother or equal, and to his younger sons as his younger brothers; that he must regard the grand princely rule "as something to be honored and held in awe," not only under Grand Prince Dmitri himself and his eldest son, but even under the other successors to the throne; that under their rule he must care not only for the Moscow votchina, but also for the grand princely rule itself; that he must serve the Grand Prince "without disobedience"; that he must go on campaigns with his boyars whenever the Grand Prince commands him to go. Of the earlier guarantees of brotherly solidarity (as opposed to the subjugation of the younger prince) there remained only two references to a mutual oneness—one in connection with the making of treaties, the other in the promise to communicate to each other whatever they heard from the lips of "peasants or pagans."

As a whole, therefore, Dmitri's treaties with Vladimir were profoundly ambiguous. The natural development of udel domain was leading to the breakdown of the Moscow principality as a single votchina in the line of Ivan Kalita into the separate votchinas of individual princely families. Yet from the very beginning this process met with energetic opposition aimed at consolidating the Grand Prince's power. The crumbling of the foundation under the old system of relations among the Moscow princes created conditions favorable for the reconstruction of these relations on a new footing, and at the same time made the need for such reconstruction more and more obvious.

The uniting of the grand princely rule and two of Moscow's udels in the hands of Grand Prince Dmitri gave him a tremendous advantage of power over Vladimir. Moreover, a number of Vladimir's princely rights and revenues were inseparable from the Grand Prince's administration of the Muscovite principality. Dmitri not only succeeded in putting a limit to the separation of the Serpukhov principality as an individual votchina in the Muscovite domain; he also managed to increase his own power in relation to its prince. The old form of the traditional seniority was being filled with new content, precisely that of the grand princely power, and as a result the line between the position of seniority in Moscow and that of grand prince of all Russia was gradually being erased. In his treaties with Prince Vladimir, Dmitri asserted the connection between his hereditary (votchina) rights to the Moscow otchina and his rights to the grand principality of Vladimir, and demanded that both be confirmed to him and to his posterity. His testament was drawn up at almost the same time as his last treaty with Vladimir, and it reveals the same tendency to merge the votchina of Moscow with the domain of the grand prince, to merge the position of seniority in Moscow with the sovereignty of grand princely rule. Having inherited from the Grand Prince of Vladimir the tasks of grand princely seniority over all the princes of Great Russia, the lords of Moscow were forging a new instrument for the execution of these tasks out of the old votchina principle.

The testament of Grand Prince Dmitri of the Don (actually his second testament; of the first, drawn up during the time of Metropolitan Alexei, we have only the closing section) is just as complicated in its significance as his treaties with Vladimir. Lying at its basis is a family riad given by the father and votchina head of the family to his sons and widowed princess. Dmitri had five sons, all of whom were "enjoined" to his princess: "You, my children, shall live as one, and shall obey your mother in all things," we read in the opening section. Again, in the closing paragraph: "and I have enjoined my children to my princess, and you, my children, shall obey your mother in all things, and shall not go beyond her wishes in any matter; and if any son of mine should not obey his mother, and should go against her wishes, my blessing will not rest upon him." In addition to the volosts and villages assigned to the princess out of the possessions of all five sons, which she was to hold during her lifetime, she was to have also her own oprichnina, made up of her own personal "acquisitions" as well as certain "grand princely additions" (*primysly*), as listed in the testament: "and I bestow upon my princess all these my own additions, and these additions my princess is free to give to any son, according to her own wishes, and my children shall not lay hands upon them." On the death of the husband the widowed princess was left as head of the family. In the event of the death of one of the sons, the princess was to divide up his udel among the other sons: "and what she will give to each one, that shall be his, and my sons shall not go beyond her wishes." It was also her responsibility to make provision for any future son, "taking part of the share of each of his elder brothers"; and by her maternal authority she was to make a partial redivision of the votchina, if the "otchina of any son should be diminished."

Not even the eldest son and grand prince was to stand outside this maternal authority. His udel was to be treated, however, in a special way. Kolomna was not to be portioned out if the grand prince should die without an heir, but was to pass *in toto* to the next older brother, "and let their mother portion out the latter's udel." Within the context of the mother's authority as head of the family, and subject to her power in questions of udel domain, the eldest son and grand prince was to take the place of the father in relation to the younger princes: "and you,

my sons, the younger brothers of Prince Vasili," Dmitri continued with his exhortation, "shall honor and obey your eldest
brother, Vasili, as a father in my place." But they were not
his vassals; Vasili must hold them "in brotherliness and without
offense."

Prince Vladimir, as the patrimonial lord of Serpukhov, stood
outside this family group. Dmitri's testament neither defined nor
confirmed his rights, since these were Vladimir's votchina rights,
while Dmitri's riad was concerned only with his own immediate
family. His testament mentions Vladimir only with respect to
his right to a third share in the city of Moscow, "which was
granted to him by his father, Andrei," and then only incidentally,
in connection with the disposal of a village with its cleared land
and timber which had "passed" from Vladimir to the Grand
Prince. The division of the Moscow principality into two votchinas stands out very clearly in Dmitri's testament.

Dmitri's princely sons were to rule their votchina in the form
of udels. The udel of Kolomna with all its volosts was assigned
to the eldest son, Vasili I. The udel of Zvenigorod was assigned
to the second son, Iuri; Mozhaisk and its volosts, and also other
"detached districts," were given to Andrei; Dmitrov was given
to Peter. Prince Ivan was left without an udel, although an
oprichnina consisting of two volosts and one village with its
cleared land was assigned to him in the testament "in the form
of an udel," and this was to be his oprichnina in the sense
Dmitri gave to this term: "My son Prince Ivan will be free
in such an udel, and whatever brother will be good to him,
to him shall he give it." His udel was a "share" only in the
broadest sense. Prince Ivan's exceptional position here, with the
assignment to him not of a real principality but of a small
oprichnina customarily granted to a daughter, is probably to be
explained by Ivan's ill health. He died in 1393. The four udel
princes also shared the villages of Moscow and Iuriev, and the
city of Moscow was granted to them with the setting aside of a
third share to Prince Vladimir. Again, as in the treaty between
Semeon and his brothers, we find a certain increase in "the
rights of seniority." In view of this "right," Dmitri granted
Vasili I an entire half of his "two shares" in Moscow—"in the

city and its suburbs" and in the revenues from the towns—with the division of the other half among the remaining three brothers. Also allocated to Vasili "by right of seniority" was the largest share in the revenues from honey. "The Dobriatinsky apiary and the village of Dobriatinsky shall be counted as Vasili's," with all the rest—"the apiaries in the other suburban districts and the revenues from the master of the horses, the master of the falcons, and the master of the hunt"—being divided among all four brothers equally, including half of the tamga (the other half, together with the vosmnichy, being assigned to Dmitri's widowed princess).

One article stood as the keystone in the arch of Dmitri's testament. This was the passage affirming Dmitri's hereditary (votchina) right to the grand princely rule: "And I hereby bestow my otchina, the grand princely rule, on my son Vasili." Dmitri's earlier treaty with Vladimir had secured this right to the grand princely family of Moscow, with its requirement that Vladimir regard the grand princely rule "as something to be honored and held in awe," not only under Dmitri of the Don, but also under Vasili I and all the rest of the Grand Prince's sons and successors. In this case the subjection of the grand princely rule to the law of votchina (or inheritance) led to an attempt (albeit cautious and tentative) to use the possessions of the grand principality as additional property to be divided among the udel princes of Moscow. Immediately following the article granting the grand principality to the eldest son, and far removed from the passage defining the composition of the udels of the three next younger sons, there is a division among them of the "purchases" of Ivan Kalita—i.e., Galich, Beloozero, and Uglich. There is an assignment also to the widowed princess, for her lifetime, of certain volosts that were part of the grand principality up to that time, specifically some districts from Pereiaslavl-Zalesky and Kostroma, as well as others from Galich and Beloozero, with allocation of a share also in the villages belonging to Vladimir and Pereiaslavl—all this quite apart from the grant to her of the volosts and villages from the udels of the four sons. The definition of Galich, Beloozero, and Uglich as "purchases" of Dmitri's grandfather had not led to their being merged into the Moscow votchina as udel domains. It had not broken the connection between these lands and the grand princely rule.

We have already noted how this definition was advanced as a justification for the disposal of these lands by testament. We have here, therefore, a characteristic uncertainty about the application of votchina law to the grand princely volosts. The reasons for this uncertainty were probably various. By developing the concept of the grand principality as his own otchina, and by including it among the things to be disposed of by testament, Dmitri automatically raised the question whether the possession of his votchina in the form of udels actually embraced the territory of the grand principality. If we compare this feature of Dmitri's testament with the content of his second treaty with Vladimir, where the Grand Prince granted Galich and Dmitrov to Vladimir "as his udel," we can say that during the reign of Grand Prince Dmitri there was a radical change in the notion of udel domain and all that this involved. The transfer of Galich and Dmitrov to Vladimir "as his udel" was not based on the latter's right to a share in a common votchina, but was simply a "grant" on the part of the Grand Prince, ratified by treaty, a "bestowal" in the spirit of ancient Kiev, made on the basis of the power possessed by the eldest among all the Russian princes. The grant of Galich, Beloozero, and Uglich to Dmitri's three sons in addition to the udels assigned to them within the Moscow votchina had this same character—not of a portioning out of a votchina, but of an arbitrary distribution of land by authority of the Grand Prince. In this connection the fate of Dmitrov deserves some special attention. According to Dmitri's testament, this city was included among the udels of the Moscow votchina. Separated from the body of Galich domains, Dmitrov was now incorporated into the Moscow possessions and stood apart from Galich.

The whole development of princely rule and princely interrelations in the Moscow principality took place under the influence of the special conditions created by the consolidation of grand princely power in the hands of the senior prince of Moscow. The significance of grand princely power and its special political aims inevitably modified the structure of princely solidarity and the real meaning of the position of seniority. The increase in grand princely power deepened the contradiction between the aims of this power and the demands and hereditary relationships of the princes of Moscow. The sons and grandsons of Dmitri of the Don lived through a period of prolonged and violent crisis in these relationships, beginning in the reign of Dmitri himself and resolved only in the time of Ivan III.

Chapter
V

The Tver Otchina Under the Descendants of Grand Prince Mikhail, Son of Iaroslav III

After its defeat in the struggle for leadership in the political life of Great Russia, the Tver principality became cut off from the outside world and from outside political interests. It is true that the old tradition of Tver and its princes as major powers continued to live for a long time in the writings of this principality, stirring the thought of its ruling and literate classes and from time to time prompting attempts to renew the struggle in order to restore the political significance of the Tver princes. But the large-scale "state" policies of Great Russia were more and more firmly concentrated in Muscovite hands, while Tver, in the words of the historian V. S. Borzakovsky, "was obliged to limit itself to narrower interests, to its own local affairs."

Tver found itself in this new situation immediately following the death of Alexander in the land of the Horde in 1338. While maintaining with difficulty its independence from Moscow, or rather from the grand principality of Great Russia, the Tver principality underwent a process of internal breakdown into separate domains, with a constant struggle against this process on the part of its local grand princes. As in Moscow, the structure of internal relationships in the Tver principality was marked by certain peculiar developments that are extremely interesting for the student of the udel-votchina system of princely rule and law.

If the testament of Prince Mikhail had been preserved, it would have shed the same light on the history of Tver as did that of Ivan Kalita on the history of the relations of the Moscow princes. The only trace we have of this document, however, is the information contained in the account of Mikhail's martyrdom that as he was preparing to leave for the land of the Horde, he sent his sons home from Vladimir, "having given them his riad and a testament dividing his otchina among them." Mikhail left his votchina to four sons: Dmitri, Alexander, Constantine, and Vasili. The votchinas of his grandsons were to become, in the line of Alexander, Kholm and Mikulin; in the line of Constantine, Dorogobuzh; in Vasili's line, Kashin. Dmitri, of course, had died earlier, in 1326. It is possible but by no means proven that this disposition of udels was actually established in Prince Mikhail's riad. But if this was the case, the possession of the Tver otchina in the form of udels did not effect the unity of the Tver principality during the early years of his sons' rule. Only after the death of Prince Alexander in the land of the Horde, when Tver's throne passed once again to Constantine, was the Kholm-Mikulin domain defined as a separate votchina. As for Prince Alexander's riad, the chronicle account of his death mentions it only in passing, stating that as he bade farewell to his boyars "he also spoke of his votchina." If we take this passage as a literal statement of fact, then we must conclude that Alexander did not actually find opportunity to compose a written testament. We have no basis for any theory as to how he might have divided his otchina among his sons in shares or udels. The scanty information about his sons given by the chronicle does not support such a division. We see here no

separate ruling princes, but a family group of heirs to the
Kholm-Mikulin principality, with. Alexander's widowed princess
at its head. From the evidence of the chronicles, the foremost
question in the life of the Tver principality at this time was
not that of the interrelationship and distribution of udel domains
within this group of princes, but another question altogether:
whether or not they were to be considered a part of the Tver
principality at all.

There are testaments of Tver princes from a later period in
which the "solidarity" of the princely house is defined with a
clarity we do not find either in the treaties between the princes
of Moscow or in any other source for the history of princely
law in the fourteenth century. In these documents the Tver
princes appear as joint bearers of a single princely power in the
Tver land, under the seniority of their "grand prince." We
may note especially the character of the Otroch Monastery in
Tver, establishing it as "a charity of Grand Prince Vasili and
all his princely nephews—Prince Vsevolod, Prince Mikhail,
Prince Vladimir, and Prince Andrei (the sons of Alexander),
Prince Eremei and Prince Semeon (the sons of Constantine),
and Vasili's son Mikhail." There is also a later renewal of this
character made in the name of "the servants of the Holy Trinity"
—Grand Prince Boris and all his "younger brothers," Feodor
the son of Feodor, Ivan the son of Iuri, Andrei the son of Dmitri,
and his own brother Feodor.

The account of the beginning of the dispute between Grand
Prince Ivan of Tver and his brothers in the early years of the
fifteenth century indicates another equally important feature of
this solidarity of the Tver princes. Under Alexander's son
Mikhail the grand princely boyars of Tver kissed the cross to
all his sons (Ivan, Vasili, and Feodor) and his grandson (Boris'
son Ivan) with an oath "that they should wish them well." But
when Mikhail's eldest son, Ivan, assumed the throne of the Tver
grand principality, he commanded "his boyars to lay aside their
kissing of the cross to all his brothers," over the protest of the
princess-mother and the younger princes.

In the family of Tver princes the rule of their common otchina
in the form of udels did not develop with any real clarity prior
to Alexander's death in 1338. Tver's strained and hostile relations

with the Horde and Moscow had apparently paralyzed the usual tendency toward subdivision into udels and votchinas, and for a time had supported the complete solidarity of its princes not only by alliances, but also in the form of shared rule. Only when Tver's ancient throne passed to Constantine on the death of Alexander was Kashin defined as Vasili's udel domain and the Kholm-Mikulin volosts assigned as the udel of Alexander's sons. Dorogobuzh must also have been defined then as the future otchina of Constantine's line. We do not know when or under what circumstances such a riad could have been composed for Mikhail's princely sons. It is entirely possible, of course, that this udel division had been determined earlier in Mikhail's testament, with its consequences not actually appearing in the life of the Tver principality until after Alexander's death in the land of the Horde.

There must have been a need to define the independence of the udel princes and to establish guarantees for the unity of Tver's resources, just as this need had confronted the princes of Moscow on the death of Grand Prince Ivan Kalita. We do not know of any treaties made between these Tver princes similar to the one between Semeon and his brothers, although references to some "settlement" following their various disputes over rights and obligations would indicate that such a treaty did exist. This question was raised sharply in the last year of Constantine's life. "In that year Prince Constantine of Tver had a controversy with Princess Nastasia and Alexander's son Vsevolod, and began to take silver from the volosts of their boyars and servants by force of arms, and this matter caused great affliction." The dispute was over the collection of tribute, as we can see from what followed. Vsevolod "could not endure this persecution," and left Tver to join Grand Prince Semeon in Moscow, and after this both parties—Constantine and his nephew Vsevolod—traveled to the land of the Horde. There Prince Constantine died unexpectedly, and his brother Vasili immediately assumed the rule of the Tver principality, his first act being to send his tribute collectors into Vsevolod's udel to exact tribute from his people.

These actions of Constantine and Vasili remind us somewhat of the oppression of the Rostov princes by Moscow described by Epifani the Wise. Although the prince of Tver had been defeated in his fight for the grand princely throne of Vladimir, he continued to claim the title of grand prince and the privileges of grand princely power within the boundaries of the Tver domains, and tried to reduce his nephews, the hereditary ruling princes of Kholm-Mikulin, to the position of vassals, placing their people directly under his own authority and making their boyars and servants answerable only to himself. Thus at the very beginning of the period when the Tver land was turned in on itself and became absorbed in its own political affairs, the solidarity of the Tver princes (both as a family and as holders of joint sovereign power) was severely shaken by the transformation of one of the brothers' udels into his and his descendants' votchina. The efforts of Tver's grand prince to deny the independence of this votchina gave rise to a bitter conflict between two lines in this princely house (Kholm and Kashin), and this tension was further complicated by the increasing influence on Tver of Moscow and Lithuania. Slowly but surely in the course of this struggle the family-votchina organization of the Tver principality was defined, with the emergence of Kashin as a separate domain under Muscovite influence, and the reduction of the other princes to the level of minor vassals of the Grand Prince of Tver as a result of his constant and determined efforts to increase his power over the whole Tver land.

II.

Alexander's son Vsevolod apparently found some support in Moscow for his fight with his uncle Constantine. In any case, it was to Moscow and Grand Prince Semeon that he went from Tver, and it was from Moscow that he journeyed to Khan Janibeg in the land of the Horde. We may suppose that his petition to the Horde was also backed by Moscow. Evidently Vasili was charged with having taken matters into his own hands in the collection of tribute from his nephew's otchina, and the Khan's anger was aroused. Prince Vsevolod was with the Horde when news came of Vasili's action, and he at once "took offense" and marched to meet his uncle, who was already on his way to the Horde with the silver he had collected. Vsevolod intercepted him on the Bezdezha River and "plundered him," acting not entirely on his own initiative, but "in the company of an envoy from the Khan." The two princes spent over a year in the land of the Horde and then returned—Vsevolod to the princely throne of Tver, Vasili to his own domain of Kashin. This did not, of course, end the enmity between them. Their dispute "laid a burden on the people of Tver," and "as a result of this disorder many Tver people were scattered" and "there was not a little bloodshed."

Beside their contest for possession of Tver's grand princely throne, the relations between uncle and nephew were disturbed even more over the question of the degree of independence from grand princely power to be enjoyed by the udel prince, especially once Vsevolod assumed the grand princely throne and his uncle was forced to be content with his own udel of Kashin. As it happened, however, Vsevolod did not remain on Tver's throne for even one year. The conflict was ended peaceably by an argument arranged through the mediation of Bishop Feodor of Tver, and "Vsevolod yielded the grand princely throne of Tver to his uncle Vasili." We can see this end of hostilities in Tver coming as a result of a change in Moscow's policy: Bishop Feodor was closely connected with the Metropolitan, and the latter was certainly a partner to Moscow's decisions. Soon after the reconciliation of the Tver princes, events occurred which were to confirm Vasili's rapprochement with Moscow and strengthen Vsevolod's connections with Lithuania. Olgerd, the grand prince of Lithuania, was married to Vsevolod's sister, Princess Uliana, and Grand Prince Semeon gave his daughter to Vasili's son Mikhail. From this time on the Kashin line of Tver princes always looked to Moscow for support and Kholm-Mikulin was always drawn toward Lithuania.

External influences on Tver and the tension between its two powerful neighbors to the southeast and to the west inevitably complicated its own internal affairs. The desire to secure its independence necessitated the unity of its military and economic forces. This urgent requirement sustained the formal solidarity of the Tver princes as expressed in the formulas of their treaty agreements, but the irreconcilable struggle between the two lines of this princely house undermined the foundations of this solidarity and encouraged the search for another method of unifying

Tver's power, namely through the development of an unchallenged sovereignty for its grand prince.

Vasili reoccupied the throne of Tver, received the Khan's yarlik confirming him in the grand princely rule, and immediately revived the policies of his brother Constantine. "And by means of this settlement he began to offend his nephew Prince Vsevolod and to afflict his boyars and servants with a grievous collection of tribute." With the open support of Moscow and the patronage of the Khan, Vasili subdued his nephew and bent him to his will. Vsevolod's appeal to the court of Metropolitan Alexei, in which he enumerated "the offenses committed against him in this settlement," only led to a more restrictive agreement, made "on the recommendation of the Metropolitan." Vsevolod tried to go to the land of the Horde with a complaint to the Khan, but the roads of Tver were in his uncle's hands, and the deputies of Grand Prince Ivan II would not permit him to enter the land of Pereiaslavl. He was forced to try to get to the Horde by a roundabout route through Lithuania. In the meantime, Grand Prince Vasili warned the Khan of his nephew's activities and made further charges against him, so that the rulers of the Horde "turned Prince Vsevolod over to his uncle without a trial . . . and Prince Vsevolod was subjected to great affliction at the hands of his uncle Prince Vasili, as were his boyars and servants, who were exposed to forced sale of property and widespread plundering, and the common people too were subjected to great extortion in payment of the tribute."

This state of affairs altered sharply following the death of Grand Prince Ivan II in 1358. When Grand Prince Dmitri of the Don was still a boy in the early years of his reign, the power of Moscow waned, and thus also Vasili's Muscovite support, while the Lithuanian pressure on Russia was increased. Prince Vsevolod traveled to visit his brother-in-law Olgerd in Lithuania.

More than ever the Grand Prince of Tver was compelled now to reckon with Lithuanian power. Vsevolod returned to Tver, arriving there at the same time as Roman, who at Olgerd's request had been appointed metropolitan of western Russia by the Patriarch of Constantinople. Roman's ill-starred arrival in Tver was designed to swing the Tver clergy to the side of Lithuania, but in the end Grand Prince Vasili and Bishop Feodor succeeded in upsetting this plan. In the meantime, however, Roman was entertained by "the leaders of Tver, and accepted gifts from the princes and boyars of Tver and from others too." Prince Vsevolod "showed him great honor, and bestowed gifts on him," and "commanded that he be allowed to travel on to Lithuania in all honor." There is some indication that Metropolitan Roman was a relative of Prince Vsevolod. At this same time Vsevolod "made a pact of peace and friendship with his brothers," and they "divided their volosts," and his (and their) uncle Grand Prince Vasili "yielded a third of the Tver otchina." This passage in the chronicle gives us only a very vague picture of what actually took place and is extremely difficult to interpret, since we have no other evidence in support of its assertions. It would seem that Vsevolod's rebellious activity had undermined his solidarity with his brothers, and that Vasili of Tver had seized and was now returning part of their shared votchina (their father's "third"), and that under the terms of this new settlement between Vsevolod and all his brothers there was a "division of volosts" among them.

III.

We have drawn attention to the destructive influence on princely solidarity of the hereditary aspect of udels, i.e., of their transformation into votchina principalities in the hands of individual family lines within a princely house. This was revealed in Tver much more strongly and vividly than in Moscow. On Alexander's death the solidarity shared by Mikhail's sons was shattered by the bitter struggle of two princely lines, and within this struggle two motives were intertwined: the clash of Tver's grand princely authority with the independence of a local udel prince, and the rivalry between the two princely dynasties over possession of the Tver otchina. The first of these two motives was the immediate occasion for their dispute, but the princes of Kholm-Mikulin shifted at once from a position of defense to one of attack. They destroyed all possibility of a compromise that would preserve the solidarity of Tver's princely forces, and vigorously sought to win control of Tver's grand princely throne itself, relying first on Moscow and then on Lithuania.

The exercise of direct grand princely sovereignty by Constantine and Vasili was what first aroused the Kholm princes. This was the starting point for the internal breakdown of Tver forces. Alexander's sons met this attempt to overthrow their princely rights not only with a defensive "settlement" of the type usually made by younger princes with a prince holding the position of seniority, but also pressed their own votchina claim to Tver's throne. Their claim was noticeably reinforced by the great popular longing in Tver for a deliverance from the Tatar yoke with the help of Lithuania. Vsevolod's brother Mikhail, prince of Mikulin, became the hero of these aspirations. Mikhail had been a threat to Vasili even during Vsevolod's lifetime, and after the latter's death he became the central figure in Tver's historical drama. The land was in the midst of a struggle to maintain and if possible increase its own local grand princely power, and this struggle was sustained by a deep desire to tear the grand principality of all Russia out of Muscovite hands and shake off both Moscow's oppression and the Tatar domination.

The possession of a common otchina in the form of udels disappeared in the course of the fight for these lofty goals, and with them also crumbled Tver's family and votchina solidarity. On the death of Vsevolod and Alexander's two youngest sons, the Kholm otchina broke down into two separate votchinas, Kholm and Mikulin, with no visible tie whatever between them. The Kholm principality was left to Vsevolod's sons Ivan and Iuri. About this particular Ivan we know only that in 1397 "he laid aside his kissing of the cross" to his uncle Grand Prince Mikhail of Tver, and went to join Dmitri of the Don's son Vasili I of Moscow, who received him with honor, granted him the city of Torzhok, and gave him his sister Anastasiia in marriage. Soon after this Vasili I of Moscow sent him as his prince-deputy to Pskov. When Grand Prince Mikhail of Tver died in 1399, Vsevolod's son Ivan "negotiated" with Mikhail's son Ivan, and on the terms of their "settlement" returned to Tver "with his princess and boyars." It is typical that Vsevolod's son Ivan was not a party to the quarrel between Mikhail's son Ivan, as grand prince of Tver, and the latter's brothers and nephews over the grand princely boyars' renunciation of their oath of fealty. This quarrel affected only Mikhail's sons, and the sons of Vsevolod of Kholm stood outside the family solidarity that had been confirmed by this kissing of the cross. The oath had obviously been designed to secure the allegiance of the grand princely boyars of Tver to the descendants of Mikhail alone, as opposed to the secondary lines of that princely house. Two years later, in 1402, Vsevolod's son Ivan died childless on the throne of Kholm, "having enjoined his otchina to Prince Alexander, the son of Grand Prince Ivan." This did not prevent his younger brother Iuri from assuming the rule of Kholm immediately after his brother's death. It was not until the winter of 1404–1405 that Iuri "went over from Tver to Moscow" and laid aside his oath to Grand Prince Ivan, who then tried to make peace with him, inviting him to return "to the house of the Holy Saviour" and live "within his father's borders." The usual explanation of this "enjoining" of Ivan's otchina to the Grand Prince's son Alexander describes this simply as a testamentary provision in favor of Alexander and a circumvention of Iuri's hereditary rights. This does not agree with the plain sense of our sources. We have no evidence as to why the Prince of Kholm assigned his otchina to the Grand Prince's son and not to Grand Prince Ivan himself, but the general sense of what was done here would indicate a very significant increase in the power of the Grand Prince of Tver.

Alexander's son Grand Prince Mikhail had consolidated this power in the hands of his own sons, and according to his testament the grand princely boyars took the oath to his sons and grandson. The secondary lines of the princely house of Tver stood outside the solidarity of the Mikulin line and the grand princely rule, which was now in its hands. Prince Ivan of Kholm did not accept the arbitrary policies of his uncle Mikhail and moved to Moscow, where he became a service prince under the Grand Prince of all Russia. When Mikhail died, Ivan returned to Kholm on the terms of a settlement with Mikhail's son Grand Prince Ivan, evidently humbling himself before the power the Grand Prince of Tver was now exercising over his younger brothers. Ivan's act of submission took the form of a riad executed before his death. Reduced to the position of a vassal, he was compelled to recognize Grand Prince Ivan and his son Alexander as having full right to the grand princely rule of Tver and to

place his otchina under Alexander's control. This was the situation when Kholm passed to Vsevolod's second son, Iuri. Iuri
refused to accept this subservient position, and, fearing capture
by Grand Prince Ivan, he fled to Moscow in the winter of
1404–1405. Two years later he carried his dispute with Ivan
to the land of the Horde, where he apparently won a large share
of the Tver otchina over and above his own domain of Kholm.
He then passes suddenly from the scene of history, with no
further mention in our chronicles. Iuri's death marked the end
of any claim to independent significance on the part of the
Kholm princes. Iuri's son Dmitri is barely mentioned in a list
of the Grand Prince's "younger brothers" found in the treaties
of Grand Prince Vasili II of Moscow with Grand Prince Boris
of Tver. Dmitri's sons Daniel and Mikhail were only very minor
vassal princes, the former serving under Grand Prince Ivan III
of Moscow, the latter living as an obedient "younger brother"
of Boris' son Mikhail of Tver and then, after Mikhail's flight to
Lithuania, entering the service of Moscow.

IV.

The princes of the junior line in the house of Grand Prince
Alexander of Tver (son of Mikhail) had consolidated their hold
on the grand princely authority and had rather quickly overthrown the claims of the senior line of Kholm to any real independence. A similar reduction in status was experienced by the
descendants of Mikhail's third son, Constantine, the princes of
Dorogobuzh. Without any direct knowledge of the contents of
Mikhail's riad, historians have assumed nevertheless that it established this domain as the otchina of Constantine's line.

The history of Dorogobuzh begins with the record of the
death of Constantine's second son. Prince Semeon died in the
plague of 1364–65, "and the udel of his otchina and his princess
were enjoined to Prince Mikhail the son of Alexander." We are
told that "enmity" arose then between Mikhail and Constantine's
son, Eremei. Eremei claimed possession of his brother's udel, and
was supported in this by his uncle Vasili, who feared any increase
in strength on the part of his brother Mikhail. Eremei and
Mikhail turned to Metropolitan Alexei to mediate between them,

and Bishop Vasili of Tver determined their case "with the blessing and permission of the Metropolitan." The Bishop "ruled in
favor of Prince Mikhail." We may suppose that Grand Prince
Constantine had divided the Dorogobuzh udel between his two
sons, Eremei and Semeon, but the exact nature of this division
is unknown. We have only the hint of an incidental observation
in the chronicles that Gorodok, which Dmitri of the Don seized
from Grand Prince Mikhail of Tver in 1368, was a part of
Semeon's udel. Semeon had left his udel in the Dorogobuzh
otchina to his wife, "enjoining" her and her possessions to Grand
Prince Mikhail. It is possible to regard this action as in fact a
seizure by Prince Mikhail of Gorodok and other places in
Semeon's udel; we may assume that Mikhail did not overlook
the sending of deputies into this area. There are no grounds,
however, for regarding this action as the transfer of the udel
by the testament of its ruling prince to Mikhail "as his votchina."
We can only guess at the real motive of Semeon's disposition.
The transfer of his hereditary udel to his widowed princess was
bound to provoke objections on the part of his brother Eremei
and arouse concern for the stability of her domain. Vasili's helplessness before the rising star of the popular prince of Mikulin
may well have persuaded Semeon to turn to Mikhail instead of
to the Grand Prince of Tver, as one who would watch more
faithfully over his widow's possessions.

But the growing strength of the Prince of Mikulin was
alarming not only the Grand Prince of Tver; it had begun to
disturb also the grand princely rule in Moscow, and the whole
situation was altered shortly after Semeon's riad was settled in
Mikhail's favor. Metropolitan Alexei and Grand Prince Dmitri
of Moscow had successfully concluded their conflict with Prince
Dmitri of Suzdal. Grand Prince Dmitri of the Don had "fortified the city of Moscow with stone . . . and brought all the
Russian princes under his will, and those who would not be
obedient to him he began to visit and afflict." Vasili of Tver
sought support in the restored grand princely sovereignty of
the Prince of Moscow, and the Prince of Mikulin was one of the
first to experience a "visitation" from Moscow. The question of
Semeon's udel was raised a second time. Grand Prince Vasili,
with his son Mikhail and Prince Eremei, brought a charge before

the Metropolitan against Bishop Vasili of Tver, saying "that he had not judged according to the truth in the matter of Prince Semeon's udel." Prince Mikhail went to Lithuania for help against Moscow, which had now taken a stand on the side of his enemies. It is very difficult to tell from the brief account of the Nikon Chronicle whether his departure for Lithuania was connected with the matter of Semeon's udel or whether there may have been some other reason as well—for example, Mikhail's construction of Novi Gorodok on the Volga, which could be understood in Tver and Moscow only as a preparation for war, and cause them to take similar measures. In any event, the rupture was complete, and the people of Tver had expressed their sympathy for Mikhail clearly enough to prompt the two grand princes to carry out a harsh repression. The struggle between Vasili and Mikhail almost immediately escalated into a struggle for the grand princely rule of Tver. The grand princes subjected the Tver boyars to a state of siege, which continued until Mikhail returned "with his host" and an army of Lithuanian reinforcements and marched on Kashin. There was no battle, however, and the princes evidently made peace, although the conditions of Mikhail's settlement with Vasili, Eremei, and Grand Prince Dmitri are not known to us. Only from later records do we know that Mikhail was grand prince of Tver after the autumn of 1366, and that his uncle Vasili was forced to retire to Kashin, where he died in 1368.

Following in the footsteps of his older brother, Vsevolod, Mikhail had entered into a struggle for the grand princely rule in Tver, and had now attained his goal, securing the throne not only for himself, but also for his descendants. He had won a complete victory over Prince Eremei of Dorogobuzh. The departure of the latter for Moscow constituted an appeal to Grand Prince Dmitri to interfere again directly in the affairs of Tver. It is possible, although later chronicle sources make no explicit mention of this, that the issue here was not just Eremei's claim to independence, but also, once more, the possession of Tver's grand princely throne. Dmitri and Metropolitan Alexei "summoned Mikhail to Moscow on friendly terms," where he was quickly "brought to trial." The case ended with the "arrest" of Mikhail and the boyars who were with him. But the Khan's envoys in Moscow "became suspicious" of the whole affair, as a dispensation of justice outside the Khan's cognizance, and Grand Prince Dmitri was forced to release Mikhail, "after binding him by the kissing of the cross." We do not know the terms of the settlement sealed by this oath, with the exception of one point that has been preserved in the Nikon Chronicle: part of Prince Semeon's udel—Gorodok—was taken away from Mikhail, and the Grand Prince sent his deputy there in company with Prince Eremei.

Eremei did not enjoy Moscow's patronage for long. In his bitter struggle with Tver and Lithuania, Dmitri abandoned the Prince of Dorogobuzh, and Gorodok was returned to Mikhail together with the rest of Semeon's udel. Prince Eremei returned to Tver in submission to Mikhail's grand princely authority, and died in his own udel in 1373. His two sons, Dmitri and Ivan, and later his grandsons Andrei and Ivan (the sons of Dmitri), were all referred to as ruling princes of Tver in unity with the other princes of the land, sharing that solidarity which is so often mentioned in Tver's official documents, but in fact this solidarity meant the complete subjugation of the younger princes as vassals of the Grand Prince of Tver, and they were soon to become simply service princes or princely boyars.

V.

The Kashin principality had also developed as a distinct domain within Tver, as the udel of Prince Vasili, the youngest of the four sons of Mikhail of Tver. When Vasili came to the grand princely throne of Tver, Kashin remained in his hands as his own votchina, where apparently even during his lifetime his sons reigned, first Vasili and then, after Vasili's death, Mikhail. As we have seen, Prince Vasili ended his days in Kashin, after having been driven from the grand princely throne by his nephew Mikhail of Mikulin.

Vasili's son Mikhail reigned as prince of Kashin after his father's death. Mikhail was married to a princess of Moscow, and like his father he sought help in Moscow in his efforts to resist Mikhail's grand princely authority. Shortly after his father's death he went to Metropolitan Alexei with his complaint against

Bishop Vasili of Tver. In 1372, at the climax of Moscow's conflict with Tver and her Lithuanian allies, Mikhail of Kashin went over to the side of Moscow, but he paid for this with the devastation of his principality. Mikhail of Tver collected a "tribute" from Kashin and forced its prince to sue for peace. Mikhail of Kashin was "restrained" and "brought to do the Grand Prince's will." He accepted this position of servitude for less than a year, and once again "laying aside the kissing of the cross" to the Grand Prince of Tver, he left Kashin for Moscow and then traveled from there to the land of the Horde. He returned to Kashin empty-handed, and died there rather unexpectedly. His son Vasili went back to Tver as an obedient servant, formally submitting to the will of Grand Prince Mikhail. Moscow had made peace with Mikhail, and the Kashin principality could only follow suit. In 1375, however, when a new storm broke over Tver, Prince Vasili and his Kashin troops were aligned on the side of Tver's enemies. Tver's defeat brought independence to the prince of Kashin, secured by the treaty made between Grand Prince Dmitri of Moscow and Mikhail of Tver: "and it is not for you to enter Kashin, and whatever concerns Kashin shall be dealt with by its hereditary ruler, Prince Vasili; nor is it for you to carry away the outlay from Kashin to Tver, or to wrong Kashin in any thing; and if you should wrong it, I shall defend it against you."

This treaty put the Prince of Kashin in a position of direct dependence on the Grand Prince of all Russia, but in fact the agreement did not have any long-lasting political consequences. Prince Vasili died childless in May, 1382, and with him the Kashin line of Tver princes came to an end. The vacant Kashin udel was transferred to the Grand Prince of Tver.

VI.

The long reign of Alexander's son Mikhail on the senior throne of Tver (1366–99) had added significantly to the grand princely power in that land. The struggle against the breakdown of Tver's power and resources through the formation of separate udel-votchinas, which had begun in the time of Alexander, Constantine, and Vasili, had been carried forward by Prince

Mikhail with very considerable success. The increase in grand princely sovereignty was so urgent and vital a question in Tver that the fight waged by its local votchina principalities to free themselves from this sovereignty evolved inevitably into a fight for the grand princely rule itself. We can apply to the situation in Tver the words of S. M. Solovyev, who said that in the struggle between the princes "the issue was this—whether to be sovereign of the land, or the servant of such a sovereign." Those princes who were too weak to fight on their own either went over to the side of Moscow or submitted to the local grand prince and became his vassals, in spite of the formal preservation of the idea of princely brotherhood and solidarity. Mikhail had reduced his nephew Ivan of Kholm to this position. Two years before Mikhail's death Ivan left him to join Moscow, only to return in a short time and humble himself before Mikhail's eldest son, Ivan. Grand Prince Mikhail had brought the princes of Dorogobuzh and Kashin under his control, in spite of the aid given them by Moscow. As we have noted, the final crisis in the struggle with Kashin, in which this udel was very nearly torn away from the Tver principality altogether, was in the end a rather unimportant incident, since the princely line of Kashin soon died out and it passed back into Mikhail's hands.

The Tale of the Demise of Prince Mikhail of Tver tells us that as he prepared for his death the Grand Prince exhorted his sons "to nourish fraternal love and honor for one another." They were advised "that a brother should love and respect his brother and not offend him, and that it was for them all to obey their eldest brother" (or "it was for them to obey their eldest brother in all things"). We are told that he spoke also to his boyars:

Remind my sons to remain in friendship with one another, as I have ordered and divided among them, to each his own part of the otchina: to my son Ivan and his sons Alexander and Ivan I assign Tver, Novi Gorodok, Zubtsov, Radilov, Vbryn, Opochka, Vertiazin; to Princes Vasili and Boris' son Ivan I assign Kashin and Ksniatin; to my son Feodor I assign the two cities of Mikulin and their volosts, as they are written in my testament; and it is for them to reign and live in such a way as not to trespass against my word and testament.

His "testament" has not come down to us, and this is an

irreparable loss, since its provisions were extremely important, if we may judge by the references to it in the chronicles. While confirming the brotherly solidarity of his sons by having the Tver boyars kiss the cross to all of them, Mikhail divided "to each one a part of his otchina." To the eldest son, Ivan, he assigned the grand principality of Tver; to Vasili he assigned the principality of Kashin; to Feodor he assigned Mikulin. But this possession of the common otchina in the form of udels had acquired a special character in view of the allocation of Tver —and therefore also the grand princely seniority associated with it—to Prince Ivan and his descendants. In this way the grand princely rule was by prior arrangement secured specifically to the senior line of Mikhail's posterity. The principality of Kashin was actually assigned to the two brothers Vasili and Boris, together with the latter's son Ivan, but this part of the text cannot be accepted as a precise record of the original document, since Boris had died four years before his father's death. He had died in Kashin, leaving a young son, Ivan, in the hands of his widowed princess. The provision of Mikhail's testament placed Ivan's family in a unique and complex relationship to his uncle Vasili, on the one hand, and to Grand Prince Ivan of Tver, on the other. Feodor received "the two cities of Mikulin with their volosts," i.e., the original udel of his father.

It is not possible to accept *The Tale of the Demise of Prince Mikhail of Tver* as an accurate record of his testament in the passage dealing with the transfer of Tver "as a part of his otchina" to Ivan and the latter's two sons. It was after assuming the grand princely rule by authority of the Khan's yarlik that Ivan took positive action to secure the grand princely rule (and possession of Tver) for his own family, setting it apart from the domain shared by all of Mikhail's sons. We have already had occasion to mention how Ivan required his boyars (the grand princely boyars of Tver) to lay aside their kissing of the cross to his brothers and nephews and swear fealty solely to himself and his own line, thus abrogating his father's testament. His brother princes complained of this to their mother, Avdotia, and her boyars joined those of the other sons and grandsons in protesting this disregard of their father's wish. Conflict arose within the family, "and from this time the Grand Prince began to plot against his mother and brothers and nephews, harboring enmity toward them."

Grand Prince Ivan had moved to free his power as grand prince from the limitations placed on it by the family-otchina system of princely relations. Regarding it as his own personal sovereign power, he made a distinction first of all between it and the traditional tutelage of the widowed princess, whose position at the head of the family had always meant control over all her sons, including even the grand prince, and second, between it and that constricting solidarity with his brother princes expressed in the requirement that the boyars "wish all the princes well" as a single body, as members of a single ruling princely house, as joint patrimonial rulers of the grand principality of Tver. How thoroughly effective were Ivan's arrangements to secure control of this power may be seen by the following incident: His brother Boris' widow took advantage of the dispute for her own purposes and went over to Ivan's side (thereby rejecting the old concept of solidarity), and her efforts to curry the Grand Prince's favor bore fruit. Ivan removed Lukoe Ozero and the Jerusalem settlement from his brother Vasili and gave them to his nephew Ivan, Boris' son. Following custom, Vasili demanded a "general trial" before Bishop Arseni of Tver, "the father of us all," but the demand was flatly refused. We also have an oblique reference to a demand on the part of the Grand Prince that the grand princely rule be acknowledged for his older son, in the passage telling us that Vsevolod's son Ivan "enjoined" his princess and otchina to Alexander. Ivan's grand princely policy met only weak opposition from the younger princes of the Tver land. Prince Iuri of Kholm made an attempt to resist in 1404–1405, but this led to nothing. After his unsuccessful appeal to the Horde against Ivan, Iuri drops out of sight in our chronicles. His son Dmitri became a subservient vassal of whom we hear nothing at all. The Dorogobuzh princes had been reduced to the same position earlier by Grand Prince Mikhail. Ivan's youngest brother, Feodor of Mikulin, is mentioned only as a participant in campaigns sent out at the command of his older brother. Most of the turmoil in Tver was connected with the Grand Prince's dealings with Kashin.

Prince Vasili tried to maintain his princely independence "and at first did not obey his elder brother, Grand Prince Ivan." This led to a campaign against him by the Tver host. Vasili fled to Moscow, and Kashin was occupied by Ivan's son Alexander. A peace was made at this time, mediated by Grand Prince Vasili I of Moscow, and Vasili of Tver once more assumed the rule of Kashin. Within two years there was another outbreak of hostilities. Ivan seized his brother Vasili and his boyars and held them "in confinement" for several months, and then let them go after making a settlement with Vasili, which was as usual sealed by a kissing of the cross. Not surprisingly Vasili broke the terms of this agreement and fled again to Moscow, and Kashin was occupied by the Grand Prince's deputies. Within a year the princes had made peace again, and again Vasili returned to Kashin. This quarrel was closely tied up with the relationships between Moscow and Tver. Tver's break with Moscow and alliance with Grand Prince Vitovt of Lithuania opened up an opportunity for the Prince of Kashin to seek the support of the Grand Prince of all Russia. The reconciliation of the grand princes of Tver and Moscow led to the reconciliation also of the brother princes of Tver. Soon after this last settlement with Ivan, we find Prince Vasili with the Tver host that marched under Grand Prince Vasili of Moscow against Vitovt.

We hear of Prince Vasili in all these reports of activities in Kashin, but there is no mention whatever of his nephew Ivan, the son of Boris. Ivan emerges only as a victim of the wrath of the Grand Prince in 1408, when the latter "marched with a host against his nephew Prince Ivan of Kashin, and Ivan fled to Moscow." The Grand Prince was reconciled with his brother Vasili, but he "seized" Ivan's mother (Boris' widowed princess) and took her to Tver, placing his deputies in Kashin and "taking tribute from that city." It may be that the question of the payment of tribute was the main reason for his conflict between the princes, just as it had been between Constantine and Vasili in an older generation, but the information we have is too meager to give us any idea why Ivan's wrath was directed at his sister-in-law and nephew, or exactly what role was played here by his brother Vasili. It may be that Boris' son Ivan made an attempt to restore the independence of the Kashin principality when he came of age and assumed its throne in 1408. This would have placed him in opposition to his uncle Vasili, which may have been the reason for the reconciliation between Vasili and Grand Prince Ivan. The younger Ivan had only one choice under such circumstances: to seek sanctuary and possible support in Moscow.

Prince Vasili paid dearly for the right to retain his position as prince of Kashin. He was forced into complete submission to the Grand Prince of Tver. A new conflict was inevitable, all the more so after Ivan was reconciled with his nephew. Once more, in 1412, "much enmity" arose between the brothers, and Grand Prince Ivan gave orders to seize Prince Vasili, his princess, boyars, and servants, and sent his deputy to Kashin. Vasili was being brought "under guard" to the signing of the treaty in Novi Gorodok when he managed to escape and find sanctuary across the Moscow border. From Moscow Vasili journeyed to the land of the Horde, and with the help of Vasili I of Moscow, who was also with the Horde at the time, Vasili apparently won the Khan's favor. At any rate, a Tatar army was with him when he attacked Kashin. Grand Prince Ivan had left his nephew, the younger Ivan, in charge of the defense of Kashin and "the gates of Tver." Vasili's attack was turned away, and he made his way back to the Horde.

After this account of the defense of Kashin, our chronicles make no further mention of Boris' son Ivan. When Grand Prince Ivan died of the plague in 1425 he was succeeded by his son Alexander. Five months later Alexander also died of the plague, and the throne passed to his son Iuri, who survived Alexander by a mere four weeks. After this series of catastrophes Alexander's second son, Boris, was installed on Tver's throne. Vasili was about to return to Kashin when he was "seized" by Boris' men, and this marked the end of his career as far as our sources are concerned. It also marked the end of the existence of Kashin as a separate principality, and thus also of any true form of udel domain in the Tver land.

VII.

It is hardly possible to regard the preservation of the appearances of princely solidarity in the treaties and charters of Grand

Prince Boris of Tver (1425–61) as anything more than a diplomatic formality. The younger princes of the Tver land, the
various hereditary rulers of local princely domains, had been
reduced to the position of dependent vassals, and the verbal
distinction between "younger brothers" and "serving princes" in
Boris' treaties had no real foundation.

Boris built his position of power as grand prince of Tver on a
close alliance with the Grand Prince of Lithuania. Placing himself under the powerful protection of Vitovt, Boris was given
full independence in the administration of the grand principality
of Tver and full dominion over its younger princes. "And by
my uncle," we read in a treaty he made with Vitovt in 1427,

it is agreed that my brothers and also all my princely kin shall be
obedient to me; I, Grand Prince Boris, am free to have mercy on
whom I shall have mercy, and to punish whomsoever I shall punish,
and it is not for my master and uncle Grand Prince Vitovt to interfere.
And if any prince should wish to go over to my master and uncle
Grand Prince Vitovt with his otchina, my master and uncle Grand
Prince Vitovt shall not accept that prince with his otchina; and if
a prince should go over to my master and uncle Prince Vitovt and be
divested of his otchina, then I, Grand Prince Boris, shall have
the rule over his otchina, and it is not for my master and uncle Grand
Prince Vitovt to interfere.

Boris' treaty in 1449 with Casimir IV, king of Poland and
grand prince of Lithuania, even more clearly equated the lesser
princes of Tver with its boyars and free servants.

And if one of my younger brothers or service princes should depart
from me and go over to you, the King of Poland and Grand Prince
of Lithuania, he shall be deprived of his otchina, and it is not for me,
as grand prince, to interfere; and if one of your service princes should
pass from you, King of Poland and Grand Prince of Lithuania, to
me, Grand Prince Boris, he shall be deprived of his otchina, and it is
not for you, as king and grand prince, to interfere. And our boyars
and free servants shall also be free to pass between us.

Thus under Boris the struggle to extend the power of the Grand
Prince in Tver ended with complete victory. The threat of a
disintegration of Tver's sovereign power into separate udel-

votchinas and of a breakdown of its territory into a number of weakly connected votchina principalities had been finally overcome.

That Tver had not fallen apart was due to the external pressures exerted upon it in its fight for independence from its two great neighbors, which had the effect of gathering all its forces around a single center. As early as the thirteenth century Tver had been the focus of the most vigorous resistance to Tatar power. This heroic resistance had remained in the memory of its people, and out of this memory of a glorious past had grown the extraordinary popularity of Alexander's son Mikhail, the restorer of its grand princely power. On the other hand, Tver had become a frontier outpost for Great Russian military activity against Lithuania's eastward advance, and in the time of Mikhail the son of Iaroslav (1304–19) Tver's princes had hopes of controlling the whole political life of Great Russia. It was not by chance that it was a prince of Tver who had been the first to call himself "grand prince of all Russia." The whole history of Tver's princes is marked by the traditions of grand princely policy. Involuntarily limited to a narrower sphere of action in their rivalry with Moscow, Tver's princes built up their grand principality as a basis for playing a new role in the history of eastern Europe. As it happened, the growth of Moscow to the southeast and Lithuania to the west forced the rulers of Tver to choose between its two neighbors, with a gradually but increasingly evident tendency to turn to Lithuania. On the basis of his treaty with Vitovt, Boris may be defined as a vassal-ally of the Lithuanian grand prince; certainly in the treaty between King Casimir and Vasili II of Moscow in 1449, the Grand Prince of Tver and all the Tver princes were considered to be on the side of Lithuania. These relations with the west placed the Grand Prince of Tver in opposition to the ancient traditions of his own land and obviously disrupted Tver's internal life. The banner of nationalism so dear to Tver was now placed in Moscow's hands, not only in the struggle against the Tatars (long the object of Tver's military activity), but also in the struggle with the Lithuanian-Polish state, where alien and non-Orthodox influences were becoming constantly more powerful. The grand princely power in Tver completed its task of building a cen-

tralized authority just at the moment in history when the basic
conditions for Tver's political importance and independent existence seemed to have been destroyed.

In the 1450's Moscow overcame the turmoil that had for so
long affected the grand principality of Vladimir and Moscow,
and entered a new phase in the building of the Great Russian
state. The Grand Prince of Tver was forced to conclude a treaty
of alliance with the Grand Prince of all Russia. This treaty bound
them both "to seek one another's welfare in all things in the
land of the Horde and in Russia, without cunning," and to help
one another with all their strength in the struggle against Lithuania, the Letts, and the Germans. Drawn into the mainstream
of Great Russian foreign policies, Tver lost the basis from which
it might have been able to withstand Muscovite influence. All
of Tver's princes, boyars, and military forces were drawn into
the circle of Great Russian interests under the leadership of the
Grand Prince of Moscow. Direct service in the name of the
Grand Prince of all Russia instead of in the name of the Grand
Prince of Tver naturally tended to pull its service princes and
boyars away from Tver toward Moscow. The closing years of
Boris' reign and the rule of his son Mikhail mark the beginning
of the end of Tver's independence.

Fate had decreed that the political successes of the Grand
Prince of Tver should work to the advantage of Moscow's task
of unification. One sign of this political success was the quiet
transfer of power in Tver on the death of Grand Prince Boris
in 1461 to his eight-year-old son, Mikhail. Alongside the name of
the Grand Prince of Tver in Mikhail's treaties with Ivan III, the
Great, of Moscow we find mention of only two princes—Iuri's
son Ivan (the insignificant minor prince of Zubtsov) and Prince
Mikhail of Kholm (brother of the Muscovite warrior Prince
Daniel), whom tradition now only very formally distinguished
as the Grand Prince's "younger brothers" in contrast to the mass
of unnamed serving princes. The Tver lands in the form of a
unified "state of Tver" had entered the roster of "those states
of which the Russian Empire was formed."

Chapter
VI

The Grand Principality
of Riazan

The Riazan frontier land followed its own strange, uneasy way of life on the southern edge of Great Russia. As early as the 1120's the Murom-Riazan region had broken away from the body of Chernigov volosts as the votchina of the junior princely line of Chernigov princes, the descendants of Prince Iaroslav (the son of Sviatoslav). In the 1160's under two of Iaroslav's grandsons this votchina dissolved into two separate principalities: Murom, ruled by Vladimir's son Iuri, and Riazan, under Rostislav's son Gleb. The connection between them was further severed as they became subordinated to the sovereignty of the grand princes of Vladimir. The Murom principality was completely suppressed. Its princes apparently never had an opportunity to resist and became Vladimir's vassals at an early time. By the time of the first decade of the thirteenth century the unstable princely throne of Riazan had also lost control of its possessions: Grand Prince Vsevolod III of Vladimir had placed his posadniks and *tiuns* [30] in every city in the Riazan land. This direct imposition of grand princely authority was main-

30. *Tiun:* a Russian court or government official in the fifteenth century. —TRANS.

tained in Riazan only by force, and aroused widespread grum-
bling and unrest among its populace. Vsevolod's sons finally
agreed to let the Riazan princes return to their votchina, and
in 1219 Prince Ingvar the son of Igor ended the disturbances by
securing the Riazan otchina for his own house and driving out
his rivals, the sons of his uncle Vladimir.

Prince Ingvar did not survive this coup for long. When Batu's
invasion struck Riazan, his brother Iuri was already occupying
the throne in his place. Ingvar's sons evidently reigned on the
throne of Pronsk. Most of the Riazan princes were killed in the
Tatar massacre. Only Ingvar's two sons survived: Ingvar, who
had been sent by his uncle Iuri to aid Chernigov, and returned
from there to the throne of Riazan when the Tatar forces moved
on; and Oleg, who languished in a prison of the Horde. Of this
younger Prince Ingvar we know only that he "restored the
Riazan land." Not even the date of his death is recorded in the
chronicles. It has usually been assumed that he was no longer
living when "the Tatars released Prince Oleg of Riazan, grandson of Igor, and allowed him to return to his own land" in 1252.
The Horde's dominion over Riazan was first established under
Oleg, with Tatar chislenniks "numbering" the land, and direct
rule imposed by the khans of the Golden Horde.

Oleg left an only son, Roman, and the latter's twelve-year
reign on the Riazan throne is not mentioned at all in our sources.
We have only the account of his martyrdom at the hands of the
Horde. It is from Roman that the later Riazan princes traced
their heritage; thus the history of Riazan began a second time
in the era of Tatar dominion. Under the Tatars Riazan grew into
a powerful principality, one of several local grand principalities
in northeastern Russia. In the fourteenth century its significance
was largely determined by its geographical position as the Riazan
frontier, the southern rampart of Great Russia. In this area it
controlled the important watershed between the Oka valley and
the upper Don. Settlers moving out from Riazan went even
beyond the southern edge of this watershed, wherever the forest
gave them cover against the hazards of the steppe country, along
the Don and Voronezh rivers to the streams and little rivers
leading into the Don, the Tikhaia Sosna, the Chervleni Iar, and
the Bitiug, and farther east along the Great Vorona and the

Khoper. At the end of the thirteenth century and throughout the fourteenth the borderline between the dioceses of Riazan and Sarai lay roughly along the Khoper. Of course, only tiny groups of settlers pushed this far to the south and southeast, to the very edge of the steppe, far from the main center of population. The real heart of Riazan lay many miles to the north. The old city of Riazan was the natural center for this settled area, although Riazanski Pereiaslavl, situated to the northwest of Riazan and farther up the Oka River, rivaled it as a center of princely power. The rise of Pereiaslavl Riazansky and its final victory over the city of Riazan tell us something about the military situation in the land as a whole. In the face of constant and exhausting danger from the south, the center of gravity of the Riazan population tended to shift northward, toward the central area of Great Russian power. The southern borders of the land touched the open steppe, where Tatar forces were in control; not only the forces of the Khan, but also restless bands of Tatar brigands whose chieftains and petty princes made frequent raids into the Russian land at their own risk and for their own profit. Military alarms were the norm for the residents of the Riazan frontier and developed in them that impetuous, "wild" nature so often criticized by the Muscovite scribes.

Pronsk was the main stronghold of Riazan forces to the south, and it soon acquired the significance of a separate princely throne. The Riazan principality could strengthen its positions in the south and develop their defensive and offensive possibilities only by seizing adjacent Chernigov volosts wherever and whenever possible and drawing their minor princes into its own sphere of influence. Riazan's relations with the west—first with Chernigov and later with Lithuania—were always of major importance.

No less unstable were the eastern sections of the Riazan land, along the Tsna River, bordering on the districts of the Meshcheriaki and Mordva tribes. A prolonged struggle with neighboring east Finnish tribes and the nomad forces of the southern steppe had created ties between the Riazan land and Suzdal as early as the twelfth century. Riazan's princes obtained reinforcements for their own inadequate forces from the grand princes of Vladimir, but paid for this with subjection to the power of Suzdal-Vladimir. In view of Riazan's position as the barrier between Great Russia and the hostile forces to the south and east, its subordination to the power of central Russia was only natural.

These long-standing relations were to have a vital effect on Riazan's future. Its exposed military position created a pressing motive for alliance with the center of Great Russia. The main artery for communication and movement of supplies was the river Oka. The strengthening of Riazan's rear and the broadening of its base of operations were essential to the welfare of the Riazan land. But the possibility of building up its strength to the north and northwest was at a very early time checked by the growing power of Moscow. As the Chernigov principality became weak and began to disintegrate, there was intense rivalry between Moscow and Riazan for possession of its volosts. Disputed areas included the towns of Lopastna, Vereia, Borovsk, and Luzha, which in treaty documents came to be called "the Riazan places," although all of them were originally Chernigov volosts. Their seizure by Moscow was probably connected with its seizure of Kolomna, the key to advance on Riazan from the north. On the other flank, the region around the juncture of the Oka and Volga rivers was controlled by Nizhni Novgorod. Riazan's expansion down the Oka was also blocked by the Murom domain, which had long since been withdrawn from Riazan's orbit and was bound now to the grand princes of Vladimir.

Such, in broad outline, was the position of the Riazan land about the beginning of the fourteenth century. Out of historical and geographical necessity and under extremely difficult conditions the Riazan principality had assumed the military and colonizing tasks of northeastern Russia, making itself responsible for the support and development of the traditions of ancient Suzdal Russia in its relations with its neighbors to the south and east until such time as the rising power of Moscow would again unify all the diverse tendencies in Great Russia's national life. The end of the thirteenth century and the beginning of the fourteenth was a time when Riazan was left to depend entirely on its own local forces; and in the meantime the center of Great Russia heaped staggering blows on it from the rear.

Our chronicle sources are amazingly uninterested in the affairs of the Riazan principality. From these sources (and unfortunately we have no other) it is often impossible to determine accurately even the most elementary facts in Riazan's history—for example, even the genealogy of its princes and the chronology of their succession.

The prince-martyr Roman died in 1270, leaving three sons: Feodor, Iaroslav, and Constantine. It is probable that Feodor sat on the senior throne of Riazan. The special principality of Pronsk was created under his brother Iaroslav. Even these facts are hard to establish, however, on the strength of the unreliable and confusing information supplied by our sources. In fact the chronicles give us no detailed knowledge of events in Riazan or of the interrelations of its princes, either at this time or in the years immediately following. After the death of Feodor in 1293, and then of Iaroslav in 1299, some form of civil disturbance shook the Riazan principality, making it possible for Prince Daniel of Moscow to seize the city of Kolomna and its prince, Constantine, who was later killed in Moscow by Daniel's son Iuri (in 1306). We have no knowledge of what took place in Riazan during the years of Constantine's imprisonment in Moscow or after his death, or of the relations that developed between his son Vasili and the hereditary rulers of Pronsk, Iaroslav's sons Ivan and Mikhail. The murder of Prince Vasili in the land of the Horde in 1308 undoubtedly simplified Riazan's internal relations. Only Iaroslav's descendants in Pronsk had survived. Ivan occupied the senior throne of Riazan, while Pronsk was left in the hands of Mikhail's son Alexander, Ivan's nephew. When Ivan was killed by the Tatars in 1327, either after he was captured by the host of the Tatar chieftain Shevkalo or in the land of the Horde, his son Ivan Krotopol succeeded him.

The lack of information about Riazan affairs is in itself evidence of Riazan's special, separate significance in the history of Great Russia in this period. The Riazan princes played no part in the struggle between Tver and Moscow, indeed they were not directly involved in any of the urgent questions then affecting Great Russian life. At the same time Riazan bore the first and heaviest blows of the Tatar onslaught, and the Tatar power was to hang over it more threateningly than over any other part of Russia. Prince Oleg spent fifteen years in prison in the land of the Horde; his son Roman perished at the hands of the Horde, a martyr for the faith; his grandsons Vasili and Ivan were also killed by the Tatars. Besides the devastating campaigns of 1237 and 1239, the Riazan land was laid waste by the Tatars also in 1278, 1288, and 1308. No matter how fragmentary or incidental our records of its Tatar relations in this period may be, they do give us some idea of the crushing weight of Tatar influence on Riazan. Because of their own involvement in civil strife, the forces of central Great Russia, including those of the Grand Prince, were in no position to aid Riazan. Far from finding friends in this direction, Riazan could only regard Moscow as a hostile power, and Moscow's seizure of Kolomna and the imprisonment and subsequent murder of Constantine could only serve to widen the breach between Riazan and Great Russia, and increase the confusion in the organization of Riazan's own local powers.

The concentration of grand princely power in the hands of Iuri III and Ivan I of Moscow placed the princes of Riazan in a position of still greater dependence. Grand Prince Iuri III led a host against Riazan in 1320 and forced Prince Ivan to make a settlement, after which we see the Riazan princes included in the ranks of the Grand Prince's "downstream host." In the reign of Ivan Krotopol (successor to Ivan the son of Iaroslav), however, there are signs that Riazan might be becoming independent of Moscow once more. Ivan Krotopol entered into his own private negotiations with the Horde, and in Riazan he made his own arrangements for the collection and payment of the Tatar outlay.

In 1340 Ivan Krotopol moved to his capital city of Pereiaslavl Riazansky with a Tatar host under the command of Tovlubi, on the first leg of a campaign against Smolensk. On the way he intercepted his cousin Alexander as the latter was going to the land of the Horde with a payment of the Tatar outlay, proceeded to "relieve him of his plunder, and took him to Riazanski Pereiaslavl, where he commanded that he be executed." From there the combined forces of Tovlubi and Ivan moved on toward Smolensk, after having been joined by the troops of Grand Prince Ivan I, under the princes of Suzdal, Rostov, Iuriev, Druts, and Fomin, as well as the personal commanders of the Grand Prince. Alexander's execution before the Tatar temnik (as a representative of the Khan) was by no means a simple case of lynching. It was a striking expression of the grand princely pretensions of Ivan Krotopol vis-à-vis the udel princes of the Riazan land.

The principality of Pronsk passed to Alexander's sons Iaroslav-Dmitri and Ivan. Iaroslav-Dmitri took the case of his father's execution to the Horde, and in 1342 succeeded in persuading the Khan to release him so that he might go in the company of the envoy Kindiak and a Tatar host "to sit on the throne of Riazan." Ivan Krotopol tried to resist, but was besieged in Pereiaslavl Riazansky. He escaped from the city but later fell into enemy hands and was killed. With his death another line in the princely house of Riazan came to an end. The whole Riazan land was now in the hands of the sons of Alexander of Pronsk. Iaroslav-Dmitri ruled after Ivan Krotopol for less than a year, and his brother Ivan died in 1350. The grand princely rule in Riazan passed then to Ivan's son Oleg, while he was still a boy, while Oleg's cousin Vladimir, also in boyhood, ascended the throne of Pronsk. The real administrators of the land at this time were the Riazan boyars.

II.

In the middle of the fourteenth century there was a substantial rise in the energies of this frontier land. Our lack of information on life in Riazan prevents us from probing very deeply into this important development. External circumstances certainly favored the longing for new power and independence. The reign of Ivan II of Moscow marked a weakening in grand princely power and a growing disaffection among the Muscovite boyars. Then came the years when the boy prince Dmitri of the Don had to struggle for control of the grand princely throne. These events in Moscow reduced its influence with the Horde, and a way was opened for successful intrigue with its ruling cliques. Riazan made every effort to draw Tatar forces over to its own side.

Grand Prince Semeon the Proud died in April, 1353. In June of the same year the men of Riazan captured Lopastna, took prisoner Moscow's deputy, and released him only on payment of a ransom. Prince Ivan of Moscow was then in the land of the

Horde with all the Russian princes, where he was engaged in a dispute with the Prince of Suzdal over the grand princely rule. Ivan returned and assumed the throne in Vladimir, as Ivan II, in March, 1354. The boy prince Oleg of Riazan could scarcely have played a leading role in the capture of Lopastna. It is more than likely that he too was in the land of the Horde during the time of Ivan's negotiations. Indeed, the chronicles emphasize the fact that "Prince Oleg was still a boy at that time" in their accounts of the capture of Lopastna, and ascribe the venture not to him, but to "the men of Riazan." Evidently the Riazan boyars saw an opportunity for energetic action and made the most of it. It may well be that this action was connected in some way with the difficulties created in Moscow by the murder of the tysiatsky Alexei Petrovich, and the departure to Riazan of "the great boyars of Moscow."

From Riazan's point of view the capture of Lopastna was only the first step in a movement toward a definite settlement of the Riazan-Moscow border. In 1358 the Tatar prince Mohammed-Khozha came to Riazan and while there sent word to Grand Prince Ivan II demanding a "separation of the Riazan land." As it happened, the demand was not satisfied. Metropolitan Alexei, the leading figure in Moscow's policy-making, had managed to build up a very considerable influence with the Horde, and the "repression" carried out by the Horde after the murder of Khan Janibeg and the transfer of power to Berdibeg brought about also the downfall of Mohammed-Khozha. Grand Prince Ivan II prevented Khozha from entering Moscow, and he was recalled by the Horde and killed "by the Khan's command." Not until the 1380's, in the time of Metropolitan Cyprian, did the men of Riazan succeed in winning a settlement of this border.

This unresolved "controversy" between Moscow and Riazan lasted for many years. The resulting tension made Riazan's position, midway between Moscow and the land of the Horde, extremely difficult and ambiguous, and did much to determine the policies of Grand Prince Oleg of Riazan. Even before this, of course, Riazan had sought aid from the Horde in the face of Muscovite aggression. Tatar reinforcements had fought on the side of Constantine in the battle that ended in his capture and death at the hands of Moscow's men. Riazan had also sought

Tatar support for the restoration of its domains along the Oka. But Tatar aid was never reliable. The rapid growth of factions among the Horde and the frequent "repressions" following shifts in power prevented any clear-cut and stable policy on matters taking place in the "Russian ulus" to the north. Small separate hordes carried out independent raids, and the Khan's authority declined sharply in this period of Tatar anarchy. In 1365 the Riazan land was raided by Prince Tagi of the Golden Horde. The Tatars razed Pereiaslavl Riazansky, but Oleg and his cousin Vladimir, joined by Prince Tito of Kozyol, Oleg's brother-in-law, attacked and defeated him near the Shushev forest on the Voina River. Repeated Tatar raids checked the desire in Riazan to break all ties with the Grand Prince of Great Russia, and at the same time undermined the significance of Tatar patronage, especially in the light of the Horde's internal divisions. Thus in spite of the strained relations between Moscow and Riazan, some ties were in fact maintained, and we see the host of "Prince Oleg of Riazan" under the command of Vladimir of Pronsk ranged against Olgerd in the latter's attack on Moscow in 1370.

But the period from 1350 to 1380 was a time when the grand princely authority of the Muscovite princes was passing through a profound crisis in Moscow's struggle with the new and rising powers of Nizhegorod and Great Novgorod, with Tver's move to win independence and supremacy in Great Russia, and with Lithuania. The outcome of this many-sided struggle was for a long time very much in doubt for those engaged in it; and without firm support from the center of Great Russia, the Riazan principality was left to defend itself and establish its own direct relations with its Tatar and Lithuanian neighbors. This tendency toward political self-determination was complicated and intensified by its border disputes with Moscow and by its own need to consolidate its base of operations through the establishment of "permanent and invulnerable borders and frontiers." In the 1370's this ambiguous position between Moscow and the land of the Horde disrupted princely relations within Riazan itself. The junior principality of Pronsk became the center of forces looking to Moscow and its grand princes, while the Grand Prince of Riazan sought to escape from Muscovite control and define his own relations with his neighbors on three fronts.

Beyond this the motives behind the break between Moscow and Riazan in 1371 are not known to us. The question we must ask is this: How was this break connected with the treaty that was at that time concluded between Olgerd of Lithuania and Dmitri of the Don? This treaty speaks of the inclusion of those princes "who will be bound by good will and the terms of a settlement to Grand Prince Dmitri and his younger brother Prince Vladimir (son of Andrei)—that is, Grand Prince Oleg, Grand Prince Roman, Grand Prince Vladimir of Pronsk, and other princes who will be bound to act in our name." The text seems to indicate that a special settlement was anticipated with the princes of Riazan and Pronsk, and suggests also that it was still an open question whether or not these princes were acting "in the name of" Grand Prince Dmitri. It is only natural to see the reason for the final break between Moscow and Riazan in Oleg's objection to being included in the number of "other princes who will be bound to act in Dmitri's name" and thereby prohibited from making independent alliances. However that may be, Grand Prince Dmitri's host marched on Riazan in December of 1371, the men of Riazan were routed near Pereiaslavl on the Skornishchev River, "Prince Oleg only barely escaping with a small druzhina," and the throne of Riazan was occupied by Prince Vladimir of Pronsk. But not for long. With the departure of the Muscovite host Oleg drove out Vladimir "by force" and resumed the grand princely rule of Riazan.

Unfortunately our sources are silent about the course of Moscow-Riazan relations after these events. This silence on the part of the Muscovite chroniclers is in itself rather significant. It is difficult to believe that these documents would have failed to mention a settlement between Dmitri and Oleg (requiring the latter to "do the whole will" of the Grand Prince) if such an agreement had in fact been made. Oleg may have relied on Tatar help to regain his grand princely rule and drive out the prince installed by Moscow. Not only had he consolidated his possession of Riazan's throne; he had also substantially increased his independence of the Grand Prince of all Russia. In the years immediately following there is no mention of his participation in Moscow's struggle with Lithuania and Tver, and his neutrality may be indicated by the role he played as a disinterested third party and judge in the dispute between Moscow and Tver, a function assigned to him in a treaty made in 1375 between Dmitri and Grand Prince Mikhail. As understood by Oleg, the local interests of the Riazan land dictated a policy of caution and neutrality. True, he had apparently gained full control of the entire Riazan region, and his dispute with Pronsk slipped into the background. Vladimir died in the winter of 1372, and we find his son Ivan actively resisting the Grand Prince of Riazan only after Oleg's death. But the 1370's were a time of extreme tension between Great Russia and the Tatar power, and Riazan could not fail to pass through these years in a state of constant alarm. In 1373 it fell victim to a devastating raid by Mamai. Grand Prince Dmitri of the Don and his cousin Vladimir the son of Andrei assembled their forces and remained on the banks of the Oka (i.e., along the border between Riazan and Moscow) "all summer," and succeeded in preventing the Tatars from crossing the river into their own land.

The Riazan land suffered the bitter fate of having to act as a buffer zone in front of Great Russia's main line of defense along the Oka. Great Russia's forces were becoming unified around the center of Moscow. Stubbornly and with increasing success they were defending Nizhni Novgorod and its lands as well as the whole Oka line against Tatar attack. Thus in the fall of 1377 the Tatar prince Arapsha advanced toward Nizhni Novgorod, devastating the country to the east of the Sura River and proceeding without opposition to subject the Riazan land to "violence." Nizhni also suffered severe losses, but the city itself was defended with valor. The events of 1378–79 were typical. It was at this time that the Tatars seized Nizhni in a surprise raid and the city was set on fire. Grand Prince Dmitri came upon another Tatar host under command of the temnik Begich, beyond the Oka and within Riazan territory, and defeated it on the banks of the Vozha River. It was not long before the Tatars took revenge, and on Riazan territory. In the face of new "violence" at the hands of a large Tatar force, Oleg was compelled (in the words of the Muscovite chronicler) "to pass over to this side of the Oka," abandoning his cities to the enemy. The Tatars set Pereiaslavl Riazansky and a number of other towns on fire and "laid waste to the Riazan land."

These events in the 1370's foreshadowed Oleg's notorious behavior at the battle of Kulikovo. For many years the Riazan and Nizhegorod frontiers of Great Russia had been sacrificed to Tatar devastation as a way of saving its central region. By the end of the 1370's, however, they had apparently outlived their usefulness as Great Russia's outer wall of defense, and now the two powerful enemies, Great Russia and the Horde, stood face to face. The battle on the Vozha had clearly shown the Tatars where the real center of Russian power lay, a power strong enough now to organize under a single command the defense of the entire western and southern borders of Great Russia. The ground had been prepared for a threatening alliance between the Horde and Lithuania, and indeed Olgerd was seeking just such an alliance. The Prince of Riazan found himself forced to clarify his position in this great conflict, which had now entered a period of crisis. In the light of Dmitri's struggle with the west, his course of action up to that time had been characterized by a kind of shrewd neutralism. Moscow had now entered into open conflict with the Horde, and the full weight of countermeasures taken against Moscow would inevitably fall on Riazan, whether Moscow was completely or only partially successful. Riazan had to reconsider its policies in the light of this new situation, and its apprehensions were aroused not least by the thought of Moscow's complete success (if such a thing could be conceived), for it was quite clear to everyone—especially after the Moscow-Tver treaty of 1375—that such a success would certainly threaten the independence of Riazan.

As it happened, Oleg took a position at the crucial battle of Kulikovo which brought down on him angry charges of duplicity and betrayal of the Russian cause. He joined Mamai and Jagiello as a way of averting the wrath of Dmitri's enemies; at the same time he kept Dmitri informed of Tatar movements. Having refused to send a host to take part in Grand Prince Dmitri's campaign against the Tatars, he had no way of avoiding a clash with the Muscovite forces when the latter returned in victory from the Kulikovo Plain. Dmitri's victory placed Oleg in a helpless position with regard to the Grand Prince of Russia. He had lost the support of the Horde and had no hope of a rapprochement with Lithuania. Dmitri decided to take advantage of this opportunity to end Riazan's independence, but the army which he assembled for the campaign against Riazan never actually set out. Riazan's envoys arrived in Moscow with the news that Oleg had left the country, fleeing with his wife and children and his entire court. Dmitri received the homage of the Riazan boyars, concluded a riad with them, and canceled the order for the campaign. His deputies were sent to administer the Riazan domain. Mamai's death and the enthronement of Tokhtamysh as the new ruler of the Horde radically altered this situation. The Russian princes, with Dmitri at their head, hastened to acknowledge the new khan, received his envoys with honor, and dispatched their own envoys to him with gifts and declarations of obedience. Apprehension in the face of this new and dreaded power had the effect of uniting all the Russian princes under Dmitri as their eldest brother. The return of the grand principality of Riazan to Oleg can be dated about this time. However, as far as we can judge from the incomplete and unreliable information of the chronicles, no formal disposition or settlement was made between Dmitri and Oleg before 1381, and very probably not until 1385.

A new Tatar campaign against Russia was mounted in the fall of 1382. Prince Oleg met Khan Tokhtamysh with a declaration of homage before he crossed the borders of Russia, and "conducted the Khan around his otchina of Riazan, wishing to gain favor not for us all," notes the Muscovite chronicler, "but for his own principality." He provided the Tatars with guides to lead them to the fords across the Oka. According to this same chronicler, Oleg assured the Khan that it would be an easy matter to take the city of Moscow and capture Dmitri as well. But the taking of Moscow and the destruction of several of its cities and volosts were costly victories for Tokhtamysh, causing his campaign to degenerate into a series of raids or "violence," ending in hasty retreat when the Grand Prince's armies finally succeeded in mounting an organized counteroffensive. This may well explain the Khan's anger at Oleg, his cruel devastation of the Riazan land, and Oleg's ultimate flight before the Tatar forces. Once more Oleg found himself between two fires. He returned to Riazan when the Tatars withdrew, but had to flee again before a Muscovite host which pillaged his land "down to the last stick," so that "it was left more desolate even than it was by the

Tatars." Our sources do not say when or how Oleg returned to his principality after this second flight, but it is reasonable to connect his return with the peace made between Tokhtamysh and Grand Prince Dmitri in the fall of 1382, with a new submission to the Tatar rule. No peace or settlement had yet been made, however, between Dmitri and Oleg. In the spring of 1385 the long-drawn-out conflict between Moscow and Riazan was resolved in bloody battle. Oleg made a raid on Kolomna, seized the city, took prisoner the Grand Prince's deputy, and then defeated the Muscovite host of Prince Vladimir (son of Andrei) in a battle "near Riazan."

These military successes did not give Oleg the slightest superiority over the forces of Moscow, but neither did they lead to a renewal of the stubborn conflict between the two grand princes. Bitter experience had shown that the Tatar threat hung equally over both Riazan and central Great Russia, while the internal affairs of the principality of Lithuania had lessened the value of the treaty that Oleg had made (probably during his absence from Riazan in 1380–81) with Jagiello. At the same time Dmitri was too burdened with other complicated problems to embark on a decisive campaign against Riazan. The long-standing hostility was finally resolved in an agreement of "perpetual peace" drawn up in 1385 under the mediation of Abbot Sergius of the Trinity Monastery. The text of the agreement has not come down to us, and the chronicles mention it in only one brief reference. We have already suggested that the provisions of the treaty of 1381 must have formed the basis also of this later "peace." According to the earlier document, Grand Prince Oleg was required to regard himself as one of Dmitri's "younger brothers," on a level with Prince Vladimir of Serpukhov; to set aside his alliance with Lithuania and subordinate his dealings with Lithuania to Dmitri's policies, both "friendly" and "hostile" (i.e., in the event of a break with Lithuania, Oleg agreed to join Dmitri and "be against it with him as one man"); to "make peace with or pay tribute to the Tatars in unity with Grand Prince Dmitri," or in the event of "enmity" to be "as one man with him against the Tatars and to do battle against them with him." The same solidarity was to hold true also in their relations with other Russian princes: whoever was a friend of Dmitri was to be acknowledged as a friend of Oleg, and whoever was an enemy of Dmitri was to be acknowledged as an enemy of Oleg—"it is for us to act as one man." In return for this the Moscow princes were obliged "to wish Oleg well in all things in the land of the Horde and in Russia, with a sincere heart," and to "watch over and not wrong" his votchina. At the same time the treaty established a new border between the domains of Riazan and those of the grand princely and Muscovite votchina.

The "perpetual peace" of 1385 was further strengthened two years later by the marriage of Oleg's son Feodor to Dmitri's daughter Sofia. The relationships established by this settlement were actually put into practice and took on real force, and did much to cement the ties of the Riazan frontier to the grand principality of all Russia. Oleg's policies had suffered a complete and decisive defeat. Riazan could not do without support from the center of Great Russia, and its fight for independence became weak and fitful. By the end of the 1380's Oleg had secured Riazan's rear flank along the lines of the Oka and the Tsna on the basis of a firm peace with Moscow and a clear settlement of their disputed border. From this time on he became absorbed in the defense of Riazan against Tatar raids and resistance to the Lithuanian advance into the territory of Chernigov. In this warfare on the southern, eastern, and western borders of his votchina, Oleg acted with considerable independence, however, and on one occasion actually broke with the grand princely policies of Moscow.

Evidently there was a weakening of Muscovite energies following the invasion by Tokhtamysh in 1382–83, and for a time there was a revival of Riazan's independent significance as a defensive barrier between Great Russia and the hostile forces of the steppe. Oleg continued to consolidate and extend the Russian colonization of the Don valley and the Meshchera region beyond the Tsna. The treaty of 1381 had already mentioned "Tatar places" that Oleg "had seized from the Tatars," and had bound Oleg not to "advance" into Meshchera. A later treaty between Vasili I and Oleg's son Feodor in 1402 guaranteed their mutual possession of the "Tatar and Mordva places" that had been seized by their fathers, and revealed that Oleg himself and also his sons and boyars had bought up land in Meshchera contrary to the earlier settlement with Moscow. It is possible that it was just such seizures (and not simply the lust for plunder) that prompted the Tatar raids on Riazan. In the 1390's Oleg shifted from a defensive stance on his southern border to more energetic and aggressive action. Thus in 1394 he "defeated the Tatars of the horde of Tokhtamysh who had come in violence into the Riazan volosts," and in 1400 he administered a heavy blow on Tatar forces in the vicinity of the Chervleni Iar. This aggressive activity tended to draw around him all the forces of frontier Russia—not only the princes of Pronsk, but also those of Murom, Karachev, Kozelsk, and Elets—and this without any direct involvement of the Grand Prince of all Russia, lesser princes simply joining the Grand Prince of Riazan as his "younger brothers" and allies.

Oleg also tried to organize these forces in an attempt to block the Lithuanian advance into Russian territory. Here he acted quite independently. His decisions were not simply unrelated to Moscow's grand princely policies; they actually contradicted Grand Prince Vasili's deferential if not wholly subordinate relationship with his father-in-law, Vitovt. Oleg's armies assisted in the defense of Smolensk against Lithuanian seizure. Prince Iuri of Smolensk was married to one of Oleg's daughters, and he was the only one of the Smolensk princes to escape capture by Vitovt in 1395, being with his father-in-law in Riazan at the time of Vitovt's attack. Oleg answered this "first capture of the city of Smolensk by the Grand Prince of Lithuania" by mounting a campaign against Vitovt. His son-in-law Iuri and also the princes of Murom, Kozelsk, and Pronsk were to join him on this campaign. Vitovt's countermarch against the Riazan volosts upset these plans, however, and Oleg had to give up his expedition and turn back to deal with the Lithuanian "oppressors." In September of 1396 Oleg renewed the struggle with an attack on Liubutsk, but Grand Prince Vasili interfered, sending envoys to Oleg and "turning him away from Liubutsk." Moscow had fallen completely under the influence of Vitovt in this period, and Vasili's tactics hindered Oleg and cost him dearly. He was forced to flee in the face of Vitovt's advance, and the Riazan land was ravaged. However, as soon as a reaction began to develop in Smolensk following Vitovt's devastating raid along the Vorskla River, Oleg marched with Iuri and his other allies to liberate the city, and Iuri was reestablished on its throne. Their armies then waged war on the Lithuanian volosts and returned "with many prisoners." Vitovt's attack on Smolensk was obviously a part of his struggle with Riazan. Oleg answered Vitovt's unsuccessful attempt to recapture Smolensk in the fall of 1401 by attacking Briansk, sending a host under his son Rodoslav. Rodoslav was defeated by the Lithuanians near Liubutsk, and was himself taken prisoner.

All the energies spent by Oleg in his conflict with Lithuania had been in vain. Riazan could not stop Vitovt's advance without the aid of the main forces of Great Russia. Liberating Smolensk from Lithuanian control had no permanent results, since Grand Prince Vasili refused to support its prince. Riazan had exhausted itself in a struggle that was really beyond its strength, and after Oleg's death in 1402 it became weaker and weaker, suppressed by Moscow's superior power.

III.

Oleg's son Feodor now assumed the ancient throne of the principality of Riazan. Feodor was related in two ways to the grand princely house of Moscow. He was married to Vasili's sister Sofia, and his daughter had been given in marriage to Prince Ivan of Serpukhov (son of Vladimir). On his father's death he visited Khan Shadibeg in the land of the Horde and received a yarlik to his "otchina and inheritance, the grand principality of Riazan." He then renewed his father's treaty with the Grand Prince of all Russia. Acknowledging Vasili I as his "eldest brother," Feodor bound himself to be at one with him in all things, "to be in agreement with him, as he should be, without cunning." Feodor was also forbidden to "join" the Tatars "in any kind of treachery"; and he accepted the obligation to inform the Grand Prince of all that he might hear "from the Horde" and "to act in agreement" with the Grand Prince in the event that the Horde should turn against him. All dealings between the Grand Prince of Riazan and the Horde were to be controlled by the Grand Prince of all Russia. Feodor had the right to send "messengers" to the Horde and to receive Tatar envoys "who did not come to him in treachery," as long as he informed

Moscow of all such dealings. The Prince of Riazan was also
forbidden to enter into any kind of treaty with Grand Prince
Vitovt of Lithuania without Vasili's prior consent.

We really know too little about the internal affairs of Riazan
to form any clear picture of its life in this period. We know of
only one princely city in Riazan besides Pereiaslavl, and this was
Pronsk. Prince Vladimir of Pronsk had been on the point of
seizing the grand princely throne of Riazan in 1372, but died that
winter, leaving his only son, Ivan, as his successor on the throne
of Pronsk. The chroniclers speak of "the Pronsk princes" in the
plural, but we do not know who they could have had in mind.
One peculiarity of the official documents of this period deserves
special attention: the treaties of 1371 and 1402 refer to the two
princes of Pronsk (Vladimir and his son Ivan) as "grand princes."
These documents were edited and copied in Moscow, so that the
ascription must have had some special significance not fully defined in our records. It is possible to connect this usage with
the claims made from time to time by these princes to the grand
princely rule of Riazan and the support of these claims by Moscow, as at the end of 1371. The treaty of 1402 emphasizes the
special position of the Prince of Pronsk. It binds Grand Prince
Vasili and the princes of Moscow "not to interfere in the affairs of the Riazan principality." Then it lays this special obligation on Grand Prince Feodor: "and it is for you to deal in friendship with Grand Prince Ivan according to the ancient treaties."
Farther on it provides for the appointment of a third person to
mediate in disputes between the grand princes of Riazan and
Pronsk, with Vasili having the right to compel the guilty party
to repay the "offended one" if he should be unwilling to pay
voluntarily—and this "without treachery" on the part of the
mediator. It is interesting to note that exactly the same arrangement for settling territorial and other disputes was fixed by a
treaty beween the Grand Prince of Riazan and the princes of
Novosil and Tarusa, who by the same treaty were all bound to
act "as one man" with Grand Prince Vasili I of Moscow.

As time went by, however, the princes of Pronsk moved in
another direction, finding support in their struggle with Riazan
not in Moscow, but in the land of the Horde. Our fragmentary
record of the events of 1408 gives us no indication of the im-

mediate cause of the clash between Feodor and Vladimir's son Ivan.

Ivan traveled to the land of the Horde and returned in the fall of 1407 "with the sanction and favor" of Khan Bulat-Saltan, and, most important, accompanied by the Khan's envoy. Evidently there had been some dispute with the Grand Prince of Riazan, which had been taken for judgment to the Khan's court. Following his turn to Pronsk, Ivan attacked Riazan with the aid of Tatar forces. Feodor was compelled to flee north of the Oka into the territory of his brother-in-law Vasili. Vasili gave Feodor sanctuary, although this caused some disagreement among Vasili's boyars and counselors, in the light of the involvement of the Tatar host. The negotiations that then took place in the presence of the Khan's envoy did not resolve the issue, and a battle was engaged. The combined armies of the two grand princes, Vasili and Feodor, were defeated by the host of Pronsk, notwithstanding the neutrality of the Tatar detachments. Here the affair ended. Ivan was about to occupy Riazan when he made peace with Feodor. Grand Prince Vasili (and probably also the Khan's envoy) acted as a mediator in this settlement.

It would be helpful if we could have more information than we do about this dispute. It was in fact a prelude to the invasion of Russia by Edigei, and the last attempt on the part of Riazan (here in the person of the Prince of Pronsk) to enter into independent relations with the Horde and find support in its struggle with the Grand Prince of all Russia. The Prince of Moscow still did not possess sufficient strength to defend the southern and western frontiers of Great Russia. The Riazan land was still exposed to Tatar raids, and the closing years of Oleg's reign had shown what little aid Riazan could expect from Moscow in its struggle with Lithuania. Moscow's grand princely power was to reach a low point in the grim years of internal disorder during the reign of Vasili the Blind. Unable to exercise control over its own destinies, Riazan made an abortive attempt to get help from the Grand Prince of Lithuania. But the treaties made with Vitovt by Feodor's son Ivan and the Prince of Pronsk, in which they agreed to "enter Vitovt's service," were only another symptom of that dominion which Lithuania was then exercising over Moscow itself, and they came in the closing years of Vitovt's life.

In the newly developed balance of power in eastern Europe after his death they lost all significance.

The grand principality of Riazan was becoming more and more closely identified with the central region of Great Russia, and had almost ceased to exist as a separate territory. On the death of Vitovt, Feodor's son Ivan again came under the direct influence of the Grand Prince of all Russia. We find Ivan's host being sent to the latter's aid in an expedition against Prince Iuri of Galich. In fact, however, Ivan's response to the disturbances within the Moscow principality was notably passive. When Iuri seized Moscow and the grand princely rule for the second time, Ivan entered into a treaty with him as grand prince, although this alliance was quickly nullified by Iuri's death. We have no evidence of any further involvement of Ivan in this dispute, and when Vasili II finally occupied the throne of Moscow there was a new treaty between these two princes on substantially the same terms as the earlier one between Ivan and Iuri.

Hard pressed by the difficulties of his relations with neighboring powers and surrounded by hostile forces, the weakened Grand Prince of Riazan was inescapably bound to the Grand Prince of Russia, while the latter was beginning again to exercise leadership in Great Russia's relations with Lithuania and the Horde. Lithuania's pressure on Riazan's western border failed to sever the tie between Riazan and Moscow. What was most typical of these relations was Moscow's continuing inability to provide fully for the defense of the Riazan land. The grand princes of Great Russia demanded the complete subordination of Riazan's relations with Lithuania to their own policies and control. But in this process they were themselves forced to make a distinction between Riazan's contacts with the west and their own, and to limit themselves to the role of intermediary between Riazan and Lithuania, which were once again dealing with each other directly and without reference to Moscow.

Thus in his treaty of 1447 Grand Prince Vasili II demanded that the Prince of Riazan enter into treaties with the Grand Prince of Lithuania only "in agreement" with himself, carefully insisting that the Prince of Riazan was to act "as one man" with the Grand Prince of Russia, and in return promising to defend the Riazan land against Lithuanian attack.

But there was as yet no complete unity in the disposition of military forces. The solidarity of the princes was qualified; it was a kind of mutual observance of brotherly equality. The Grand Prince of Riazan was to engage personally in a campaign only in the event that the Grand Prince of Russia himself "mounted his horse"; and if the latter simply sent one of his lieutenants, then the same would hold for the Prince of Riazan.

A similar equality existed in the event of an attack by Lithuania against Riazan. Grand Prince Vasili promised to "defend" Riazan against all enemies whom it was itself "unable" to beat back; in return the Prince of Riazan promised not to enter into any separate alliances. The Grand Prince of Russia was obliged to defend Riazan against Lithuania in person only if the Grand Prince of Lithuania personally led a campaign against Riazan; whereas if the Lithuanian grand prince sent his lieutenants against Riazan, then Vasili could also send his lieutenants. This qualification of the princes' military "solidarity" becomes important when it is considered in the light of the stipulation that the Prince of Riazan was "to act as one man" with the Grand Prince of Great Russia in the face of Lithuanian aggression. In the eyes of Moscow, at least, this was indeed a very relative "equality." In 1449 Vasili II made a treaty with Casimir, grand prince of Lithuania and king of Poland, in which it was agreed that if the Prince of Riazan should "despoil" Casimir, the latter was to inform Vasili of the offense; and if the Prince of Riazan should refuse to "make amends" for such violence when ordered to do so by Vasili, then Casimir had the right to "punish" the Prince of Riazan, and Vasili was bound not to interfere. But then Vasili also acknowledged the right of the Prince of Riazan to serve Casimir "if it seemed good to him," promising that he would not "be angered at him for such a thing, nor try to dissuade him."

Thus Riazan's waning independence was sustained not so much by its own power as by the powerlessness of the central region of Great Russia in the face of the looming might of the grand principality of Lithuania. The Grand Prince of Great Russia was in no position simply to conquer Riazan, and so was content with the submissiveness of his "younger brother," so long as he did not become the instrument of hostile powers or obstruct his own policies as grand prince of Russia and ruler of Moscow.

Our chronicles continue to be silent about the internal affairs of Riazan even in these last years of its independence. We know enough, however, to say that here too, as in Tver, the process of centralization of princely power accompanied the loss of independence. This process is difficult to trace in the few facts that have come down to us. Let us consider the treaty made between Feodor's son Ivan and Iuri of Galich. We find here a definition of the domains of the Grand Prince of Riazan which does not agree with the picture of an independent "grand prince" of Pronsk that we get in the treaties made earlier by the Grand Prince of Riazan with Vasili I of Moscow and Vitovt. The Prince of Riazan demands that Iuri guarantee "his otchina principality of Riazan, Pereiaslavl, and Pronsk, and all the volosts attached to Pereiaslavl and Pronsk along the Oka River." For a clear understanding of the relationships reflected in this treaty we would need to have access to a much wider collection of texts and documents than that provided in the chronicles. In this same treaty Grand Prince Ivan of Riazan repeats the provisions of former agreements that the princes of Moscow should not "interfere" in the affairs of "the Riazan princes," but special emphasis is laid on his obligation to "maintain friendship" with the Prince of Pronsk and his brothers. The definition of the Riazan otchina as including "Pereiaslavl and Pronsk and all the volosts attached to Pereiaslavl and Pronsk" gives us reason to say that this reference to a pact of "friendship" with the princes of Pronsk could mean that Ivan had already brought Pronsk "under his control." However, the treaty also repeats the provision that all conflicts between the princes of Riazan and Pronsk are to be referred to the Grand Prince of Moscow for "judgment," which must be regarded as genuine evidence of the independence of Pronsk in its relations with Riazan. The chronicles give us no information about the last years of the Pronsk principality. They do not even tell us when Ivan, the "grand prince" of Pronsk, died; and there is no mention of his sons—presumably the "brothers" referred to in the treaty with Iuri. Only the genealogies of the sixteenth century give us a glimpse of the later Pronsk princes. On the strength of this information it is really impossible to say when and under what circumstances the Pronsk domain ceased to be an independent principality. It is a fact, however, that Prince Vasili of Riazan (son and successor of Prince Ivan) was in possession of Pronsk, and that before his death he bequeathed it (together with his grand princely rule) to his own eldest son, Ivan.

Thus the unification of Riazan under a single grand princely power took place at a time when Riazan had become completely dependent on the power of Moscow, with all its internal affairs subject to Moscow's strict control and "safeguards." In full possession of the Riazan land, the Grand Prince of Great Russia did not oppose but evidently encouraged the centralization of this frontier territory as a way of gaining more effective control of the defense of his southern border.

Grand Prince Ivan died leaving his eight-year-old son Vasili on the throne of Riazan and securing his right to the principality by "giving him into the hand" of Grand Prince Vasili II of Moscow. In 1464 Ivan III of Moscow gave his sister Anna in marriage to the young prince and let him go back to Riazan, "to his otchina and grand principality." Vasili ruled as "grand prince" for nineteen years, but was in fact a vassal of Moscow. Before his death in 1483 he assigned Pereiaslavl Riazansky, Rostislavl, Pronsk, and the whole grand principality of Riazan to his eldest son, Ivan, giving Perevits and the city of Riazan to his younger son, Feodor. These two brothers entered into a treaty modeled on the Muscovite treaties between a grand prince and his udel brothers, but with considerably more power given to the Grand Prince over his younger brother in the city of Riazan.

This treaty marked the end of Ivan's negotiations with his brother Feodor, and was made in the closing years of Ivan's life. It was intended primarily to confirm their hereditary possession of their domains, and also, in the event that Riazan's throne was left vacant, to guarantee the transfer of the grand princely rule to Feodor with the transfer of Ivan's domains to Ivan III of Moscow. But this was a mere formality. No political or territorial arrangements on the part of the Riazan princes could disturb the policy of extending Muscovite sovereignty as it was being finally achieved under Grand Prince Ivan III.

From the time that Vasili II finally secured his possession of Moscow's throne, the princes of Riazan were nothing more than

"obedient servants" of the Grand Prince of Great Russia. Prince
Ivan of Riazan (the elder son of Vasili) was bound to Moscow
by a treaty made in the first year of his reign. The Prince of
Riazan acknowledged both Grand Prince Ivan III and his son
as his "elder brothers." He was obliged to "act as one man" with
them against Lithuania and the Tatars, and renounced all claims
to Moscow's acquisitions to the south of the Oka. While preserving the outward forms of grand princely dignity in his treaty
with his brother Feodor, and even acting as if his power had
been increased, Prince Ivan was in fact an obedient vassal of
Moscow. The Riazan host marched in Moscow's campaign against
Lithuania, and in his peace treaty with Grand Prince Ivan III
Prince Alexander of Lithuania inscribed Prince Ivan and his
brother Feodor of Riazan "on the side of" Ivan III, thereby requiring that all his disputes with them be handed over for "disposition" to the Grand Prince of Moscow. The daughters of
Princess Anna of Riazan were completely under the influence of
their uncle Ivan III, all the more so in that their mother was still
alive. Grand Prince Ivan of Riazan died in 1500, leaving his five-
year-old son Ivan on its throne. Prince Feodor died in 1503,
"giving his otchina" to Ivan III of Moscow, who then transferred it by testament to his son Vasili III. The grand principality of Riazan was in the hands of the rulers of Moscow from
the end of the fifteenth century onward, and the history of the
last prince of Riazan, ending with the abolition of this domain
as a separate principality, is the history of the "rebellion" of a
vassal prince against the power of a grand prince who already
controlled all the administrative and military forces of the land.

Chapter

VII

The Grand Principality
of Nizhegorod

The historical process in Riazan was so characterized by violence and unrest as a result of its vulnerable position between three enemies—the Tatars, Moscow, and Lithuania—that its internal political organization as a "grand principality" was unable to develop any real permanence. There is no basis for speaking of an udel system (in the strict sense of this term) in the Riazan land. But while our view of Riazan as a land without a well-developed political structure may well be determined simply by our ignorance of the events in its history and of the nature of its princes' interrelationships, our view of the grand principality of Nizhegorod as a similarly undeveloped territory is based on at least one solid fact: this principality lived out its short life under extremely tense and violent conditions.

In his study of the development of the eastern frontier of Great Russia, the historian is confronted with the same problems as he is in the study of Riazan; the information available in our sources is fragmentary, confused, and oblique. The story of how this territorial-political unit first came into being in the middle of the fourteenth century, with Nizhni Novgorod as its urban center, is very obscure and difficult to explain. Suzdal was the

only ancient city in this land with a glorious past. The other
"princely" towns were evidently fortified posts that were built
for particular strategic purposes. This was especially true of the
two cities that together with Suzdal are usually regarded in
the chronicles as making up the Nizhegorod land as a whole—
Volga Gorodets and Nizhni Novgorod. Volga Gorodets was
older than Nizhni. The first reference we have to it in the
chronicles comes under the year 1172. It was probably built
either by Vsevolod Big Nest or by Andrei Bogoliubsky; or perhaps even by their father, Iuri Dolgoruky. In the twelfth century
and at the beginning of the thirteenth, Gorodets was a staging
point for the grand princes of Vladimir in their activities along
the Volga. The "mouth of the Oka" was another of their key
points, and this led to the construction of Nizhni Novgorod there
in the thirteenth century.

When Vsevolod's son Sviatoslav "placed his nephews in the
other cities in the order their father Iaroslav had established,"
Prince Andrei had received Volga Gorodets and Nizhni Novgorod as his portion. He returned to these cities from abroad as
to his own otchina in 1256, after a reconciliation with his
brother Alexander, and at this time also received Suzdal as his
domain. But this unification of several domains in Andrei's hands
did not yet constitute a "Suzdal-Nizhegorod principality." It is
even possible that Andrei received Suzdal not in addition to
Gorodets and Nizhni Novgorod, but in exchange for them. Such
a theory would help to explain the subsequent fate of Gorodets
and Nizhni, and would be more in keeping with their special
significance for the Grand Prince's power. The chronicles identify Andrei as prince of Suzdal from 1256, and name Suzdal as
his place of burial. His sons also reigned in Suzdal as their otchina,
first of all Iuri, then Mikhail and Vasili, while Gorodets and
Nizhni did not form a part of their otchina. From our sources
it is impossible to say exactly when and under what circumstances
Gorodets and Nizhni came into the hands of Andrei III, the son
of Alexander Nevsky. The earliest direct connection we have
of this younger Andrei (Alexander's son) with Gorodets—the
first reference to him as "prince of Gorodets"—appears in the
account of his death: "and they came and laid him in Gorodets,
in the Church of St. Michael the Archangel." But this Andrei

was never the udel prince of Gorodets. We see him almost constantly either fighting for the grand princely rule of Vladimir
or in possession of it. He left no sons, and so the question of his
votchina never arose. Nor do we have any evidence that he
possessed Nizhni Novgorod, although he exercised control over
it as grand prince. The grand princely boyars who established
Prince Mikhail of Tver on the grand princely throne tried also
to confirm his rule over Nizhni. We must assume, therefore,
either that Prince Iuri III of Moscow (Mikhail's rival in the
struggle for the grand princely rule) won final control of Nizhni
Novgorod (and also, perhaps, of Gorodets) when he won the
grand princely throne, or that the princes of Suzdal had reestablished their otchina rights to Nizhni and were fighting on
the side of Iuri and against Mikhail. Mikhail of Tver did not take
possession of Nizhni, and under his sons the quarrel between
Tver and Moscow ended in 1328 with the transfer of the grand
princely rule to Ivan Kalita and the assignment of "Vladimir and
the Volga land" to Vasili's son Alexander of Suzdal. This must
be regarded as the time when the territory of the grand principality of Nizhegorod was first defined. The land was to be more
fully developed under Alexander's brother Constantine.

We have seen something of Alexander's broad ambitions: he
tried to win control of Vladimir and its territory, and to join
these lands firmly to his own Suzdal domains, which would then
have embraced the whole of eastern Great Russia—the Suzdal-
Nizhegorod region along the Volga. But on his death the territory of the grand principality of Vladimir went to Grand Prince
Ivan Kalita and the throne of Suzdal passed to his (Alexander's)
brother Constantine.

Constantine was the real organizer of the grand principality of
Nizhegorod. In the period from 1332 to 1340 our chronicles give
no precise information about the state of affairs in the Suzdal-
Volga region. The Nikon Chronicle reckons the years of Constantine's reign only from the time of Ivan Kalita's death, and
this circumstance, combined with a passing mention of the fact
that Prince Semeon was in Nizhni at the time of his father's
death and burial, has led historians to conclude that it was only
then that Constantine became "grand prince of Suzdal, Nizhegorod, and Gorodets." If we are to accept this conclusion (drawn

from the rather scant data available), then the grand principality of Nizhegorod must be regarded as having been established and formally defined by the Khan's sanction as well as the agreement of the princes at the "great assembly" of all the Russian princes in Moscow in 1341. Soon after this the separate episcopal jurisdiction of Suzdal was reconstituted. The revival of local political life in the middle of the fourteenth century on the eastern frontier of Great Russia was directly related to Russia's military and colonizing activity. In the second half of the twelfth century and the first quarter of the thirteenth, the Mordva had carried on a stubborn resistance to Russian expansion. This struggle was interrupted and suppressed by the imposition of Tatar rule. Russia was brought under the power of the khans of the Golden Horde, and both the Mordva and the Kama Bulgars were subdued by the Tatars. After the invasion, however, a new order came into being, and questions of landhold, trade, and princely rivalry began to disturb the Volga region with new force. The position of Nizhni Novgorod on the border between Russian and foreign territory gave it an extraordinary strategic and administrative significance, and at a very early time had defined its role as a major trading center on the Volga River. Moscow was becoming the commercial and military center of Great Russia, but it was not yet strong enough and was still too absorbed in other matters —its western relations, its own complicated internal struggle, and its dealings with the Golden Horde—to spend much of its energies or devote much attention to affairs on its eastern frontier. Under these circumstances Nizhni Novgorod and the princely house installed on its throne acquired significance for a short time as an independent center of power.

In the middle of the fourteenth century Nizhni Novgorod's revived importance as a staging point for Great Russia's expansion to the east is clearly reflected in the fragmentary and meager chronicle accounts of the history of the Nizhegorod land. In 1350 Prince Constantine began construction of the Church of the Transfiguration in Nizhni, or rather the reconstruction of the Cathedral of the Transfiguration, originally built by Iuri II in the early part of the thirteenth century. According to a Nizhegorod tradition, Constantine brought to this church an ancient ikon of the Saviour originally brought to Russia from Greece.

This work of church building was connected with the transfer of the ancient throne of the Suzdal principality from Suzdal to Nizhni Novgorod. Local tradition has preserved a memory of Prince Constantine as an energetic colonizer of the Nizhegorod land. "And he commanded the Russian people to settle along the Oka, the Volga, and the Kudma Rivers and in the villages of the Mordva, wherever they were willing to go." His volosts—which included Nizhni Novgorod, Suzdal, Gorodets, Iurievets on the Volga, Shuia, and Berezhits at the mouth of the Kliazma—became Great Russia's barrier against alien forces and a center for the organization of further Russian colonization to the east. Like Riazan, the grand principality of Nizhegorod developed as an outpost of Great Russia, and like both Tver and Riazan it depended on the support of Great Russia's power and resources. In this close relationship between Great Russia's central and frontier lands we can see the real basis for the attempts of the lesser grand princes to acquire the power and title of grand prince of Vladimir and all Russia. The indivisibility of the grand princely rule of Great Russia and possession of Vladimir had again emerged clearly in the reign of Prince Alexander, and his brother Constantine took the first opportunity that presented itself to "contend with the Prince of Moscow for the grand princely rule."

His chance came with the death of Grand Prince Semeon the Proud. As a major rival of Semeon's brother Ivan, Constantine established important ties with Lithuania and Great Novgorod. In 1354 his son Boris was married to a daughter of Olgerd, and we see Novgorod envoys supporting his petition to the Horde for possession of the title of grand prince of Vladimir. On this occasion, however, the influence of Moscow prevailed: "the Khan did not listen to them," and gave the grand princely yarlik to Prince Ivan. Constantine's forces were not subdued at once, but they had no strength to keep up the fight, and were eventually forced to make peace with Ivan. Their reconciliation took place not long before Constantine's death, and at this time the men of Novgorod also made their peace with Moscow. The chronicle says of Prince Constantine that he "reigned for fifteen years, and defended his otchina with honor and might against the violence of other princes and against the Tatars." After his death his son Andrei went to the land of the Horde. The Khan "bestowed on him his father's throne, the princely rule of Suzdal, Nizhni Novgorod, and Gorodets." At a meeting with Grand Prince Ivan II in Pereiaslavl, Prince Andrei of Suzdal acknowledged himself as a "younger brother" of the Grand Prince and made a peaceful settlement with him. The peace with Moscow and the agreement not to challenge its power were perhaps an extension and ratification of the "friendship" that Andrei's father had "entered into" with Grand Prince Ivan, and were characteristic of Andrei's reign. Both in the Suzdal-Nizhegorod land and elsewhere, however, there were still active elements of power and points of view hostile to Moscow as the center of grand princely sovereignty. Andrei's brother Dmitri stood at the head of these forces.

Andrei's brothers had quite probably been placed in a certain "order" by their father's riad, each one receiving an udel in the common otchina, with Suzdal assigned to Dmitri and Gorodets to Boris. We have no direct knowledge of the riad that Constantine must have made for his sons, nor of the treaty agreements made between these sons. In fact, the position of seniority was not settled on Andrei. Pressure from Moscow had radically distorted the relations between the princes in Suzdal-Nizhegorod. The brothers acted separately, each one pursuing his own goals. Unrest in the land of the Golden Horde greatly complicated the status of grand princely rule and created new possibilities for bold intrigue on the part of the Russian princes, destroying all stability in their emerging political relationships. The death of Grand Prince Ivan II in November, 1358, and the transfer of his title to his little son Dmitri inevitably increased the element of confusion. Both of the foundations on which their relations then rested had become weakened at the same time—the significance of the Khan's "sanction" and the power of the bearer of grand princely rule. A swift and bloody succession of khans following the murder of Berdibeg brought first Kulpa to power, then after six months Neurus, and in the spring of 1360, Khidyr. The princes of Russia could not fail to be affected by this instability in the power that lay behind their own rule. The political organization of the Russian ulus was only just established after the violent upheaval that brought Nevriui to power when authority was transferred to Khan Khidyr. Khidyr gave the yarlik to the grand principality of Vladimir to Constantine's son Dmitri, and Dmitri ascended the throne of the grand principality on June 22, 1360, acclaimed by Metropolitan Alexei and all his fellow princes as well as by Great Novgorod.

In the meantime, confusion in the land of the Horde was growing steadily worse, and just as it had assured Dmitri's success, so it now led to his downfall. Khan Khidyr was murdered by his son Timur-Khoza, and the temnik Mamai then rose against Timur. The royal dynasty of the Golden Horde seemed to be at an end. The princes of Sarai acclaimed Amurat, Khidyr's brother, as khan. Mamai advanced his own candidate, Abdul. The Russian princes acknowledged the rule of Amurat, and Dmitri of Moscow and Prince Dmitri of Suzdal submitted their dispute over the grand princely rule to his judgment. The Khan's yarlik was given this time to Dmitri of Moscow, and Dmitri of Suzdal, who was on the point of seizing Pereiaslavl Zalesky, was forced to seek refuge in his own otchina after his two-year reign on the throne of Vladimir. Having occupied the throne of Vladimir, Dmitri of Moscow then obtained a yarlik also from Amurat's rival Abdul, the khan of Mamai's horde. In the court of Khan Amurat at Sarai this action was regarded as treachery, and Amurat issued a new yarlik to the grand principality in the name of Dmitri of Suzdal, sending it to him by Prince Ivan of Beloozero in the company of Tatar envoys. Dmitri of Suzdal was about to occupy the throne of Vladimir for a second time, but within two weeks an army from Moscow drove him out of the city and pursued him into Suzdal, forcing him to sue for peace. Moscow's victory was complete. Not only had it overthrown the attempt of the Prince of Suzdal to seize the grand princely throne; it had also checked the growing hostility of the other princes. Grand Prince Dmitri of Moscow "had his way" not only with Dmitri of Suzdal, but also with Prince Constantine of Rostov; at the same time he drove the princes of Galich and Starodub out of their principalities.

The actual conditions of the peace made between the princes of Suzdal and Moscow have not been preserved in our sources. Indeed, the whole record of events between 1363 and 1365 is full of omissions and in places quite confused when the texts of different chronicles are compared.

Prince Andrei's entry into a monastery and then his death in 1365 prompted a new outbreak of local disturbances. Rival claims to the princely throne of Nizhegorod were advanced by Constantine's sons Boris and Dmitri. Like the earlier conflict between the princes of Moscow and Suzdal over the grand principality, this contest was largely inspired and sustained by the anarchy among the Tatars. The struggle for the khanate of the Golden Horde marked the beginning of a period of decline in Tatar power. Certain Tatar princes, to use the expression of the chronicles, "became puffed up," and began to assert their own rights and privileges. Thus Bulat-Timur seized the Great Bulgar territory and "carried away the whole Volga River route," while the Tatar prince Tarai ruled independently over the Mordva land. Loosed by this anarchy, Tatar bands began to move across the Russian frontier, and the Riazan and Nizhegorod volosts suffered more and more as a result of these eruptions. The central authority of the khan, weakened and dispersed, fell into the hands of men who obtained the title by force and retained it only for short periods of time.

Disorder in Russia was bound to be encouraged by the hasty granting of yarliks to the various pretenders to Russian princely thrones. Prince Boris succeeded in finding support among the Horde for his claim to Nizhni Novgorod and was formally installed in the Nizhegorod principality by the Khan's envoy. But Dmitri's son Vasili Kirdiapa was also in the land of the Horde at this time, in the court of Khan Aziz, having gone there immediately after the death of his uncle Andrei. Kirdiapa now brought the yarlik to the grand principality of Vladimir to his father, Dmitri of Suzdal. It may be that these grants of Nizhni Novgorod to Boris and of the grand principality of all Russia to Dmitri were two parts of a single plan. In any case, Dmitri was apparently aware of the futility of all these political maneuvers. Keeping his hold on Suzdal, he tried now to subdue his brother and win control over Nizhegorod by turning to Grand Prince Dmitri of Moscow. The Grand Prince was unable to bring the two brothers to an agreement. Boris rejected the intervention of the

Grand Prince in his dispute with his brother Dmitri. Metropolitan Alexei, the real molder of Muscovite policy at this time, then brought the full force of both the ecclesiastical and the secular power against him. Nizhni Novgorod and Gorodets were removed from the jurisdiction of Bishop Alexei of Suzdal and placed under the immediate control of the Metropolitan. Abbot Sergius appeared in Nizhni as an envoy from the Metropolitan and the Grand Prince, with a summons commanding Boris to appear in Moscow and present his case in the Grand Prince's court. Boris' refusal to comply with this order brought excommunication to the city of Nizhni Novgorod. "On orders from Metropolitan Alexei and Grand Prince Dmitri," Abbot Sergius closed all the city's churches. In the meantime the Grand Prince's army was moving from Moscow toward Nizhni, being joined on the way by the host of Prince Dmitri of Suzdal. Prince Boris could only submit. According to the terms of the settlement made with his brother, he returned to his udel of Gorodets, and Dmitri assumed the throne of Nizhni Novgorod. Helped by Moscow, Dmitri had finally restored the unity of the Suzdal-Nizhegorod land. His capital city was Nizhni, and in all likelihood his son Vasili Kirdiapa ruled in Suzdal. Boris, of course, ruled in Gorodets under his brother's sovereignty. The grand principality of Nizhegorod did not, however, stand on a par with the grand principality of Vladimir and all Russia; it was rather a part of this larger political system, which had Grand Prince Dmitri of Moscow at its head. Unfortunately, there is no trace in our sources of treaties between Dmitri of Moscow and the Grand Prince of Nizhegorod. As far as we can tell, their relationship was one of political unity involving the subordinate "solidarity" of the Grand Prince of Nizhegorod with the Grand Prince of all Russia.

This system of relationships was determined at least in part by the very location of the Nizhegorod land on the eastern frontier of Great Russia. Here too, as on the western and southern borders, the weakening of the internal bonds of Vladimir-Suzdal Russia had given rise to the independent organization of local forces to resist the pressure of hostile neighbors, to preserve and strengthen positions won through earlier colonization, and to carry this colonization still further. The breakdown of the world that had been very nearly welded together around the center of the Golden Horde only served to make Great Russia's neighbors to the south and east that much more dangerous, and led first to greater defensive measures on Russia's part, and then gradually to further Russian expansion. Attempts at local political organization on the eastern frontier were from the start inevitably influenced by the need to have the reliable support of the forces of central Great Russia. The Nizhegorod princes made an attempt to seize "the grand principality of Vladimir and all Russia" and revive the age-old and apparently forgotten tradition of the seniority of the Suzdal throne, and when they were defeated in this, they sought aid and protection from the new center of Great Russia, the growing and powerful city of Moscow. These determining factors in the history of the Nizhegorod frontier are clearly reflected in the life of Dmitri of Suzdal.

An end to disorder in Nizhegorod could come only through submission to Moscow and recognition of its supremacy. Grand Prince Dmitri of Suzdal established his ruling authority in Nizhni Novgorod with Moscow's aid, and he closely identified himself with the grand princely rule in Moscow, cementing these ties by giving his daughter Evdokia to Dmitri of the Don in marriage.

From this time on, our sources reflect Nizhni's growing commercial and military significance, although they do not permit us to look as closely as we would like into the organization of life in the Nizhegorod land. Thus as evidence of substantial trade through Nizhni we have only the chronicle accounts of attacks by Novgorod river pirates and the reports of clashes between the forces of Russian princes and the Kama Bulgars. Novgorod pirates made two raids on Nizhni during Dmitri's reign in Nizhegorod. In 1366 they slaughtered a "great multitude" of local Nizhegorod people as well as visiting Tatar traders (Tatars, besermen, and Armenians), plundering their wares and sinking their boats, and then proceeded down the Volga to the Kama River to pillage Bulgar towns. Novgorod pirates made another, larger raid in the 1370's. They devastated Kostroma and Nizhni Novgorod, attacking both bersermen and Christian traders in these cities, plundered towns on the Kama River, and then went farther down the Volga, taking what they could from traders along the way. Undoubtedly the growth of trade along the Volga through the main center of Nizhni Novgorod was the occasion for this increased activity on the part of roving pirate bands.

The development of new trade along the Volga naturally raised the question of the defense of the Volga towns and volosts and their trade route against Tatar, Bulgar, and Mordvian attacks. This commercial activity was therefore closely connected with colonization, which from the middle of the fourteenth century pushed slowly but surely down the Volga River. Dmitri's reign in Nizhegorod was marked by new clashes between Russian forces and the non-Russian world of the lower Volga. The Tatar prince Bulat-Timur had become a dangerous neighbor to the southeast, building up power as he seized control of almost the whole of the Volga waterway and consolidated his dominion over the Kama estuary. As it happened, however, his power was to crumble at the first real test. In 1367 he made a raid on the Nizhegorod volosts along the Volga, plundering as he went, but was stopped by news that Boris and Dmitri had come out against him. The Russian host pursued the Tatars, caught up with them, and defeated them. Bulat-Timur managed to escape to the land of the Golden Horde, but was executed there by command of Khan Aziz.

The internal breakdown of the Tatar world made the struggle against its separated forces much easier. The military activities of the Russian princes along the Volga did not at first bring them face to face with the main power of the Horde; from time to time they were even supported by the Khan. Thus after the death of Bulat-Timur, Prince Dmitri's troops marched against the Bulgar prince Asan in the company of the Khan's envoy, drove Asan out, and placed another prince (Makhmet Saltan) on the throne of the Bulgar principality. Several years later a Russian army again marched against the Bulgars, this time against both the "Bulgar princes" Asan and Makhmet, and without the participation of the Khan's envoy. Dmitri's troops brought the Bulgar princes to submission with the help of an army sent by Grand Prince Dmitri of Moscow, and forced the Bulgars to pay a heavy tribute. The Bulgar princes were also compelled to "seat a darug and customs officer" of the Russian

Grand Prince alongside their own Bulgar tax officials, which meant, as far as we can tell from this rather cryptic report, that they were made subject to the Grand Prince's agents in matters of trade, and had to acknowledge his right to certain customs revenues. A Nizhegorod host also marched with the troops of Dmitri of Moscow against the Mordva, laying their land waste in revenge for Mordvian attacks on Russian volosts.

The military activity of the Russian princes along the eastern frontier of Great Russia gave rise to the construction of a stone fortress in Nizhni Novgorod in the 1370's, and of a new dependent town called Kurmysh on the Sura River. The grand principality of Nizhegorod was more and more closely bound to the grand principality of Great Russia as military pressure was directed against enemy peoples along the Volga, and the Nizhegorod frontier was inevitably brought into greater conflict with Tatar forces. In this Nizhegorod acted not as an independent political power, but as the cutting edge of the forces of Great Russia. Great Russia's conflict with the Tatar world was coming to a head just as the Golden Horde, torn apart by internal strife, found a leader and unifier in the person of the temnik Mamai.

From about the middle 1370's the Nizhegorod frontier could again feel the weight of the Golden Horde behind the activity of its hostile neighbors. Mamai's envoys approached Russia with powerful military detachments, and Russian settlers clashed with Mamai's troops as the latter moved northward. In one encounter the men of Nizhegorod killed some members of a Tatar troop and took the rest as prisoners back to Nizhni, where they too were killed. The Tatars responded with a raid on the Nizhegorod volosts and the destruction of its settlements on the east bank of the Riana River. A year later Grand Prince Dmitri of Moscow set out "in great strength" to defend the city of Nizhni in response to a summons from its prince, who had just learned that the Tatar prince Arapsha was marching against him with his host. Arapsha halted his advance, and then attacked the Russian host by surprise with the aid of Mordvian princes, who led the Tatars to the Russian position by a secret route at a time when Dmitri had returned to Moscow and the Russian forces had lowered their guard. The Russian host was cut to pieces on the Riana River in August, 1376, and Nizhni was left

completely exposed. Dmitri fled to Suzdal; the Nizhegorod boyars retreated to Gorodets. The city was captured and sacked by
the combined Tatar and Mordvian forces, and its volosts
plundered.

The Russian princes paid off their score with the Mordva as
soon as the Tatar raiders withdrew, but the threat of further
Tatar attacks remained. As a first step in his massive assault
on Russia, Mamai sent an army on a raid against Nizhni in
1378, when its prince was absent from the city. Again the city
was without defense, and after refusing a tribute offered to them
by Dmitri the Tatars again burned Nizhni and plundered its
surrounding area. This raid was evidently connected with an
expedition against central Russia being carried out at the same
time by the Tatar prince Begich, whom Grand Prince Dmitri
met and defeated on the Vozha River in the Riazan principality.
This partial success did not accomplish anything, however. Mamai
now controlled all the forces of the Golden Horde, and his
power hung over Russia like a black cloud. Although Nizhegorod
had received more active support and protection from central
Great Russia than Riazan, like Riazan it was too exhausted by
the blows it had received to join energetically in Grand Prince
Dmitri's expedition against Mamai. Moreover, it was reasonable
to expect a Tatar diversionary thrust against Nizhni like the
raid of 1378, when Begich marched against Russia through the
volosts of Riazan. We do not find Nizhegorod princes with
their troops in the Russian army at the battle of Kulikovo. Subsequent events were to bear out Nizhegorod's apprehensions.

Tokhtamysh's invasion began with a move against Nizhni
Novgorod. The Khan sent his army into the Bulgar lands, where
Russian merchants were seized and plundered and their vessels
used by the Tatars as a means of crossing the Volga. Prince
Dmitri of Nizhegorod made haste to pay homage to the Khan.
There could be no thought of resistance without major support
from Moscow, and of course at this time Dmitri of Moscow was
himself unable to prevent Tokhtamysh from marching on Moscow. Vasili and Semeon, the two sons of Dmitri of Nizhegorod,
had gone to the Khan with their father's gifts and had remained
in the land of the Horde, evidently as hostages. After his campaign Tokhtamysh allowed Semeon to return to his father with

a Tatar envoy, but he took Vasili Kirdiapa back with him to
the land of the Horde. For a time Russia was humbled again
before the Tatar power, and the Nizhegorod princes were eager
to go to the land of the Horde to assure the Khan of their
submission. Prince Dmitri of Nizhegorod was apparently approaching the end of his life, and the Khan was faced now with
the need to choose a successor. Dmitri's sons and brother were
all in the land of the Horde at the time of his death in the summer
of 1383. His eldest son, Vasili, remained there for several more
years as a hostage, while the yarlik to the grand principality
of Nizhegorod was bestowed on his uncle Boris, who then
returned to his throne accompanied by his son Ivan and his
nephew Semeon.

The grand principality of Nizhegorod was coming to an end.
Its successes and failures under Dmitri were in fact only a
reflection of the changes in the strength and position of Moscow
at the center of the Great Russian grand principality. The enthronement of Boris with the Khan's sanction must be regarded
as in part a consequence of the temporary weakening of grand
princely power in Great Russia following the invasion by Tokhtamysh. Dmitri's sons Vasili and Semeon, brothers-in-law of
Grand Prince Dmitri of Moscow, had evidently been removed
from their votchina, the throne of Nizhegorod, without the
Grand Prince's consent. Their relations were made plain after
Kirdiapa's escape from the Horde. The escape itself was not a
success. He was intercepted on his way north by a Tatar envoy
and once more imprisoned. In the following year (1387), however, Khan Tokhtamysh allowed him to return to Russia, granting him full right to the throne of Gorodets. His brother Semeon
was apparently ruling at Suzdal, under the sovereignty of his
uncle Boris. On Vasili's return the two brothers began working
at once to regain the grand principality of Suzdal-Nizhegorod,
and like their father they found support against Boris in Grand
Prince Dmitri of Moscow. The massing of the Suzdal and
Gorodets hosts with Muscovite reinforcements at the gates of
Nizhni forced Boris to yield to his nephews and return to
Gorodets. Boris had yielded only under pressure from Grand
Prince Dmitri of Moscow, however, and when Dmitri died he
journeyed at once to Tokhtamysh, spent over a year in the land

of the Horde courting the Khan's favor, and then returned again with the yarlik to the grand princely rule of Nizhegorod.

Our sources give us no clue as to why Boris found himself so constantly at odds with the Grand Prince of Moscow. It may be that the mere fact of his acceptance of the Khan's yarlik without the consent of the Grand Prince of all Russia was sufficient cause. The general situation in eastern Europe, coupled with the conditions on the eastern frontier of Great Russia, whose special significance in the growing conflict with the Tatars and other alien powers had already been made clear during the reign of Dmitri of the Don, made it absolutely essential to eliminate every element of dissension in Nizhegorod's political life. Recent events had shown that the Horde also clearly appreciated the strategic importance of Nizhni as a military post controlling the Volga River route and the eastern flank of the line along the Oka. A series of heavy Tatar blows had brought Nizhni Novgorod into a state of complete subjection to the power of the Khan.

The relations established by Grand Prince Vasili I of Moscow with the Horde gave him an opportunity to resolve the Nizhegorod question without a clash with the Khan and even with his help. This time the Grand Prince did not simply join Dmitri's sons Vasili and Semeon in their fight to overthrow their uncle Boris. Instead, he "laid aside his kissing of the cross" to Prince Boris, traveled to the land of the Horde "to pay homage and offer many gifts" to Khan Tokhtamysh, and asked that the grand principality of Nizhegorod "be taken from Grand Prince Boris" and granted to himself. Vasili's lavish gifts and subservience won him the desired yarlik, and he returned to Russia with the Khan's envoy and a Tatar detachment. We do not know the precise details of this affair, but evidently the change was well prepared for in Russia, since according to the chronicles the Nizhegorod boyars renounced Boris at once and delivered him in chains to the Muscovite and Tatar leaders. Vasili arrived in Nizhni after Boris' seizure. The matter was not yet ended, however. An envoy from the Khan came to Vasili with a summons to appear once again in the land of the Horde, and it was after this journey that Vasili finally returned with a confirmation of his title to Nizhni Novgorod and Gorodets.

Our collections of chronicles present this story of the collapse of Nizhegorod's independence in brief and fragmentary passages. We get only a vague hint of the fate of Dmitri's sons Vasili and Semeon, in a reference to Semeon's flight to the Horde. We have no direct information as to how the authority of the Suzdal-Nizhegorod princes was constituted after their subjugation by Moscow. We do know that they retained possession of Suzdal, probably in accordance with the Khan's wish, while Nizhni Novgorod and Gorodets were transferred to the grand principality. Certainly there could be no restoration of the former relationships when Nizhni and Gorodets were detached from Suzdal and turned into possessions of the grand principality of all Russia. The bond that had held the grand principality of Nizhegorod together was now broken.

Boris spent the rest of his life in Suzdal, and was buried there "in his otchina." We may assume that his nephew Vasili Kirdiapa lived with him in Suzdal, and also Semeon when he returned from the Horde. But this hint of a shared rule of the Nizhegorod principality had no real basis in fact. Once confirmed in his possession of Nizhni Novgorod, Vasili I of Moscow acquired the rights of the "entire principality and rule" connected with it. Dmitri's sons, of course, were unable to reconcile themselves quietly to the loss of what they considered to be their own otchina. The dispute flared up again almost at once. Again we must take note of the complete inadequacy of the information provided in our various chronicle texts; not, of course, because of some simple accident in the preservation or copying of these sections of the chronicles, but rather because of a quite obviously deliberate suppression of facts by later Muscovite redactors in the name of their peculiarly Muscovite outlook.

Soon after Boris' death his nephews fled from Suzdal to Khan Tokhtamysh in the land of the Horde. Grand Prince Vasili of Moscow almost intercepted them on the way, but they managed to escape. Once again, however, the Horde was troubled by its own internal disorders and was in no position to become directly involved in Russian affairs. We hear nothing more of

Vasili Kirdiapa, and the chronicles even disagree on the date of his death.

Semeon tried to continue the struggle with Tatar assistance. In October, 1395, he succeeded in capturing Nizhni with the aid of a Tatar host. The city was devastated. As the Grand Prince's army approached, the Tatars retired, and again Semeon went to the land of the Horde. Grand Prince Vasili I sent his host farther down the Volga under his brother Iuri, and for three months this force waged war in the Bulgar land. The chronicles note that no one could recall when Russia had penetrated so far into Tatar territory. Semeon found sanctuary and military support among local Tatar forces controlling the Mordva and Bulgar volosts, which were enjoying increased independence as the power at the center of the Horde declined. His stubborn and violent efforts to regain his otchina lost momentum when the Kazan kingdom began to take shape and Semeon betrayed the Russian cause, going over to the Tatar side to fight against Russia. The presence of a claimant to the Nizhegorod throne on the side of the border Tatars only heightened the tension on Russia's eastern frontier. Vasili I of Moscow made a number of attempts to take Semeon prisoner; this had been the purpose of Iuri's expedition. Now the Grand Prince sent his men to seize Semeon's family, who had managed to join him. Semeon's wife and children were indeed captured and taken back to Moscow. The hopelessness of his position and the seizure of his family finally forced Semeon to negotiate with Grand Prince Vasili I and submit to him. He was exiled to Viatka, where he died in December, 1401.

The grand principality of Nizhegorod had been created by the conditions on the Great Russian frontier, and it retained power and importance as long as it was involved in defense or the seizure of new land for colonization or in military campaigns aimed at the protection of Russian trade routes. The transfer of these tasks into the stronger hands of the Grand Prince of Russia led to the rapid decline of Nizhegorod's independence; the "grand principality" was left in ruins as a minor votchina possession of the Prince of Suzdal. For a time it led also to an outbreak of adventurism on the part of the Nizhegorod princes, for which there was ample opportunity in the unstable conditions of frontier life. Semeon's cousins Ivan and Daniel (the sons of Boris) followed in their father's footsteps. These two "hereditary lords" of Nizhni Novgorod marched on Russia in 1411 with the "Kazan princes" (actually the princes of the towns of Bulgar and Zhukotin), and defeated the army that Grand Prince Vasili I sent out against them under his brother Peter. Later Prince Daniel led the Tatars in a raid on Vladimir, and the capital city of the grand principality was pillaged. Our chronicle collections speak about these events in an obscure way and with obviously deliberate omissions. The attack on Vladimir by Daniel's commander Semeon Karamyshev and the Tatar prince Talych, whom "Daniel had brought up secretly," could have been successful only with the backing of Nizhni Novgorod, which Daniel must have occupied after defeating the Grand Prince's army there. The chronicle texts do not mention the capture of Nizhni, however, and minimize the results of Daniel's victory. Later information about Daniel would seem to confirm our interpretation of the vague and superficial account of the matter given in our sources. In 1402 the Nizhegorod princes traveled to the land of the Horde to appear before Khan Zeleni-Saltan, Tokhtamysh's son, and returned "having been confirmed in their otchina." In 1414 Grand Prince Vasili's brother Iuri marched against Daniel and his brother Ivan in Nizhni Novgorod. The Suzdal princes fled down the Sura River, Iuri was greeted submissively by Nizhni's inhabitants and boyars, and the city was taken without a battle. Daniel and his brother eluded capture beyond the Sura. Putting these pieces of evidence together, we have reason to say that Prince Daniel ruled in Nizhni from 1411 to 1414. Two years later Boris' sons appeared in Moscow in full submission. Then in 1418 they fled again, and there is no further reference to them in our chronicle collections. Grand Prince Vasili placed Ivan's son Alexander in Nizhni, and gave him his daughter in marriage, but Alexander died soon after, and Nizhni Novgorod was henceforth administered by the Grand Prince's deputies.

The old traditions of independence and political power lived on for a long time in the minds of the Suzdal princes. Grand Prince Vasili's son had to deal with new pretenders to the throne of Suzdal, which greatly complicated the civil strife in

Moscow in the early years of his reign, and later Suzdal princes were to be the foremost upholders of the traditions of udel princes. But the grand princely claims of Suzdal had lost their basis both in history and in the events of real life on the eastern frontier of Great Russia. These claims were to survive only in the general outlook and strictly local stature of later Suzdal princes.

Chapter
VIII

Grand Princely Policy Under the Successors of Ivan I

Ivan Kalita's successors pursued the task of defining and enlarging the meaning of grand princely power, building on his achievements. The information we have about life in the princely court of Moscow is too limited, of course, for us to assess exactly the direct and more or less conscious role played by the grand princes themselves in the subsequent working out of this political enterprise. It should not be exaggerated. The rather small number of facts we do have at our disposal for answering this question suggest rather that Ivan's successors were secondary and for the most part passive figures in that task of molding political relationships and sociopolitical thought which was eventually to make the grand principality of Great Russia a major state power. The testament of Semeon the Proud is a perfect illustration of the narrow "family" concept of princely domain. The pale figure of the "tender and quiet" Ivan II remains in the shadow of the events of his time, while his son Dmitri was little more than an instrument of the

policies of the metropolitan court and Moscow's boyar class
during his boyhood years, and displayed no brilliant individuality
in later life. Behind the official actions of the grand princes
stood other guiding forces that built up the grand principality
in both theory and practice in a way often contrary to the
traditions of votchina domain characteristic of the ancient
princely law. Very gradually and hesitantly, these old traditions
of princely domain were to give way to new attitudes and views
among princely and other social classes until the votchina principle itself, having broken down the political organization of Great
Russia through the practice of udel domain with its consequent
division into separate votchinas, would at last, in the form of a
developed monarchy, become the foundation of the autocratic
sovereignty of the Muscovite tsars. This process of gathering
power around a single center was deeply influenced by Great
Russia's foreign relations under the pressure of the need for
self-defense and the desire to establish relations with other lands
which would secure its own trading, colonizing, and (in the
broad sense) national interests. Thus Moscow's first real success
in its struggle for greater and more centralized political power
was the emergence of the grand princes of Russia as leaders in
Great Russia's international affairs, both in war and in peace,
accompanied by corresponding modifications of the internal
organization of princely rule and of the princes' mutual
relationships.

The foundations of this new statehood were gradually
fashioned under the constant pressure of the great international
struggle being carried on in all parts of eastern Europe. A
review of the main events in this struggle is necessary for any
explanation of the formation of the Great Russian state, since
the struggle affected the Russian state in the most fundamental
way over a period of centuries.

Semeon the Proud inherited the form of grand princely
sovereignty developed by his father. His grand princely rule
was ratified by the Khan's yarlik, which gave all the Russian
princes "into Semeon's hand." It was also acknowledged at the
"great assembly of all the Russian princes" held in Moscow in
1341. In the treaty made with his brothers "on his father's
tomb," Grand Prince Semeon secured his position of leadership

in the external affairs of the Moscow principality and in the disposition of all its military forces, and also won acceptance of the right of the eldest prince in the house of Moscow (and "Grand Prince of all Russia") to a number of tax revenues "by reason of his seniority." This too, of course, enhanced his primacy. Beyond the borders of the Moscow principality, however, his real power extended only over the minor princes of the Vladimir grand principality. The Rostov, Iaroslavl, and Belo-ozero princes were part of the Grand Prince's "downstream host," and Constantine of Suzdal is also mentioned. On the other hand, the grand principality of Nizhegorod, which came into being during the reigns of Semeon and Ivan II, set itself in opposition to the grand principality of Vladimir. There was also an increase in the independence of Riazan, which insistently demanded a definition of its territorial and political powers "by means of fixed bounds" setting Riazan apart not only from the "Moscow votchina," but also from the "grand principality." Tver, Moscow's ancient rival, was already established as a territorial and political entity in its own right, and in its difficult position between Moscow and Lithuania it was now inclined more to enter into alliances with the latter. In its struggle to prevent the grand princes of all Russia from interfering in its own local affairs and from subjugating Tver to Moscow, supposedly on the grounds of the traditional seniority of the grand princes of Vladimir but actually on the basis of a "seniority" deeply marked by the elements of monarchy, Tver now sought the active support of the Lithuanian grand principality.

All the attention and energies of Russia's grand princely power were being focused on its affairs in the west. The gathering of west Russian lands under Olgerd's rule seemed to contemporaries to be part of a broad design to subjugate the whole of Russia. Border clashes between Moscow and Lithuania were from the beginning complicated by the disturbing effect these conflicts had on internal relations on both sides. Russian princes sought protection in eastern Russia from Lithuanian attack and seizure, and by his flight to Semeon in 1345 Olgerd's brother Iavnuti had shown the way to those who were dissatisfied with the Grand Prince of Lithuania. But more and more acutely Moscow was feeling the effects of the support that local separatist tendencies in Pskov, Novgorod, Tver, and Riazan found in their ties with Lithuania. Olgerd's political horizon took in much of northeastern Russia, and in the light of later events he anticipated the policies of Vitovt. Family relationships can give us some idea of the way Lithuania exercised influence on decisions and interprincely relations in Great Russia. Olgerd was related to the princes of Tver through his wife and to the princes of Nizhegorod through his daughter, and Gedymin's son Liubart was related to the princes of Rostov. Of course these ties did nothing to ease the tension or hostile rivalry between the two grand principalities. The two powers came together in battle in the very first year of Semeon's reign, over the question of Smolensk. Olgerd had failed in his attempt to seize Mozhaisk, recently a volost of Smolensk, even though his raid was made at a time when Semeon had apparently not yet returned from the land of the Horde. Olgerd's thrust on Mozhaisk was in answer to a campaign against Smolensk the year before made by Russian armies and a Tatar host under the leadership of Tovlubi. Lithuania's claims to Smolensk and the northern Chernigov volosts had met with opposition in these areas, with the forces of resistance counting on help from Moscow (and the Grand Prince) as well as from the Tatars. The minor local princes were being drawn toward Moscow. Thus a Russian campaign in 1340 included the princes of Druts and Fomin; and in 1341 the Prince of Briansk gave his daughter to Prince Ivan II of Moscow; while Semeon's unsuccessful father-in-law, Prince Feodor of Dorogobuzh, at one point occupied the throne of Volok.

Olgerd pursued his goals—the strengthening of the ties between Smolensk and Lithuania, which had been broken in the time of Gedymin, and the extension of Lithuanian power over the region of Chernigov—with the utmost caution and always with an eye on Moscow. In 1349 he finally decided to prepare a decisive blow against Moscow, and sent his brother Koriad to Khan Janibeg to persuade the latter to join him in a campaign against Semeon, but Semeon's envoys convinced the Tatar ruler that Olgerd, having laid waste the votchina of the Grand Prince of Russia and thus also the Khan's ulus, was in fact one of the Khan's enemies, and the Lithuanian envoys with their druzhina

were delivered into Moscow's hands. Olgerd was forced to abandon his broad plan and conclude a new treaty with Semeon
in order to obtain the release of Koriad and his men. We do
not know the price Olgerd paid for this "peace and friendship,"
but a year later we find Semeon mounting another offensive
against Smolensk. Olgerd's envoys met Semeon on the river
Protva, and some peaceful settlement was made. Semeon continued his advance on Smolensk, however, moving with his
army to the Ugra River, where the Smolensk envoys came out
to meet him. After eight days of negotiations Semeon dispatched
his own envoys to Smolensk and made peace with its leaders.
It may be that this treaty of 1350 guaranteed Smolensk's position
as a domain completely independent of the Grand Prince of
Lithuania. Only after the death of Grand Prince Semeon did
Olgerd find opportunity to wage war freely on the lands of
Smolensk and Chernigov. Our information concerning affairs
in Smolensk after Semeon's time is very meager, but it does give
us grounds for saying that by this time it was no longer Tver,
but the power of the grand prince of Russia (now concentrated
in Moscow), that had taken over the defense of Great Russia
on its western frontier.

This task was vastly complicated by the relationships existing
within Great Russia. The armed forces of Tver and Riazan,
Pskov and Great Novgorod did not take part in Semeon's
campaigns. Moscow's relations with Novgorod were extremely
strained, as they were also under Ivan Kalita. Semeon's journey
to the land of the Horde on his father's death and his successful
negotiations there, leading up to the Khan's confirmation of his
right to the grand princely throne, must certainly have involved
great expense as well as promises of increased payments of the
Tatar outlay, surcharges, and "gifts" in the future. Indeed,
Semeon's first action on his return was to send men into the
Novgorod volosts of Torzhok "to collect tribute," and there
his deputies and "armed tribute collectors" began to "act with
violence." The men of Novi Torzhok sent a complaint to Novgorod with an appeal for help. The Novgorod boyars then
appeared in Torzhok, arrested the Grand Prince's agents, prepared the city for defense, and sent an envoy to Semeon with
the protest: "You have not yet sat on your throne among us,

and already your boyars are acting with violence in our land."
But the preparations for war with the Grand Prince led to a
revolt on the part of the people of Novi Torzhok, who did not
have faith in Novgorod's strength and were afraid of the Grand
Prince's power. They drove out the Novgorod boyars and freed
the Grand Prince's deputy and his tribute collectors. Semeon
did in fact arrive in Torzhok "with all the downstream host,"
and the men of Novgorod, although they had mustered all their
forces for battle, sent envoys to the Grand Prince and "concluded a peace" with him "according to the ancient treaties and
with a grant of full freedom to Novgorod." For this they paid
the Grand Prince a "general levy" from the whole Novgorod
land, plus a thousand rubles from the city of Novi Torzhok. A
deputy of the Grand Prince was installed in Novgorod.

But Semeon lacked the power to act as a leader in the defense
of Novgorod and Pskov against German and Swedish attacks.
Once again in the early 1340's, as it had done before under
Prince Alexander, Pskov reacted to the constant threat of
invasion by the Livonian order of knights by "renouncing"
Great Novgorod and the Grand Prince of Russia and "giving
itself up" to Lithuania, acclaiming Olgerd as its prince. Olgerd
then placed his son Andrei on its throne. But neither Andrei
nor his father was in a position to lead the defense of Pskov
personally or to assign adequate forces for its protection. Only
the small druzhinas of the Lithuanian deputies aided Pskov in its
struggle with the Germans, so that in the end Pskov rejected
Prince Andrei and again found itself in the camp of Olgerd's
enemies. In the same year (1348) the leaders of Pskov renewed
their political ties with Great Novgorod in the Treaty of Bolotovsk, in which Pskov was no longer defined as Novgorod's
dependent town, but instead as its autonomous "younger
brother." This treaty also restored the bonds between Pskov
and the grand principality of all Russia.

Novgorod had accepted the deputy sent by Grand Prince
Semeon in 1341. In the years that followed, Semeon was occupied with the administration of the downstream land and with
his relationships with the Khan and Lithuania, and five years
passed before he came to Novgorod and "sat on its throne."
The situation on the Novgorod frontier was increasingly threat-

ening. Olgerd controlled Pskov and was contemplating a move against Novgorod. Olgerd's activities in the south soon absorbed all his energies and attention, however, and he then lost Pskov. But this only meant that a still more serious threat for Novgorod appeared from another direction: Sweden.

King Magnus II of Sweden had begun to wage war in the Izhor region, had taken Orekhov, and was threatening to march in full force against Novgorod. Novgorod's appeal to Semeon for help was in vain. Semeon was delayed for a long time by his "dealings with the Khan," and then after having started out for Novgorod he changed his mind and returned to Moscow. Semeon's brother Ivan was sent to Novgorod, but was not received, and returned to Moscow "without the bishop's blessing or the homage of the people." The men of Novgorod had to fall back on their own forces; only Pskov, which had just secured a new position for itself in the treaty of Bolotovsk, gave Novgorod some military assistance. Novgorod had to beat back the Swedes and defend itself from German attack relying almost wholly on its own forces. The Grand Prince of Russia could not afford to send his troops to the far northwest. It was at this time that Olgerd was engaged in his attempt to win the Horde to his side against Semeon; then came Semeon's expedition against Smolensk. The threat of attack by Lithuanian forces influenced all the decisions of Russia's grand princely power.

This threat clearly undermined the effectiveness of grand princely power in Novgorod. It had also greatly complicated Semeon's relations with Tver. Here, with the death of Prince Constantine of Tver in 1345, a conflict flared up between the princely houses of Kashin and Kholm which completely tangled the already complex web of Tatar, Lithuanian, and Muscovite political interests. The disorder seemed quite beyond the strength of Russia's grand princely power, and for a time blind centrifugal forces were in control. The shock that brought these forces sharply into focus was Semeon's unexpected death in the plague of 1353.

The period from 1350 to 1370 was a time of serious crisis in Moscow's position of leadership in northeastern Russia. Immediately after Semeon's death, Prince Constantine of Nizhegorod, with the support of Novgorod, began to "strive for the grand princely rule" with Semeon's brother Ivan. It was not until just before Constantine's death that he and Ivan were reconciled, and for a year and a half the men of Novgorod "were not at peace with the Grand Prince," although "there was no wickedness between them." We may conclude from this that the Grand Prince had no power either to punish the Novgorod boyars for their action in going to the support of Constantine, or to bend them to his will. Their relations were restored only when Ivan and Constantine were reconciled. After Constantine's death his son Andrei acknowledged Ivan II as his elder brother. After Ivan's death in 1358 a new conflict for the grand princely rule was to break out and be resolved only with great difficulty.

Equally confused were Moscow's relations with Riazan, which had seized Lopastna and was insistently demanding a settlement of the Moscow-Riazan border. In Tver the civil strife was moving in the direction of a victory for the princes of Mikulin, who were hostile to Moscow and sympathetic to Lithuania. Behind all these upheavals in the life of Great Russia lay the constant threat of intervention on the part of Lithuania or the Horde. Again the control of Great Russia's external relations had slipped out of the hands of her grand princes, and individual territorial powers were setting themselves against Moscow's central authority, defending and extending their independence, arbitrarily defining their own relations with the outer world, and seeking alliances and aid from the Horde and Lithuania in their efforts to resist the demands of the grand princes of Great Russia.

II.

During this difficult time in Moscow's history a powerful political figure was administering the affairs of the grand principality of Great Russia. This was Metropolitan Alexei. His leadership in matters of grand princely policy carried the sovereign power of the grand princes safely through the serious difficulties that arose in the reign of the "gentle and quiet" Ivan II and during the boyhood of his son Dmitri. As head of the Russian church, Alexei injected a particular ideological content into this grand princely policy, giving it a religious and also a nationalistic character. The very fact of Alexei's accession to the metropolitan see was a major victory for the grand princely court. Here was a representative of Moscow's ruling class, a man drawn from the Grand Prince's own court, at the head of the Russian episcopate. Alexei was a son of the boyar Feodor Biakont, who had come from Chernigov to enter the service of Prince Daniel (son of the illustrious Alexander Nevsky), and of whom it is said in the genealogies that during the reign of Ivan I "all Moscow was behind him," which may be taken to mean that Feodor was at that time tysiatsky of the city. These genealogies trace a number of boyar families from Biakont, for example, the Pleshcheevs, the Fomins, the Zherebets, and the Igniatevs. None of these families stood in the uppermost boyar class, but they all occupied a secure position in the class of Moscow's free serving men, some of whom, like Fomin, held office in the court of the Metropolitan. Alexei's brother Alexander (from whom the Pleshcheev family traced its origins) and his nephew Danilo were boyars of Grand Prince Dmitri of the Don.

Alexei may be regarded as a child of the Grand Prince's court and its class of boyars and free servants. There is evidence that he was a godson of Ivan Kalita. His early entry into a monastery at the age of twenty did not sever his connections with society and was not a withdrawal from the world. Alexei was enrolled in one of the monasteries in Moscow and his acceptance of monastic vows was evidently intended as a preparation for future service in the episcopate. From 1340 on he stood at the head of the metropolitan court and its administration, as deputy metropolitan. With the consent of the Grand Prince, Metropolitan Theognost prepared Alexei to be his successor, and familiarized him with the work of the metropolitan see in the more than twelve years of his service as deputy. In December, 1352, Theognost consecrated Alexei as bishop of Vladimir, and with Grand Prince Semeon he sent a legation to the Patriarch of Constantinople to secure Alexei's appointment as his successor. Alexei's candidacy for the office had by this time been very well prepared both in Constantinople and in Russia. The Muscovite legates returned after both Theognost and Semeon had died, bringing Alexei a summons to go to Constantinople for his consecration. Grand Prince Ivan II quickly arranged for Alexei's journey, on the eve of his own departure for the land of the Horde to receive the yarlik to the grand princely throne. Alexei then spent almost a year at the Patriarch's court in "vain attempts" to obtain consecration, and only in June, 1354, was he sent on his way with formal jurisdiction over the metropolitan see of Kiev and all Russia. The Russian bishops sent letters to the Patriarch acknowledging Alexei as worthy of the metropolitan office—all but Bishop Moisei of Novgorod. Whatever its causes may have been, the opposition of the Bishop of Novgorod was a serious matter, not only for the metropolitan court, but also for the Grand Prince, who was fighting for power in the western regions of Great Russia against the influence exercised there by the Grand Prince of Lithuania. The whole question of Muscovite-Lithuanian relations was bound up more and more with the ecclesiastical-political policies of the Russian metropolitan court, as a consequence of Olgerd's energetic and successful expansion into Russian territory in the 1350's and the inevitable effect this had on the relations of the west Russian church with the Moscow-Vladimir metropolitan see.

As head of the Russian church and the guiding force behind the political decisions of the Great Russian grand principality, Alexei was immediately confronted with a whole series of major and challenging problems. He had occupied his see as the Grand Prince's candidate; now fate had made him the virtual ruler of the Great Russian grand principality. In all his relations, whether with ecclesiastical or secular powers and whether within Great Russia or beyond its borders, Muscovite political interests became inseparable from the tasks and concerns of the metropolitan court.

The certificate of consecration that Alexei received from the Patriarch defined the relationship of the Russian metropolitan to the patriarchal court very carefully and precisely. An important document in the history of Russian-Byzantine church relations, the certificate emphasized the large size and population of the metropolitan district of Kiev and all Russia. The administration of this see was an important part of the work of the ecclesiastical authorities in Constantinople, and for this reason the Patriarch had hitherto consecrated for the Russian jurisdiction only the most capable and trustworthy men drawn from the ranks of the Byzantine clergy, carefully selecting those who were not only gifted and vigorous preachers, but also well acquainted with ecclesiastical and civil law. The patriarchal certificate took note of the fact that Alexei's appointment was an exceptional case, justified by his unusual personal qualities, by his excellent preparation for the office, and by the almost unanimous testimony on his behalf from Greeks as well as Russians, beginning with Grand Prince's Semeon and Ivan II and Metropolitan Theognost himself. The certificate made it plain that such an exception must not be taken as a precedent. On the contrary, the patriarchal see was in future not to allow or approve of the consecration of any Russian-born candidate to the Russian metropolitan jurisdiction. The certificate stressed the point that this present exception was quite extraordinary and not altogether without hazard to the church. It therefore set forth measures designed to guarantee and provide for the close supervision of Alexei's activities by the Byzantine church. Alexei was required to travel personally to Constantinople every two years, or to send a reliable representative from among the clergy of his see, for the purpose of receiving final judgment on all major ecclesiastical questions that may have arisen in Russia. The whole document is marked by a fear of excessive independence on the part of a metropolitan who had not been drawn from the ranks of the clergy in Constantinople and was not bound to the Byzantine world by ties of education and tradition. The vision of a strong national Russian episcopate obviously alarmed the patriarchal see. This was understandable. Constantinople was well aware of the fact that the Russian metropolitan court had taken up a position in support of and thus subject to the local secular power. The Patriarch must see to it that the Russian metropolitan would be not simply a representative of Russian political interests but above all a representative of the power and authority of the Patriarch and his Sacred Council, a servant of the Greek Orthodox Church, which according to Byzantine tradition was governed by the Patriarch in Constantinople.

As it happened, however, the relations between Alexei and the Patriarch developed far differently than this certificate anticipated. After his consecration Alexei journeyed to Constantinople only twice, and apparently sent his legates only at times

when he himself felt the need to ward off some blow being
prepared by his enemies or stood in need of patriarchal influence
to support his own policy. And indeed this support was essential
to him in his work of consolidating the power of his see.

Growing dissatisfaction with Moscow's new strength and its
sweeping claims was inevitably reflected in ecclesiastical circles
under a metropolitan so closely allied with Moscow's grand
princely policies, especially under one who had been named to
this office by the Grand Prince and had come to it from Moscow's boyar class, only to take into his own hands the actual
administration of the grand principality. Alexei formally confirmed the bond between the metropolitan see and the grand
princely rule by obtaining permission to transfer the metropolitan residence from Kiev to Vladimir. He remained metropolitan
"of Kiev and all Russia," since Kiev retained its significance as
the location of his original seat, but Vladimir was defined as the
Metropolitan's second see and the place of his residence and
burial. The manner in which this question was resolved con-
formed perfectly with the basic interests of both the Metropolitan
and the Grand Prince. For both it was absolutely essential that
the Russian metropolitan see retain its "Kievan" character even
as the residence was moved to the north. The loss of Kiev as a
center of church life would threaten the loss not only of Kiev
itself and the southwestern dioceses, but also those of Tver,
Novgorod, and Pskov, not to speak of Smolensk; these areas
were not yet prepared to regard Moscow as the primal city
in ecclesiastical matters. It is almost certain that this question
of the composition of the metropolian see of Kiev and all Russia
confronted Alexei from the time of his very first visit to
Constantinople.

The political destinies of southwestern and western Russia
naturally led to an attempt to free the ecclesiastical administration
of these areas from subjection to metropolitan authority in Moscow. Efforts had been made to create a special metropolitan see
in Galich at the beginning of the fourteenth century, and it was
not until 1347 that Theognost had managed to bring to an end
what had come to be the separate jurisdiction of Galich. Soon
after this, however, and only shortly before Alexei's consecration
as metropolitan, the question of the separation of the west Rus-

sian church from the northern metropolitan see was again raised
sharply. Even before Theognost's death, Theodoret appeared in
Constantinople as a candidate for a new west Russian metropolitan see. Unsuccessful in Byzantium, Theodorit took advantage
of the existing schism between the Byzantine and Bulgarian
churches and went to Ternov, where he was consecrated as
metropolitan by the Bulgarian patriarch, and then occupied the
see of Kiev. The fact that Theodorit's action coincided with
the conflict between the Metropolitan in Vladimir and the
Bishop of Novgorod further complicated an already difficult
situation. Patriarch Philotheus of Constantinople acted decisively.
He sent letters to the west Russian dioceses ordering Theodorit
removed from office under penalty of complete expulsion "from
the Christian state," and threatening similar excommunication
to all who should accept him into communion. Bishop Moisei of
Novgorod received two patriarchal letters almost simultaneously,
one calling for his obedience to Metropolitan Alexei, the other
containing an account of the Theodorit affair and forbidding him
to accept Theodorit's authority or to enter into communion with
him. After this a patriarchal exarch who had been sent to Russia
in the company of Metropolitan Alexei presided at the latter's
enthronement over the see of Kiev and all Russia, evidently at
Kiev itself. Theodorit disappears from the scene and we know
nothing more about him.

We cannot fail to see the hand of Grand Prince Olgerd behind
Theodorit's attempt. The main reason for its failure was Theo-
dorit's consecration by the Bulgarian patriarch, and this ecclesias-
tical difficulty was removed by advancing a new candidate for the
see of Kiev: Roman, who was related to Olgerd's wife, Uliana.
There is evidence that in the role of metropolitan designate,
Roman made an attempt to occupy the see in Kiev prior to
Alexei's return from Constantinople in the summer of 1354.
Roman was rejected by the church in Kiev, and then appeared
before the Patriarch in Constantinople after Alexei's consecration
and departure for Russia. Roman was made metropolitan of
Lithuania, assuming jurisdiction over the dioceses of Novgorod,
Polotsk, and Turov. He was not satisfied with this, however,
and soon began to "manifest wider ambitions," trespassing on
the rights of Metropolitan Alexei. A dispute arose over control

of Kiev and the south Russian dioceses as well as Tver. The quarrel was brought before a patriarchal council under Patriarch Callistus, after the fall of Philotheus, and Roman appeared in Constantinople to defend his claims. Alexei was also summoned. The council confirmed the fact that Alexei had been made metropolitan of Kiev and all Russia and declared that he should retain this title. As metropolitan of Lithuania, Roman was given jurisdiction over "the dioceses of Little Russia" (the Ukraine) with the exception of Kiev, Kiev still being regarded as the prime seat in Alexei's see. This fundamentally inconclusive resolution of the question shows that the patriarchate was unwillingly yielding to Lithuanian pressure. In a later decree issued in Philotheus' second reign as patriarch, the unity of the Russian see was restored, with the explanation that this division had been permitted for a time in response to many pressing demands. There can be no question about the existence of these "pressing demands," since whenever the church's life is ordered on a national basis, each political power demands its own special episcopal organization and will not readily accept ecclesiastical jurisdiction from beyond its borders. Byzantium, of course, found it difficult to accept fully the canonical validity of such nationalistic tendencies, without denying the supranational or ecumenical character of its ecclesiastical empire; on the other hand, Moscow and Lithuania found themselves in stubborn conflict over the very much unresolved questions of territorial and political boundaries, and every attempt to define the limits of their ecclesiastical jurisdictions led inevitably to "perplexities and disorders." Olgerd insisted that his Lithuanian-Russian state was not subject to Alexei's spiritual authority and that the west Russian church had been acknowledged as an independent metropolitan see. The patriarchal council began to fear that if Alexei's authority were upheld, it might well mean the complete breaking away of the Lithuanian-Russian state from the Greek church, or at least from the Byzantine patriarchate, as had happened in the days of Theodorit. Callistus had attempted a compromise, but this certainly did not end the dispute.

Roman rejected the inconclusive settlement, refused to accept his certificate of appointment to the see, and left Constantinople. Arriving in Kiev, he proclaimed himself metropolitan of Kiev and all Russia, and he retained possession of Kiev until his death in 1361.

The fact that the northern metropolitan could not exercise authority over the Orthodox churches on the borders of the Lithuanian-Russian state threatened the grand principality of Great Russia in two ways. The west Russian metropolitan district inevitably came to support the policies of the Lithuanian grand princes in the same way that the metropolitans in Vladimir supported Muscovite political interests. In addition, episcopal authority centered in Kiev was used by the rulers of Lithuania to consolidate their control over Russian lands and extend Lithuanian influence beyond the borders of lands under their direct rule. The battle between the two grand principalities on the soil of Tver had begun even while the two metropolitans were still in Constantinople. Later, in 1358, when Alexei made an attempt to establish his authority in southern Russia (an attempt in which both the church and the grand principality paid out large sums of money), Roman made use of his own ecclesiastical and political connections in Tver to make a visit to that city, precisely as an answer to Alexei's action in the south, which Roman naturally regarded as a "trespass" within his jurisdiction.

III.

All these ecclesiastical-political relationships were closely bound up with the fundamental antagonism between Moscow and Lithuania. The struggle between Metropolitans Alexei and Roman was played out against the background of Olgerd's basic policy, which from 1350 through the 1370's was aimed at a vigorous expansion to the east. This eastward expansion began at the time when the power of the Great Russian grand principality was paralyzed by internal conflict, following the succession of Semeon by his brother Ivan II. Lithuania occupied Rzhev. Lithuanian armies made war in the Briansk and Smolensk volosts, and the civil strife that broke out in Briansk after the death of its prince set the stage for its seizure by Olgerd. As soon as "the Grand Prince of Lithuania began to rule over Briansk," Metropolitan Roman seized episcopal authority there too, in a volost that was actually within Alexei's jurisdiction. In Moscow, and as a result of Muscovite influence in the court of the Patriarch also, Roman was accused of prompting Olgerd's attack on Alexin, one of the Metropolitan's towns. From this time Orsha and Belaia were in Lithuanian hands, and within three years Olgerd had also taken Mstislavl. A tight ring of Lithuanian forces surrounded the principality of Smolensk, and now Lithuanian power was a constantly increasing threat to the borders of Tver and Moscow.

The Smolensk principality was to survive for another fifty years, swinging its allegiance back and forth between Moscow and Lithuania. The Chernigov region, however, which had become broken up into minor votchina principalities and scarcely felt the influence of the center of Great Russia, now became the arena for Olgerd's major successes. The western part of this territory came under the direct control of the Lithuanian princes in the 1360's and 1370's. It was here that the principalities of Olgerd's sons came into being: the principality of Briansk and Trubchevsk under Dmitri, the principality of Chernigov and Novgorod under Koribut, and the principality of Starodub and Rylsk under Narimont's son Patriki and his successors. In the eastern part of this region the descendants of Rurik reigned as minor princes in their otchinas, and Olgerd made every effort to turn these princes into vassals, sometimes by force and sometimes through the ties of marriage. In a letter to the Patriarch of Constantinople, Olgerd spoke of Kaluga and Mtsensk as his volosts, and complained of their seizure by Moscow following the "treachery" of Olgerd's service prince Ivan of Kozelsk. For a long time eastern Chernigov was to continue to waver between Moscow and Lithuania, and for many years its princes were to serve first one, then the other, and at times even both sides at once.

In the 1350's and early 1360's the grand principality of Great Russia was too oppressed by its own internal political crisis to resist the pressure from Lithuania with much energy. The chronicle collections give us only scattered hints of such an attempted resistance. There is a reference to a battle between a combined Tver and Mozhaisk host with Lithuanian forces over control of Rzhev, and a report of a campaign by Smolensk troops against Belaia. Lithuania's eastward advance greatly complicated and indeed disrupted relationships within Great Russia. In Tver the local conflict between the princely houses of Kashin and Mikulin was caught up in the struggle between Lithuania and Moscow over Tver, and from 1366 the Mikulin (Lithuanian) party gained the upper hand. Grand Prince Mikhail of Tver became engaged in a stubborn and prolonged war with Moscow, and this secured Olgerd's freedom of action in the Chernigov region. Olgerd gave aid to Mikhail only occasionally and in limited ways, directing his main energies to the south and to the support of Keistut against the Germans.

Once again these hostilities between Moscow and Tver took the form of a struggle for the grand princely rule of all Russia, although this was probably not true at the outset, since Moscow and not Tver took the first aggressive action. With Metropolitan Alexei as its guiding spirit, the grand princely power in Moscow had just ended its conflict with Prince Dmitri of Suzdal, with Dmitri and the other lesser princes of Great Russia being brought to "do the will" of Grand Prince Dmitri, the son of Ivan II. Great Novgorod had also acknowledged his grand princely authority, although it insisted on the right to exercise "its ancient freedom, without giving offense," and then on its right to take its own defensive measures against external enemies. Moscow's relations with the grand principalities of Tver and Riazan continued to be strained.

As it gained in power, Moscow was becoming more aggressive. One of the chroniclers, undoubtedly writing in the tradition of Tver, has made this eloquent entry under the year 1367:

In the same year Grand Prince Dmitri walled up the city of Moscow with stones, and began to accomplish many things; he brought all the Russian princes to do his will, and those who did not submit he began to afflict, among them Prince Mikhail of Tver, and for this cause Prince Mikhail withdrew to Lithuania.

Moscow's attempt to take the Tver grand principality out of Mikhail's hands and restore it to Vasili of Kashin was not successful. Tver repulsed the attack of the Moscow-Kashin host, and in the fall of that year Mikhail returned from Lithuania with Lithuanian reinforcements and made peace with Dmitri of Moscow and his uncle Vasili. Dmitri's counselors and boyars did not trust Mikhail, however, and tried to trap him, "inviting him to come to Moscow with a promise of safe-conduct." When this attempted seizure also failed, Moscow moved its armies against Tver once more, and in the face of this show of strength Mikhail was forced to flee again to Lithuania. Olgerd came to the aid of his brother-in-law in 1368. He sent a large Lithuanian army to join the regiments of Tver and Smolensk, and in a swift move they took Dmitri by surprise, demolished his outposts, and appeared before the walls of Moscow before the Grand Prince's host could be mustered. The princes of Moscow withstood the siege, but Dmitri was forced to yield to Mikhail. His "intrusion" into Tver had led to a war with Lithuania, and Dmitri now decided to take further aggressive action. His armies waged war in the Smolensk volosts, and advanced toward Briansk. Dmitri's counselors felt that Olgerd's campaign against Moscow in 1368 had been only a warning thrust, and that, occupied as he was in the south and west, Olgerd would not concentrate sufficient forces on his eastern border for a decisive battle with Moscow. Another attempt was made to subdue the Prince of Tver. The Grand Prince's army advanced again into Tver, in violation of the recent treaty, and again Mikhail withdrew to Lithuania. In September, 1370, Grand Prince Dmitri personally led an army into Tver "with much strength," capturing Zubtsov and Mikulin (the votchina city of the Prince of Tver) and "utterly subduing its boyars and leading men."

It may be supposed that the general strategy of the war against Moscow which was to consume so much of Mikhail's energies in the years to come was drawn up in Vilna. At this same time the Golden Horde began to emerge from its state of anarchy, under the strong hand of Mamai. Mikhail went from Lithuania to visit Mamai, and obtained a yarlik to the grand princely rule of Vladimir. He then made his way into Russia accompanied by the Khan's envoy. Grand Prince Dmitri set up barricades on all routes, however, and only a message of warning from friends in Russia saved Mikhail from being taken prisoner. Again he had to take refuge in Lithuania, where Olgerd was mounting another campaign against Moscow. Mikhail's recent failure to take possession of Vladimir did not put a stop to this campaign, and Olgerd marched with Mikhail to the gates of Moscow, but now the massing of the Great Russian host under Andrei's son Vladimir (of Serpukhov) with reinforcements from Riazan led to the declaration of a truce, and then a treaty calling for "perpetual peace." Mikhail was bound by this treaty, but this new setback did little to check his ambitions. Again he journeyed to the land of the Horde to make yet another attempt to secure possession of the grand princely throne on the strength of the Khan's yarlik and with the help of a Tatar envoy.

He soon returned to Tver with the desired yarlik and the envoy Sarykhozha, and from there tried to occupy the capital city of Vladimir. But Grand Prince Dmitri took his own measures. He had made the boyars and people of Vladimir kiss the cross in a solemn promise that they would neither join Mikhail nor let him occupy Vladimir's throne. Now with lavish gifts he bribed the Khan's envoy to come over to his side, and Mikhail found himself abandoned. The Grand Prince of Lithuania renewed the truce with Moscow, guaranteeing a new "perpetual peace," and entered into an alliance of marriage with its ruling house. Dmitri's subsequent journey to the land of the Horde resulted in the return to him of the grand princely yarlik, and the refusal of any further aid to Mikhail on the part of the Tatars. The desperate nature of Mikhail's position seemed only to redouble his energies. He evidently made an attempt to take the grand principality by sheer force, with the hope that success would end Olgerd's hesitation and restore their alliance against Moscow. He managed to occupy several of the Grand Prince's cities—Kostroma, Uglich, Mologa, Bezhetski Verkh—placing his deputies in them, and won at least qualified acceptance in Great Novgorod.

None of these successes brought any permanent results. During this time Dmitri was with the Horde, preparing a heavy blow against his rival. Continuing to strengthen his position in Russia, Mikhail now sent his son Ivan to obtain support from the Horde for his various concerns. Dmitri of the Don was able to take advantage of Mikhail's heavy debts to the Horde and in effect "redeemed" the young prince by paying Mikhail's obligations and having Ivan delivered into his hands. He then returned to Russia in triumph "and great honor, with a new confirmation of his grand princely rule," and with young Prince Ivan held as a hostage. Without Tatar or Lithuanian support, Dmitri's enemies in Russia were helpless. Moscow's dispute with Riazan was quickly ended with the defeat of Riazan's army near Skornishchev, the flight of Prince Oleg, and the installation of Prince Vladimir of Pronsk on Riazan's throne. It is true that Oleg reoccupied his throne soon after the withdrawal of the Grand Prince's army, but from now on he was a submissive Muscovite vassal.

Mikhail's position was more difficult than ever. Again he found support in Lithuania, and led Lithuanian troops against Pereiaslavl Zalesky, Dmitrov, and Kashin, subjugating his uncle Vasili of Kashin just as the latter was about to go over again to the side of Moscow. Mikhail lost Novgorod, however, which was not prepared to accept his deputy once Mikhail had lost the yarlik to the grand principality of Vladimir and all Russia. With these same Lithuanian forces Mikhail went on to capture Torzhok, but it was not long before his deputies were driven out of this city too by the men of Novgorod. Mikhail countered with a campaign against Torzhok in which the city was completely devastated. Mikhail's Lithuanian support was beginning to place Dmitri in a dangerous position. The Lithuanian host evidently appeared on Great Russian soil, and now Olgerd joined it "with much strength." Olgerd's defeat in battle near Liubutsk in June, 1372, put an end to any further military action in Russia on his part and led to a new peace with Moscow. Dmitri had succeeded at last in separating Great Russia's external affairs (its relations with the Horde and Lithuania) from his struggle with the Prince of Tver. As it happened, however, his relations with the Tatars were still too strained for this to be a very stable peace. The events of 1372 were significant chiefly in that they brought an end to the war with Lithuania and deprived Mikhail of any further Lithuanian support.

In the next several years all of Dmitri's attention was to be centered on the relations of the grand principality to the Tatar world. The Nizhegorod and Riazan frontiers were kept in a state of almost constant alarm, and were quite incapable of sustaining the defense against Tatar attack without aid from the region that lay behind them to the northwest. The rulers of Great Russia repeatedly moved their armies up to the line of the

Oka and beyond, "on guard against the Tatar hosts," and sent military aid also to Nizhni Novgorod. Little by little the ground was being prepared for the decisive clash between Great Russia and the Tatars which was to come on the Kulikovo Plain.

Having lost the support he once had in his alliance with Lithuania, Mikhail was now compelled to limit himself to internal matters for a time. He strengthened the fortifications of Tver and made peace with Dmitri. He ransomed his son Ivan from prison in Moscow, recalled his deputies from the cities of the grand principality wherever they were still in residence, and entered into a "settlement" with Moscow. We do not know the terms of this settlement, but in any case it turned out to be little more than an armistice. Mikhail took advantage of Dmitri's difficulties to strike another blow, resting his hopes this time on the growing hostility between Moscow and the Horde of Mamai. In July, 1375, a Muscovite traitor named Nekomat went to the land of the Horde and brought back to Mikhail a new yarlik to the throne of Vladimir with a Tatar envoy to support and enforce it. Mikhail immediately "laid aside his kissing of the cross" to Dmitri, sent his deputies to Torzhok, and dispatched a host against Uglich.

These actions were to bring about his final downfall. Dmitri stirred up the whole of Great Russia against Tver—all the "downstream" princes joined him, as well as the Novgorod regiments, and even a troop from Kashin. Mikhail's trust in Tatar and Lithuanian support was misplaced. He was forced to sue for peace and agree to a settlement that brought a full stop to the struggle he had carried on for so many years. In this treaty Mikhail acknowledged himself as Grand Prince Dmitri's "younger brother," on a par with Vladimir of Serpukhov; submitted to the conditions of a subordinate solidarity with the Grand Prince; renounced (in his own name and in the name of all the Tver princes) every claim to the grand principality and Great Novgorod; accepted the independence of Kashin; and was compelled to subordinate his dealings with the Tatars and Lithuania to the policies of the grand principality. In short, this treaty made only one distinction between the Grand Prince of Tver and an udel prince of Moscow, to the effect that disputes between the two grand princes should be submitted for arbitration by a third party to Grand Prince Oleg of Riazan in the event that their boyars could not reach agreement, as was the case also in disagreements between Tver and Muscovite citizens in the "common court." Dmitri's votchina of Great Novgorod was included in this treaty with Tver, and thus the relations between Tver and Novgorod were regularized in this treaty and not by a separate agreement. Mikhail's domains in Tver were set over against the territory of the Grand Prince's Moscow votchina, the grand principality as a whole, and Great Novgorod. A unique twofold political structure was established. Not long before this, in Dmitri's treaty with the Lithuanian envoys in 1371, Mikhail had been inscribed "under the name of" Grand Prince Olgerd. Now he was compelled to lay aside his kissing of the cross to Olgerd and acknowledge Tver's organic relationship to the grand principality of Great Russia, in which he occupied a position similar to that of the udel prince of Serpukhov, but the political identity of the grand principality of Tver (or the "Tver state," as it will be called later) remained a vital reality. In fact, the treaty of 1375 was only a preparation for the eventual restoration of the Tver principality as a part of the grand principality of Great Russia; it did not actually establish this relationship. But the acceptance in principle of the need for such a relationship was a major step in the territorial and political self-definition of Great Russia.

IV.

In these difficult years of intense external and internal struggle, the grand princely power of Great Russia found an energetic and gifted leader in the person of Metropolitan Alexei. Alexei had made it clear that he was determined to pursue the policies of Metropolitans Peter and Theognost, to strengthen the ties between the ecclesiastical activities of the metropolitan see and the policies of the Grand Prince of Moscow. Under his leadership this connection was very clearly defined, thanks to the unique position he occupied in Moscow, which a Greek writer has described (evidently on information received from Muscovite envoys) in the following terms:

. . . before his death Grand Prince Ivan II not only placed his son Dmitri, the present grand prince of all Russia, under the Metropolitan's care, but also entrusted the Metropolitan with the administration and welfare of the whole principality, for he was unable to trust anyone else because of the multitude of enemies without, standing ready to attack from every side, and of enemies within who envied his power and sought opportunity to seize it.

With the metropolitan see occupied by a product of Moscow's princely court, a child of its boyar class and a pupil of Metropolitan Theognost, the traditions of the metropolitan court as they had developed under Maxim were now strengthened and defined in the spirit of Muscovite policy. Alexei's personal "desire to protect the child entrusted to him and preserve the country and its sovereign power in his name" only added a greater comprehensiveness to the basic goal of his activity: "to bring unity to the secular power" and at the same time preserve the unity of the Russian see. This linking of the task of the secular power with the ecclesiastical policies of the metropolitan see considerably broadened the scope of grand princely rule and had the effect of attaching a particular ideology to its policy. At the end of the 1360's and the beginning of the 1370's Alexei found himself involved not only in the administration of affairs within Great Russia, but also in a fierce struggle with his Lithuanian adversaries in Byzantium. In 1370 and 1371 there was a lively correspondence between Russia and Constantinople in which Alexei very vigorously upheld a point of view that was to become extremely important in the subsequent development of Muscovite political theory.

This point of view was crystallized in the heat of polemical thrust and counterthrust. The double aspect of Alexei's activity —as political leader and as head of the church—inevitably provoked criticism, all the more so in that his ecclesiastical authority was used to serve the interests of the secular power, as for example in the Nizhegorod affair to which we have already referred. Alexei succeeded in reunifying the metropolitan see of Kiev and all Russia on the death of the Lithuanian metropolitan Roman in 1361. The political significance of his ecclesiastical authority was increased both inside Great Russia and in the west

Russian lands. In addition, Metropolitan Alexei managed not only to overcome the Patriarch's original distrust, shown at the time of his consecration, but even to gain considerable influence in the patriarchal court. He convinced Philotheus that it was in the interests of the patriarchate for the Russian metropolitan to occupy this position of broad power and influence. The Patriarch gave this view strong support, and only insisted that the power of the Russian metropolitan be seen as a reflection of the sacred authority of the ecumenical patriarch. "The metropolitan whom I have appointed," Philotheus wrote in a letter to Grand Prince Dmitri, "bears the image of God and shall stand for me in your presence, so that anyone who is obedient to him and desires to show him love, honor, and respect will be manifesting his obedience to God and to our wishes, and the honor offered to him will pass on to me, and through me directly to God Himself." The Metropolitan's position was thus supported by the whole force of patriarchal authority: ". . . whomsoever the Metropolitan shall bless or favor for any good cause, for his piety or devotion, that one I too shall hold as blessed, and so it shall be with God also."

This readiness of the Patriarch to give full support to the Metropolitan's actions acquired extraordinary significance as the latter's blessings and interdictions became effective political weapons in Russia. In a communication addressed to Alexei the Patriarch expressed his "special love for and perfect trust in him," and urged him to turn to the patriarchal see not only in ecclesiastical matters but also in matters of state, since in the Patriarch's words, "this great and numerous people" which looks to Alexei "as its father, teacher, and intercessor before God, and depends on him in all things," stands in need of "much care and supervision." No documents have come down to us in which Dmitri or Alexei address themselves to the Patriarch in matters of state, although the existence of such correspondence is suggested in the Patriarch's letter. The Metropolitan and the Grand Prince had evidently written to him about Russian princes who had broken their vows and treaty agreements.

The struggle waged by Alexei and Dmitri for the grand princely sovereignty of Vladimir and all Russia had recently come to an end; the princes of Suzdal, Rostov, Starodub, Galich, and Beloozero had all been brought "to do the Grand Prince's will." The struggle with Olgerd had continued, with Olgerd being joined by Prince Sviatoslav of Smolensk and Mikhail of Tver. Sviatoslav became a Lithuanian vassal and was inscribed "as one man" with Grand Prince Olgerd, while the Prince of Tver was inscribed as acting "in the name of" Olgerd. A new clash with Riazan was also now at hand.

Under Alexei's leadership the grand princely authority strove to give political substance to the traditional seniority of the grand prince of all Russia—"to bring unity to the secular power." Local principalities and at least a part of the Russian population regarded this policy as an "encroachment" on their ancient rights and tolls, but then it could be defended as a strengthening of the real solidarity of the Russian princes "in friendship and alliance" under the Grand Prince's leadership. In their correspondence with the Patriarch, the Grand Prince and the Metropolitan can be seen as vigorous proponents of the union of the princes in a brotherly and subordinate solidarity with the Grand Prince, to be consolidated by treaty settlements and the mutual exchange of sacred vows in the face of disobedient violators of the peace.

In addition to his letters in reply to the Grand Prince and the Metropolitan, the Patriarch sent two other communications addressed to and intended to be circularized among all the Russian princes. In one he called upon the princes of the Russian land in general terms to manifest the proper respect, honor, obedience, and submission to the Metropolitan, who was to be regarded as the representative of the Patriarch's pastoral authority, indeed as the Patriarch's personal deputy, and as their "father and teacher of souls." In the other letter he drew certain practical conclusions from these general premises and indicated their political applications. The Patriarch had adopted the view of the grand princely government regarding the necessary solidarity of all the princes of the Russian land as confirmed in treaties "by sacred vows and by the kissing of the venerable and life-giving cross," but with a special interpretation and application of this theory which had evidently been suggested to him by Moscow. The whole purpose and meaning of the union of all the Russian princes under the supreme command of the Grand

Prince of all Russia lay in their joint struggle against "the enemies of the cross," against those alien to the Russian faith who "godlessly worshipped the element of fire"—i.e., Lithuania. Grand Prince Dmitri's war with Olgerd was represented as a holy war being waged in the name of the God of Christianity, as a fulfillment of their obligation "to fight on God's side and destroy His enemies." Among the Russian princes, however, there were those who had "despised and violated God's commands and their own vows and promises," and had united with the "unclean" Olgerd against Grand Prince Dmitri. For this cause, the Patriarch noted, the Metropolitan had laid an excommunication upon them, which he confirmed, since "they had acted contrary to the interests of Christian society." But then he also made it clear that the excommunicated princes ought to be forgiven by the Metropolitan and reconciled with the great army of the church as well as with the Grand Prince against "the enemies of the cross," that is, against Grand Prince Olgerd and the Lithuanian forces. After this general letter a special communication was sent to Prince Sviatoslav of Smolensk advising him that his alliance with Olgerd against Dmitri was a "grievous sin against his faith and the Christian religion," and urging him to repent sincerely and make his peace with the Metropolitan.

Metropolitan Alexei was adapting and making good use of the concepts of the Byzantine school. The idea of a "sacred Christian state" (against which Olgerd's Russian allies had so grievously sinned that they deserved excommunication) was used to give spiritual significance to Moscow's policy. Orthodox Russia was seen as a part of the political body of the church. The sovereign power of the Grand Prince and of the Metropolitan of all Russia were seen as the instruments of its organization and defense.

That the whole ideological content of Patriarch Philotheus' letters, insofar as they referred to Russian affairs, originated in the letters he received from Metropolitan Alexei is clear from the break in the Patriarch's relations with the Russian metropolitan in the years immediately following.

Philotheus' attack on the Russian princes who had made alliances with Olgerd brought a sharp response from the Grand Prince of Lithuania. Olgerd countered the accusations brought against him by Alexei by charging that the grand principality of Great Russia had violated a peace sealed by a kissing of the cross with its treacherous seizure of his brother-in-law Prince Mikhail of Tver, with its confiscation of the domains of his son-in-law Prince Boris of Nizhegorod, and with its attack on another son-in-law, the Prince of Novosil. Olgerd accused the Metropolitan of "blessing the Muscovite bloodshed" and of approving those among his serving princes who had violated their kissing of the cross and had gone over to the side of Moscow, releasing them from their vows. Olgerd also reproached the Patriarch for allowing Alexei to do all these things with his own blessing. Contrary to the general line of the Patriarch's letters, Olgerd maintained that the Metropolitan ought to have blessed those Muscovite princes who went to the aid of Lithuania in its war with the Germans. Olgerd ended with a complaint that the Metropolitan had neglected his jurisdiction in west Russia and a request that the Patriarch appoint another metropolitan for this region, having jurisdiction over "Kiev, Smolensk, Tver, Little Russia,[31] Novosil, and Nizhni Novgorod."

Even more weighty objections to preservation of the ancient unity of the Russian metropolitan see came to the Patriarch from another direction. King Casimir of Poland turned to the Patriarch at this time with a request that he consecrate a special metropolitan for Galich, since as part of the territory under his rule "Little Russia was now perishing without God's law." Casimir threatened him with the assertion that a refusal would force him "to baptize the Russians in this region into the Latin faith."

A party of envoys from Grand Prince Mikhail of Tver also appeared in Constantinople with complaints against Alexei and a demand that he be called to trial. The Metropolitan's excommunication had affected Mikhail and his brother princes in Tver as well as the bishop of the Tver diocese. The political struggle in Russia was now having a direct influence on its ecclesiastical

31. The term Little Russia, first used in the late thirteenth or early fourteenth century, was applied to Galich, Volhynia, and the Turov land for both political and ecclesiastical matters.—ED.

affairs. Metropolitan Alexei equated faithfulness to the church with faithfulness to a vow of allegiance to Dmitri's grand princely sovereignty.

The Patriarch was confronted with a link between the policies of the Muscovite sovereign and the activities of the Russian metropolitan which had actually made him an instrument of Muscovite strategy. The role he had been playing threatened to compromise patriarchal authority not only in the Lithuanian state, but also in the whole sphere of Lithuanian influence, not to speak of the threatened loss of Russian lands to the Latin church.

In May, 1371, Patriarch Philotheus ratified the election of Bishop Anthony, Casimir's candidate, as metropolitan of Galich, with the transfer into his jurisdiction of the dioceses of Vladimir, Peremysl, Turov, and Kholm, all of which were then under Polish rule. In August of the same year he sent a letter to Alexei informing him of the accusations brought against him. The Metropolitan "had established himself in one place, leaving all other areas without pastoral leadership, instruction, or spiritual supervision," and had not visited Little Russia for a number of years. The Patriarch also censured him for his "sinful dispute with Prince Mikhail of Tver." The Metropolitan was also informed of Anthony's consecration to the metropolitan see of Little Russia. Finally, he was summoned to trial, at which he might appear in his own name or in the person of representatives sent to Constantinople to act for him. Having taken this step, however, the Patriarch then proceeded with great caution, avoiding open conflict with either side and the resulting subordination of his actions to the interests of one or the other. His letters to Alexei describe the charges against him in a tone of self-justification. The trial was at first postponed, and in the end never took place. The idea of a formal trial in the patriarchal court was never accepted in Moscow, and subsequent events led to the overthrow of this combined Lithuanian-Tver attack on the Great Russian grand principality. Evidently information received in Constantinople from an envoy who had been sent to confer with the Metropolitan in Russia made clear to the Patriarch the true relations between the two warring powers and the need to take these relations into careful consideration. The

Patriarch suddenly changed his tone, and no longer insisted on the appearance of the parties at a trial. Letters were sent to Alexei and Mikhail urging them to be reconciled and even proposing that his envoy and representative, who was then visiting the Metropolitan in Russia, act as mediator. Grand Prince Mikhail was advised in plain terms to ask forgiveness of the Metropolitan and strongly urged to uphold his kissing of the cross to Dmitri. The Patriarch was forced to rest content with fresh explanations and self-justification now on the part of Alexei, who countered the charges of Casimir and Olgerd by pointing to the latter's uncompromising hostility as the reason why he could make no personal visits to Kiev and his western dioceses, a hostility that had developed as a result of Great Russia's refusal to let Olgerd pursue his ambition "to seize power for himself in its land."

The Patriarch had yielded—for a time. In fact, however, these actions did not reflect his real attitude toward Alexei. Even now he repeatedly reminded Alexei that he had been made metropolitan "not of one part but of the whole of Russia," and that it was his duty to show all the princes of the Russian land the same pastoral love rather than "to love some as his own sons" and others not. The Patriarch urged Alexei to deal dispassionately with the grand princes of Moscow and Lithuania and to be reconciled with Olgerd, so that the way might be opened for him to exercise his jurisdiction over the west Russian church and "the people bearing Christ's name" then living under Lithuanian rule. Thus not only in west Russia but also in Byzantium there were forces opposing the tendency to transform the metropolitan see of Kiev and all Russia into a national, Great Russian institution that would support the power of Great Russia's grand prince and act as an instrument of its secular policy. These forces will hold the upper hand under Alexei's successors, under the influence of the general course of political life in eastern Europe, until the final victory of the national concept of the Russian church and its metropolitan see is signaled by Alexei's canonization under Metropolitan Jonas, the heir to his ideas.

It had been hoped that the "perpetual peace" made between Olgerd and Dmitri and then Dmitri's peaceful settlement with Mikhail would put an end to this whole episode. Olgerd, however, could not reconcile himself to the presence of the Russian church in the lands under his rule, and the matter of Alexei's relationship with the west Russian dioceses was soon raised again with new force, under circumstances that are only very obscurely hinted at in our chronicle sources. Evidently Olgerd took advantage of the way the question had been handled in the Patriarch's conciliatory letters and confronted Alexei with a blunt demand: Go to Kiev and make your residence there, or agree to the election of a special metropolitan for the see of Kiev. Alexei's refusal occasioned new accusations and denunciations in the Patriarch's court. Philotheus sent his trusted monk Cyprian to Russia to make an investigation. Contradictory reports of subsequent events in the patriarchal court make it practically impossible for us to arrive at a clear picture of what actually happened after that or to come to any correct understanding of the actions taken.

Philotheus' earlier representative in Russia, Johan Dokian, had gone to Moscow, and once there had evidently yielded rather easily to Alexei's influence. The new patriarchal legate now went to Lithuania and carried on his negotiations with Alexei from there. At his urging the west Russian princes sent envoys to the Metropolitan, promising to end the dispute and accept him as their pastor, and Cyprian persuaded Alexei to make the decision to go to Kiev. The Metropolitan's preparations for this trip were interrupted, however, and the journey was not made, since after his meeting with the Lithuanian envoys Alexei "felt that the Patriarch's instructions and the Lithuanian request were hostile to his interests, and he flatly refused to make the journey to Kiev." New and more violent complaints and charges were brought against Alexei, all with the aim of securing a special metropolitan for Kiev. With Olgerd at their head the west Russian princes decided not to accept Alexei even if he wanted to come to Kiev, and sent a communication to the Patriarch asking for the consecration of another man. Their candidate must certainly have been acceptable to Byzantium, since he was none other than the legate Cyprian. Their petition naturally contained a number of charges against Alexei, and of course earlier correspondence offered ample material for this purpose. The impossibility of reconciling Alexei's political activity with his title of "Metropolitan of all Russia" was all too clear. The Patriarch yielded to the appeal of the Lithuanian princes and on December 2, 1375, Cyprian was consecrated as metropolitan of Kiev and Lithuania. This did not signify a formal division of the metropolitan see into two parts; the Patriarch reaffirmed the position that there could be only one metropolitan over Russia, as required "by law, by the common good, and by custom," and in order that Cyprian should assume the whole Russian metropolitan jurisdiction on the death of Alexei.

These arrangements were typical. The patriarchal court genuinely valued the unity of the Russian metropolitan see. This unity was a guarantee, essential to the interests of the patriarchate, against the complete nationalization of the Russian church and its subordination to the secular powers of either of the two grand principalities. A metropolitan of all Russia who would deal with the political interests of both Moscow and Lithuania in a nonpartisan way and thus be independent of these secular powers in the formation of his own policy was regarded by the patriarchate as the best support for its own "ecumenical" authority. Constantinople knew how to bring men to this office who would not follow in the footsteps of Alexei, but would pursue the path of compromise between the see of Moscow-Vladimir and that of Kiev and all Russia which had already been marked out in the later letters of Patriarch Philotheus.

The political situation in eastern Europe after the middle of the century—in the closing decades of the fourteenth century and in the early years of the fifteenth century—had created conditions favorable to this departure from the tradition established under earlier Russian metropolitans, and this rupture in the Russian jurisdiction brought about serious disorders in the church following the death of Metropolitan Alexei on February 12, 1378. Olgerd had died the year before, and in the general situation created by these events the division of the see marked the beginning of Great Russia's open conflict with the Tatar world and the growing power of Lithuania under Vitovt.

V.

We have tried to demonstrate the important role played by Metropolitan Alexei in the gradual development of a national-political ideology out of those modest beginnings that can be seen in the concept of an "all-Russian" collection of chronicles which originated in the metropolitan court at the beginning of the fourteenth century. After a temporary success, the attempt to understand the political struggle in terms of the medieval theory of a conflict between "Christendom" and "the enemies of the cross," and to use this theory in a way that would serve the interests of the Great Russian grand principality, had apparently miscarried. It had left deep marks, however, on the political thinking of the Muscovite aristocracy. It had struck too deeply into Russian soil to pass without a trace. From the end of the 1360's the struggle with Lithuania became much more intense, and in the mind of the Russian people it took on the character of a national fight for survival. In the letters of Alexei it even acquired the significance of a confessional war, which only heightened the aggressive element in grand princely policy and placed an even more clear-cut ideological foundation under the claims of the grand principality to control over the destiny of the whole of Great Russia. This ideology had the effect of drawing Russia's grand princely power onto a historical stage that extended well beyond the borders of the little world of Great Russian politics and, what was of the utmost importance at that time, it confronted the Orthodox people of west Russia with an urgent choice. Where were they to find the center of their national life, in Vilna or Moscow? We have no evidence of a conscious or precise articulation of this question on the abstract level in the writings from this period. A number of characteristic events in the history of Lithuanian-Great Russian relations do bear witness, however, to a wavering of west Russian powers between Moscow and Lithuania which at the time made understandable the warning given to the Lithuanian assembly by Casimir that it should not rely too heavily on Russian elements in the Lithuanian state, since it must recognize how hostile they were to Lithuania, how ready they were to help bring about not simply a victory over Lithuanian elements in the event of a war with Moscow, but their complete annihilation.

Olgerd's death marked the beginning of a time of unrest and internal decline in the grand principality of Lithuania. Violent disputes arose among the Lithuanian princes over Olgerd's transfer of the heart of his domain—the Vilna region and the lands of White Russia—to Jagiello and his brother (his sons by a second marriage), together with the throne of Vilna and its title to seniority among the princes of Gedymin's line. The older brothers rose up against Jagiello. After having been assigned to Pskov by his father, Olgerd, Andrei had left Polotsk and gone to his city, and the men of Pskov had received him as their prince by a kissing of the cross. Now Andrei went over to Grand Prince Dmitri of Moscow, who "received him in friendship." For some time Andrei continued to rule in Pskov as a vassal of the Grand Prince of Great Russia. Anticipating support among the Lithuanian princes, Dmitri decided to make war. In 1379 his regiments marched with his cousin Vladimir and Prince Andrei of Pskov against the Chernigov land, and Andrei's brother Dmitri "did not enter into battle against them," but left his city of Trubchevsk with his family and boyars and went over to Moscow, where he was received "in friendship" and was given Pereiaslavl Zalesky as his domain, "with all its revenues."

The Russified Lithuanian princes looked to Moscow for help in regaining their principalities and unseating Jagiello. But their hope that the campaign of 1379 marked the opening of a major offensive on the western frontier was not realized. The clouds of a new Tatar invasion had been gathering over Russia since the early 1370's. The storm was about to break, and efforts to withstand it now absorbed all of Russia's forces. The situation on the west remained extremely tense, and indeed danger threatened equally on both sides. There were bound to be fears that the forced peace with Tver of 1375 would be set aside by Mikhail at the first opportunity. Dmitri of Moscow was also involved in "hostility" with Novgorod, a conflict that was ended only at the beginning of 1380. To the east the Riazan and Nizhegorod lands were being subjected to a series of Tatar attacks. At the end of the seventies Dmitri was by no means in control of all the forces of Great Russia, and only the internal weakness of the Lithuanian principality saved him from a worsening of the situation on his western borders, and in fact gave him the vitally needed support of some of the Lithuanian-Russian princes at the moment of his clash with Mamai. On the other hand, the defection of Olgerd's two sons to Moscow was bound to alarm Jagiello and appear as a sign of the wavering of the whole northern Chernigov region. If we remember that another of Olgerd's sons, Dmitri Koribut of Novgorod-Seversk, was also hostile to Jagiello, and that his rule was not accepted by Prince Liubart of Volhynia or the sons of Koriatov in Podolsk, we may understand the significance for Jagiello of the threat from Moscow. In this time of internal strife in the eastern (Russian) sections of the Lithuanian state, the Russian grand principality stood ready to support every element dissatisfied with the power of Vilna and to seize those domains that by ancient tradition had been connected with the grand principality of all Russia.

The internal affairs of both grand principalities were closely bound up with their long-standing rivalry and hostility. The Moscow-Lithuanian conflict had always been connected with the work of internal political organization which each state carried on independently, and this fact made war a bitter but inevitable factor in the process of their territorial and national self-definition.

Their struggle was also bound up in a complicated way with their relations with the Tatar world. A common enemy often unites; in this case it divided. In an earlier period the "Russian ulus" of the Tatar khans had been supported from time to time by Tatar forces in its struggle with Lithuania. Now the conflict between Russia and the Horde had come to a moment of crisis. The almost uninterrupted civil strife among the Golden Horde in recent years had undermined its dominant position and brought anarchy to the Tatar world. All this was painfully reflected on the frontiers of Great Russia and compelled the Grand Prince to stand in a position of constant military readiness in the face of increasingly frequent and devastating Tatar raids. The Grand Prince's army maintained the defense of the Nizhegorod land and pushed forward Russia's advance along the Volga valley, and extended its line of defense along the Oka River. This long history of border clashes was leading inevitably to a serious break with the Golden Horde.

The influence of the temnik Mamai had been growing steadily since the early 1360's in the chaotic political situation in the land of the Horde. It was in Mamai's territory that Prince Mikhail of Tver had received his yarlik to the Grand Principality of Vladimir. It was "Mamai's Tatars" who had been pillaging the Riazan and Nizhegorod lands. With the Khan's throne secured, the temnik Mamai ruled the Horde until he himself became the chief khan. For a long time disorders both in the land of the Horde and in Russia prevented him from establishing definite sovereignty over the "Russian ulus." When Dmitri had journeyed to visit Khan Mamai in 1371 and honored "Prince Mamai and his khans, princesses, and princes" with gifts and his oath of obedience, he had received the yarlik to the grand principality at what was from Dmitri's viewpoint a somewhat reduced and thus more or less reasonable cost. Now that he had established himself in power, however, Khan Mamai was not satisfied with the outlay that had been fixed in his settlement with Dmitri, and indeed this tribute had probably not been paid to him after 1373, when Dmitri succeeded in breaking Tver's alliance with the Horde and Lithuania. Year by year there is reference in the chronicles to the "hostility" between Russia and Mamai, a tension that was to culminate on the banks of the Vozha River and on the Plain of Kulikovo. After the defeat of Prince Begich on the Vozha, a decisive battle became inevitable. The time was ripe for a new attempt to arrange a Tatar-Lithuanian alliance against Moscow, and this was precisely what Olgerd had had in mind. Khan Mamai gathered the armies of the Horde for the campaign, and in negotiations with Jagiello plans were made for a joint Tatar-Lithuanian attack on Moscow. The Khan's envoys appeared before Dmitri demanding a restoration of the amount of the Tatar outlay as established earlier under Khans Uzbek and Janibeg. It is likely that even during these negotiations an open battle had already been decided upon, especially in the minds of Moscow's enemies. For both Mamai and Jagiello it was vitally important to inflict a decisive blow on the Russian grand principality.

The history of the events surrounding the battle of Kulikovo has had its own special treatment in the various literary documents that serve as our source material. A sound basis for the analysis of these documents was established in a study by Shakhmatov. We must agree with Shakhmatov that three different sources lie at the basis of our chronicle accounts. One is the *Story [Povest] of the Slaughter of Mamai*, written soon after the actual event to extol the victory won by Dmitri and his host. This "story" was written in Moscow "in an ecclesiastical milieu," notes Shakhmatov, and, we might add, in a milieu that sought to uphold the legacy of Metropolitan Alexei and had as its central figure the Abbot Sergius of the Trinity Monastery. Another source was an account that Shakhmatov calls "an official report of the Grand Prince's campaign," written by a member of the Grand Prince's court. The third source—*The Tale [Slovo] of the Slaughter of Mamai*, as it is called by Shakhmatov—appeared probably in the court of Prince Vladimir of Serpukhov, and in very rhetorical language extolled the exploits of Vladimir, his wife's brothers (Olgerd's sons), and a captain from Volhynia named Dmitri Bobrok. Elements of all three sources are found in the texts of our chronicle collections, interwoven and complicated with layers of revision by later hands—insertions, explanations, and transpositions.

The mood in Rusia on the eve of the battle with Mamai was evidently much like that which pervaded Hellas on the eve of the battle of Marathon. Hardly anyone believed in the possibility of victory, and Dmitri was unable to assemble the whole of Great Russia's military strength. Neither the Novgorod host nor the troops of Nizhegorod and Tver were with him. Only the obviously embroidered *Story of the Slaughter of Mamai* in the Nikon Chronicle brings a Tver force under Prince Ivan of Kholm and a regiment from Pskov under Olgerd's son Andrei onto the Kulikovo Plain. Neither of these pieces of information is corroborated by other texts, and it is difficult to see how participation in the battle on the part of Tver and Pskov could have passed unnoticed in the basic accounts of this engagement as well as in the Pskov Chronicle. There was no metropolitan in Moscow. Tradition has placed Abbot Sergius in the center of the wave of spiritual energy which was so necessary to the success of any military exploit under such circumstances. It was not for nothing that Metropolitan Alexei had named Sergius as his successor. Exercising broad influence in the land by the force of his own personal spiritual charm and the authority surrounding a *starets*,[32] Sergius had come into the religious life out of the boyar class, like Alexei before him, and stood equally close to the grand princely court, where his brother Stefan and later his nephew Feodor were confessors to the Grand Prince and his older boyars. Under Alexei he had become an active participant in the affairs of the Metropolitan. Sergius had declined the see on Alexei's death, but it was inevitable that he should have great spiritual authority during this time of ecclesiastical disorder.

Tradition has described Olgerd's two sons and Vladimir of Serpukhov as the other main centers of military energy at this crucial moment. No matter how obvious the tendency to exaggerate the role of these princes may be in our sources, we have no basis for saying that their judgment had no basis in fact, since there is no contradictory evidence, and the view that they did play an important role has a certain internal probability. The overthrow of Dmitri by the united forces of Mamai and Jagiello would not have served the interests of Olgerd's sons. Moreover, they had brought with them to Moscow their own military forces and skills and much experience in fighting with the Tatars for the Russian land, as well as vital information about the state of affairs in the Lithuanian-Russian state which was bound to diminish the fear of an attack by Jagiello and at the same time hasten a move against Mamai before the Lithuanian and Tatar forces could come together. Jagiello was evidently in no position to hurry to meet Mamai, involved as he was in his dispute with his uncle Keistut and the general disorder shaking the Lithuanian grand principality, and instead of joining Mamai he moved back from Odoevo into Lithuania to face a bitter struggle with Keistut and Vitovt.

The victory of the Russian armies on the Plain of Kulikovo brought an end to Mamai's career, but it did not result in any immediate, decisive change in the relations between Russia and the Tatars. Nor did it lead to any sudden changes in Great Russia's internal affairs. This does not detract from its great

32. *Starets:* a charismatic monk or elder.—TRANS.

historical significance. The battle of Kulikovo is one of those events to which both contemporaries and people of later times have attached great symbolic meaning. In the traditions of generations closest to them as well as in the constructions of later historians, such events may become subject to very inaccurate evaluation, may become overgrown by legend that is partly the result of exaggerated style and partly due to deliberate attempts to modify the original account. The role of Dmitri of the Don as the leader of Great Russia, not only in a national war of liberation from foreign domination, but also in a religious war between "Christendom" and the "pagan Turk," has been elaborated in the colored perspectives of popular memory and the literary reworking of *The Story of the Slaughter of Mamai*. But the real foundations of Dmitri's commanding position in Russia were laid in the preceding decade of war with the Lithuanian-Russian state and of defensive operations in the face of Tatar raids. This position of leadership then acquired its spiritual and ecclesiastical overtones from the ideology that has been connected with the names of Metropolitan Alexei and Abbot Sergius.

Great Russia was unified in the course of this great struggle on two fronts. On the eve of the battle of Kulikovo, Dmitri had succeeded in breaking Tver's alliance with Lithuania and the Horde and forcing it, as a part of the territory of Great Russia, to acknowledge his grand princely sovereignty. The Nizhegorod principality was even more closely dependent on Moscow. In the years immediately following the battle of Kulikovo, Riazan also entered into a "perpetual peace" with the Grand Prince on conditions similar to those accepted by Tver in 1375. The fact that the two "grand princes" of Tver and Riazan were put on a level with Prince Vladimir of Serpukhov (a "younger brother" of the Grand Prince) acquired special significance when Vladimir was separated from the immediate circle of Muscovite "brother princes," and instead of being the possessor of a share in the common Moscow votchina became the ruler of his own votchina principality. In this position he was no longer a participant in the joint rule of Great Russia, and as time passed he was to become more and more a landholding prince subject not so much to the seniority of his "elder brother" as to his sovereign and absolute power. In its attempt to apply the principle of votchina rule to the grand principality of all Russia, Dmitri's testament displayed all the more clearly the tremendous significance of this moment in history, when the grand principality was seeking in the now modified forms of its traditional "seniority" and "solidarity" a way to organize the political unity of the land on new foundations. This slow task of building up grand princely sovereignty was carried forward under the constant threat of external dangers, and these too helped to foster the development of national unity and internal political order.

The immediate results of the Kulikovo battle tended for a while to increase rather than decrease both the external and internal forces opposing the development of a unified power in Moscow. Great Russia now entered a difficult period of conflict with foreign powers which made abundantly clear the unsuitability of its traditional internal organization for any successful resolution of its political problems. The old order was moving toward a sharp crisis, which was to come violently in the reign of Vasili the Blind (1425–62). Under Ivan Kalita and Semeon and Dmitri of the Don the power of the Grand Prince rested chiefly on his alliance with the Metropolitan of all Russia and the solidarity of the votchina princes within the Muscovite principality. Both of these foundations of his power underwent severe trial at the end of the fourteenth century and in the first half of the fifteenth century.

Chapter IX

The Breakdown of the Udel-Votchina System

The period in Russian history extending from the death of Metropolitan Alexei and the battle of Kulikovo to the resolution, about the middle of the fifteenth century, of the disorders that shook the grand principality in the time of Vasili the Blind is characterized by a certain unity in its general features and thus lends itself naturally to comprehensive study. There were, first, Russia's unsettled relations with the Tatars, who, in spite of periodic recovery of power under Tokhtamysh and Edigei, were in a state of decline; second, Russia's strained relations with Lithuania in the time of Vitovt's rise to power and ultimate overthrow; and finally, a period of ecclesiastical and civil disorder within Great Russia itself, when the Russian metropolitan court departed from the traditions laid down by Alexei and interprincely relations entered the final stage of conflict between the disintegration of the land into separate votchinas on the one hand and centralization of political power on the other.

We have no evidence on which to base a close analysis of the immediate effects of the battle of Kulikovo. The mood in which Great Russia anticipated this test of strength was evidently not dispelled by the victory. Everyone expected that Mamai would gather "his remaining forces" and make another "sweep" through the Russian land. Riazan was in the hands of the Grand Prince's deputies, and Great Russia stood face to face with the Tatar world, waiting for the expected blow of vengeance. The situation was suddenly altered with the overthrow of Mamai by Tokhtamysh. Negotiations were now possible. In the autumn of 1379 the new khan sent envoys to Dmitri of the Don and to all the Russian princes to inform them of his coronation. The Khan's envoys were received with honor by all the Russian princes, and during the following winter and spring they sent their own emissaries to the land of the Horde with homage, gifts, and presentations. Dependence on the Golden Horde was restored by common agreement of the Russian princes, who in November, 1380, bound themselves together in a close alliance. From the meager information of our chronicle sources we may assume that the Russian princes also took measures for the defense of their land at this same time. Tatar movements were watched more closely than ever. Later, when news came of the advance of Tokhtamysh's army, Dmitri was to encounter disagreement among his princes, and their "doubt and lack of solidarity" were to convince him that resistance was out of the question. These differences were undoubtedly aired also at the meeting of the princes in 1380. In spite of their peaceful overtures at the beginning of Tokhtamysh's reign, neither the Russians nor the Tatars had any real hope of a peaceful settlement. The Tatar envoy sent to Russia to summon the princes to the land of the Horde decided not to go beyond Nizhni Novgorod, and having sent a courier to Moscow, he returned to Tokhtamysh. The news he took back to the Khan could not have been comforting. The spring of 1381 passed, and still the Russian princes had not decided to appear in the land of the Horde. There is no record in our sources of the reason for this general indecision, but certainly the rout of Mamai must have aroused considerable hostility toward the "Russian ulus" among the princes of the Horde.

Toward the end of the summer of 1382 Tokhtamysh organized an expedition against Russia. The references in the chronicles to measures taken by the Khan "to assure that no warning of the attack would reach Russia" merely reinforce the comment regarding the "doubt and lack of solidarity" among the Russian princes. Dmitri left Moscow for Pereiaslavl Zalesky, and from there went round Rostov to Kostroma. Moscow was left virtually without defense. Its garrison was led by a Lithuanian prince named Ostei, who died a victim of Tatar treachery when he accepted an invitation to negotiate. Moscow was taken by the Tatars and sacked, while other Tatar detachments seized and plundered Pereiaslavl, pillaging and taking captives also in the volosts of Vladimir and Zvenigorod, Mozhaisk, Dmitrov, Iuriev, and Volok. Near Volok Prince Vladimir assembled an army and defeated the Tatar raiders. On hearing of the gathering of Russia's military forces, Tokhtamysh retreated from Moscow and left for the land of the Horde. On his way he took Kolomna and devasted the Riazan land.

This appearance of Tatar power in Russia had extremely important consequences. It showed how powerless Moscow was to take advantage of the victory of Kulikovo. At the price of major concessions in its border dispute with Riazan, and after prolonged negotiations that included another military confrontation, Moscow finally managed to conclude a "perpetual peace" with Oleg and confirm its alliance with him. The grand principality of Riazan remained an independent political entity, however, and continued to conduct its own diplomacy with the Tatars and Lithuania without reference to the policies of the Great Russian grand principality. The Nizhegorod princes made full submission to Tokhtamysh at the time of his campaign in Russia, and in the years following they were controlled more by the Khan than by the Grand Prince of all Russia.

When Tokhtamysh had stood before Moscow, Grand Prince Mikhail of Tver had sent an envoy to him with many gifts and a promise of submission, and a request that the Tver land be spared from Tatar pillage. For this he received the Khan's sanction and yarlik. His treaty with Dmitri of the Don made in 1375 was at once abrogated. Mikhail lost no time in again advancing his claim to the grand princely throne of Vladimir. Following Tokhtamysh, he journeyed to the land of the Horde "along byways, and not by the main routes . . . hiding himself from Grand Prince Dmitri," with a view to gaining "the grand princely rule of Vladimir and Novgorod." Prince Boris of Gorodets also made his way quickly to the land of the Horde.

Dmitri awaited the Khan's summons. Only after the arrival of the Khan's envoy in Moscow with a message concerning peace and a "conferral of the Khan's sanction" did he send his son Vasili to the land of the Horde to vie with Mikhail for possession of the grand princely rule. The Khan confirmed Dmitri on his throne. Tokhtamysh evidently saw in the conflict of the two rivals a guarantee of his own rule. He held Mikhail's son Alexander and Dmitri's son Vasili as hostages. Dmitri never again wavered in his obedience to the Tatar power. The Khan could now be reasonably certain that the Grand Prince's closest advisers—with the boyar Feodor the Cat in the position of greatest influence—were determined to preserve "good will toward the Horde."

The old relations seemed to have been restored. In the 1380's and early 1390's the Grand Prince was again regarded as the Khan's *ulusnik*,[33] with his authority sanctioned and upheld by the traditional yarlik. This restoration of the Khan's "sanction" and of Russia's dependence on the Horde helps to explain the "perpetual peace" with Riazan, the subsequent removal of Prince Boris from Nizhni Novgorod and restoration of Nizhegorod's dependence on Moscow, and the state of peace between Tver and Moscow in Dmitri's closing years. Similar fluctuations in grand princely power were to be seen also in Moscow's relations with Great Novgorod. At the beginning of the 1380's Novgorod was again left to itself, and at once there was a revival of its old ties with Lithuania. In 1383–84 the Novgorod boyars accepted Prince Patriki (son of Narimont) as a ruler over those dependent towns that had been assigned to Narimont and his sons "as an otchina and patrimony" in a treaty made earlier by Novgorod with Gedymin. This did not, however, signify a break with the grand principality. It was a sign rather of Novgorod's need to have a prince and his army to defend its borders. Since it could not get this protection from Moscow, Novgorod looked for help wherever it could be found.

Soon another aspect of Novgorod-Moscow relations emerged. Unable to defend itself against the Grand Prince's forces, Novgorod was made to bear a very large share of Moscow's "Tatar expenses." The end of the "litigation" with the Horde over the

33. *Ulusnik*: a ruler of an *ulus*; see n. 25.—TRANS.

grand princely rule marked the begining of extensive payments of tribute to the Khan. "In that same spring a heavy tribute was demanded throughout the grand principality from every prince, with no discount allowed, at the rate of fifty kopeks from every village, and the gold was then sent to the Horde, and from Great Novgorod the Grand Prince took a general tribute." The men of Novgorod were subject to the same general tribute as the rest of the grand principality, but its collection by the Grand Prince's boyars did not go smoothly. "The Prince's tax was withheld" by many in the Novgorod land, and the tribute collectors frequently met open resistance. This led to a campaign that winter under Dmitri's command. The campaign ended in a peace with Novgorod which compelled its boyars to pay a huge fine for its "guilty persons" over and above the full payment of its general tribute.

The attempt to drive the Tatars out of Russia which culminated in the victory of Kulikovo had not strengthened the Grand Prince's power, but rather had weakened it temporarily. Only after the reestablishment of dependence on the Horde was there a restoration of the old balance of relationships within the Great Russian grand principality, and even then it was a very qualified and uneasy equilibrium. In the next few decades the heritage of Ivan Kalita and Dmitri of the Don underwent a period of severe crisis.

Dmitri died in May, 1389, having bestowed "the grand principality as his otchina" on his son Vasili. Dmitri was trying to apply the votchina principle to possession of the grand princely throne, with the hope that the Golden Horde would acknowledge his son's possession of this right. On August 15, 1389, Vasili I was in fact installed on the throne of the grand principality in Vladimir by the Khan's envoy. A temporary falling out of the young prince with Vladimir of Serpukhov was quickly brought to an end.

Vasili's treaty with Vladimir at this time mentions the possibility of an acquisition by the Grand Prince of Murom and Torusa. The first important act of the grand princely court under the new prince was the obtaining of a yarlik from the Khan granting direct possession of Nizhni Novgorod, Gorodets, Murom, Meshchera, and Tarusa, i.e., of all the major outposts used for defense of the eastern frontier and advances to the southeast. This step in grand princely policy was almost certainly prepared during Dmitri's reign, on the strength of relations that had been built up between Dmitri and Tokhtamysh. But before these new rights could be established and exercised, there were to be sharp and important changes in the relationships of all the major powers in eastern Europe.

II.

These changes came from both east and west, and greatly altered the circumstances in which Great Russian policy was formulated. The power of Tokhtamysh had been broken in a conflict between the Khan and Timur (Tamerlane), another Tatar khan, and Timur's vassal Timur-Kutlugh. His territory was pillaged by Timur's army in 1395. Tokhtamysh fled into southern Russia, seeking refuge under Vitovt, and the land of the Golden Horde was placed under the nominal rule of Timur-Kutlugh, although in fact it was in the hands of Prince Edigei.

Tokhtamysh's downfall disrupted the stable relations that had developed between Moscow and the Golden Horde. This change in Moscow's Tatar relations was explained later as being a result of changes that took place about this time in the circles immediately surrounding Grand Prince Vasili. Abbot Sergius of the Trinity Monastery died in 1391; the prominent boyar Danilo died in 1392. Another boyar had also passed from the scene, Feodor the Cat, whose "good will and good deeds with respect to the Horde" were later to be mentioned by Edigei. The Grand Prince was now surrounded by new men, with the Grand Prince's treasurer, Koshkin, regarded as the "senior" member of this circle. Vasili I did not travel to the land of the Horde to visit the new khan, Timur-Kutlugh, nor did he visit his successor in 1400, Khan Shadibeg. Direct contact with the Horde was broken off for ten years or more. The Great Russian grand principality was drawn into the sphere of Vitovt's activity.

The position of Olgerd's sons Andrei and Dmitri in Moscow, as men closely connected with the court of Serpukhov (Vladimir had married their sister), may well explain the strong Lithuanian influence in Moscow at this time. It is true that the conflict with

Jagiello, which broke out with new violence when his uncle Keistut rose against him and occupied the city of Vilna in 1381, had had the effect of distracting Andrei and had forced him to go to Polotsk, where he managed to remain in power even after Jagiello's victory, and where he appeared later as a leader of Russian elements in a revolt against the Krevo Pact, uniting Lithuania with Poland. During this period away from Moscow, however, Andrei of Polotsk never lost touch with the principality of Pskov. His son Ivan reigned there as his vassal, and when the collapse of the revolt against Jagiello led to Andrei's imprisonment, he soon obtained his freedom (in the early part of 1394) under a surety given by Vitovt, who now had control of the whole of Lithuania. Andrei then returned to Pskov and remained on its throne until the alliance between Vitovt and Grand Prince Vasili was terminated. A living symbol of the complicated east and west Russian relations, colored as they were by the ethnic, ecclesiastical, and cultural ties of these two territories and at the same time by their political hostilities, Andrei found the ground cut from under his feet when Vitovt and Vasili clashed. He left Pskov to join Vitovt, and died in a battle with the Tatars on the Vorskla River. His brother Dmitri had returned to the throne of Briansk after laying aside his kissing of the cross to Vasili and swearing fealty to Jagiello and his queen, Jadviga. He too died in the battle on the Vorskla. During the time that these two princes served and were "provisioned" by Grand Prince Dmitri of Moscow, an influential group of west Russian exiles grew up around them. Among these exiles we have the names of Olgerd's "grandsons" (the sons of Andrei), the boyar Peresvet of Briansk, and the boyar Dmitri Bobrok, who according to later genealogies became the son-in-law of Dmitri of the Don.

The struggle against the Tatars for the independence of the Russian territories of the Lithuanian state had been the main occupation of the Russified Lithuanian princes and their Russian boyars, and this made their alliance with the forces of Great Russia both natural and easy. Now these same concerns, together with their family ties with west Russia and Lithuania, had the effect of drawing them around Vitovt, as he fought against the incorporation of the Russian-Lithuanian state within the kingdom of Poland.

In 1386 Dmitri's son Vasili had fled from the Horde into the Podolsk area and had joined the military men of Volok, taking part in a campaign against Volhynia under Vitovt. A group of envoys selected from Moscow's "senior boyars" arrived to seek his return, and a number of Lithuanian boyars journeyed back to Moscow with him. We do not know the precise nature of these negotiations, but the generally accepted view is probably correct, that an agreement was reached on the marriage of Vasili to Vitovt's daughter Sofia. This marriage took place soon after Vasili I's coronation as grand prince in 1391. Vasili's connection by marriage with Vitovt brought him very much under his father-in-law's influence, and this relationship was to continue with variations and moments of complete breakdown throughout Vasili's reign as grand prince. His subordination to Vitovt was supported by Metropolitan Cyprian and later by Metropolitan Photius, both of whom pursued their ecclesiastical and political activities as "metropolitans of all Russia" on principles quite unlike those of Metropolitan Alexei.

Vasili I's close relationship with Vitovt came in the midst of an extremely complex international situation. At first Vitovt was bound to appear to Moscow as an adversary of Moscow's old enemy Jagiello, and as a much-needed ally in the struggle against the Tatars. Jagiello's alliance with the Tatars on the western frontier was a dangerous threat. The Great Russian grand principality had first come into conflict with Jagiello's eastern policy on Novgorod soil. Moscow's forces were inadequate to defend its own eastern and southern borders and at the same time deal with the frequent clashes and the constant threat of war with Lithuania, and Novgorod had become increasingly independent. Already on several occasions it had attempted to organize its own military activity by provisioning exiled Lithuanian princes. But Novgorod had not succeeded in bringing these princes under its full control. The newly arrived princes were still oriented toward the Russo-Lithuanian state, and their temporary appearances on Novgorod soil brought little help to the land. On the contrary, they brought about new internal disorders and raised all the more sharply the question of Novgorod's relations with Lithuania and Moscow. Novgorod had never really been able to rely on its own forces, and its alliances with the

Lithuanian princes could acquire real significance for the defense of Novgorod only if their forces were supported by the armies of the Lithuanian grand prince, which would in effect take the place of the "downstream regiments," which could be counted on less and less to come to Novgorod's aid. Novgorod's treaty with Gedymin had led only to unsuccessful attempts to place first Prince Narimont and then Patriki in charge of Novgorod's military affairs.

Matters did not end there, however. In 1388 Prince Olgerd's son Lugven sent envoys to Novgorod with his claim to the dependent towns ruled by Narimont, and later was received with honor in the Novgorod land. Lugven stood at the head of the Novgorod army in its conflict with Pskov, and in 1390 he turned back a Swedish attack on Oreshek. Although the city had received him from the hand of Jagiello, Lugven never actually sat on Novgorod's throne. In his oath of allegiance to Jagiello in 1389 (Jagiello was then ruling as king of Poland and Lithuania), Lugven calls himself "guardian of the boyars and people of Great Novgorod" under Jagiello's command, and promises Jagiello and his queen, Jadviga, that "together with the people of Novgorod" he will remain loyal to them and to the Polish crown, as long as he shall "have the people of Novgorod under his guardianship." Having in principle acknowledged the merger of his Lithuanian-Russian grand principality with Poland, Jagiello now transferred to the "Polish crown" the lands united under his grand princely rule through his vassal princes. Novgorod was about to be placed in a position of complete dependence on Poland, provided Lugven's "guardianship" succeeded in withdrawing it from its traditional position as a part of the grand principality of Great Russia. At this point, however, Olgerd's son Dmitri occupied Briansk and laid aside his oath to Dmitri of Moscow, and it happened that Lugven was not able to separate Novgorod from Great Russian rule. His arrival in Novgorod was evidently connected in some way with the breakdown of relations between Novgorod and Moscow, and occurred at a time when the Russian grand prince had no deputy in the city. In 1390 Novgorod "made a settlement of peace on the old terms" with Moscow, and accepted Vasili's deputy, at the same time retaining Lugven as a provisioned prince of its dependent towns. This extremely ambiguous situation, so differently interpreted in Moscow and in Lithuania, was bound to give a new foundation to Novgorod's independence. It is hardly accidental that Lugven's departure from Novgorod in 1392 was followed at once by new and increased demands on the part of the Russian grand prince, new "hostilities" over these demands, and the simultaneous appearance in Novgorod of Prince Constantine of Beloozero and the Lithuanian prince Roman.

Pskov did not take the part of Novgorod in these matters. Evidently after Andrei's departure for Lithuania, his son Ivan reigned in Pskov as his deputy. The relations between Pskov and Novgorod were definitely strained. Open "hostilities" had broken out in 1390. Prince Lugven marched on Pskov with a Novgorod regiment, and the expedition ended with a truce. In a peace established with the Germans in 1392, however, the men of Novgorod did not include Pskov, and the latter had to enter into negotiations separately. It was not so much that Pskov was oriented toward Moscow as that it found itself in the hands of forces opposed to Jagiello. Prince Andrei's return to Pskov "out of exile" was accompanied by a new outbreak of hostilities with Novgorod. Princes Roman and Constantine fought a battle with Andrei and his son near Pskov. The attack on Pskov was repulsed, but no treaty was made.

Lithuanian influence weighed heavily over the western regions of Great Russia. Powerless to overwhelm and drive the Lithuanian forces beyond the borders of that still undefined world called "all Russia," of which it considered itself the center, the Great Russian grand principality was now moving in the direction of a rapprochement with those Russian elements of the Russo-Lithuanian state that were related to eastern Russia by ties of nationality, culture, and religious faith, encouraging as much as possible their dissatisfaction with Lithuanian domination and supporting them in their struggle against the pagan and, subsequently, Roman Catholic rulers of the Lithuanian state. Vitovt relied chiefly on the power of his own traditionally Lithuanian lands, but he too sought closer ties with the Russian and Orthodox elements of his domains, and even adopted the Orthodox faith when he acquired control of south Russia. His very first steps, then, brought him into a circle of relationships that prepared the way for closer ties also with Moscow. In 1391 Vitovt became the father-in-law of Grand Prince Vasili of Moscow. In the following year he was placed at the head of the Lithuanian grand principality according to the terms of the Treaty of Ostrov. In fact this abruptly altered the whole situation. From this time on Vitovt acted in full agreement with the policies of Jagiello and Olgerd. Acting in Jagiello's name, he gave orders for the liquidation of the independent principalities in the Russian sections of Lithuania, and his general political strategy during these years in no way opposed the principles of the Union of Krevo. All the more remarkable, then, was the position he managed to occupy in eastern Russia in the 1390's.

Made ruler of Lithuania by consent of Jagiello, "king of Poland, grand prince of Lithuania, and hereditary prince of Russia," Vitovt worked energetically to extend his influence and direct control over Lithuania's Russian territories. In this he not only was unopposed by Moscow and Tver, but had their open support. His immediate goal was the subjection of Smolensk and Great Novgorod. In 1395, at a time when eastern Russia was threatened by the presence on its borders of the dreaded Timur, Vitovt took advantage of civil strife among the princes of Smolensk to summon them to his camp for a settlement of their dispute, seized them, and replaced them by his own deputies. Prince Iuri of Smolensk escaped and found refuge and support with his father-in-law, Grand Prince Oleg of Riazan, but Moscow took the side of Vitovt in this affair. In the spring of the year, when "Vitovt carried out his first seizure of Smolensk," Grand Prince Vasili and Metropolitan Cyprian visited him there, and in the summer and fall Vasili thwarted Oleg's attempt to mount a campaign against Vitovt and did nothing to prevent the latter from devastating the Riazan land. Indeed, after this Riazan expedition Vasili received his father-in-law in Kolomna with full honor.

This rapprochement between the grand princes of Lithuania and Great Russia placed Novgorod in a most difficult position. Its dispute with Vasili I had not been smoothed over, despite the fact that hostilities had been formally ended (with concessions on the part of Novgorod) in 1393. Novgorod had sent envoys to Vasili with a "promise of obedience regarding the ancient customs" and had submitted also to the Metropolitan, permitting the collection of a "general tribute" in its volosts and the exaction of other forms of princely revenue. But then the men of Novgorod proceeded to arrange a peace "according to the old customs" with Vitovt also. This action made any permanent peace impossible. Novgorod's independence of Russia's grand princely power had increased significantly as Moscow neglected its affairs in the northwest. "Lord Novgorod the Great" now had the opportunity and in fact was compelled to define its relationships with its neighbors as a self-determining power and to rely wholly on its own strength in the conduct of wars and the making of treaties. It was in this period that democratic government in Novgorod reached its fullest development. While still acknowledging the need for princely power, mainly for military purposes, the leaders of Novgorod more and more frequently tried to replace the sovereignty of a ruling prince by the limited authority of a visiting prince whom they would "provision with Novgorod bread" in their neighboring dependent towns. Novgorod's alienation from Great Russia reached its highest point, and the end of the fourteenth century brought unprecedented suffering to the city.

In 1397 a "joint embassy" of envoys from Grand Prince Vasili and Vitovt appeared in Novgorod and demanded that the city break its peace with the Germans. The people of Novgorod refused, insisting on the independent nature of their policies and treaties with the grand princes of Russia and Lithuania and the Germans. The real reason for this demand on Novgorod is not quite clear. Neither Vitovt nor Vasili, least of all the latter, was thinking at that time of war with the knights of the Livonian order. Perhaps its meaning can be discerned in the light of Novgorod's reply: it may be that this demand was a denial of Novgorod's right to carry on its own independent foreign policy. In any case, it served as a pretext for beginning to carry out a plan that very probably had been drawn up when the two grand princes met in Kolomna. It is difficult to understand subsequent events without positing some agreement between Vitovt and Vasili I regarding a division of the Novgorod domains.

Vasili sent his boyars into the Dvina valley, calling the people of the Dvina land to detach themselves from Novgorod and "yield" to him. All of the boyars and landholders of the Dvina land kissed the cross to Vasili, although they secured certain administrative powers for themselves according to the terms of a special charter. The Grand Prince occupied Volokolamsk, Torzhok, Vologda, and Bezhetsk. At this same time (October, 1398) Vitovt concluded his remarkable Treaty of Salino with the Livonian order, by which he yielded Zhmud to them and gave up all claims to Pskov, even promising to aid the knights in their efforts to subjugate the Pskov land, and in return received a commitment of aid from the order in his campaign to subdue Great Novgorod.

Vitovt's envoys arrived in Novgorod with a declaration of war, charging the city with failure to acknowledge Vitovt as its grand prince. The proposed attack on Novgorod was not carried through, however, and Vitovt's allies wavered in their support of his aggressive policy. It was more to the advantage of the knights to get Vitovt embroiled in a quarrel with Jagiello than to strengthen him in the conquest of Novgorod. Nor is it likely that the German knights ever had any serious thought of conquering Pskov. The seizure of the Dvina land and other Novgorod domains turned out to be short-lived, and even before Vitovt gained the freedom of action he needed in the Treaty of Salino, Novgorod's army had carried out a return expedition into the Dvina territory and had cruelly punished its inhabitants for their defection. After this Novgorod concluded a new peace with Vasili "according to the ancient terms."

The fact that the Grand Prince rather quickly dropped his ambitious plans for occupation of the Novgorod land can hardly be explained by that city's military successes alone. Vasili's almost complete subjection to Vitovt threatened to reduce Moscow's power substantially. The Grand Prince's policy became more independent, and when Vitovt sent his "conditions for peace" to Novgorod with the sacrifice of Pskov to the Germans, the men of Pskov again found support in the Grand Prince of Great Russia, and Novgorod renewed the "ancient terms" of its treaties with Moscow. In the summer of 1399 Pskov was hastily fortified. Olgerd's grandson Ivan had already left the city the previous spring, with "the laying aside of his kissing of the cross" to Dmitri. With the arrival of winter it was evident that the Great

Russian grand principality was prepared to support Pskov and Novgorod against Vitovt. Vasili's brother Andrei arrived in Novgorod, and in answer to a petition from Pskov, Vasili sent Prince Ivan of Kholm to its defense. "In that winter Vitovt broke his peace with his son-in-law Grand Prince Vasili, and with Novgorod, and with Pskov." In Moscow Vitovt's policies began to be regarded in a new light, perhaps as a result of his new relations with the Tatars.

III.

Vitovt's ambitions in the north came to nothing as his attention was drawn more and more to the south. His relations with the Tatars had tied up his forces along that front and prevented him from launching an attack on Novgorod. Great Russia's submissiveness toward Vitovt may well have been determined not only by Vitovt's personal influence over his son-in-law, which had the support of Metropolitan Cyprian, but also by the rupture between Great Russia and the Horde and Moscow's reliance on its pact with Vitovt as a defense against Tatar power. An agreement between Moscow and Lithuania to take joint action against the Tatars must surely have been another matter negotiated at the meeting in Kolomna. Certainly Vitovt held in his hands an effective instrument for the continued disruption of the balance of power among the Horde. Khan Tokhtamysh had fled to him for protection and now resided with his court in Kiev. Beginning in 1397, Vitovt revived the ancient Russian custom of making expeditions into the steppe country and establishing military outposts in the territories thus acquired, settling them with fugitives from other lands and armies that he had taken captive. But his plans went even beyond this. He dreamed now of destroying the Golden Horde, and gathered his forces for a huge campaign. He persuaded Pope Boniface IX to proclaim a crusade against the Tatars in Poland, Lithuania, and Wallachia, and also secured the support of the Teutonic knights.

This plan for a major war with the Tatars could not fail to affect Vitovt's relations with Moscow and Tver. Mikhail's son Ivan of Tver visited Vitovt at the end of 1397, and there was an exchange of envoys between Vitovt and Vasili I in 1398. The border fighting between the Tatars and Great Russian forces along the Riazan and Nizhegorod frontiers had continued throughout this period, but the grand princely government in Moscow did not respond warmly to Vitovt's proposals. In Moscow the sanctuary offered by Vitovt to the fugitive Tokhtamysh, with Vitovt's enticing promise to restore him to his khanate, was regarded with the utmost suspicion. There are passages in the Russian chronicles that give us an indication of the treacherous plans ascribed to Vitovt by those who opposed his influence on Russian affairs. Vitovt, they said, would reestablish Tokhtamysh over the Horde and then with his help bring Moscow and the whole Great Russian grand principality under Lithuanian rule, thereby resolving also in his own favor the questions of Novgorod and Pskov.

The significance of the defeat of Vitovt's armies on the banks of the Vorskla River has often been exaggerated. It certainly disrupted his plans for a massive attack on the Tatar world. It also shattered the dreams of the Salinsk conference, and Vitovt's relations with Poland began to develop once more largely in terms of solidarity with Jagiello; a solidarity based on new principles, incidentally, since Vitovt was to be acknowledged as the holder of the grand princely sovereignty now only during his lifetime. But if we do not attach undue importance to the broad ambitions ascribed to Vitovt by neighbors disturbed by his growing power (and in the minds of his enemies in Great Russia these ambitions were blown up to fantastic proportions), and if we look rather at his actual strength, we may say that Vitovt's position was not seriously affected by his defeat on the Vorskla.

It was not this military setback that destroyed Vitovt's plans in northern Russia in 1399, but the temporary uniting of Russian forces against him. Coinciding with the change in Lithuanian-Polish relations on the death of Queen Jadviga, the defeat on the Vorskla made it impossible for Vitovt to act decisively. Soon Novgorod and Pskov made treaties of "perpetual peace" with him, but their submission did not restore Vitovt's power over these free cities. In Pskov we find Prince Daniel (of the house of Rostov) ruling as a representative of the Grand Prince of all Russia. Novgorod also was deprived of Lithuanian support. The disturbances arising in Smolensk, where part of the population was on the side of Vitovt and another part called for the restoration of the city's hereditary prince, gave Iuri an opportunity to repossess Smolensk with help from Riazan, and Vitovt's campaign against Smolensk in the fall of 1401 ended in failure and the conclusion of a "peace on the ancient terms" with Prince Iuri, with whom the men of Novgorod also hastened to make a settlement. At this same time, but without declaring war on Novgorod, Vasili renewed his attempts to seize the Dvina territory and Torzhok. Once again, however, the Grand Prince failed to secure the Novgorod volosts, although none of the chronicle texts reveal the circumstances in which this conflict was resolved.

Evidently Vasili's hasty reconciliation with the men of Novgorod, which came soon after this, had something to do with the revival of Lithuanian attacks on the Smolensk region. To allow his conflict with Novgorod to flare up again would only mean to drive it into the hands of Vitovt. Vasili refused to come to the aid of Smolensk, however, although his reconciliation with Novgorod and Prince Iuri's settlement certainly must have given Smolensk some hope of support from Great Russia.

Shortly after this, when Olgerd's son Lugven seized the Smolensk town of Viazma and Vitovt took Smolensk itself, Iuri looked to Moscow for help, and once again we see Vasili I avoiding direct conflict with his father-in-law. Negotiations between the two grand princes made it likely that Vasili would deliver Iuri to Vitovt, and the Prince of Smolensk quickly fled from Moscow to Novgorod—possibly assisted by elements in Moscow—and was received there. A common danger had brought the two grand princes together, and again there was a possibility of a division of the Novgorod domains. The men of Novgorod made a pact with Iuri on the basis that with him they would defend themselves against their enemies "as one man," and for this they gave him thirteen dependent towns. They anticipated an attack by Vitovt and evidently also feared Vasili's wavering policy. Again all the cautious neutrality of the grand princely government in its dealings with Vitovt helped to bring about an overthrow of the Lithuanian prince's plans.

Vitovt began his military campaign with an attack on the Pskov volosts in the beginning of 1406, after the taking of

Smolensk. The Grand Prince's brother Peter went to Novgorod and Pskov to prepare their defenses, and the Grand Prince's army advanced with Tatar reinforcements sent from Khan Shadibeg. Lithuanian pressure had again not only consolidated the Russian forces, but also forced them to drop their struggle with the Tatars and seek support from the Horde against a common enemy. Vitovt was checked. Both sides avoided a decisive engagement. A truce was declared, although the "hostilities" lasted for three more years. The Grand Prince of Great Russia now began to assume the defense of his western territories with greater boldness. Prince Peter's arrival in Novgorod meant the end of Iuri's position as an independent prince. He left for Moscow, and there received Torzhok as his city, not from Novgorod, but at the hands of the Grand Prince. During this period we find Constantine, the Grand Prince's youngest brother, in Pskov, as leader of that city's defense against German attack.

The increased activity of Moscow on the western frontier quickly revived the old vacillation of the Russian elements in the Russo-Lithuanian state. Lesser princes again began to come over from western Russia to Moscow, counting on Great Russian support in their conflict with Vitovt, in which the Polish land-holding boyars, Vitovt's main support, were more and more heavily oppressing the Russian and Russified elements of the land. And yet this growing tension led to no sharp, decisive conflict. The campaigns of both grand princes were characteristically inconclusive—in 1406 along the Plava River and in the vicinity of Viazma, and in 1407 along the Ugra River. Each of these campaigns ended in the same way: an armistice for a year, then a new armistice, and then a peace "on the ancient terms," which was in fact an indefinite truce that in no way resolved the complex and age-old antagonisms. Vitovt was bound by his ties with both Polish and Russian forces, just as Vasili was by his ties with Novgorod, Nizhegorod, Tver, and Riazan. Just how far the Lithuanian grand principality was from being a well-defined national and international power is evident from the fact that Prince Lugven returned to Novgorod in 1407 to occupy the same dependent towns that had been his before, and until 1412 retained them under his own rule and that of his deputies, in the meantime leading the Novgorod army against the Swedes. In this same period we find Vasili's brother Prince Constantine in Novgorod as the Grand Prince's representative and deputy. Novgorod's willingness to provision Lugven did not mean that Lugven had turned against Vitovt, nor was it regarded as a violation of Novgorod's "settlement" with Vasili. The democratic city of Novgorod guarded its independence on both sides, and whenever it had the strength and opportunity it increased its freedom, gradually seeking a breach of the ancient "terms and customs" and the end of its ties with the Great Russian grand principality. Sometimes support from Lithuania furthered this process; at other times the threat from Lithuania slowed and weakened it.

No matter how turbulent life in Great Novgorod may have been in the first decade of the fifteenth century, this period marked an easing of the tension Novgorod experienced in its position between the two great grand principalities, since their major interests at this time lay in other directions. On the one hand, the Polish-Lithuanian union was forming and gathering strength for the great battle of Grunewald (Tannenberg); on the other hand, a new Tatar storm hung over the grand principality of Russia.

The breach between Moscow and the Horde after the invasion by Tokhtamysh did not lead to a continuation of the liberating movement begun on the Plain of Kulikovo. On the contrary, the Lithuanian threat (judging from the general tone of the references to Vitovt in the chronicles) led to a situation in which the attitude of "good will toward the Horde" acquired new force in Moscow, with the awareness that Vitovt was a more dangerous enemy that the Tatars. Relations with the Horde were resumed during the reign of Khan Shadibeg. The Khan sent a Tatar host to help Vasili in his struggle with Lithuania in 1406. His replacement by another of Edigei's favorites, Bulat-Timur, occurred during the period of prolonged unrest on the Nizhegorod frontier, when the Nizhegorod princes were trying to return to their otchina and secure it for themselves, and in a time of increased hostility toward Vitovt. The government of the Grand Prince attempted to end the Tatar support of the hereditary Nizhegorod princes, and also to use the power of the Horde against its powerful neighbor to the west, dispatching urgent petitions and appeals to the rulers of the Horde. The supreme khan, Edigei, was aware of the difficult position of "the senior grand prince of this great ulus" and of the opportunity he had to make demands upon him. The Horde was evidently also aware of the fact that a restoration of its power over the Russian ulus could not be brought about simply by negotiations and decrees. Edigei followed the example of Tokhtamysh. A raid in 1408 brought him to the walls of Moscow. Vasili left the city in the hands of his cousin Vladimir of Serpukhov and his brothers, and moved with his family to Kostroma. Tatar detachments spread havoc in the towns and volosts of the grand principality. For three weeks the Tatars held their position before Moscow. The city withstood the siege, but the Grand Prince was unable to organize his forces to defeat the enemy. Edigei retired with the booty and ransom he had extracted from the boyars of the city, but only on receiving news of an attack on his capital by another Tatar prince.

This raid clearly revealed the desperate position in which the Great Russian grand principality found itself, too weak to unify the land against the Tatars even when the latter were themselves weakened by internal strife. It is also true, of course, that Edigei failed to reap any permanent advantage from this raid, his only gain being the plunder he seized. Not until after the fall of Edigei and the transfer of Tatar power to Jalal ad-Din (the son of Tokhtamysh) did Vasili journey to the land of the Horde "with great riches." This step was forced upon him by a renewal of ties between the Tatars and the princes of Nizhegorod and Tver.

For Russia the reign of Vasili I was a period of instability and painfully strained relations that exhausted the land. Repeatedly conflicts would break out which the grand princely power had neither the energy nor the means to resolve decisively. Moscow swung wildly from one alliance to another, lacking the strength to bring about any definite settlement of the complicated problems arising out of Great Russia's relations with other nations. Leadership over the destinies of Great Russia was the end and justification of Muscovite sovereignty both in the minds of those who bore it and in the view of the Russian people as a whole, but time and again this leadership was to slip out of Moscow's hands, obviously beyond the grasp of this as yet immature political organism. The demands of leadership and the need for the unity and strength of a centralized authority had been raised too soon, when the organization of the Great Russian grand principality was passing through only the very first stages of its evolution into new political forms. The premature test of Russia's powers proved to be too much for it, and had the effect of checking and delaying the process of unification. At the same time it clearly and urgently posed the need for unification, and hastened the crisis in the old order.

Attempts at constructive political activity on the part of Moscow's rulers were not completely thwarted in this period of extremely difficult external relations. In the second decade of the fifteenth century Grand Prince Vasili completed the task of bringing Nizhni Novgorod under his immediate rule. The Riazan land, however, continued to find only weak and occasional support in Moscow. As the chaos in Nizhegorod was gradually and with difficulty brought to an end, Vasili prepared a new invasion of the Dvina territory. Again the attempt was beaten back. His relations with Great Novgorod continued on the basis of what Novgorod called "the ancient terms and customs," but these ancient terms of submission now concealed "the full freedom of Novgorod," which was constantly widening with the growing independence of the Novgorod democracy. Novgorod was not formally detached from the grand principality of Vladimir; it continued to receive the Grand Prince's deputies. But then side by side with them it retained and provisioned west Russian princes in its dependent towns, and "downstream" princes too, who would from time to time come to Novgorod after quarrels with the Grand Prince. Moreover, as we have seen, Novgorod carried on its own independent relations with Vitovt, the Swedes, the Livonian order, and its "younger brother" Pskov, with the Grand Prince's representatives in Novgorod and Pskov playing no visible role in these affairs. The question of Tver's relationship to the grand principality was also raised sharply. In the first quarter of the fifteenth century Tver ended the last of its udel disputes, which of course had been supported and aggravated by Moscow, and this process of internal concentration of power in Tver made it too more independent in relation to the grand principality of all Russia. During the reign of Mikhail's son Ivan, Tver occupied its own independent political position between Moscow, the Tatars, and Lithuania.

After his father's death and just two weeks after the Tatar victory on the banks of the Vorskla, Grand Prince Ivan of Tver found himself face to face with the massive strength of the Horde. His father had held the position of a vassal in relation to Timur-Kutlugh, and now Ivan sent envoys to receive his yarlik to the grand princely rule of Tver from Khan Shadibeg. At this same time Tver was drawn into the union of Russian forces against Vitovt, when under the threat of Lithuanian attack the Grand Prince of all Russia was forced to renew relations with the Horde. The Tver host took part in the first engagement with Vitovt in 1406, but the armistice that followed exposed the basic differences in the positions of Tver and Moscow. Vasili conducted negotiations with Vitovt and agreed to the armistice and settlement without reference to the Tver princes or to Ivan, and in the treaty document he inscribed Ivan's name below the names of his brothers. This met with violent protest. The Tver princes and boyars withdrew their forces, and Ivan renounced his alliance with Vasili on the grounds that the Muscovite princes had not considered the Tver princes as equals, had not given due respect to the name of Tver in the phrasing of the treaty document, and had concluded the peace "without the counsel" of the Tver princes, thus treating them as servant princes or vassals. Tver took no part in the expedition against Viazma along the Ugra River in 1407, but when Edigei made his attack on Moscow the Grand Prince of Tver avoided taking part in the siege of the city as he was commanded to by the Tatar general, and for this the Tver land was burned and plundered. Our chronicles explain these actions on his part as a sign of a tentative healing of the breach with Moscow, but at this time any direct participation with Tatars in a raid on Russian soil would even in Tver have been psychologically impossible. The desire to maintain the fullest possible independence from the grand princely power of Great Russia inevitably moved Tver along the now familiar path of alliance with Lithuania. Internal strife soon broke out again in the Tver principality, encouraged of course by Moscow, which could not afford to

miss any opportunity to bring Tver under its control. The path
from Tver to the grand princely court of Lithuania had long
been marked out by ties of marriage. In 1411 Ivan's son Alexander visited Vitovt in Kiev. A year later an alliance between
the grand princes of Lithuania and Tver was ratified, with the
provision that "they be in all things as one," and a Tver regiment
subsequently took part in the Polish-Lithuanian war against the
Livonian knights.

This rapprochement between Tver and Lithuania had no
great political significance, however, in view of the close relations established also between Vitovt and Vasili after their temporary rupture. In 1412 Jalal ad-Din was installed as khan of the
Golden Horde. Vitovt now had a friend in the Horde, for
he had given Jalal ad-Din and his father, Tokhtamysh, aid and
refuge in their time of exile in Kiev. In this same period Vasili
was renewing relations with the Tatars. Journeys were made to
the Khan in an effort to win Tatar support for Vasili's plans for
Tver and Nizhegorod. From 1412 on, therefore, Tver's contacts
with Lithuania and the Horde lost much of their danger for the
Grand Prince of Great Russia. But then Tver's refusal to enter
into full and active cooperation with Great Russia in the latter's
military activities inevitably tended to neutralize Moscow. This
refusal may well have played a role not only in Vasili's renewed
dependence on the Khan, but also in the decline of elements in
Moscow opposing Lithuanian policy and in the new wave of
Lithuanian influence in the Muscovite court.

The closing years of Vasili's reign were marked by new ties
between Lithuania and Moscow. This growing Lithuanian influence was determined not only by Great Russia's complex and
difficult external relations, but also by the violent tensions in its
own princely house. As we shall see, Vasili I had good cause
to view the future with alarm. His family and his successor on
the throne could expect little security. On his death the throne
would pass to an infant son, since his older son, Ivan, had died
in 1417. Shortly after Ivan's death a testament was made in which
Vasili's younger son, born in 1415, was committed to the care
of his mother, Grand Princess Sofia, who was to be to him as
a father. Vasili regarded Vitovt, his father-in-law, as the natural
guardian of his little son and widowed princess. His last testa-

ment was drawn up in 1423, with the same "enjoining" to Vitovt of Sofia and her son. In this year Vitovt was visited by Sofia, and also by Metropolitan Photius. These visits had political significance, since we know that Photius carried Vasili's testament with him to Vitovt. It was presented to the Lithuanian grand prince during negotiations for a new ratification of the earlier testament.

Also in 1423 Muscovite and Tver detachments took part in Vitovt's campaign against the Germans, and in the following year Vitovt called on Great Russia for help in fighting off a Tatar raid. Vitovt wished to consolidate his victory at Grunewald by drawing Lithuanian, Polish, and Russian forces into his various military enterprises, and had managed to involve at least Pskov and Novgorod in his war with the Germans. But these commercial cities, so often at war with the Germans themselves, were now on the defensive and looking for peace. In the early 1420's both Novgorod and Pskov made treaties with their German neighbors. Pskov had even agreed not to go to the aid of Vitovt. This action aroused Vitovt's anger, and fearing retaliation, Pskov turned to Vasili for help, with the request also that Vasili act as mediator between them. The Pskov Chronicle notes that although Vasili did answer their request by sending princely deputies, "nothing good was accomplished." This powerlessness on the part of the grand principality of Great Russia was determined by its own internal chaos; a complex political crisis was brewing.

IV.

As we have seen, the alliance between the metropolitan see of "all Russia" and Great Russia's grand principality had taken on special significance in the time of Metropolitan Alexei, and by its very existence was bound to raise a series of sharp, complex questions concerning not only the relations of the metropolitan see with the patriarchate of Constantinople, and of the metropolitan with local churches and secular powers in other Orthodox and Russian lands, but also of the relationship of ecclesiastical and secular power in general. A more general question would also be raised: the real meaning at that time of the concept "all

Russia," now that this term had entered into the titles of both the metropolitan and the grand prince. For the metropolitan see it had a very definite meaning—it referred to the sum total of all the Russian dioceses. For the grand principality, however, it was a matter of varying interpretation and obviously did not refer to the borders of the grand principality of Vladimir, which in its treaty documents set itself apart from the neighboring local grand principalities in Great Russia, from the Novgorod volosts, and above all from the territories of west Russia. In the usage of the grand princely court, the term "all Russia" expressed the desire for the exercise of sovereignty beyond the borders of the Grand Prince's immediate domains. In short, it expressed Moscow's pretensions to the position of grand princely "seniority" in relation to all the local political powers of Great Russia, including such "younger brothers" as Tver and Riazan; to direct control over Novgorod and Pskov; to the sole right to deal directly with the Horde; and to protect the Smolensk and Chernigov lands against Lithuanian seizure—a defensive function that at the first opportunity could turn easily into direct aggression. This school of thought in Moscow tended to interpret the concept "all Russia" in the broadest sense, which would include the same territories as came under the jurisdiction of the Russian metropolitan. Alexei's attempt to put the struggle between Moscow and Lithuania on ecclesiastical and confessional grounds, to explain it as a struggle between Orthodox Christianity and the "idolatrous" Olgerd, naturally led to a nationalistic and confessional outlook on the international situation in eastern Europe. All of Alexei's energies had forged a firm link between the term "all Russia" as a religious concept and the broadest possible definition of the aims of the prince's secular power in order to secure Russia's defense against alien religious and political powers and unite Russia around a single political center. The influence of the Russian metropolitan became a major factor not only in the interprincely relations within Great Russia, but also in its relations with other nations and in the formation of the political outlook of Moscow's ruling group.

To keep this great power in its hands and maintain its national-political character was a matter of the utmost importance for the grand princely throne of Great Russia. The way to accom-

plish this was clear. Efforts must be made to transfer the metropolitan jurisdiction to another candidate from Russia as a successor to Alexei. A man must be chosen out of the same class
of serving officials in the grand prince's court from which Alexei
himself had been drawn, and indeed Alexei had named an experienced colleague to take his place: Abbot Sergius of the
Trinity Monastery. Sergius had declined an independent political
role, however, feeling that it was "not within his bounds," and
chose to remain at the monastery.

Grand Prince Dmitri had his own candidate in the person
of Archimandrite Mikhail (better known as Mitiai, which we
may conclude was his secular name), whom he regarded as
more suited for the worldly and public aspects of a metropolitan's career. Mitiai was a priest from Kolomna who had
become confessor to Grand Prince Dmitri and all his senior
boyars, then chancellor of the Grand Prince's printing house,
and then archimandrite of the Cathedral of Our Savior in Moscow. His candidacy not only caused violent agitation among the
people of Moscow, but also raised a number of basic questions,
above all the question of the unity of the see.

This question had been settled in advance, it would seem,
by the provision made by the patriarchal council when it appointed Cyprian metropolitan of Kiev. After Alexei's death the
temporary division of the metropolitan see was to be ended and
Cyprian, hitherto metropolitan of Lithuania and Little Russia,
was to become the new metropolitan of Kiev and all Russia. In
Moscow, of course, Cyprian was regarded as an ally of the
Grand Prince of Lithuania, and thus a political enemy. The grand
princely government refused to accept him.

The question of Alexei's successor had been raised officially
even during Alexei's lifetime. Unfortunately the accounts of the
matter in our sources do not give us sufficient information as to
just how this happened. They do not indicate, for example,
whether the question of the uncanonical nature of Cyprian's
consecration was raised at the beginning, as it was to be later
in the conciliar decree of Patriarch Nil. Cyprian was convinced
that Grand Prince Dmitri wanted the division of the metropolitan see in order to put his own candidate at the head of the
church in Great Russia, but it is extremely doubtful that Mitiai

ever had the approval of Metropolitan Alexei. Dmitri hoped to secure the see for Mitiai by an arrangement similar to that which had brought Alexei to office, that is, by winning the Metropolitan's approval of his candidate and by making a prior agreement with the Patriarch. As it happens, neither *The Story of Mitiai* in the chronicles nor Cyprian's letter to Sergius and Feodor gives us any clear idea of the role played in this affair by Alexei. Considered as a whole, however, the information we do have leads us to the conclusion that Alexei probably did not ever formally approve Mitiai's candidacy. Sergius' refusal to accept the office and the general lack of agreement over Mitiai greatly confused a situation that was difficult enough without these added problems.

An envoy was sent to Constantinople to prepare Mitiai's case in the patriarchal court. Patriarch Makarios rejected Cyprian's claims and transferred the rule of the Russian church to Archimandrite Mitiai, summoning the latter to Constantinople to be consecrated as metropolitan of Great Russia. This step was obviously not in harmony with Alexei's basic ecclesiastical and political policies, and we may suspect that it was not just the personal character of the Grand Prince's candidate, but also matters of principle, that had given rise to the disagreement between Alexei and Dmitri over the question of the Metropolitan's successor. Although not in episcopal orders, Mitiai began to administer the affairs of the see by the authority of the Patriarch, and had hopes of being raised to the episcopate by a local Great Russian council of bishops before his departure for Constantinople. This move was blocked, however, by Bishop Dionysius of Suzdal. Mitiai's candidacy had lost almost all the support that Alexei had enjoyed in a similar situation. Mitiai did not have the official approval of his predecessor; he did not hold the rank of bishop of Vladimir, and he did not have the universal support of the Russian bishops. The purely political significance of his candidacy became increasingly clear as it was seen to be urged only by the Grand Prince. The dissent in Moscow and Mitiai's delayed departure gave his opponents time to mount opposition against him in Constantinople. This opposition came from two directions: from Dionysius and from Cyprian. Dionysius had been made bishop of Suzdal by Metropolitan Alexei in the time of Dmitri's close alliance with the Prince of Suzdal, who was in fact his father-in-law. There are no grounds for regarding Dionysius as an enemy of Moscow or for the discovery of some political motive in his conduct toward Mitiai. A protégé of Alexei and close friend of Abbot Sergius, Dionysius could have himself aspired to the metropolitan see, counting on the support of influential elements in the Muscovite clergy who were hostile to the Grand Prince's candidate.

Dionysius had openly opposed Mitiai. After his appointment to administer the see, Mitiai made it clear that he would crush this opposition by force when he returned from Constantinople. As we shall see, the question of Nizhni Novgorod and Gorodets was raised again in this dispute. Dionysius made preparations to go to Constantinople to defend his position and press his attack on Mitiai. Dmitri immediately had him placed under guard, and he was not released until Abbot Sergius gave assurances on his behalf. Dionysius then "broke his word and betrayed his saintly intercessor" and followed Mitiai to Constantinople. Mitiai's unexpected death en route prevented them from meeting in the Patriarch's court.

Dionysius arrived in Constantinople when the retinue that had accompanied Mitiai had already succeeded in producing a man named Pimen as the Grand Prince's new candidate for the Great Russia see. Dionysius' protests and charges made against the envoys who had accompanied Mitiai came too late to prevent Pimen's nomination. We can see from a presentation of Dionysius' arguments found in a later patriarchal document that he was definitely unwilling to accept the division of the metropolitan see of all Russia as it was then accepted by the Grand Prince. Dionysius had made an impression in Constantinople as a man with real understanding and knowledge of the canons who would vigorously defend them in the deliberations of the patriarchal council, and he was given the title of archbishop of Suzdal, with a special guarantee and definition of his jurisdiction. Dionysius now appeared in Russia in the unusual role of a fully empowered patriarchal legate, entrusted with ecclesiastical authority reaching far beyond the borders of his own diocese. We find him in Novgorod enforcing a patriarchal condemnation of the *Strigolniki*,[34] and later combating the same heresy in Pskov, and thus performing pastoral duties in the name of the Patriarch outside his own diocese but within the territory of the metropolitan see of all Russia. This unusual arrangement would undoubtedly have had the effect of furthering Dionysius' candidacy for the office of metropolitan whenever the occasion for such an advancement should present itself. Such an occasion could only be the removal of Pimen and Cyprian in favor of a new metropolitan of "all Russia."

The affair was to develop in another direction, however. Dmitri of the Don did not accept Pimen and had broken also with Cyprian (whom he had been on the point of accepting at last), and in the summer of 1383 he sent Dionysius to Constantinople to be made metropolitan in Pimen's place, i.e., to be made metropolitan of Great Russia, with "letters of accusation" against Mitiai's unwanted successor. In Constantinople this new delegation was received with perplexity and consternation: here was the zealous guardian of the canons being drawn into the struggle for the metropolitan see, for which there were already two claimants having patriarchal blessing. Moreover, he came now as a candidate of the Grand Prince, accepting that very solution to the question of a divided see which he had formerly opposed and which the patriarchal council had always wished to avoid. Patriarch Nil did not decide the matter at once, but sent two bishops to investigate Pimen's case in Russia, with power to remove him if the accusations were well founded and put Dionysius in his place. Dionysius then set out for Russia as metropolitan designate, but Olgerd's son Vladimir of Kiev seized him en route, and he died there in prison a year later.

In his opposition to Cyprian, Dionysius was no longer able to remain in the position of a staunch defender of the unity of the metropolitan see. Adherence to this principle was Cyprian's main strength. He had always defended and now at last he secured his right to succeed Alexei in the seat of Kiev and all

34. *Strigolniki:* members of a reforming religious sect that opposed corruption among the clergy of the Russian church. Like the sect of the Old Believers, it existed without priests and developed a practice of lay preaching; it did not survive the sixteenth century.—TRANS.

Russia. His victory acquired special significance in the history
of Great Russia and its grand principality, since Cyprian connected the unity of the see with an effort to establish the metropolitan's independence from the grand prince in all matters of
church policy. After Alexei's death Cyprian had proposed a
visit to Moscow, and when Dmitri refused to grant him permission to come to the city he got through to Moscow secretly,
having forewarned Abbot Sergius and his nephew Abbot Feodor
of the Simonov Monastery of his plans, and inviting them to
meet with him. He was seized in Moscow, however, and sent
back to Lithuania. While in Moscow, Cyprian had been informed
that the Grand Prince's own metropolitan designate, Archimandrite Mitiai, was administering the affairs of the Great Russian
see. Cyprian was evidently also told that Mitiai had received this
jurisdiction with the approval of Alexei and the Grand Prince.
Cyprian himself was denounced as a "Lithuanian." He answered
this by excommunicating all who had taken part in this plot
and brought such dishonor on his sacred office, made his way to
Constantinople, and took his case before the Patriarch and the
patriarchal council. Here, however, during the inquiry into his
charges, the canonical validity of his own consecration as metropolitan was questioned, and he was forced to agree to remain
in that part of the metropolitan district which had been entrusted
to him and to leave Kiev, in order to diminish the seriousness
of the charge against him. It was decreed that Pimen should be
made metropolitan of Kiev also, and that Cyprian, "because of
his obedient submission," be left to rule the see of Little Russia
and Lithuania.

Cyprian's letters to Abbots Sergius and Feodor showed that in
them he had found champions of the concept of metropolitan
unity. It is to their influence that we must ascribe the unexpected
turn of events in the spring of 1381, when Feodor, the Grand
Prince's confessor, was sent to Kiev to call Cyprian to the see of
Kiev and all Russia. Cyprian arrived in Moscow on the Feast of
the Ascension (May 28, 1381), and toward the end of the year
the Muscovite envoys returned from Constantinople with Pimen
—only to be met with disgrace, punishment, and exile by Dmitri's
orders. The Patriarch, however, took Pimen's side and sent
"many letters" to Moscow opposing Cyprian. The patriarchal

conciliar decree of 1389, on which our knowledge of this affair is based, can scarcely be correct, however, when it states that Dmitri's subsequent actions—the expulsion of Cyprian from Moscow and the sudden acknowledgment of Pimen as metropolitan—were determined by the intervention of the Patriarch. According to our chronicles, the Grand Prince had his own good reasons for profound dissatisfaction with Cyprian and open suspicion of his motives. At the time of Tokhtamysh's campaign in Great Russia, in August, 1381, Metropolitan Cyprian was left in the besieged city by the Grand Prince to help maintain order. Cyprian had failed in his efforts to stop the riots and looting brought on by panic, and had left for Tver, where he remained until the beginning of October. The negotiations between the Grand Prince of Tver and Tokhtamysh took place in Cyprian's presence, and with Cyprian's knowledge Grand Prince Mikhail of Tver left for the land of the Horde to try to obtain a yarlik to the "grand princely rule of Vladimir and Novgorod." Cyprian had thus embarked at once on the path of making a distinction between his own policies and those of the Grand Prince. In his own eyes he was not the metropolitan of Moscow, but of all Russia. Grand Prince Dmitri now returned once and for all to his original position. He decided that there must be a metropolitan for Great Russia alone; and, summoning Cyprian from Tver, he forced him to "descend" from Moscow to Kiev, and "with great honor and love" Pimen was recalled from exile to occupy the seat from which he had only recently been removed.

Archbishop Dionysius' return from Constantinople to Russia in 1383 again raised the question of Pimen's unlawful occupation of the Russian see. Dmitri made an attempt to salvage his position in relation to the church by agreeing to accept Dionysius in Pimen's place, but Dionysius' imprisonment and then death cut short this new effort to establish a lawful separate metropolitan for Great Russia. Dmitri now had to be content with Pimen, if only to avoid Cyprian's restoration in northern Russia. The only alternative was to bring forward a new candidate, but matters were too confused and Pimen's candidacy had been carried too far for this to be accomplished quickly. In fact, Pimen's compromised position and Dionysius' death opened the way for Cyprian. The representatives from Constantinople who had been accompanying Dionysius on his journey back to Moscow (the metropolitans of Adrianople and Jannina) now arrived in Moscow without him, fully empowered to investigate the confused question of the Russian metropolitan see. They were able only to carry on the investigatory side of their mission, however, and final resolution of the matter was to be left to a patriarchal council in Constantinople.

It was not until the spring of 1385 that Pimen finally set out for Constantinople, and we know that he did not travel in the company of Abbot Feodor (the Grand Prince's envoy) and the Greek metropolitans. Our sources give no information about Dmitri's intentions or the instructions he may have given to Feodor. The abbot evidently had rather broad powers, since there is no indication of any specific proposal by the Grand Prince's government with regard to the arrangement of the see. Abbot Feodor and the Greek legates presented their charges against Pimen to the Patriarch, accusing him of obtaining his office by subterfuge. Feodor also carried on certain independent "verbal" negotiations with the Patriarch at this time, which gives us reason to suppose that while the Grand Prince had decided not to confront the Patriarch with demands for a new metropolitan, the Russian grand principality was making efforts to find an acceptable way out of the situation that had been created. If this assumption is not accepted, then we are left with the very unlikely conclusion that the agreement made at this time between Feodor and Pimen (in which Pimen placed Feodor in the see of Rostov with the rank of archbishop) was an arbitrary act not in accordance with the Grand Prince's wishes. Feodor's action here is explicable only if we assume that he had received some instructions to this effect from Moscow, i.e., that if absolutely forced to it, Feodor was to accept Pimen, just so long as Cyprian did not return. Feodor was in fact compelled to accept Pimen when it became evident that no other solution was possible and it was a matter of choosing between Pimen and Cyprian alone.

The Patriarch prolonged these negotiations endlessly, and in the spring of 1387 Cyprian was sent back to Lithuania on some imperial commission, with instructions to return after a year for a final judgment of the case. The matter now took a direction against Pimen and in favor of Cyprian, and Pimen's deposition could be foreseen well before the case was finally settled. Pimen and Feodor decided not to wait for the judgment, and after entering into their agreement (against the Patriarch's wishes) they secretly left Constantinople and returned to Moscow. Here Pimen continued to exercise his sacred duties, ignoring the Patriarch's summonses and prohibitions, until a new decree on the Russian see was published by Patriarch Anthony, Nil's successor. The decree stated that in accordance with the canons, Pimen must now be regarded as deposed, and that the unity of the metropolitan see of Kiev and all Russia was forever reestablished "in its ancient order and structure," with Cyprian as the sole legitimate metropolitan. This development forced Pimen to undertake a third journey to Constantinople—against Dmitri's advice, according to the evidence of the chronicles. Fate saved Cyprian from further conflict. Pimen died before he reached Constantinople, and even before Pimen's death Dmitri's life had also come to an end. Under the new grand prince, Cyprian was accepted as metropolitan without objection.

V.

Thus in the period of serious military reverses in the 1380's this ecclesiastical controversy ended by depriving the Great Russian grand principality of the influential support of the metropolitan of all Russia. The grand principality had clearly suffered another defeat. For many years to come the Grand Prince's political solidarity with and reliance on the metropolitan see would have to be abandoned. The power to name metropolitan candidates who were acceptable to the secular power had slipped out of the Grand Prince's hands. There was a break now in the development of the tradition established by Metropolitan Alexei, which had given his see very much the character of a Great Russian state church.

Although Cyprian may not have been as much an enemy of Moscow and a "Lithuanian" at heart as he was accused of being in Moscow, nevertheless he was a man alien to the ruling class of Moscow and its traditions and general outlook. Cyprian was a Bulgarian who had made an outstanding career for himself

In Byzantium. Even as metropolitan of all Russia he remained a representative of the Byzantine school in ecclesiastical matters, and by no means did he equate the interests of his see with those of the Great Rusian or Lithuanian grand princely powers, much less subordinate the church's interests to those of the secular powers. Once established in Moscow, Cyprian pursued the task of consolidating his metropolitan authority with great consistency, and achieved considerable independence in his administrative policies within the church. Unfortunately, the case of Bishop Evfimi Vislen of Tver remains very obscure in our sources. Vislen had been made bishop of Tver by Metropolitan Alexei when the conflict between Mikhail of Tver and Grand Prince Dmitri was about to end in Dmitri's favor with the treaty of 1375. Mikhail developed a growing "dislike" of Bishop Evfimi, but was not able to secure his removal from the see of Tver until 1387. Evfimi's departure into a monastery at that time did not mean his renunciation of his office as bishop of Tver, and thus no opportunity was given for his replacement by someone acceptable to Mikhail. One of Cyprian's first actions after his installation in Moscow was to settle this controversy in Tver. The manner in which it was handled was characteristic. Cyprian did not summon the two parties to come before his court in Moscow. Instead, he himself went to Tver with the two Greek metropolitans who had accompanied him to Moscow and two Russian bishops. There he convened a synod and carried out the investigation before a joint assembly of his ecclesiastical court and the Tver boyars' *duma*,[35] with Grand Prince Mikhail at its head. Many charges were brought against Evfimi by both the secular and ecclesiastical powers in Tver, and Mikhail insisted on the appointment of a new bishop. After making certain necessary formal attempts to reconcile the two sides, Cyprian had Evfimi deprived of his episcopal jurisdiction by a synodal decree, and chose his own proto-deacon Arseni as Evfimi's successor. Arseni did not immediately accept this advancement. He feared "enmity and a great outcry," undoubtedly because of Cyprian's decision to place his own man in the see of Tver and not one chosen by Mikhail. Cyprian was pursuing his two main goals, which consisted, first, of handling the case without the inter-

35. *Duma:* council or assembly, usually of princes and/or boyars.—TRANS.

ference of the Grand Prince of all Russia, and second, of elimi-
nating the influence of local secular power in the appointment
of a bishop to a vacant see.

Cyprian based his actions here on relationships between the
ecclesiastical and secular powers as well as between the Russian
metropolitan see and the Byzantine patriarchate, which had been
regarded as norms in the correspondence of Patriarch Philotheus
with Alexei. The metropolitan see was not a national Russian
institution; much less was it an instrument of Great Russian
political power. It was an independent organ or instrument of
the Ecumenical Eastern Church. In a number of instances it
moved in full agreement with the grand prince in his handling of
ecclesiastical affairs in Russia, but this happened only when their
interests coincided. The real basis for the metropolitan's authority
lay not in the grand prince, but in the power of the patriarch
in Constantinople, by whom all disputes in Russia were finally
settled.

In Moscow the rather well-developed concept of a national
Russian metropolitan see was not easily set aside. This was reflected in the famous controversy over the mention of the
Emperor's name in Cyprian's order of worship and the lack of
respect given to patriarchal authority in Russia. In 1393 Patriarch
Anthony reproached Grand Prince Vasili I for actions brought
to his attention by Dmitri the Athenian, who was in Constantinople in connection with the affairs of the Russian church
as the legate and envoy of Metropolitan Cyprian and Grand
Prince Vasili. The Patriarch reprimanded the Grand Prince for
not showing due respect to the representatives of the patriarchal
court and not honoring the Patriarch's name, as was the custom
under former grand princes, and for not permitting the Metropolitan to mention "the Emperor's divine name" in his liturgical
prayers. Anthony threatened the Grand Prince with the wrath
of God if he would not "honor the Patriarch as Christ Himself,
and show respect for his words, letters, and communications, and
for those sent to Russia in his name." Russia must not become
separated as a self-governing, national entity, in either the ecclesiastical or the political sense, but must see itself as part of the
Ecumenical Church and the great Eastern empire. The Grand
Prince must not say: "We have the church, but as for an em-

peror, we do not have one nor do we want one." The Byzantine emperors were the church's organizers; by their laws they confirmed the church's canons regarding right doctrine and the proper establishment of Christian ways of life; the emperor was the supreme lord and ruler of the universe, which was not so of other local rulers and princes. "It is impossible that Christians should have the church but not the emperor, since empire and church have the closest unity and communality, and it is impossible to separate one from the other." Russia was part of a great whole, of the whole Christian East, with the Byzantine emperor standing at its head, "the emperor and autocrat of all the citizens of Rome, that is, of all Christians," who ruled side by side with "the ecumenical patriarch."

As a part of this whole, Russia was to organize its political life in such a way that the rule of the grand prince was set side by side with the rule of the metropolitan of all Russia, recognizing that the latter had his own tasks and his own methods. This independence on the part of Metropolitan Cyprian could be seen in the fact that his attitudes toward the secular powers of northeastern and western Russia did not always coincide with those of the Grand Prince. On the other hand, his influence must be regarded as one of the main reasons for the vacillation and obvious instability of Vasili's policy.

In their approaches to Novgorod and Suzdal, the interests of the metropolitan see and the grand principality were very much the same. Both powers acted together, although in the case of Great Novgorod only at first. Later the Metropolitan pursued his own goals here quite apart from the policy of the Grand Prince.

Evforsin had succeeded Dionysius as archbishop of Suzdal. He was consecrated in Constantinople, probably by Pimen at the same time that Feodor was made bishop of Rostov. Following Dionysius' example, he too obtained a patriarchal letter attaching Nizhni Novgorod and Gorodets to the diocese of Suzdal. Cyprian and Vasili I objected to this, however, asserting that Dionysius had possessed only "the right of a patriarchal exarch" in these territories. The Patriarch sent a legation to Russia to look into this question. The result of the inquiry is not known, although later (under Metropolitan Jonas) Nizhni and Gorodets were under the immediate jurisdiction of the Metropolitan. The Grand Prince's interest in this dispute between the Metropolitan and the Archbishop of Suzdal was connected, of course, with his acquisition of the Khan's yarlik to Nizhni, and with the beginning of the consolidation of grand princely power in that region.

Even more characteristic were Cyprian's relations with Novgorod. From his predecessor he had inherited a controversy between the metropolitan see and the people of Novgorod over the rights of the metropolitan in Novgorod's ecclesiastical courts. The growth of the Novgorod democracy inevitably had led to attempts to redefine and limit the dependence of the bishop of Novgorod on the power of the metropolitan. This episcopal dispute took on political significance partly as a result of the close ties between the metropolitan and the grand principality, and partly because of the arrogation by "Lord Novgorod the Great" of the right to choose its own archbishop, a right which by tradition belonged to the local ruling prince. The elevation of the Bishop of Novgorod to the rank of archbishop and his later adoption of the specially embroidered archepiscopal vestments as a mark of his office had already made it necessary for the Patriarch of Constantinople to remind the Archbishop of Novgorod that these marks of honor did not in any way reduce his dependence on the metropolitan see.

A sharper question raised in this dispute was that of the metropolitan's judicial rights. The people of Novgorod had applied to the metropolitan court the legal principle of venue established in their treaties with the Grand Prince ("and you, O Prince, shall not bring people of Novgorod to trial in the 'downstream lands'"), and it had become a custom for the metropolitan to make periodic visits to Novgorod for a period of one month for the purpose of holding court and receiving his ordinary revenues and fees. But this practice did not exclude the older procedure; it had not completely supplanted the "summons" to go to the "downstream lands" and appear for trial in the metropolitan's residence in Moscow. In 1385 the people of Novgorod vigorously opposed this summons to trial in Moscow, and the dispute over this question quickly spread to others, and finally involved a rejection not only of the right of summons, but also of the month-long session of the metropolitan court in Novgorod.

In this same year a law concerning civil and ecclesiastical courts was passed "in the Novgorod veche, in its princely court," and sealed by the kissing of the cross of the whole Novgorod land. Not only the civil courts (those of the posadnik and tysiatsky) but also the ecclesiastical court of its ruling archbishop must be conducted in the presence of two boyars and two serving persons from each party in any given litigation, and no citizen of Novgorod was to bring a charge against a fellow citizen in the metropolitan court. This was the beginning of an open conflict with the metropolitan see, one that had special meaning for the grand principality, since a weakening of ties between Novgorod and Moscow brought the threat of increased western, Lithuanian influence in Novgorod. It was not for nothing that the Novgorod envoys made use of the Lithuanian argument when they were defending their claims in the court of the patriarch. If you of the Greek church will not yield to our demands, they said, then we shall be forced to convert to Roman Catholicism. Among other demands made at the time of his dispute with Novgorod in 1392–93, Vasili I was to require that this veche decree on the courts be handed over to the metropolitan and revoked. The men of Novgorod met this demand only after "much spilling of blood" and a "peace according to the old terms" had been made with Vasili, at which time they received a letter of pardon and blessing from the Metropolitan. This did not end the matter. In the years immediately following we see the Bishop of Novgorod appearing in Moscow whenever he is summoned by Cyprian, and we see the Metropolitan being received by Novgorod with great honor. But the people of Novgorod stubbornly opposed the month-long session of the metropolitan court in their city. The controversy dragged on, and led to the confinement of Bishop Jonas in the Chudovsky Monastery in Moscow for three years.

The most important feature of this dispute, however, was Cyprian's extraordinary circumspection with regard to Novgorod, a caution that was very far from being in harmony with Vasili's Novgorod policy. The Metropolitan did not resort to the harsh measure of excommunication, and did not break with

Novgorod in the years when Vasili and Vitovt were bringing pressure against it and Vasili was fighting for control of the Dvina territory. The real motives for Cyprian's behavior are difficult to establish from the brief and fragmentary accounts of our chronicles, but his action suggests a deliberate separation of the policy of the metropolitan see from that of the grand principality. Even after Novgorod's refusal to allow him to hold sessions of his court there following its concession in surrendering the veche statute, Cyprian gave not an order of excommunication but his blessing to the city as he departed, in spite of his "displeasure" with the people and their bishop. Again, in the hostility between Vasili and Novgorod that broke out when the Grand Prince "refused to accept its bishop's entreaties and good words, or the homage ·of the Novgorod envoys, and did not set aside his enmity toward Novgorod, and gave it no peace," the Metropolitan "let his spiritual son [Bishop Jonas] and the Novgorod envoys depart for Novgorod in honor and with his blessing." Again at the end of the 1390's, when Novgorod found itself at war with both the Lithuanian and the Russian grand princes, Cyprian did not press the ecclesiastical question, and it did not then enter into the demands made on Novgorod by Grand Prince Vasili. Not until 1401 was Archbishop Jonas actually seized and prohibited from further exercise of his duties. This action was taken against the Bishop personally, and there was no interdiction laid upon Novgorod as a whole. After more than three years of negotiations this episode ended with Jonas' release and return to his see, without any resolution of the basic question in the Metropolitan's favor, although Cyprian had both law and the authority of the patriarch behind him.

In his struggle with Lithuania, Vasili I received none of the support from the Metropolitan that his father did from Alexei. Vitovt's great influence in Moscow was undoubtedly encouraged by the Metropolitan, who sought to further his significance as metropolitan of "all Russia" without relating this effort directly to the rivalry between Lithuania and Moscow. In his dealings with Lithuania, Cyprian, metropolitan of Kiev as well as of "all Russia," scrupulously avoided those complications that would diminish his importance in western Russia, as had happened in the case of Alexei. The sharp opposition of Christian Russia to pagan Lithuania used by Alexei to sustain a political struggle and a nationalistic ideology had moved onto another plane with the establishment of Roman Catholicism in Lithuania. Metropolitan Cyprian did not openly oppose the Roman church or this Roman Catholic state. His ambition was to eliminate this ecclesiastical schism and become the head of a large local church embracing not only eastern Russia, but also the Russo-Lithuanian state and the Russian lands of the Polish crown. Free from the nationalistic aspirations of Great Russia, Cyprian was oriented not toward the nationalization of confessional antagonism, but toward a resolution of this problem through the unification of the Russian church. At the beginning of 1397 Patriarch Anthony sent Jagiello and Cyprian a reply to their urgent proposal that he summon a council to discuss the conditions for this ecclesiastical unification. The Patriarch's evasive and cautious answer would indicate that Byzantium, at that time hard pressed by the "infidels" (Moslem Turks), had embarked on a path of intrigue, and hoped to make a union with the Catholic West in return for its military aid against the Moslem world. Cyprian's desire for unification of Orthodox Russian people was not altogether opposed to Byzantine policy, and Byzantium found him to be a champion of material aid from Russia in the form of collections of money to meet Constantinople's expenses in its struggle with the enemies of Christianity to the east.

Cyprian's independent position between the grand princes of Lithuania and Great Russia and his refusal to let his close ties with Byzantium be undermined by the national interests of Great Russia placed him in direct opposition to the traditions of Metropolitan Alexei. A statute promulgated by Vasili I and Cyprian dealing with "the ecclesiastical houses and all the church's volosts, lands, waters, and revenues" comes down to us as a memorial of the internal relations between the metropolitan see and the grand princely power in Great Russia. The statute reveals Cyprian as a defender of the independence of the metropolitan in ecclesiastical matters and also of his secular power. Owing to the lack of documents from an earlier period, it is difficult to say precisely which sections of this document belong to Cyprian and which represent the renewal or confirmation of provisions made by earlier metropolitans. The statute was issued in the name of both the Grand Prince and the Metropolitan, and it took the form of an official summary of points on which they agreed, so that it has something of the character of a treaty. It defines the status of the Metropolitan's domains within the territory of the grand principality as similar to the position of the domains of the udel princes. His domains and privileges were in general "to be as they were under Metropolitan Alexei." People attached to ecclesiastical institutions ("ecclesiastical people") were to pay an *obrok* (quitrent or tax) to the Grand Prince (according to the terms of an obrok charter) "whenever tribute is paid to the Tatars"; but if there was no Tatar tribute, then no obrok was to be paid. When the Grand Prince himself set out on a campaign, then the Metropolitan's boyars and servants would march under the leadership of the Metropolitan's captains, although under the banner of the Grand Prince. This was obviously an older tradition, since there was a provision that those who had not served Metropolitan Alexei, but "had recently been attached to the new metropolitan," should march in campaigns under the Grand Prince's captains in accordance with their places of residence. The Metropolitan was not to make deacons or priests of servants of the Grand Prince and persons in his care; he must take candidates for the clergy only from the sons of priests. Complaints against the Metropolitan's officials (deputies, desiatniks, volostels) were to be taken to the court of the Grand Prince. The principle of venue was the same as that found in treaties between princes. The judicial immunity of the Metropolitan's villages and "monastery settlements" was confirmed. Here, as in the treaties between princes, much depended on the financial and military power of the Grand Prince. The collection of tribute, in the amount fixed by the obrok charter, was determined by the payment of the Tatar outlay. The Metropolitan's regiments were to enter into campaigns in which the Grand Prince himself had "mounted his horse." Of course there was no mention of independent external relations on the part of the Metropolitan. In fact, however, Cyprian acted as a separate political power in his contacts with centers outside Great Russia, and this modified his dependence on the Grand Prince in secular and political matters and gave it the quality of an interdependence ratified by treaty.

This relationship of the ecclesiastical and secular powers may be regarded as a reflection of the udel-votchina system. The weakening of the old bonds of political solidarity that had once existed between the metropolitan see and the grand principality was bound to bring the question of the nationalization of the see into the foreground, not only in the light of the general political interests of the Great Russian grand principality, but also as a way of unifying local power over the internal resources and forces of the land.

The ecclesiastical and political activity of Metropolitan Cyprian was not simply a product of his own personal drive and ambition. What he did was determined by a number of complicated forces —not only by the general situation in eastern Europe, divided then into the Great Russian grand principality and the Russo-Lithuanian state, but also by the ecclesiastical and political policies of Byzantium. The Great Russian grand principality was being forced to modify its earlier position. The death of Cyprian (in September, 1406) coincided with a break in the peaceful relations between Vasili and Vitovt. Vitovt immediately brought forward his own candidate for the see, in the person of Feodosiia of Polotsk. To block this move Moscow appealed to the Patriarch to consecrate a metropolitan "following the ancient tradition," urging that "according to God's will he be chosen and sent" by the Patriarch in conjunction with the patriarchal council and the Byzantine emperor. A Greek prelate named Photius was duly consecrated, and grudgingly accepted by Vitovt.

Photius was not destined to maintain the good relations with the Lithuanian grand prince established under Cyprian, nor was he able to prevent controversy and disorder from threatening the unity of the see. The situation was now complicated by Vitovt's firm resolve to obtain a separate metropolitan for western Russia, and in this he was supported by at least a part of the west Russian clergy. A strong-willed and demanding metropolitan, Photius irritated his clergy and society in general by his insistent efforts to restore in full all his revenues and ecclesiastical properties. More than ever Lithuania was interested now in having a metropolitan resident in Kiev, for the proper administration of ecclesiastical affairs in Lithuanian Russia and in order to put a stop to the use of Lithuanian funds to meet the expenses of the Metropolitan in Moscow. Vitovt's actions immediately made it clear that this was not simply a matter of defending the interests of the south and west Russian church. Irritated by the failure of his plan to have Feodosiia made metropolitan of all Russia, and having taken a personal dislike to Photius, whom he accused of breaking his promise not to neglect the care of the Lithuanian church and not to leave it without his personal presence in Kiev, Vitovt refused to let Photius come to that city in 1414 and forced him to return to Moscow. The Metropolitan's deputies were also expelled and sent back to Moscow, and "he gave the towns belonging to the metropolitan see of Kiev and its great cathedral churches with their volosts and villages" to his own Polish boyars. With the support of a number of bishops in the Russo-Lithuanian state, Vitovt then secured the election of a Bulgarian, Grigori Tsamblak (a nephew of Cyprian), to the see of Kiev. The Patriarch's refusal to consecrate Grigori resulted in his consecration by a synod of local bishops.

The ensuing four-year break in relations between Photius and Vitovt did not lead, however, to Photius' adoption of the ecclesiastical-political views and aspirations of Moscow. When Tsamblak was removed from his see at the beginning of 1419, Photius again began to exercise his rights as metropolitan of all Russia. In the summer of 1420 he journeyed into Lithuania with a patriarchal legate in order to unify his see, and in the second decade of his career he finally established peaceful relations with Vitovt, taking advantage of a new rapprochement between Moscow and Lithuania, which he himself had undoubtedly encouraged. Photius' relations with Moscow were also being gradually defined and settled during this period, but not without difficulties and occasional violent conflicts. When he arrived in Moscow he was confronted with a series of disputes over the church's votchina domains, those possessions and revenues that had been guaranteed not long before in the statute drawn up by Grand Prince Vasili and Metropolitan Cyprian. In this conflict over church property Photius emerged as an authoritative pastor who would not hesitate to demand the Grand Prince's submission and obedience in the name of Christ, since, as he put it, "even if I am a sinner, I am teaching that which has been laid down by the apostles."

An able and energetic ecclesiastical administrator, Photius had not become directly involved in the political struggle that was going on around him at this time. His one political act was to participate in the sending of envoys to Vitovt in 1423 to present Vasili's testament. Vasili's death (in February, 1425) placed Photius in a completely new position. It became necessary for him to engage directly in the struggle for control of the grand prince's throne. He defended the hereditary rights of the young Prince Vasili II, and managed to survive the new crisis that now broke out in the interrelations of the Russian princes.

VI.

The reduction in the power and influence of the Russian grand principality in the last two decades of the fourteenth century and the first quarter of the fifteenth was not just the result of its strained external relations and its break with the metropolitan see. The deep roots of the violent crisis that was about to shake the sovereign power in Moscow lay in the very structure of this power, in its close ties with the ancient and traditional family relationships within the princely votchina of Moscow, and in the prevalence of these votchina principles throughout the whole political outlook and life of Great Russia in that period.

We have seen the signs of increasing votchina disintegration in the Muscovite principality during the reign of Dmitri of the Don, and how the reaction to this process on the part of the grand princely power led to the development of its absolute sovereignty over the country's military and physical resources, as it consolidated and elaborated the principles laid down in the testament of Ivan Kalita and the treaty that Grand Prince Semeon made with his brothers. As possessor of the position of seniority, the Grand Prince not only labored, to the limit of his powers and on every possible occasion, to check the disintegration of his sovereignty into udel and votchina domains, but also made successful attempts to use this patriarchal family principle as a convenient form for determining the relations between ruler and ruled and to consolidate the rudimentary bonds of political unity in Great Russia. Inevitably this patriarchal principle became a two-edged sword. In this same period we see in the relations between domains within the Muscovite principality an increase in the tendency toward votchina disintegration as a result of the very conditional nature of any unification of military forces and the awareness that the unity of financial resources and institutions was only temporary—designed to stand only until such time as God would overthrow the Horde. The attempt to adapt the principle of votchina domain to the grand principality itself threatened to make its territory subject to votchina division, and the application of the patriarchal institution of "seniority" to the Grand Prince's relations with the local grand principalities of Great Russia tended to arouse the opposition of these "younger brothers" and destroy the "solidarity" of the princes' forces.

The inconsistency of the udel-votchina system with the basic political tasks and requirements of the grand principality became increasingly painful. Only the complete collapse of Great Russia's internal relations was to bring this old system to an end. Only the harsh resolution of this crisis in the cruel civil strife of the second quarter of the fifteenth century was to open the way to a synthesis of the principle of votchina domain and the political power of the grand principality in the Muscovite monarchy or autocracy.

The reign of Vasili I was full of internal friction between the various Muscovite princes. Unfortunately we must again take note (as we have had to do much too often in the history of Great Russia in this period) of the fragmentary and incomplete nature of the information provided by our sources.

Possession of the different shares of the Muscovite principality was complicated in the time of Vasili I by the setting apart of the Serpukhov principality and the question of the distribution to be made to Dmitri's youngest son, Constantine, who was born only a few days before his father's death. Dmitri's last testament, drawn up just before Constantine was born, provided that should God give the Grand Princess a son, she should give him a share of the Muscovite domains, taking some part of each of the udels of his older brothers for this purpose. There is reason to believe that Dmitri actually made some disposition for his youngest son himself. In the first testament of Grand Prince Vasili I we read that he gave Constantine "the Toshna and the Ustiug region as his udel," and he did this, we are told, "according to the testament" of his father. This did not constitute the whole of Constantine's udel, of course, but what else was assigned to him cannot be definitely established. This grant of a share to the youngest son gave rise to too many complications, and after many changes and new treaty agreements his domain was dissolved among the other Muscovite princes, who for a long time "strove" with each other over Constantine's volosts.

The problem of the allocation of domains to the various Muscovite princes was made all the more difficult by the fact that Dmitiri's testament raised the question of the application of the votchina principle to the territory of the grand principality, just as at an earlier time his treaties with Prince Vladimir of Serpukhov, with the "conferral" upon Vladimir of Galich and Dmitrov "as his udel," had opened the way for claims by the younger princes for a share in the lands seized by the Grand Prince. Although actually inspired by his own action, these claims threatened to undermine his policy of centralization of power over the cities and volosts of the grand principality with its elimination of local princely rule in favor of direct rule by the Grand Prince. Appearing simultaneously with the first successful attempts to build up centralized power, these claims could scarcely be satisfied with the very limited concessions made during Dmitri's reign. The question of the composition of Vladimir's domains was bound to be raised again, since Vladimir was an active participant in the defense of the Muscovite lands and the grand principality, and an energetic supporter of grand princely sovereignty. To be set apart in his own votchina principality meant that he would simply be serving another person's interest, indeed not just the Grand Prince's interest, but also that of other members of the Grand Prince's family who would share in the Grand Prince's newly acquired domains. All these questions and claims were raised on Dmitri's death, when his final riad was put into effect. In view of Moscow's strained relations with Novgorod, Lithuania, and the Tatars, its princes' strife was now posing a very serious threat to the stability of the Russian grand principality.

Within a year of Dmitri's death there was "hostility" between Vasili I and the Prince of Serpukhov. Shortly after Vasili's installation on the grand princely throne, Vladimir gathered his court and separated from the Grand Prince, moving first to his own city of Serpukhov, and from there to Torzhok. The princes were reconciled when Vasili granted Volok and Rzhev to Vladimir as a part of his otchina. But this was only the beginning of a division and redivision of domains that was to be characteristic of Vasili's reign. These divisions destroyed the stability of traditional udel domain, carrying it further and further from its original foundations (the father's riad, the hereditary nature of each udel or portion, and the system of relations among the princes based on custom and law) onto the new ground of arbitrary treaty agreements. The disposition of a domain now took the form of a "conferral to a prince as his udel" or "as his udel and votchina," becoming nothing more than a concession to the demands of this or that party to a dispute over a given volost, either on the part of the Grand Prince or by one of his "younger brothers." The traditional provisions for rule by udel and the actual territorial composition of the princes' domains entered a transitional period when the stability of the udel-votchina system and the traditional concepts of possession of a domain were gradually destroyed.

The treaty of 1390 did not end the negotiations between Grand Prince Vasili and his older cousin Vladimir. About 1405 a review of the grand princely domains took place, and the Grand Prince exchanged Gorodets for Volok and Uglich for Rzhev, adding several other volosts in each case. The outstanding role played by Vladimir in the defense of Moscow and the grand principality gave him a double reason for demanding an increase in the size of his domains, and his growing family (there were now five sons) must also have added impetus to his demands. Before his death (in the spring of 1410) Vladimir "gave a riad to his sons and princess," in which the complex nature of his domains was clearly set forth. Vladimir "enjoined" his third share in the city of Moscow to all five of his sons, the revenues thereof going to each one in turn for the space of one year, while to his eldest son, Ivan, he also assigned a number of sources of court income "by reason of his seniority." What Vladimir considered to be his and his sons' otchina (Serpukhov, Borovsk, Iaroslavl, Radonezh, and Peremysl) he divided among his sons, listing also certain other volosts as an additional distribution to them of lands he had received "from the udel of Grand Prince Vasili"—Kozelsk, Gorodets, and Uglich.

In other respects the interrelations of the princes and the forms of princely domain set forth in this testament were quite in harmony with tradition. At the head of the family stood the widowed princess mother, who was to govern the domains placed in her possession (during her lifetime only) both in the realm of the administration of justice and in the business of the collection of tribute. Vladimir's sons were to rule their otchina in udels, each one transferring his udel to his widow for her lifetime use and to his sons in the form of a hereditary domain. No prince had the right to alienate an udel or dispose of it by testament in the event of a lack of male heirs; in such a case the udel was to be divided equally among the remaining brothers. Quarrels between the brother princes were to be settled by an assembly of their boyars and by the final decision of the Princess Mother, who was placed under the guardianship of the Grand Prince, to whom his princess and all his children were "enjoined." The Grand Prince was to care for them and supervise the execution of the Princess' wishes, seeing to it that their otchina and its udels suffered no loss.

The division of Vladimir's domains among his five sons put an end to whatever significance his principality may have had, and reduced his sons to the position of minor vassals of the Grand Prince. The plague of 1426–27 spared none of his sons. The last survivor of this princely house, Iaroslav's son Vasili, appears to have been a rather important figure among the princes of Moscow, but his position as a ruling prince was compromised by the violence that upset the relationship of the Muscovite princes in the time of Vasili the Blind.

Although the structure of ruling relationships set forth in Vladimir's testament gave no firm and stable organization for the Serpukhov principality, it gives us an indication of the views on princely law as they had developed in that time, and of the historical conditions in which it was drawn up. We have here not an udel of the Moscow otchina, but a separate votchina principality, repeating in its own internal structure the relations of the Muscovite family as a whole. Vladimir's sons were to rule their otchina in the form of udels on the principles of the traditional family-votchina law, and they were united within the family group not only as a result of their joint rule of their domains and the seniority of the Princess Mother and Vladimir's eldest son, but also because of their political ties with the grand principality. However, the seniority of the Prince of Serpukhov over his younger brothers was devoid of political significance, and thus of any real power, since it was wholly qualified by the dependence of this entire group of local princes on the power of the Grand Prince. The only thing still binding these princes and their domains together as a political and administrative unit was their collective payment of tribute into the Grand Prince's treasury at the time of a Tatar outlay. The Grand Princess of Serpukhov and her sons were to collect this tribute "whenever the Grand Prince made a payment of tribute to the Horde," each one from his udel "according to the obrok," which was precisely set forth in the testament. Then together they were to send their tribute to the treasury of the Grand Prince, paying it in a lump sum, with one boyar from each udel assigned to carry out this task. There is no trace here of a retention of financial powers on the part of Serpukhov; this is nothing more than a roundabout way of carrying out the Grand Prince's demand for payment of "the unavoidable tribute." Under such circumstances there was really nothing to prevent the breakdown of the Serpukhov principality. Without real power, its princes became first vassals, and then princely landholders bound to service. This process was affecting other principalities besides that of Serpukhov; the only difference here was that the process was altered and hastened by the plague.

VII.

Prince Vladimir's quarrels over volosts with the Grand Prince came about partly as a result of Vladimir's place as a member of Moscow's ruling family and partly because of his active participation in the struggle to build up Moscow as the center of the grand principality. The ambiguity of his position—as prince of his own votchina of Serpukhov and a member of Moscow's princely house—created a contradiction between his concern to make Serpukhov a stable and independent principality and his desire to strengthen his position there by participating in the joint rule of the Muscovite principality and acquiring udels or portions of lands newly added to Moscow as a result of his campaigns with the Grand Prince. The latter course was all the more attractive in that the direct heirs to Dmitri's otchina were engaged in their own dispute over and redivisions of their domains as a result of the setting apart of an udel for Dmitri's youngest son, Constantine. This apportionment had necessitated a series of exchanges of volosts between Dmitri's sons, ratified in treaties and agreements, which, since they had no clear basis in their father's riad, introduced the principle of arbitrary "conferral" into their relationships as rulers of the land.

It was against this background of "volost madness" that now possessed Grand Prince Vasili, his younger brothers, and his cousin Vladimir that hostile relations soon developed between them, especially between Vasili and his brothers Iuri and Constantine. Only one of Vasili's treaties has come down to us, one made with Andrei and Peter. What is striking about this treaty is its lack of real content. It simply confirms the traditional arrangement that the princes "be as one man in their concern for one another's welfare," and reaffirms their mutual "watchful care" of one another's domains (in spite of the fact that the treaty did not include Iuri or Constantine). We also have evidence of the relations between these brothers in Vasili I's testaments. In the first the Grand Prince "enjoins" his princess and his son (Vasili) to Vladimir of Serpukhov and his two brothers Andrei and Peter. In the second they are committed to his father-in-law, Vitovt, to his brothers Andrei, Peter, and Constantine, and to Vladimir's sons in Serpukhov. In the third they are committed to these same persons with the exception, again, of Constantine. Iuri is mentioned nowhere in these documents, and was evidently alienated from Vasili throughout the latter's reign as Grand Prince. We know, however, that he did march at Vasili's command in campaigns against Novgorod, the Dvina territory, and the Volga Bulgars. There is no clear indication in our sources of the cause of their quarrel. We have no record of treaties between Vasili and Iuri. Historians have usually connected all these facts with another feature of Vasili's testaments: in his first and third provisions Vasili bestowed the grand principality on his son in a rather qualified way, with the words "and God will give the grand principality to my son." Certainly we have no direct evidence that Iuri was advancing his claims to the grand princely throne during Vasili's lifetime, but it is at least reasonable to suppose that even then Iuri did not wish to have his name inscribed below that of his nephew, or to accept Vasili's eldest son as his own "elder brother" and thus as grand prince. This theory can be supported by analogy with Constantine, who in 1419 broke away from Vasili and moved to Novgorod because the Grand Prince "thought to inscribe his name beneath that of his son Vasili." The theory may also be supported by the apparent absence of any treaty between Vasili I and Iuri, where the use of the "younger brother" formula would have been unavoidable.

The dispute between Prince Iuri and Grand Prince Vasili I was more than a simple quarrel over volosts. Iuri's attack on his nephew after the father's death was not unexpected. It was the logical consequence of strained relations and rival claims already defined. We have no way of knowing precisely when or under what circumstances the question of these rival claims of uncle and nephew were first raised, but undoubtedly both claimed a right to the position of seniority in the princely house of Moscow. Historians have developed the theory that there was a replacement at this time of the old mode of succession within a "patrimony" by a "new" votchina succession, in which princely power was passed from father to son directly, to the exclusion of secondary lines. But we must not lose sight of the fact that votchina succession was even then a very ancient concept of princely law, although it referred to those votchina principalities established as a result of a father's assignment to his sons of hereditary domains or udels in the common otchina with the subsequent breakdown of this common otchina in the changes occurring with each passing generation. We should not confuse this type of territorial votchina succession with succession in the possession of seniority within a group of princely brothers and cousins. The latter form of succession was a principle not in the law of domain, but in the law of family relationships. It was a family right, and in the minds of the princes it carried with it powers and concerns more of a political than of a territorial nature. From the very earliest times we see a series of attempts to connect grand princely seniority with a specific throne within the principality and thereby to assimilate the succession in seniority to the votchina succession within one line of the princely house. We see this in the setting aside of the Polotsk otchina for the "descendants of Rovgolod," and even more clearly in the struggle of the older line of Monomakh for a votchina right to "the golden throne of Kiev" and that seniority in the brotherhood of Russian princes which became connected with it. What the sons of Monomakh had been unable to do in the south was finally accomplished in the north by the descendants of Prince Daniel of Moscow, who had built up a great otchina around the seat of their patrimony, gained the grand princely rule of Vladimir and all Russia, and now stood at the head of the Great Russian land. They had established dominion over Great Novgorod, had brought under their grand princely sovereignty the neighboring principalities of Tver, Riazan, and Nizhni Novgorod, and for three generations had retained the succession to the grand princely rule within their family. Throught this period of early growth the question of relations between an uncle and a nephew had arisen only once, under Dmitri of the Don, when Vladimir of Serpukhov recognized his cousin's son Vasili as his "elder brother." Even here, however, there was nothing "new." This was simply another example of the denial of the position of seniority to a representative of a secondary line who had become settled in his own separate votchina.

Iuri's pretensions were based on quite different and genuinely new ground, and a lengthy dispute now flared up among Dmitri's descendants. This new ground had been created by the truly unprecedented provision of Dmitri's testament that applied the votchina principle to the grand princely rule and its territory. Dmitri had "bestowed" the grand princely rule of Vladimir upon his sons, together with Galich, Beloozero, and Uglich. These domains still stood apart from the Moscow votchina, as did also Pereislavl Zalesky and Kostroma, which were not to appear as distinct votchina domains until the testament of Vasili the Blind, although Dmitri disposed of these too in his riad to his sons.

Beyond this, Dmitri took a long step toward cementing the connection between the grand principality and the principle of votchina domain and inheritance by creating a grand princely udel standing as a special domain within the Muscovite votchina, which could not under any circumstances be divided among his sons, but must pass undivided to whichever one of them became grand prince.

Dmitri's riad had in view only his own sons, the next generation of rulers of the Muscovite votchina. His testament was bound to raise a new question for succeeding generations. Its application was clear and simple in the event of the death of the elder son without children. But what was to happen if he died leaving an heir? Which would take precedence, the votchina principle or the principle of seniority? Dmitri had introduced a new element into Muscovite princely law by permanently connecting the grand principality with the domains of Moscow and Kolomna, as "the Grand Prince's udel." This had led to the merging of political succession in the grand princely rule with votchina (territorial) inheritance as determined by the father's riad. And behind this new principle there loomed the fact that Moscow and not Vladimir was the real center of grand princely power over all Russia.

Moscow had acquired its significance as a result of its strategic location and as the place of residence of both the grand prince of all Russia and the metropolitan. Its central importance had emerged first in the reign of Ivan Kalita, then it was defined and consolidated under Dmitri of the Don. Henceforth the grand principality was to be inconceivable apart from Moscow. Moscow was to be the real support and organizing center of the grand prince's power, as the votchina of the house of Daniel— or, more precisely, of the house of Dmitri of the Don. But its possession was to be subject to the traditional family-votchina principles. On the father's death the widowed princess mother was to take the position of head of the family, and Moscow and its suburbs were to be under the joint rule of the heirs to the otchina, with Moscow's volosts given into their possession in the form of shares or udels. There was the familiar prospect of votchina disintegration, and only a very qualified unification of the military and financial resources of the principality as a whole. This structure of internal relations made the Moscow principality an unstable basis for grand princely policy, and the Grand Prince's position as leader of Great Russia's political life was undermined by inner contradictions. The profound incongruity between the formal organization of princely rule and the actual political tasks of the grand principality was the basic cause of the sharp crisis that began to develop in the time of Vasili I and broke out in violent conflict in the reign of his son Vasili the Blind. The crisis was to be resolved finally, after new violence in the bosom of this family in the reign of Ivan III, by the liquidation of the udel-votchina system.

Iuri's struggle with Vasili II, the Blind, was a struggle for Moscow. The grand principality of Vladimir had become the grand principality of Moscow. It was a struggle also for the position of seniority in the princely house of Moscow, a position now inseparable from the grand princely rule. Their conflict revealed with new force the need to rebuild the entire structure of family-votchina relations on new principles that would be appropriate to grand princely rule. This task had to be accomplished if all the long years of building by the lords of Moscow were not to end in nothing. The merging of the grand principality and the Moscow otchina into a single Muscovite state recognized as the votchina of a sovereign grand prince, and the transformation of the princely family of Moscow into a "reigning house" or dynasty of Muscovite sovereigns, with a corresponding reorganization of its internal relationships; these were to be the results of the crisis through which this princely family passed in the time of Vasili the Blind and Ivan III. History had carried the descendants of Daniel toward this goal in the latter half of the fourteenth century and throughout the fifteenth century. The disorders in the reign of Vasili the Blind showed that this historical process was coming to a head, and hastened its final resolution.

These disorders originated in the relations that had developed in the time of Vasili I, and they broke out immediately after his death. Before his death, of course, he had named his ten-year-old son (Vasili II) grand prince in his place. Metropolitan Photius and his boyars were appointed as the young prince's guardians. The struggle had begun, and several phases in this conflict deserve special study. On the very night that Grand Prince Vasili I died, Photius sent to Zvenigorod for Prince Iuri, where it was learned that Iuri had withdrawn to Galich and had already begun to marshal his forces there. The other Muscovite princes and boyars responded by rapidly mustering an army and making an advance on Iuri, who retreated to Nizhni. The expedition did not reach the point of armed conflict; a truce was declared and negotiations were started. Vasili II was supported not only by the boyars of Moscow, with Photius and Grand Princess Sofia at their head, but also by his uncles Andrei, Peter, and Constantine, and by "all the princes and boyars of his land." Appeals were made also to Vitovt, into whose "care" Vasili I had committed his son. It was agreed that Photius should make an effort to reach an agreement with Prince Iuri, but Iuri had no desire for peace, and insisted on an extension of the truce. Only under threat of the Metropolitan's wrath did he agree to send his boyars to Moscow for further negotiations. These talks resulted in an agreement that "it was not for Prince Iuri to seek the grand princely rule on his own initiative, but through the Khan; and whosoever the Khan should appoint, that one would be grand prince of Vladimir and Great Novgorod and all Russia."

This is all that the chronicles tell us. Our sources omit a number of facts that would help to explain what happened after this. It would seem that on this occasion the matter was handled without recourse to the power of the Khan. Iuri had decided against battle mainly because of the Lithuanian power standing behind Vasili II and secured by the intermediation of Photius and Princess Sofia. The subordination of Great Russian grand princely policies to Lithuanian influence in this period and then the dispute over possession of the grand princely rule in Lithuania following Vitovt's death, with the transfer of power there to Svidrigailo, together with the fact that Svidrigailo and Iuri were married to sisters, will give us some idea of the significance of this Lithuanian support.

The grandson was destined to pay dearly for his grandfather's "care." Taking advantage of his influence in Moscow, Vitovt began to renew his attacks on Pskov and Novgorod. In 1426 he invaded the Pskov land and forced its capital city to pay a heavy sum in return for peace. Appeals for help sent out by

Pskov to Novgorod and Grand Prince Vasili II were unanswered. Then in 1428 Vitovt marched against the Novgorod volosts and compelled the men of Novgorod to sue for peace "on the ancient terms," with the payment of a huge tribute. Great Russia's powerlessness in the face of Lithuanian pressure on its western frontier was reflected in the lack of unity among the western cities. Novgorod decided not to help Pskov, and limited itself to fruitless diplomatic overtures. Pskov made peace with Vitovt "without Novgorod," and agreed not to aid the latter. Neither city was supported by the forces of the Grand Prince. Vasili did send an envoy to Vitovt to protest the violation of his otchina in Novgorod, and did allow Pskov to have a prince in return for its homage, but was unable to take really effective steps on their behalf, and "kissed the cross to his grandfather Vitovt, promising him that he would send no aid" to either city.

This left the rulers of Moscow free to press their attack on Iuri. It was not until March of 1428, however, that they succeeded in bringing him to a settlement on the Grand Prince's terms. The treaty concluded at that time abrogated the provisional measures taken in 1425 in the very first phase of their conflict. The Grand Prince's deputies, volosts, village officials, and tiuns would henceforth "superintend" Iuri's otchina and the villages of his boyars, until such time as Iuri should agree to make a treaty accepting Vasili II as his elder brother and binding him not to violate Vasili's domains in Moscow and Kolomna, in Nizhni Novgorod and Murom, or in any part of his grand principality, either during the reign of Vasili II or under the latter's sons.

The treaty of 1428 only established another truce, however, although it did provide that the princes should "at all times be as one man and seek one another's welfare." It was concluded a month after the death of Prince Peter of Dmitrov, who left no son to succeed him. Peter's death created another occasion for strife over possession of the vacant principality. Vasili's treaty with his uncle Iuri makes no mention of Dmitrov, although this question must have been in their minds at the time of this settlement. From what we know about this principality later on, it is apparent that the Grand Prince simply seized Dmitrov and made no division of its volosts among his uncles.

The treaty of 1428 established a very temporary and fragile peace. The calm lasted for about two years. In 1430–31 two extremely important events took place. Vitovt died in October, 1430, and this was followed by the death of Metropolitan Photius in July, 1431. The grand principality was left without an authoritative leader in Moscow, and in Lithuania power shifted to Iuri's brother-in-law Svidrigailo. Iuri at once "violated his peace" with Grand Prince Vasili II, returning his copy of the treaty of 1428 to Moscow and making a declaration of war. The princes decided now to take their case to the Horde for the Khan's judgment. Unfortunately the next stage in their controversy is set forth in our chronicles in a very confused and contradictory manner, with much abbreviation and revision of the original text, so that it is difficult to establish the sequence and meaning of events with any certainty.

The arguments used by the princes in support of their claims are very interesting. According to the chronicles, Prince Iuri based his claim "on the chronicles and ancient records and on the testament of his father, Grand Prince Dmitri." His chief argument—the reference to "his departed father's testament"— shows that he was seeking not only the throne of the grand principality, but also the Grand Prince's udel of Moscow-Kolomna, and therefore that he was refusing to admit that Dmitri's testament (which had provided that this udel should pass to the next eldest brother in the event of Vasili I's death) was invalid once an heir to the votchina had been born to Vasili I. This argument stemmed naturally from the already established connection between the Moscow-Kolomna domains and the grand princely rule, but it sharply contradicted the votchina tradition. Even among the persons close to Prince Iuri there was some doubt about the lawfulness of such a claim, and an attempt was made to resolve the question by separating Moscow from the Kolomna udel, with an acknowledgment of Vasili II's votchina right to Kolomna and the retention of Moscow alone as the residence of the grand prince.

The weakness in Iuri's argument lay in this confusion of votchina law with succession to the grand principality. As the representative of the Grand Prince (who was still not of age), the boyar Vsevolozhsky denied Iuri's claim and advanced Vasili's rights "on the basis of his otchina and patrimony," supporting his argument by citing the Khan's sanction, already secured for his son by Grand Prince Vasili I, and by pointing to the young Prince Vasili's political reliability in contrast to Iuri, the "half brother" of Svidrigailo of Lithuania. Complicated by the struggle between leading factions in the Horde, the princes' quarrel was not as quickly resolved as some of the chronicle texts would indicate. The Russian princes and boyars were in the land of the Horde from the fall of 1431 until the following summer. Finally, in June of 1432, the Khan allowed the princes to return "into their otchinas," at the same time "attaching" Dmitrov and all its volosts (i.e., the entire Dmitrov udel) to the domains of Prince Iuri. The question of the grand principality was left open, at least formally, and it was not until three months later that the Khan's envoy installed Vasili II on the throne of the grand principality.

Once confirmed as grand prince, Vasili II resumed possession of Dmitrov and the struggle broke out again, this time in armed conflict. Iuri attacked quickly and smashed Vasili's hastily assembled troops, forcing him to seek refuge first in Tver and then in Kostroma, where Iuri took Vasili prisoner and received his homage. Iuri then ruled as grand prince in Moscow, and on the advice of his trusted boyar Semeon Morozov he returned the Kolomna udel to Vasili. This action had an immediate and characteristic result: the boyars and free men of the grand princely court in Moscow "began to renounce Prince Iuri in favor of Grand Prince Vasili II and to move from Moscow to Kolomna." Prince Iuri was defeated in his attempt to divide the indivisible. He had failed to separate the grand princely rule from its territorial basis, closely tied as this was to the real seat of power in the grand principality—the grand princely court of Moscow. Iuri's sons could see that all was lost. They murdered Morozov and forsook their father. Iuri was forced to admit that "he had not gained possession of the grand principality," and made peace. According to this new treaty, Iuri bound himself to accept Vasili II "as his eldest brother" and to support him "in the position of seniority." He was compelled to renounce his claims to the grand principality and to all Vasili's domains, including Peter's votchina of Dmitrov. He was even obliged to give up the yarlik to Dmitrov which he had received from the Khan. He was also prohibited from having any further direct dealings with the Horde. Vasili's only concession was to grant him the right not to participate in campaigns against Lithuania.

Iuri concluded this treaty in a fit of rage against his sons Vasili Kosoi (Squint-Eyed) and Dmitri Shemiaka, who had forsaken him. He was obliged not to receive them back or "be concerned for their welfare," and Vasili Kosoi and Dmitri Shemiaka settled in Kostroma. An attempt by the Grand Prince's host to drive them out of Kostroma was defeated, and it is interesting to note that Iuri and his commanders evidently took part in this battle against Vasili II. The struggle was renewed with fresh bitterness, and Vasili II, twice defeated in the Rostov region, was forced to flee to Great Novgorod, and from there to Nizhni. Once again Iuri was installed in Moscow. This time Vasili's strength seemed completely shattered, and the younger princes hastened to join the victor. The two sons of Andrei of Mozhaisk, Ivan and Mikhail, again acknowledged Iuri as grand prince, as did also Prince Ivan of Riazan. Iuri's younger sons, Dmitri Shemiaka and Dmitri the Younger, went in pursuit of the Grand Prince, who apparently had no recourse but to seek refuge with the Horde.

All these successes on the part of the opponents of Vasili II collapsed with Iuri's unexpected death. Moscow had surrendered to Iuri in Holy Week of 1434; he was dead on the fifth of June. His eldest son, Vasili Kosoi, moved to occupy the grand prince's throne, but his brother princes did not accept him and made haste to reconcile themselves with Vasili of Moscow. Recently "forsaken by all," Vasili once more reigned "in his otchina on the grand princely throne of Moscow." In his treaty with Dmitri Shemiaka, Vasili II consolidated his hold not only on the Moscow-Kolomna domains and the grand principality, but also on the udel of Dmitrov and Vasili Kosoi's udel of Zvenigorod, which the Grand Prince "seized for himself." Dmitri Shemiaka once again divided the Galich votchina with Dmitri the Younger, and in addition to Galich, Ruza, and Vyshgorod he received Rzhev and Uglich from the Grand Prince "as his udel and votchina," i.e., what had formerly been the udel of his uncle Constantine, while Dmitri the Younger received Bezhetsk. Dmitri Shemiaka also gave up Viatka. Vasili II was reconciled with Vasili Kosoi after further military engagements, with a settlement made in the spring of 1435. The Grand Prince did not return the Zvenigorod udel to Vasili Kosoi, nor did he set aside another udel for him within the Galich otchina. Instead, Vasili Kosoi was given as his udel and otchina the city of Dmitrov with its volosts. He reigned there for only one month. His next act shows that he was angered over his exclusion from the Galich otchina. After seizing Kostroma and from there sending a "declaration of hostility" to the Grand Prince, he marched into Galich, gathering his forces as he went, including the men of Viatka and the members of Dmitri Shemiaka's court. From Galich, Vasili Kosoi moved against Ustiug, where a sharp resistance against him was cruelly punished. Vasili Kosoi's aggressive action made the Grand Prince also suspect Dmitri Shemiaka, who was sent into safekeeping in Kostroma, while he himself marched against Vasili Kosoi with Dmitri the Younger and Prince Ivan of Mozhaisk. Considerable help was received from Lithuania, since Vasili II was joined also by Prince Ivan of Druts. With these reinforcements Vasili Kosoi was beaten and taken prisoner. His stormy political career was at an end. He was blinded for his treachery, and although he lived until 1448 he was unable to take any further active part in the affairs of the land.

These events marked the end of the first stage in this period of Muscovite unrest. The relationships built up under the old traditional order had been violently confused and disrupted. The unity of the princely house of Moscow was shattered by the new separation of one of its udels as the separate votchina of the Galich princes. In place of princely relations governed by tradition and law, we now have outright seizure, the definition of domains by way of "conferral" and "settlement," and warfare characterized by increasing barbarity, treachery, and violence. An outworn social order was in its death throes.

VIII.

Having crushed Vasili Kosoi and subdued Dmitri Shemiaka, Vasili II could feel that he had ended the sedition, but not many years passed before it broke out again. This time it exploded with redoubled force, more deeply implicating the lesser princes of Great Russia and developing into a much more complicated situation that now involved the Tatars, Tver, and Great Novgorod, as well as Lithuania.

The affairs of the grand principality were in a state of chaos. Moscow was completely ineffectual. It is true that the Prince of Riazan did not withdraw his military aid from Vasili II in the latter's struggle against Iuri, but then he also acknowledged Iuri as grand prince when Iuri held Moscow for the second time. Internal strife threatened to destroy Moscow's significance as the center of grand princely power, all the more so in view of the Lithuanian influence on Moscow established first in the reign of Vasili I and heightened by Vitovt's guardianship of Vasili II. We see Vasili accompanied by Metropolitan Photius and the grand princes of Tver and Riazan at the court of Vitovt at Trokakh in the famous "coronation" assembly of 1430. The Grand Prince of Tver had in fact already made a treaty with Vitovt in 1427, in which he had declared himself to be "on his side," with the obligation "to assist him in all things without reservation." As we have already noted, these connections between Lithuania and Tver became so firmly established that in 1449 Grand Prince Boris was to renew the treaty with Casimir providing for Tver's subordinate dependence on the Lithuanian state, and force Grand Prince Vasili II to admit that the Tver princes stood definitely "in the ranks of" the Lithuanian prince.

Under these circumstances it is easy to see why the question of the appointment to the metropolitan see after Photius' death could not be settled according to the wishes of the Grand Prince of Great Russia. The new Lithuanian prince, Svidrigailo, sent Bishop Gerasim of Smolensk to Constantinople to be consecrated as metropolitan, and Gerasim was duly installed in the Russian see. The rulers of Moscow had their own "metropolitan designate," Bishop Jonas of Riazan, but although Gerasim failed to make an appearance in Moscow, they made no attempt to send Jonas to Constantinople. Gerasim was evidently waiting for a victory by Iuri, which would make it possible for him to enter fully into his office as metropolitan of all Russia. The suppression of the Muscovite disorder and the death of Iuri removed this possibility, and in the summer of 1435 Gerasim also perished, a victim of Svidrigailo's anger over some "treachery" said to have been committed by the Metropolitan. Vasili II now sent Bishop Jonas to be consecrated by the Patriarch. In Constantinople, however, broader and more important aims (the proposed union with the Roman church) led to the consecration of a Greek bishop, Isidore, to the Russian see. The metropolitan was not to be a potent political force in Great Russia again until after Isidore's deposition, the rupture with Constantinople, and the subsequent complete nationalization of the Russian see.

Great Novgorod pursued a cautious and neutral course in the disorders among the Muscovite princes. Vasili II found sanctuary there when he was compelled to flee from his uncle Iuri. The people of Novgorod were greatly alarmed by this action and raised an army, but they were not drawn directly into this storm. Soon another visitor appeared in their midst, Iuri's son Vasili Kosoi, seeking assistance in his efforts to mount a new offensive. He revenged himelf for their refusal to support him by plundering the Novgorod volosts. When Grand Prince Vasili was again established on his throne in the winter of 1435, Great Novgorod entered into a treaty with him by which the Grand Prince gave up his possession of the "Novgorod otchina," i.e., all the lands seized from Novgorod by grand princes in former times (Bezhetsk and the lands of Volokolamsk and Vologda), and agreed to send his boyars at an appointed time "for a division of the land," with the Novgorod boyars agreeing to return to Vasili II the ancient and disputed "princely tolls." Once he had settled finally with Vasili Kosoi, however, the Grand Prince did not carry out this "division," and did not "execute justice," "refusing to restore any part of the Novgorod otchina to the people of Novgorod." His demands increased and the promised concessions were abrogated, and in 1437 the people of Novgorod were forced to pay him a general tribute "from all the Novotorzhok volosts from which tribute had been levied in times past." The development of Great Novgorod's political independence had been undermining the Grand Prince's "toll," and the demands made by the grand principality on Novgorod "not to withhold these tolls, but to pay them in accordance with the ancient sacred vows," gave place now to direct efforts to restore the rights that had been either completely abrogated or for a time suspended.

Moscow's insistent demands and the constant disputes over the volosts of the "Novgorod otchina" that had been seized by the grand princes and placed under their own direct rule inevitably set the stage for new "hostilities." In 1441 Vasili II pillaged the Novgorod volosts, in the face of stiff resistance put up by combined Novgorod and Zavolochie forces. Vasili moved against these forces with a troop from Pskov and the host of Tver. Novgorod was forced to sue for peace, making a payment of 8,000 rubles and accepting the obligation to pay the Grand Prince's rents and tolls "on the ancient terms." The long-standing and radical instability of Novgorod's relations with the grand principality gave Dmitri Shemiaka an opportunity to stir up new unrest. The chronicles have preserved only a brief and incomplete account of this attempt on his part to take advantage of Novgorod's dissatisfaction with Vasili's demands, but we can assume that it was this kind of activity on Dmitri Shemiaka's part that prompted Vasili to make a campaign against him immediately after concluding his treaty with Novgorod. Dmitri Shemiaka fled into the Novgorod hinterland, and then invited Novgorod to accept him as its prince on terms of its own choosing. Novgorod's evasive reply forced Dmitri Shemiaka to submit to the Grand Prince, with Abbot Zinov of the Trinity Monastery acting as mediator. The next outbreak was brought on not by Moscow's relations with Novgorod, but as a result of its dealings with the Tatars. The complications of the grand principality's external relations were becoming more and more deeply entwined with its unstable internal situation.

Once powerful under Mamai, Tokhtamysh, and Edigei, the Golden Horde was again entering into a period of decline. Large splinters of Tatar power were breaking away from the Horde, but even as this process began to weaken Russia's ancient foe, it had the immediate effect of bringing Tatar forces closer to hand. The lesser hordes forming out of Kipchak's empire were moving toward the borders of Russia in search of a new center of operations. In the fall of 1438 Khan Kuchuk-Makhmet drove his brother Ulug-Makhmet out of the land of the Horde, and Ulug-Makhmet settled in Belev. In his search for sanctuary, Ulug-Makhmet "began to submit to the will of the Russian princes," promising that if he gained control of the Golden Horde "he would watch over the Russian land" and would not send his envoys into Russia "to gather the outlay or for any other purpose." But Grand Prince Vasili II sent Dmitri Shemiaka and Dmitri the Younger out against him with orders to drive him back out of Russian territory. This resulted in the defeat of the Russian host, however, and Ulug-Makhmet occupied the ancient city of Nizhni Novgorod, where he was to remain until the autumn of 1445. The Grand Prince's commanders had intended to fortify the "lesser town" of Nizhni and stand siege, but lack of food forced them to set fire to the town and retreat to Moscow. From his captured outpost Ulug-Makhmet made raids on Russian soil up to the very gates of Moscow, setting fire to Kolomna and attacking also Murom. About the same time the Tatar prince Mustafa came into the Riazan land, and prepared to spend the winter in its chief city. Grand Prince Vasili sent a host against him, reinforced by a regiment of Riazan foot soldiers, a troop of Riazan cossacks, and detachments from Mordva. The Tatars were defeated and Mustafa killed.

This movement toward Russia's borders of obviously quite large and well-equipped fragments of Tatar power gave rise to a new practice that was to have important consequences. There now began to appear in the Grand Prince's armies Tatar service princes and other persons of royal blood from the Horde with detachments of their own servants and soldiers. As early as 1445 Vasili sent two such Tatar princes on a campaign against Lithuania. There is also mention at this time of a Tatar service prince named Berdydad. Having driven Vasili's forces out of the suburb of Nizhni, Ulug-Makhmet now sent his sons Mamudek and Yakub against the Grand Prince. Dmitri Shemiaka did not come to Vasili's help, Berdydad failed to move quickly enough to join the battle, and the Grand Prince was defeated near the

Spas-Evfimi Monastery and taken prisoner, along with Prince Mikhail of Vereia and many of their boyars.

Unfortunately we do not know exactly what took place then between Ulug-Makhmet and Vasili II. Some of our chronicles have evidently deliberately avoided giving a description of the conditions of their settlement; others mention a huge ransom paid (in the amount of 200,000 rubles) with the added comment, "and God knows what else." Ulug-Makhmet had released Vasili, Mikhail, and their boyars on extremely harsh conditions, but many Tatar princes with large bodies of their own people accompanied Vasili and Mikhail on their return to Russia.

Fantastic rumors spread over the land, and were used by Dmitri Shemiaka to frighten Prince Ivan of Mozhaisk into thinking that Vasili II "had kissed the cross to the Khan, that a khan would soon rule in Moscow and in all the cities of Russia, and that Vasili himself would rule in Tver." Later Vasili was to be reproached for his alleged betrayal of the Russian cause: "Why did you bring the Tatars into the Russian land and give our cities to them, and provision them on our volosts? And why did you befriend the Tatars and speak with them beyond measure, while Christians you afflicted without restraint or mercy, giving their silver and gold and all their possessions to the Tatars?" In the day of Vasili's worst affliction—when he was blinded and driven into exile—we shall see two of Ulug-Makhmet's sons, Kasim and Yakub, in the ranks of Vasili's supporters, bringing their forces "to seek out the Grand Prince and defend him, in return for the good that he had done to them in the past and for the bread he had provided, for much good had been done to them by him."

Precisely what was this "good" that bound these Tatar princes to such faithful service in Vasili's name? After making his agreement with Vasili and releasing him, Ulug-Makhmet had moved against Kazan, a small city under the rule of the princeling Azi-Alibeg. Ulug-Makhmet took Kazan, but was then killed by his son Mamudek, who became the founder of the Kazan Khanate. Mamudek's brothers Kasim and Yakub were in Vasili's service, and we are told that they fought for him "with all their strength" against every enemy, above all against the Nogai and Kazan Tatars. We do not know anything about the terms on which they were "provisioned for service," but of course this silence is no accident, just as it is not accidental that our sources tell us nothing about the period when Kasim's kingdom came into being. Only a later treaty between Ivan III and Prince Ivan of Riazan informs us that Vasili II had "made a settlement" with the Tatar prince Kasim, in his own name and for the Prince of Riazan, which defined the position of Vasili and the Prince of Riazan as rulers of the Meshchera land.

It is in these relations with the Tatars that we find the real foundation for the furious attacks made on Vasili. His use of Tatar forces in the defense of the Russian land and as a support for the power of the grand prince was widely opposed. There is a clear indication of the impression that Vasili's close relations with the Tatars made on Russia in the obviously deliberate suppression of the details of these connections in our chronicles, which of course are the products of later editing and revision.

Grand Prince Vasili II returned from imprisonment surrounded by Tatars and burdened with a heavy debt that was to bring tremendous hardship to the peasant classes. On the news of his imprisonment panic swept through Moscow. The Tatars were expected to arrive at any moment. The Grand Princess fled to Rostov and the boyars began to leave the city. The common people refused to be swayed by the cowardice of their leaders, however, and began to erect fortifications in preparation for a siege. But the Tatars did not advance against Moscow. Instead, Dmitri Shemiaka appeared, having been informed of Vasili's defeat and imprisonment by a special messenger from Ulug-Makhmet. The Grand Prince's agreement with the Tatars prevented Dmitri Shemiaka's seizure of Moscow and the grand princely rule at this time. On November 17, 1445, Vasili II returned to the throne, but not for long. The horror produced by his return with Tatar forces and obligations created a mood that foreshadowed his overthrow. Dmitri Shemiaka won Prince Ivan of Mozhaisk over to his side, secured the support of Grand Prince Boris of Tver, made contacts with boyars, merchants, and monks in Moscow who were ill disposed toward Vasili, and in February, 1446, seized the Grand Prince as he arrived at the Trinity Monastery on a pilgrimage and had him blinded and exiled to Uglich. Grand Princess Sofia was banished to Chukhloma.

This new "onslaught of evil" threatened completely to destroy the grand principality of Great Russia. Intoxicated by their quick and easy victory, Dmitri Shemiaka and his friends now began to dream of dividing up the grand principality among themselves in the form of large independent domains. Prince Ivan of Mozhaisk, who had gone over to Dmitri Shemiaka but then left him when he was granted possession of Suzdal, now returned to him with the provision that his possession of Suzdal be confirmed. This was sharply opposed by the heirs of the Suzdal otchina, Iuri's sons Vasili and Feodor, who had made a treaty with the Grand Prince securing their possession of the Suzdal "patrimony and otchina"—which included Suzdal, Nizhni Novgorod, Gorodets, and Viatka. Grand Prince Boris of Tver had already taken advantage of the unrest in Moscow to make attacks on the Novgorod volosts.

But an increasingly significant popular support of the grand principality began again to take effect, as it had the first time that Vasili II lost his hold on Moscow. The exiled grand prince was soon to be restored a second time. The boyars and serving princes tried to conceal Vasili's children from Dmitri Shemiaka, but he forced Bishop Jonas, the metropolitan designate, to bring them back to Moscow from Murom, where the boyars had taken them, and then broke his promise to give them (and their father) freedom and "a substantial otchina." Instead, he sent them to join their father in exile in Uglich. This only stirred up opposition against Dmitri Shemiaka. The supporters of Vasili the Blind were gathering beyond the Lithuanian border around Prince gathered their forces to join Vasili the Blind in Uglich. One by one Dmitri Shemiaka's entire court forsook him. Bishop Jonas' urgent protests and the unrest in Moscow's boyar class forced Vasili of Serpukhov and Prince Semeon Obolensky. Prince Feodor also fled Moscow to join them. The princes of Riapolovsk Dmitri Shemiaka to release Grand Prince Vasili from his confinement in Uglich and grant him Vologda as his otchina, having bound him, of course, by the usual "kissing of the cross and the threat of excommunication." The Grand Prince set out at once for the Kirilov Monastery in Beloozero under guise of making a pilgrimage, and there Abbot Trifon released him from the vow he had made under duress. From there he went to visit Grand Prince Boris of Tver, and confirmed his alliance with Boris by betrothing his seven-year-old son, Ivan, to Boris' five-year-old daughter, Maria.

The freeing of the Grand Prince encouraged his supporters. Moscow was taken without a battle, and Vasili the Blind then moved southward from Tver against Dmitri Shemiaka and the Prince of Mozhaisk "with great strength." The army of Vasili of Serpukhov joined him from beyond the Lithuanian border, and he was reinforced also by the two Tatar princes Kasim and Yakub. Dmitri Shemiaka was forced to retreat into his own domain of Galich and sue for peace. Their reconciliation did not bring any real settlement of the issue, however, and their kissing of the cross with the threat of excommunication was of no effect. In the years to come Dmitri Shemiaka made several futile and violent attempts to regain Moscow, and each one touched off new outbreaks of fruitless strife, intended by Vasili to subdue Dmitri Shemiaka once and for all and put an end to his efforts not only to arouse every possible element of dissatisfaction within the grand principality, but also to support these elements by agreements with Vasili's enemies beyond the borders of the Russian land. Tatar raids that shook Great Russia at the end of the 1440's and the beginning of the 1450's were brought about not only by the fact that (as in earlier times) princely "discord" made it easy for the "pagans" to "bring havoc on the Russian land," but also Dmitri Shemiaka's direct contacts with Kazan. In this period he was constantly urging other princes, the cities of Novgorod and Viatka, and the boyars and servants of the Grand Prince himself to join him in the cause of liberating Moscow from its subjection to Vasili's Tatar allies.

Vasili the Blind did not rely on military power alone to counter Dmitri Shemiaka's intrigues. He submitted his dispute to the judgment of a sacred council, to which he presented Dmitri Shemiaka's treaty and armistice documents and evidence of Dmitri Shemiaka's violation of all the principles of "solidarity." The hierarchy took action against Dmitri Shemiaka in a detailed letter of condemnation, threatening him with excommunication if he did not meet the conditions established in the various articles of his solemn agreements. This action on the part of the bishops marshaled the opinion of Russia's leading circles in support of the Grand Prince. On his consecration to the metropolitan see, Jonas addressed an encyclical letter to all princes, boyars, and military commanders and to "all people bearing the name of Christ," describing Prince Dmitri's acts of treachery and noting the excommunication to be laid upon him by the sacred council if he should renew his attacks on the Grand Prince and "bring this Christian realm to ruin and bloodshed."

At the same time Vasili the Blind was making a series of treaties that had the effect of isolating Dmitri Shemiaka within the general brotherhood of princes. Prince Ivan of Mozhaisk had tied his fate to Dmitri Shemiaka's, but Vasili's agreement with Boris of Tver forced both Ivan and Dmitri Shemiaka to seek peace with Moscow through the mediation of Mikhail of Vereia and Vasili of Serpukhov. In the end a peace was concluded only with Ivan of Mozhaisk, who submitted to the Grand Prince as a result of the mediation of Boris of Tver and on his surety. Ivan did not yet break completely with Dmitri Shemiaka, however, and insisted on Dmitri Shemiaka's inclusion in this agreement. In the beginning of 1448, with the renewal of hostilities between Vasili and Dmitri Shemiaka, Ivan of Mozhaisk once more stood on the side of the Grand Prince's enemies, who still harbored their ambitious plans. Ivan carried on negotiations with Grand Prince Casimir of Lithuania as Dmitri Shemiaka conferred with the Tatars, in an attempt to set up an alliance for the seizure of the Russian grand principality. Ivan bound himself to give Rzhev and Medyn to Casimir if the latter could help place him "on the grand princely throne of Moscow." The real reason for Ivan's anger lay in the fact that he had been deprived of Bezhetsk, which the Grand Prince had almost given him on an earlier occasion. Vasili II now succeeded in finally separating Ivan from Dmitri Shemiaka by granting him Bezhetsk. He could now settle with each of them separately.

Dmitri Shemiaka carried on his hopeless fight alone for some months. He was confronted now by a grand prince who was at peace with all the major forces of Great Russia, even though he did not yet possess absolute authority over them. The attitude of the Grand Prince of Tver to Muscovite affairs could best be called one of friendly neutrality. Vasili the Blind also made a treaty with the Grand Prince of Riazan in which the latter acknowledged himself to be a "younger brother" of the Grand Prince of all Russia, renounced all independent external relations, and promised to observe the principles of full solidarity. Prince Mikhail of Vereia had withdrawn from his brother Ivan of Mozhaisk when the latter went over to Dmitri Shemiaka, and ruled in his volosts of Vereia and Beloozero as a faithful vassal and "younger brother" of the Grand Prince. In 1447 Vasili II received a two-year advance payment of the outlay from Mikhail's domains and in return added half of the land "beyond" Beloozero and an additional hundred villages to Mikhail's domains. Vasili II had another faithful vassal in Vasili, the last prince of the house of Serpukhov, who had again united that otchina into a single domain. In addition to Serpukhov, Mikhail had received "as his votchina and udel" the domains of Dmitrov and Sukhodol.

Forsaken even by Ivan of Mozhaisk, Dmitri Shemiaka still placed some hope in Novgorod, at least as a final sanctuary. Great Novgorod had broadly developed its practice of "provisioning" princes who came to the city either from Great Russia or from Lithuania, and it valued its freedom in external affairs. Dmitri Shemiaka went to Novgorod therefore in 1450, after Vasili II had made a successful campaign against Galich and "had set his deputies throughout the whole of the Galich otchina." The men of Novgorod accepted the fugitive prince as they had done once before, when he returned from his unsuccessful attempt to seize Ustiug. Not even the exhortations of Metropolitan Jonas had any effect. The Metropolitan declared that Dmitri Shemiaka could not be received in the Novgorod churches, since he had been excommunicated for his actions; he insisted not only that Novgorod should refuse to give him sanctuary, but also that it should stop supporting his military activity, as it had done when it guarded Dmitri Shemiaka's family and treasury during his raid on Ustiug. All this was to no avail.

But Dmitri Shemiaka was doomed. His stormy career ended with his "unjust" death in July, 1453, as a result of a "cruel poison" given him by a representative of the Grand Prince's court.

Dmitri Shemiaka's death marked the end of this bloody drama with its cruel civil strife, its blindings, deportations, betrayals, and violence. This period was not like the Time of Troubles at the beginning of the seventeenth century. It did not touch the great masses of people, nor did it destroy the developed structures of social life. But by the end of Vasili's reign the traditional political organization of Great Russia with its age-old forms of interprincely relations was obviously scorned and shattered. Seizures of another prince's domains, forced "conferrals," the buying and selling of volosts and vows sealed by the kissing of the cross, bloody and cruel acts of vengeance, the continuous intrigues of princes and boyars and even of visiting cloth merchants and monks who had the misfortune to fall into the Grand Prince's hands, the Grand Prince's Tatar sympathies and alliances —all these things had the effect of shattering the established structure of relations in the life of the Russian princes. The udel-votchina system was now corrupted, undermined, and indeed destroyed. The Muscovite family of princes was broken. Most of the uncles and cousins of Vasili II had passed from the scene. Among the hereditary rulers of udels in the Muscovite principality, only Andrei's sons Ivan and Mikhail and Prince Vasili of Serpukhov had survived. From the viewpoint of the grand principality the struggle to end this disorder and eliminate its causes had now become simply a campaign to "take over the votchinas of its enemies." The ending of this disorder was directly connected with the organic process already working from within to reconstitute the Great Russian grand principality, on the principles of hereditary monarchy, as the Muscovite state.

Chapter
X
The Gathering of Power

Ivan III is usually regarded as the real founder of the Great Russian state. We must remember, however, that he built on a foundation already firmly laid. Ivan himself was a product of the closing years of his father's reign both in his style and in his basic ambitions, which is not surprising, for even as a boy (Ivan was born in 1440) he had been drawn into political life in his father's stubborn fight for power. From the time he was eight years old he was a representative of the grand princely power both in campaigns and at court. From the beginning of the 1450's we see him acting as grand prince and his father's co-regent. In these years his personality took shape and a ruling class was formed around him with which he was to begin his own independent reign in 1462. Ivan's policy with regard to his younger brother princes (those of his own family as well as those more distantly related), and also his treatment of the democracies of Great Novgorod and Pskov and the principalities of Tver and Riazan, were a direct continuation of the measures taken in the 1450's to put an end to the princely strife in Moscow's ruling house. As we have tried to show, these measures also had the effect of destroying the foundations of the udel-votchina system and led to the building of political power over Great Russia on new principles. Ivan III was to complete this task after another, less violent, but still turbulent crisis in Moscow in the

1470's. But it was in the 1450's that the new political type of a "terrible tsar" was first developed in its basic outline, a figure to be fully realized later in Ivan III, in Vasili III (about whom Herberstein has said that there has scarcely been any sovereign in the course of history with greater power), and in the latter's son Ivan the Terrible.

The first hint of this new type, which made a strong impression on Muscovite society, was the attempt of Vasili II to strengthen his hand against foreign and domestic enemies by enrolling Tatar princes in his service. In the course of this struggle for greater power, some other trends began to emerge, especially the cruel methods used to punish those charged with sedition against the Grand Prince, the rapidly growing pretensions to unlimited freedom in the exercise of grand princely power, and the increasing disregard of laws that had hitherto determined the conduct of princely affairs.

The unity and the autocracy of the Muscovite sovereign was the result of the gathering together of the scattered elements of power over the territory of Great Russia and its population. In the last ten years of his reign Vasili the Blind established a firm foundation for the Great Russian state by building up its central core, which was the state of Moscow.

Dmitri Shemiaka's death gave Vasili II a free hand. The Grand Prince took quick advantage of the next opportunity to be rid of Ivan of Mozhaisk. Although he had been received by the Grand Prince "in friendship and alliance," and had been granted his own votchina and share in the otchina of the grand principality, Ivan had refused to join in an expedition against the Tatars, whose raids had been devastating the Russian land, and for this "unrighteousness" Vasili marched against him, occupied Mozhaisk, and set his own deputies over Ivan's votchina. Ivan fled with his family to Lithuania.

That this was something more than a simple act of vengeance or an attempt to forestall some new "sedition" is indicated by the fate of Prince Vasili of Serpukhov. "Unrighteousness" was found even in this faithful supporter of the Grand Prince's power. Vasili of Serpukhov had had his domains considerably increased as a result of grants made by the Grand Prince. Bezhetsk, once in the hands of Ivan of Mozhaisk, was evidently transferred to

him after Ivan's flight to Lithuania, with the addition also of
Zvenigorod. It may be that a quarrel arose out of the demand of
Vasili of Serpukhov for more land. All we know, however, is
that in July of 1456 he was "taken" to Moscow and then exiled
to Uglich. His son Ivan and his second wife fled to Lithuania.
Vasili of Serpukhov was to remain a prisoner until his death in
1483. Not long before the death of Grand Prince Vasili II there
was a conspiracy among the younger boyars and courtiers left
in Serpukhov, who were in touch with the exiles in Lithuania, to
free their prince from his imprisonment in Uglich, but "their
thought was exposed," and the cruel punishment that followed
impressed Moscow as a terrible new manifestation of the Grand
Prince's power.

The Grand Prince's heavy hand lay also on the princes of
Suzdal. Even during Dmitri Shemiaka's lifetime Grand Prince
Vasili II had succeeded in sowing discord among these princes.
Vasili Kosoi and Dmitri the Younger had been on the side of
Dmitri Shemiaka in Suzdal, but the Grand Prince's treaty with
their third cousin Ivan Gorbat (son of Vasili Kirdiapa of Gorodets) was kept in force, and in return for his promise not to
join Dmitri Shemiaka (under threat of excommunication and the
transfer of his "whole udel and votchina" to the Grand Prince
and his heirs), Ivan Gorbat was granted possession of Gorodets
on the Volga, the votchina in Suzdal previously ruled by his
father. Our sources are silent about the subsequent fate of these
domains. We only know that Vasili Grebenka (Ivan Gorbat's
brother) reigned in Pskov from 1448 as a vassal of the Grand
Prince, and then after Dmitri Shemiaka's death took part in a
new struggle against the Grand Prince, standing at the head of
the army of Novgorod. In 1458 Grand Prince Vasili sent a host
against the men of Viatka, which had been one of the main
sources of Dmitri Shemiaka's military strength, and Viatka was
brought "under his full control." Our sources do not give us a
complete picture of the way Vasili the Blind finally ended this
period of sedition and civil strife. There are many gaps and
silences in the accounts of the events of this troubled time in our
chronicles. The final result, however, is clear. Grand Prince
Vasili may be called an absolute monarch in the domains of the
Moscow-Vladimir grand principality. Prince Mikhail's udel of

Vereia did not detract from the absolute nature of this monarchy, any more than the udels of Prince Andrei and Prince Vladimir were to limit the sovereignty of Vasili III and Grand Prince Ivan the Terrible in a later time. Drawing strength from the core of his grand princely domains, Vasili II proceeded to consolidate his power over Novgorod, Pskov, and Riazan.

In 1456 Vasili II mustered his princes and generals with a huge army for a war on Novgorod. Once again the attack was justified on the grounds of "unrighteousness." The men of Novgorod had been "disobedient" to him and had sheltered "his maligners and deserters." The campaign forced Novgorod to submit and do homage to him, with the payment of a tribute "for his expenses," according to the terms of the treaty of Iazhelbits, which formally reestablished Novgorod as an integral part of the grand principality. The people of Novgorod were required to hold the grand princely rule "as something to be honored and held in awe," and agreed to observe the Grand Prince's "ancient tradition and toll," which was set forth in a special section of the treaty. Its main provisions were (1) that the official treaties of Great Novgorod "should be sealed by the Grand Prince," and that henceforth "there should be no perpetual treaties" made by Novgorod; (2) the restoration of the grand princely court in Gorodishche, "with boyars of the Grand Prince as well as boyars of Novgorod as judges"; (3) that if these judges should differ, appeal should be made to the Grand Prince and the posadnik, at such time as the Grand Prince should be present in the city; (4) the courts of the Grand Prince's deputies were not to be taken over by Novgorod, and in Novgorod and its volosts a summons to court must be issued by the officials of both the Grand Prince and Novgorod; (5) the restoration as a norm of the Grand Prince's right to a "general tribute . . . whenever such collection of tribute might be deemed necessary by the Grand Prince"; (6) that henceforth Novgorod should not shelter the Grand Prince's "maligners"; and (7) that the Grand Prince was to hold authority in Novgorod "in accordance with the ancient traditions and tolls," as these had been defined in various earlier treaty documents.

The chronicles give almost no information as to how or to what extent the terms of the Iazhelbits treaty were put into effect.

Undoubtedly the treaty aroused a great deal of opposition in Novgorod, and there can be no thought of its full implementation. Later, in 1471, it was necessary for Ivan III to reconfirm the grand prince's "ancient rights" as fixed at Iazhelbits. Not until 1460 did Vasili II visit Novgorod "to look into all his rights there," and the situation was strained. "The people of Novgorod were on guard." A wave of disturbances passed through the city. Some unidentified "rascals" tried to kill the boyar Feodor Basenok, and the people of the city assembled in a veche against the Grand Prince. Only with difficulty did Archbishop Jonas succeed in quelling the uprising. Great Novgorod had passed through the first convulsion leading to its death as a political power. Whatever may have happened in 1460, one thing was certain: Novgorod and Pskov had been fully restored as component parts of the grand principality of all Russia. In subsequent negotiations with the Germans regarding an armistice with these two cities, the Grand Prince took the initiative. In 1461 he sent his deputy to Pskov "neither on the request of that city nor in accordance with the ancient tradition," and the people of Pskov received him and installed him on their princely throne.

Riazan was no longer a problem; it was now completely subject to the Grand Prince's rule. Before his death (in 1456) Grand Prince Ivan of Riazan had committed his eight-year-old son and the Riazan principality "into the hand and care" of Grand Prince Vasili II, and the latter had taken the lad into his household in Moscow and transferred the administration of Riazan to his own deputies. The old "traditions" of interprincely relations were now retained only between Moscow and Tver. Moscow-Tver relations had been reestablished in the mid-1450's, after Tver's long and close association with Lithuania. The treaty between Grand Prince Vasili and Grand Prince Boris of Tver now confirmed their full solidarity "against the Tatars, the Poles, the Lithuanians, and the Germans," and Boris acknowledged "the grand principality of Moscow and Great Novgorod" as the "votchina" of Vasili and his sons. Boris did not, however, acknowledge Vasili as his "elder brother." Their "brotherhood" in this treaty was still a relationship of equals. A return to the times of Dmitri of the Don and the provisions of the treaty of 1375 was still not possible.

Moscow's great success lay in the fact that Tver, once wholly on the side of the Russo-Lithuanian state, was now once more allied with the grand principality of Great Russia. For this Moscow could thank not so much its own new power as the internal difficulties of the Polish-Lithuanian state. Great Russia's western relations were still characterized by the qualified and basically unstable equilibrium established by Vasili's treaty with Casimir in 1449, although the terms of this treaty had been for the most part abrogated. During this same period (in the 1450's) Great Russia was virtually free from dependence on the Golden Horde. It was not with the Horde or its khans that Vasili had to reckon, but with Kazan and Said-Akhmat, the khan of the Sinaia and Nogai hordes. The Kazan kingdom had only just organized itself in its new location and had not disturbed the Russian border to any great extent. Our sources give us no information about the relations that developed between Moscow and Kazan in the time of Mamudek, but evidently the heavy obligations undertaken by the Russian grand prince were not transferred from Ulug-Makhmet to his son Mamudek, and the organization by Khan Kasim of a separate kingdom hostile to Mamudek tended to reduce the effectiveness of raids by Kazan forces. Said-Akhmat, however, frequently made raids on Muscovite territory. The defense of the southern border was to become the main task of the grand principality. A practice originated under Dmitri of the Don, the moving of observation detachments up to the Oka while holding sufficient forces in reserve to repel any Tatar attack, was to become more and more common. This was true also on the Riazan frontier to the east. These tactics were to be carried out with difficulty, however, and developed gradually through a series of bitter reverses.

Such, then, was the position of the grand principality toward the end of the reign of Vasili II. The core of his domains, the main territorial basis of his grand princely power, lay in the central Moscow-Vladimir region of Great Russia. This territory was now developing into the Muscovite state, the patrimonial votchina of the grand princely family, and its development may be studied in the testament of Vasili the Blind, composed not long before his death in 1462. Vasili's testament represents an original compromise between the old ways and the new conditions of political life. In form we have before us a father's traditional riad. His definition of family relationships is still firmly planted in the soil of the "ancient traditions and ways." The Grand Prince's sons—Ivan, Iuri, Andrei the Elder, Boris, and Andrei the Younger—are "enjoined" to their mother, Princess Maria, with the exhortation: "and you, my sons, must live as one, and obey your mother in all things as standing in my place, the place of your father." And farther on: "and you, my sons, must obey your mother in all things; do not go beyond her wishes in any thing, and if any son of mine should not be obedient to his mother, and should go against her wishes, then by blessing will not be upon him."

But the relative positions of members of the grand princely family with respect to rule over its domains had been altered radically. Vasili's testament completed the merging of the Muscovite votchina with the territory of the grand principality, and it can be regarded as a division of a votchina in the form of udels only in a very qualified sense. There is no formula here: "And I have hereby made a distribution to you my sons and princess. . . ."

By the will of his father it was the eldest son, Ivan, who received "the otchina and grand princely rule," and the territory of the grand principality of Vladimir was already synonymous with the grand prince's udel in the Muscovite votchina. Ivan's personal domains are listed in this testament as being a one-third share in Moscow, Kolomna, Vladimir, Pereiaslavl Zalesky, Kostroma, Galich, Ustiug, the Viatka land, Suzdal, Nizhni Novgorod, Murom, Iuriev, Veliki Sol, Borovsk, Sukhodol, Kaluga, and Alexin—all with their volosts roads and villages and with their "ancient rights." His territory had never before included all these lands. There are really no grounds for calling this the udel of the eldest son and grand prince. It may be more accurately defined as the votchina of the grand prince as sovereign, with the udels of the younger brothers standing alongside it.

There were four such udels. Iuri received Dmitrov, Mozhaisk, Medyn, and Serpukhov, plus a number of volosts over and above the districts attached to these towns. Andrei the Elder received Uglich, Bezhetsk, and Zvenigorod. Boris received Rzhev, Volok, and Ruza. Andrei the Younger received Vologda, and also the Kuben and Zaozero volosts. The princes' inheritance was completed by the granting to them of certain villages and volosts as "detached" domains and by the confirmation of their possession of lands acquired through the testament of Princess Sofia, and also of Iuri's possession of all that Princess Maria (mother of Prince Vasili of Serpukhov) had granted to him. The widowed Grand Princess received as a lifetime possession Rostov, with several villages and volosts in different districts, and she also retained her own acquisitions—the dependent town of Romanov and the villages purchased by her and held as her oprichnina. This possession of districts or towns set between lands held by others (*cherespolositsa*) was provided for and explained by saying that just as the Grand Princess controlled the courts and collection of tribute in all her separate villages and volosts, so it was also with the princes, "each one having the right to judge in those villages given to him . . . no matter whose udel they might be in."

The city of Moscow was divided up in a complicated way in "annual" shares. A third belonged to Grand Prince Ivan. Iuri was assigned the "yearly share in Moscow" that had belonged to Constantine (youngest son of Dmitri of the Don); in addition he was to divide with his brother Andrei the Elder ("each shall have a half in each year") the third share that had belonged to Vladimir of Serpukhov. Boris received the yearly share once held by Prince Ivan of Mozhaisk. Andrei the younger was given the yearly share of Prince Peter (Dmitri's fourth son). Of the Muscovite tamga, a third was assigned to the Grand Prince and the other two-thirds went "half and half" to Iuri and Andrei the Elder together, and to Boris and Andrei the Younger together, with a half of the revenues to be separated from each third and assigned during her lifetime to the Princess Mother. The testament did not anticipate the vacancy of any of these udels. This ticklish question may have been side-stepped deliberately, but the continued provision for a possible partial redistribution of udels by authority of the Princess Mother in the event of a loss by any son of a part of his domains bears witness to the vitality of the tradition of udel domain. Another sign of the continuing predominance of family-hereditary over political-state concepts can be seen in the fact that Vasili's testament "en-

joins" his widowed princess and her sons to Casimir, king of
Poland and grand prince of Lithuania, placing them in his
"protection."

As presented in the testament of Vasili the Blind, the order
of relationships in the Muscovite family of princes seems almost
too traditional to apply to the actual state of affairs in the grand
principality at that time. But Grand Prince Vasili had given a
completely new definition to his son's udels, one that clearly departed from tradition. He had not so much divided a common
votchina among his heirs as distributed to each a share drawn
from the great complex of grand princely possessions, the basic
mass of which remained under the immediate control of the
Grand Prince. This testament was composed at a moment in the
history of Great Russia when fate was urgently posing the
question whether or not the family-votchina forms of rule and
princely relations could be retained in the face of the constantly
growing need for centralized power. The inconsistency of the
various provisions of this riad appears with special clarity in its
regulations concerning the collection of tribute. Thus:

and when my sons shall begin to live in their udels, let my princess
and my son Ivan and my son Iuri and my other sons send assessors,
and let their assessors list their udels under oath, and according to
this inventory let them assess a tax on all plows and all persons, and
in this way let my princess and my sons collect the outlay and make
payment to my son Ivan from their udels.

If we remember that Muscovite Russia had been scarcely touched
by the khan's power for the past ten years, this provision for
the work of inventory and assessment may be regarded as a
major step in the development of the economy of the grand
principality. The collection of tribute was still formally connected with the payment of the Tatar outlay, and also, as in
old times, with the notion that if "God should change the
Horde," then the payment of such tribute into the Grand
Prince's treasury would be discontinued, and it was certainly not
accidental that the inventory should be carried out by the
"assessors" of each prince. But this effort to organize the collection of revenue was really designed to guarantee the Grand
Prince's income from the udels; the "unavoidable tribute" had

in fact died out or degenerated into "Tatar expenses," i.e., into an element in the general cost of administering the grand principality.

Vasili's provision for the subdivision of udels was therefore something left over from the past; it no longer fitted the actual circumstances of Russian life. Was it to be applied to the domains of the Grand Prince in the sense that the Princess Mother had the right to "draw" from his domains in order to make up any reduction in the votchina of one of the udel princes? This question was bound to become an issue the moment one of the udels was reduced. And behind it lay another question, centering on the limits of the mother's power as against that of her eldest son: the question of the basic organization of the ruling family. Under the terms of Vasili's testament, as in the testament of Dmitri before him, the family had two heads. Alongside the injunction that the princes were not to go beyond their mother's wishes in any matter and that they should obey her "in the place of their father" stood another command: "that they must honor and obey their eldest brother, Ivan, as in their father's place."

Vasili's eldest son had himself been grand prince and co-regent with his father from boyhood. But in this co-regency—obviously influenced by the Byzantine example of confirming succession to the throne by attaching a successor to the emperor as a kind of joint sovereign—there was not yet any clear displacement of the votchina notion of family rule by the concept of a succession within the sovereign rule of a state. Grand Prince Vasili could not free himself from traditional ideas in this matter, any more than the later autocratic monarchy was to free itself completely from these old traditions in its dynastic concept. Vasili was not placing the sovereignty of the grand prince outside the limitations of the traditions of family rule; he was simply limiting the votchina right to this sovereignty to his own family, to his own descendants. In his treaties with lesser princes he placed his "votchina, the grand principality of Moscow and Great Novgorod," under the rule of "his sons Grand Prince Ivan and Prince Iuri and his younger sons," and wherever possible he saw to it not only that these lesser princes acknowledged his own position as their eldest brother, but also that they "regarded his sons Ivan and Iuri and their younger brothers" as their "eldest brothers" too, and that they "held them also in honor and awe." The final victory over the breakdown of the grand principality into isolated and weak udels was to be accomplished in the very bosom of the grand princely family itself.

II.

As far as the exercise of grand princely power in Moscow was concerned, the accession of Ivan III was of little significance. It represented no real change in policy. Grand Prince Ivan III completed the task of gathering the power and rebuilding the internal relationships of the Muscovite state on new foundations. He brought about the political unification of Great Russia and left his successors as hereditary rulers over every state in the Muscovite land.

Ivan III began by changing the status of the Vereia and Iaroslavl principalities, and carried out this work in unhurried, gradual stages. First he renewed the treaty with Prince Mikhail of Vereia, reaffirming the position that had been defined for Mikhail under agreements with Grand Prince Vasili II. In this treaty Mikhail acknowledged his cousins Grand Prince Ivan and Prince Iuri as his elder brothers, and Andrei the Elder as his equal. Mikhail's votchina of Vereia and Beloozero was confirmed, as well as the Grand Prince's grant of Vyshgorod, with a number of new volosts added. It is very characteristic that the meaning of this part of the treaty document was defined in a note made on its reverse side: "This possession of Vyshgorod was given to Mikhail after the death of Grand Prince Vasili II." Obviously this settlement was meant to serve as a deed of gift. It was soon revised, however. Mikhail was forced to "surrender" Vyshgorod to Ivan, along with the added volosts given to him under the first treaty; in short, to give back all that the Grand Prince had originally conferred on him "out of his otchina" as Mikhail's "votchina and udel."

It was not long before this second treaty was replaced by a third, in which Prince Mikhail's position was reduced even further. He was now defined as among "the youngest in the whole brotherhood of the Grand Prince." For about twenty years

Mikhail was then left in peace. In 1482, however, this last treaty was also revoked. The time had come for important new steps in the liquidation of the udel-votchina system. The position of the younger generation had to be defined. Ivan's son now appeared as grand prince beside his father; Prince Mikhail also had his son Vasili at his side. A new treaty was made in which Prince Mikhail gave up his otchina of Beloozero to the Grand Prince "and surrendered his deed to this otchina." Mikhail retained possession of this domain during his lifetime, however. On Mikhail's death Beloozero was to pass to the Grand Prince or one of his sons, as determined by the Grand Prince, and Mikhail's son Vasili was not to enter into this votchina or seek to obtain it by subversion.

In 1484 Vasili fled to Lithuania, after falling into disgrace in connection with the complications in court relations arising out of Ivan's second marriage. Vasili became involved in this matter through his marriage to Maria Paleologue, a niece of Grand Princess Sofia (the daughter of Vitovt). Grand Prince Ivan then took possession of Vereia, which we must suppose had been given to Vasili by his father, Mikhail, after the young prince's marriage to Maria. Grand Prince Ivan returned Vereia to Mikhail, this time, however, as part of his own grand princely otchina and not as Mikhail's votchina, and to be ruled by Mikhail only during his lifetime. Vasili's votchina rights to Mikhail's other domains (to his shares in Moscow and Iaroslavl) were also abrogated, since Mikhail "had provided that all of his votchina be given to the Grand Prince after his lifetime." Thus the incorporation of Mikhail's entire udel-votchina within the body of the Grand Prince's immediate domains was guaranteed even before Mikhail's death.

Just before his death in 1486, Mikhail ordered that a testament be drawn up to the effect that he was conferring upon his lord, Grand Prince Ivan III, his hereditary shares in Moscow, Beloozero, and Iaroslavl with their suburbs and villages (apart from those he had given to the church or had sold to his boyars). Vereia was not even considered worthy of mention. This document was presented to Grand Prince Ivan by Vasili Romodanovsky, one of Mikhail's boyars, and was altered at the Grand Prince's request. Romodanovsky returned to Mikhail with a new draft of the testament composed by the Muscovite officials and the blunt command that Mikhail "write his testament in this way." In the new draft the reference to Beloozero was not "I confer my otchina . . ." but "I have conferred and given this my otchina in my lifetime . . ." As for his share in Moscow and Iaroslavl, the new text read: "I have conferred and given this my entire otchina after my lifetime . . ." There is the added statement that Vereia had been conferred on Mikhail by the Grand Prince as part of the Grand Prince's votchina, and had been given to Mikhail during his lifetime only, so that on his death this votchina would belong to the Grand Prince "in all respects."

Thus at the Grand Prince's command the Muscovite officials had carefully eliminated from Mikhail's testament even the external features of a free disposition by testament, which clearly would not have corresponded to the real situation. Mikhail was simply ratifying in the form of a testament the transfer of all his ruling rights to the Grand Prince, a transfer that had in fact been fully accomplished in their earlier treaties. This transfer of rights by way of treaty agreement made under pressure exerted by the Grand Prince naturally placed all of Mikhail's grants and dispositions of property on shaky ground. When he listed them in his testament he added the proviso: "and if these towns and villages are needed by my lord the Grand Prince," the Grand Prince shall either give money for them or shall give "his own lands in exchange for these." The increase in grand princely power led to an intensified policy of territorial expansion, and it is to this policy only that we can apply the expression "the gathering of lands." The practice of filling out the grand prince's personal domains by the exchange or purchase of small parcels of land was now well established. The grand prince "exchanged" towns with the metropolitan and the younger princes more or less at will, so that all these transactions had a compulsory character. Thus in the testament of Vasili the Blind we read: "and should my son Ivan wish to make an exchange for the towns of Kolomna belonging to my son Iuri, and should my son Iuri exchange these towns with him, then let my son Ivan make the exchange with his brother for these towns without offense."

The degeneration of udel domain into properties granted at will by the grand prince also posed the question to what extent the younger princes' testamentary dispositions had any validity once their hereditary rule had yielded to the hereditary and direct rule of the grand prince. Did the legal acts undertaken by the original local princely power survive such exchanges? Prince Mikhail was concerned that the Grand Prince should "not tamper with his courts" and should not "infringe" or "violate" his deeds and grants of land, but he had little faith in the Grand Prince's good will. Ivan was in a position now to settle such questions in any way he pleased.

The local votchina principalities were in fact overshadowed now by a truly awe-inspiring power. Its methods and capabilities were clearly revealed in the 1460's, in the liquidation of the hereditary domains of Iaroslavl. Unfortunately we know about this only through the passing observations of a local chronicler who under the year 1468 has added this bitter comment to his account of the discovery of the miraculous relics of the ancient princes of Iaroslavl:

Since these miracle workers appeared to be of no value to the princes of Iaroslavl, they bade farewell to their whole otchina forever, handing it over to Grand Prince Ivan III, and the Grand Prince gave them certain volosts and towns in exchange for their otchina, and the Grand Prince's secretary, Alexei Poluektovich, made a deposition concerning this otchina to the elder grand prince [i.e., to Vasili the Blind] on the basis of ancient tradition, asserting that it was not really theirs.

Having dismissed a major element in local "tradition" in this way (very much in the manner of the "revision of lands and persons" carried out later by Ivan the Terrible), the grand princely power proceeded with the reconstruction of other local institutions and relationships: "And after that," we read in the same chronicle,

in the city of Iaroslavl a new miracle worker, Ivan Sushchey, appeared as administrator of the land; and whoever had a good town, that town was taken from him; and whoever had a good village, it was taken from him and inscribed in the name of the Grand Prince; and whoever was himself a good man, whether boyar or boyar's son, Ivan inscribed him as his own.

The Muscovite power had vigorously undertaken the task of subordinating to its own needs the possession of land and those elements of the population most fit for service. The local chronicler reaches a pitch of irony in his reference to the Muscovite deputy: "and it is impossible to recount or calculate the vast number of other wonders he performed, inasmuch as he was the devil incarnate."

The suppression of the Rostov princes came in the 1470's. Like the princes of Iaroslavl, they had long been reduced to the position of service princes, and had become accustomed to function as the Grand Prince's military commanders or deputies. They still ruled, however, over their own "half" of the Rostov votchina. In 1474 they sold it "in its entirety" to Grand Prince Ivan, and he assigned his new acquisition to his mother, who already held the other "half" of Rostov under the testament of Vasili the Blind.

The Grand Prince's votchina was steadily growing, swallowing up the minor votchinas of the udel princes. His direct control over the territory and population of the Moscow-Vladimir grand principality grew more aggressive and more embracing. The Muscovite state was coming into being. And yet the old traditions of the udel-votchina system were still alive within the grand princely family.

Ivan III had evidently made no treaty with his brothers "on his father's grave." In September, 1472, his brother Iuri died without an heir, and the question of the fate of his udel immediately caused sharp disagreements among the surviving brothers. Indeed, there was conflict even before his death. Iuri's testament has come down to us. Of course he makes no mention in it of his own udel (there could be no disposition of an udel without an heir), but he does portion out certain towns and villages and his movable property among his mother, his brothers, and his sister, and provides for grants to his monasteries and boyars, and makes a list of debts to be paid.

The text of a treaty made by Andrei the Elder with Grand Prince Ivan also dates from this period, just before Iuri's death. In it special attention is given to conditions governing possession of the third share in Moscow and to the princes' relations with the city's general population and "enrolled" persons. Under the

testament of Vasili the Blind one of the Moscow thirds had been
given jointly to Andrei the Elder and Iuri. Now we see in this
treaty between Andrei and Ivan a confirmation of these methods
of governing Moscow that had placed it mainly in the hands
of grand princely administrators, with a retention of Andrei's
rights to his share in Moscow's revenues. We find reference to
the "supervision as one man" of persons engaged in commerce
and of all residents of the city. There is also a revival of the
"joint supervision" of all enrolled persons, with a prohibition
against purchase of their lands. If any prince should engage in
such purchases from common citizens or from servants of the
court without having special permission from the Grand Prince
to do so, he must return such property for joint taxation in
accordance with the tradition. These features of the treaty testify
to confusion in the minds of the princes concerning their joint
possession of Moscow and their relations to serving persons and
persons subject to taxation. The text of this treaty was composed
"at the behest" of the widowed princess mother.

By early 1473 Grand Prince Ivan was already making treaties
with his brothers in connection with Iuri's udel—in February
with Boris and in September with Andrei the Elder—which had
the effect of securing this udel as an indivisible possession of the
Grand Prince. This was not done without difficulty. The chronicles note the brothers' anger at the Grand Prince "for not having
given them shares in their brother Iuri's domain as part of their
udels," and their efforts to obtain such a division did not end
with the treaties of 1473, in spite of the fact that they then
received some compensation for their loss. The Grand Prince
conferred Vyshgorod on Boris "as it had been given to Prince
Mikhail," and Grand Princess Maria had given Andrei the Elder
some of her own purchases—the suburb of Romanov, the lands
around the mouth of the Sheksna, and a "salt well" in Rostov.

The question of Prince Iuri's votchina took on a special
urgency as the status of the Grand Prince's brothers within the
emerging Muscovite state was changed. In the face of stiff resistance the grand princely power was gradually isolating the bearer
of the title of grand prince from his family, elevating him above
all other members of the family.

In the treaties of Ivan III we no longer find the ambiguous

terminology that in his father's documents still represented the grand prince's domains as one among several udels in the Moscow votchina. Here the udels of the "younger brothers" are clearly distinguished from the votchina of the grand prince, i.e., the grand principality. While preventing the secondary lines of this princely house from making any claim to his domains by placing his own brothers above them, Ivan at the same time worked consistently to secure the hereditary rights of his own posterity—first those of his son Ivan and then the rights of any other sons that God might give him. By the 1470's Ivan's eldest son was already hailed as grand prince and elder brother by the Grand Prince's brothers Andrei and Boris. Not only in his joint rule of Moscow, but also in his management of the military and financial resources of the grand principality and his dispositions of its cities and volosts, Grand Prince Ivan III pursued his own arbitrary policies, setting aside the independent princely rights of his brother princes in favor of his own self-determined "power of conferral."

The question of grand princely "acquisitions" was also posed sharply at this time. The Grand Prince's seizures of land and power were constantly increasing the boundaries of his immediate domains. Whenever this required the use of considerable military force, the princely brothers would take part in the campaign with their own regiments, but the acquisitions were always added to the domain of the eldest brother. One feature of the treaties of 1473 stands out as especially significant. Ivan exacted a promise from his brothers "not to trespass" against any land that he had acquired or might yet acquire. They were also bound to recognize these acquisitions not only in his own reign, but also in the reign of his son and that of any other children that God might give him. There is no trace in these treaties of a corresponding formula securing the acquisitions of the younger princes, although such a formula was customary in the treaty documents of former times. This is hardly a superficial detail or the result of some editorial slip. The chronicles have preserved the memory of profound dissatisfaction on the part of the Grand Prince's brothers at his refusal to share his acquisitions with them: "With them he seized Great Novgorod.

but it was to him that everything accrued, and he gave them
no share in it."

A new family crisis was brewing. Ivan's brothers took advantage of the next occasion when he stood in special need of
their military support to press their demands upon him: "In accordance with their father's command and testament the Grand
Prince must deal justly with them and show them favor, and
grant them Prince Iuri's udel as their votchina, and must make a
settlement with them." The older brothers, Andrei the Elder and
Boris, turned for help to those who had been entrusted with
this responsibility in their father's testament: their mother, Metropolitan Gerontius, and King Casimir of Poland. They appealed
to Casimir to "judge their cause and help them in their struggle
with the Grand Prince." They were defending their traditional
rights in a way that was quite in the spirit of ancient times, but
which scarcely exposed the grand principality to any real danger.
Counting on the fact that Moscow was being weakened by this
internal strife, Casimir accepted the summons to interfere and
tried to assemble a massive coalition against his dangerous neighbor, entering into negotiations with Khan Akhmet of the Golden
Horde as well as with the Livonian order of knights and with
Sweden. In fact, the attacks by Sweden and the Livonian knights
on the Novgorod and Pskov volosts had no important results,
and Casimir himself was hindered by unrest in Lithuania. Only
Khan Akhmet was able to mount an expedition against Russia.
Caught by the Tatars before he had an opportunity to settle
with his brothers, Ivan was unable to marshal his forces. After
their appeal to Casimir at the end of 1479, Andrei and Boris
had "withdrawn" from him and moved into the region of Novgorod. They had set up headquarters in the Veliki Luki region
and had sent their families to Vitebsk, where Casimir gave them
sanctuary. Ivan III was forced to make concessions. Through the
Metropolitan and the widowed princess mother he assured the
brothers that he would accept their conditions. Andrei and
Boris then came quickly to the Grand Prince's help, and their
arrival decided the conflict with the Tatars. Khan Akhmet could
not face a battle with the unified Russian forces and quickly
retreated from his position on the Ugra.

The events of 1480 not only marked the end of Great Russia's subservience to the power of the khan and the transformation of the grand principality of all Russia into a sovereign and autocratic (in the root meaning of the word) state; they also hastened and guaranteed the complete reversal of the breakdown of power under the udel-votchina system and the establishment of an absolute monarchy.

Once out of danger, Ivan failed to keep the promises he had made to his brothers. Andrei the Elder did receive part of the otchina of Iuriev-Mozhaisk, but then only in the form of a conferral on the part of the Grand Prince, and not as a subdivision of the vacant udel among the brothers arranged according to tradition by the Princess Mother.

The treaties made by Ivan III with his brothers in the 1480's confirmed them in the position they had been given under the treaties of 1473. The udels of the younger brothers were set sharply against the possessions of the Grand Prince and heir to the throne "in each of his grand principalities." His brothers were bound to "watch over" these grand princely domains—not only his votchina of Moscow-Vladimir, but also those of Great Novgorod, Tver, and Pskov—under Ivan III, under his son Ivan, under his princess, and under his younger sons. The new treaties completely subordinated the younger princely brothers to the Grand Prince in all military matters as well as in external affairs, prohibiting them from settling any question "by subversive agreement." The provision of the earlier treaties dealing with the collection of tribute was also confirmed. Once again this collection was connected with the payment of Tatar expenses, although in fact it was now simply a method of meeting the regular expenses of the Grand Prince's treasury.

The possession of udel-votchinas was a survival from a dying age. The princes ruled over their votchinas in complete subjugation to the Grand Prince. They occupied the precarious position of landed gentry living under the constant threat of grand princely disgrace for some "unrighteousness," which of course meant the loss of their otchina "for the fault committed." The principle of the hereditary nature of votchina principalities was not denied, but there was a vigorous assertion of the Grand Prince's claim to udels that fell vacant, and in his testament Ivan

III elevated this claim to the level of a general norm in Muscovite princely law. The younger princes could no longer even think of having a share in the Grand Prince's acquisitions. It was by his own sovereign will that the Grand Prince decided for what purpose and to whom land was to be given, and such grants were made now not as the satisfaction of a right, but at his own personal discretion.

A number of events in the closing decades of the reign of Ivan III helped to consolidate this new growth in grand princely power. Before his death in 1481 Andrei the Younger made a testament in which he listed his lands and indicated "to whom this was given and from whom that was received." In this list there is mention of his own votchina—his "yearly share" in Moscow, with Vologda and the Kuben and Zaozero lands— but only to say: "and the whole of this my votchina is in the hands of my lord and eldest brother, Grand Prince Ivan III." A formula was now found for expressing the inescapable fact that the wishes of the prince making a testament really counted for nothing. There is no sign in this text of the words "I confer" or "I give." Indeed, even the word riad does not appear. Henceforth the udel princes will say: "and as for my votchina, it lies before my lord the Grand Prince," or "and should my princess leave no posterity, then my votchina lies before God and before my lord the Grand Prince."

The Volok udel passed from Prince Boris to his sons in 1494, and it was not until after their deaths (in 1504 and 1513) that their shares reverted, as vacant domains, to the Grand Prince. Ivan III continued to regard his brother Andrei the Elder with suspicion. Both sides were on guard, and when trouble came between them in 1488 Andrei prepared to take flight. In the early 1490's their strained relationship ended in a sudden catastrophe. The struggle with the Tatars flared up again in 1491, and when the Grand Prince ordered his younger brother to join him on a campaign against them, Andrei refused. In the fall of that year Ivan gave orders that his brother be seized and held in prison for the rest of his life. Andrei died in prison in 1491. His sons ended their lives in exile.

In the last years of Ivan's reign there were really no udels or votchina principalities left in the territory of the Moscow

Vladimir grand principality. The whole land was now welded together into a single votchina under the rule of a single sovereign.

III.

The core of Great Russia had been united by the rulers of the grand principality into the monarchy of the Muscovite state. This process had gone hand in hand with the subjugation of the rest of Great Russia to the grand prince's sovereignty, under the strong pressure of foreign relations, which were becoming more and more strained as time went by.

Moscow's position in relation to surrounding nations had become extremely complicated in the 1460's. The khanate of Kazan was growing to the east. At the same time, the disorders that had begun there with Mamudek's murder of his father were spreading, and with each new outbreak Moscow was drawn more and more into Kazan's affairs. Ibrahim, Mamudek's son, was now the khan of Kazan, and his brothers Kasim and Danyar were in the service of Moscow, as were other Tatar princes and royal persons seeking sanctuary in Russia as a result of the strife and discord in their own courts. The proximity of the khanate of Kazan and the character of this disturbing center of Tatar power, now settled on land once occupied by the old Bulgar kingdom and obstructing Moscow's routes of trade and colonization, tempted the grand principality to attack and subdue it. Some of the leading men of Kazan were dissatisfied with Ibrahim and called for his replacement by a khan appointed by Moscow. In 1467 Ivan III accepted the invitation and marched against Kazan. His attempt to place Kasim on its throne failed, however, and the Muscovite army was forced to retreat hastily in the face of Ibrahim's superior strength. Border warfare began, with the ravaging of Russian volosts by the Tatars and Russian bands moving into the Kama valley and against the Finnish settlements along the Volga and Cheremshan. The situation along the eastern frontier was very unstable. There was no clear-cut line of fortifications, and the land was settled by a Russian population that had no close ties with Muscovite power and a foreign (Tatar and Finnish) population always ready to reach out to Kazan. Constant military and political activity was required in order to build up an effective system of government in this area. On several occasions local rebellions were supported by Tatar princes from Nizhni Novgorod or Galich. Viatka had become a center for river pirates, and was another center of military power hostile to the Grand Prince and oriented toward Kazan.

The close connection between the growth and concentration of power in Moscow and the task of national defense and self-definition appears very clearly on these eastern borders. The Grand Prince's unsettled relations with Kazan called for a firm stand. Trouble was constantly threatening from this direction. When Ivan made his campaign against Novgorod in 1478, Ibrahim attacked Viatka and Ustiug. In return, Ivan could make only a small-scale raid on the Kazan volosts. Not until the resolution of the grand principality's internal crisis in 1480 was Ivan free to act in the east. In 1486 he advanced on Kazan with a huge force and the Khan quickly sued for peace.

The prolonged struggle with Mamudek and Ibrahim had made it clear that Russia's eastern frontier could not be stabilized without the permanent subjugation of the khanate of Kazan to the power of the grand prince. Not even in Ivan's time, however, was the grand principality strong enough to bring this about. The closing years of Ivan's reign (after Ibrahim's death in 1486) were taken up with various new and more or less successful attempts to install Muscovite vassals on the Kazan throne, chosen from among the Tatar service princes who had been so eagerly received and "provisioned" by Moscow for the military aid they could supply and as agents of political intrigue. The results of this policy were not really permanent, but the situation in the east was eased somewhat at a time when the Grand Prince was still occupied with the gathering and organizing of Great Russia's power from within.

Tatar troubles also determined the policy of the grand principality in the south. As of old, the task of defending Russia against the roving Tatar forces of the steppe fell naturally on the Riazan principality. Muscovite deputies governed Riazan in the early years of Ivan's reign, while its boy prince Vasili lived in Moscow as a ward of the Grand Prince. When Vasili reached the age of fifteen, Ivan gave his sister Anna to him in marriage and let him occupy the throne of Riazan, where Vasili then ruled as a Muscovite vassal for nineteen years (1464–83), to be succeeded by his son Ivan, who ruled until 1500 in the same position of dependence on Moscow. At the end of the reign of Grand Prince Ivan III, Riazan was being governed by Vasili's widow, Princess Agrafina, who was informed by Ivan that her service people had now been "inscribed in his service." The Princess was also ordered to punish severely any who should disobey this command, and threatened with direct interference by the Grand Prince if she refused to cooperate. Indeed, it was only this kind of cooperation on the part of Riazan's ruling house that so long delayed the establishment of the Grand Prince's direct sovereignty in this land.

The borders of the Great Russian state had always been in doubt. On the eastern frontier the defensive struggle had slowly but surely changed into an offensive operation designed to clear the routes of trade and colonization. The Tatars had virtually blocked all expansion to the southeast, so that colonizing and trading activity had shifted northward, going around the khanate of Kazan and following the routes of the ancient movements out of Novgorod. The sovereignty of the Grand Prince replaced Novgorod's control of Perm from 1473 onward, and toward the end of the reign of Ivan III the rule of the minor princes of Perm gave way to government by the Grand Prince's deputies. As early as the 1460's Muscovite boyars were traveling with "scouts" along the Ugra and bringing local minor princes into submission. In the 1480's Moscow undertook a defense of Perm against Vogul (Finnish) forces, organizing a number of local northeast Russian forces for this purpose.

The situation on the western border of Great Russia was equally unstable. The compromise of 1449, intended to limit the spheres of Lithuanian and Muscovite influence, had in fact resolved nothing. The wavering of the ancient "sovereign principalities" of Chernigov, Tver, Novgorod, and Pskov between Moscow and Lithuania continued. In several cities along the frontier between Novgorod and Lithuania, for example in Rzhev, and in a number of centers in the Veliki Luki and Kholm regions, there had even appeared a form of joint Lithuanian and Muscovite rule. In order to define its western borders and its power in that area, the Great Russian principality eventually had to establish direct control over Great Novgorod, Pskov, and Tver.

The treaty of Iazhelbits had laid the basis for the subjugation of Novgorod. The *Life of St. Jonas* (archbishop of Novgorod) tells us that Grand Prince Vasili II prepared his decisive blow against Novgorod because "he had not received all due honor" from its people. The biography goes on to say: "And since it was to him that grand princely power over the Russian princes had been committed, so for this cause he sought to raise his hand against Great Novgorod." This biography was compiled by a contemporary of Jonas about the end of 1472, and it shows that the question of the grand prince's "dominion" over Novgorod had been in the minds of Moscow's rulers and the leaders of Novgorod long before Ivan III began to take steps to bring it into full effect. The issue had been raised by the treaty of Iazhelbits, and then aggravated by the disorders in Novgorod following this settlement. It may be that the *Life of St. Jonas* puts the matter correctly when it states that the conflict was eased somewhat by Jonas' representations before the Grand Prince on Novgorod's behalf. At any rate, the death of this spiritual leader in November of 1470 marked the beginning of the complicated story of the fall of Novgorod.

The boyar party that controlled Novgorod's policies (with the Boretsky family at its head) had its own plan of action. It decided to seek help against Moscow in Lithuania. Two closely related events in the early stages of this new approach to Lithuania were to lead to the ultimate failure of the Boretskys' plan. The contacts with Lithuania had obviously begun even before Archbishop Jonas' death, since within three days a Lithuanian prince (Mikhail) arrived in Novgorod in answer to an appeal to King Casimir. Novgorod was to have a Lithuanian governor "of the Orthodox Christian faith." From the accounts given in our chronicles, the scheme worked out by Prince Mikhail and the Boretskys involved giving the widow of Novgorod's deceased posadnik to Mikhail in marriage, with the acknowledgment of Mikhail as Novgorod's ruler. This would confirm the tie between the boyar party and the ruling powers of Lithuania, and also would consolidate the boyars' hold on Novgorod. It is possible, of course, that this was never a formal agreement. It may well have been simply a rumor, originating either in Novgorod or in Moscow. Casimir's position in relation to Novgorod was extremely difficult. Direct action was possible only with the help of the Orthodox princes and boyars of the Lithuanian state, precisely that group of descendants of Rurik and Gedymin with their Russified boyars whose suppression was the next item on the agenda of Casimir's domestic policy. Mikhail was one of the leading men in this circle, and its candidate for the grand princely throne in Lithuania. The steps being taken in Novgorod could scarcely have pleased Casimir. A powerful governorship was about to be created for the leader of the Orthodox Lithuanian forces.

The whole matter was further complicated by the church question. On the death of Jonas the cathedral chapter of St. Sofia chose Jonas' protodeacon and sacristan, Theophil, as his successor. The candidate of the Lithuanian party, the chief sacristan, Pimen, was passed over. Theophil's relations with the Lithuanian party were ambiguous. He began to make preparations for a journey to Moscow for consecration by Metropolitan Philip, but he also took part in the negotiations with Casimir. This latter activity was probably forced on him by his rivalry with Pimen, who was seeking support in the Lithuanian party and had agreed to be consecrated by the Lithuanian metropolitan. This plan was still further complicated by the fact that the Russo-Lithuanian metropolitan see was occupied by a Uniate disciple of Isidore who had not been accepted by the leaders of west Russian Orthodox circles, including Mikhail and his brothers and other Lithuanian boyars. It is true that Metropolitan Grigori had shortly before this secured approval of his rank as metropolitan of Lithuania, and even of his right to jurisdiction over all Russia, from Patriarch Dionysius of Constantinople. But this had brought a sharp protest from Moscow and raised the threat of schism. Under these circumstances the agreement made between the boyars of Novgorod and Casimir could not acquire much force, even when cast in the form of a treaty providing for the appointment of an Orthodox Lithuanian as governor of Novgorod (with the city remaining "in the hands of its free men") and the defense of Novgorod against Grand Prince Ivan by the full power of the Lithuanian king.

The city was divided, and alarm spread when news came that Ivan was stirring up the men of Pskov. Moscow's first step was not a military expedition, however, but an admonition from the Metropolitan concerning the "just and awesome" sovereignty of the prince who stood at the head of the Novgorod "otchina and patrimony." The Metropolitan called on Novgorod to submit "in accordance with tradition to the powerful hand of the faithful and just sovereign of the Russian lands." Philip also reminded Novgorod of the great sin of "yielding to the Latin temptation." Torn by internal disagreement and its suspicion of Muscovite power, Novgorod apparently made no reply. Grand Prince Ivan III then raised "the whole land" against it in an army that included his brothers and dependent princes as well as the Tatar prince Danyar and the hosts of Tver and Pskov. At the same time he sent another army against the Dvina territory.

The matter ended quickly with the defeat of Novgorod's main forces on the Shelon River by the first wave of Russian forces, and the rout of the Dvina regiments under Prince Vasili Shuisky by another Muscovite detachment. The settlement that followed repeated the Iazhelbits treaty almost word for word. "For its transgressions" Novgorod was obliged to pay another huge tribute.

In chronicles reflecting the viewpoint of Moscow, this peace in 1471 is given the character of a generous "conferral" on the part of the Grand Prince, a kind of amnesty declared for those involved in the "Novgorod transgression" as a result of the intercessions of Metropolitan Philip, the Grand Prince's brothers, and his boyars. The reconciliation still took the old form of a treaty settlement "according to the ancient traditions and rights," but this was a restoration of the Grand Prince's "ancient rights" and not those of Novgorod. Primarily this was a confirmation of the terms of the Iazhelbits treaty. There was a full acknowledgment of the fact that all acts of the Novgorod veche were made in the name of the Grand Prince; there was a guarantee of the judicial authority of the Grand Prince's deputies. The treaty of 1471 was directly connected with the composition of the Novgorod Charter, which was drawn up "according to a draft presented to our lord the Grand Prince," and in which it was provided that "the posadnik shall make no final judgment in the absence of the Grand Prince's deputy, but shall conduct the trial jointly with the Grand Prince's deputy and tiun, according to the ancient tradition." The treaty contains a direct reference to the Novgorod Charter: ". . . and this settlement in Novgorod omits mention of the courts, since the Charter will bear the name and seal of the Grand Prince." The active role of the Grand Prince's deputies in Novgorod's courts and government increased in proportion to their control over Novgorod's revenues.

From Moscow's viewpoint the conditions laid down in the treaty of 1471 seemed very moderate; in his own way the Grand Prince handled the ancient rights of Novgorod quite cautiously. There was a definite political purpose in this. In view of Novgorod's internal divisions, Grand Prince Ivan was in a strong position, and it was not in the grand principality's interest to unite the Novgorod factions by a sudden and overly harsh application of pressure. While appearing to spare the deep instincts of the common people of Novgorod, Ivan aimed crushing blows at the leaders of the Lithuanian party, completely disorganizing them and frustrating their plans.

After the events of 1471, Ivan's Novgorod policy passed through two stages. For some time he strengthened his hand gradually by a partial observance of the traditional forms for the exercise of grand princely power in Novgorod; the "ancient traditions" were at least formally upheld. Later he moved decisively to extend the "state" over Great Novgorod, as part of his own votchina.

Within Novgorod's "ancient traditions and rights" significant powers and privileges had been reserved for its ruling prince, but these powers were limited in such a way that they could be exercised only as the rights of a local, elected ruler. Its princes could take full advantage of their privileges only if they were actually present in Novgorod, and then only with the cooperation of the posadnik and other officials chosen from the ranks of the citizens of Novgorod. When the grand princes of all Russia became also the princes of Novgorod, the inevitable absenteeism of Novgorod's ruling princes prevented their active participation in the city's internal affairs; its independence was further increased, of course, by the Grand Prince's involvement in his own internal struggle and in his relations with powers to the southeast and southwest of Great Russia. In fact, the "ancient rights" of the ruling prince of Novgorod had fallen into decline, yielding more and more to the "rights" of the Novgorod democracy. The people of Novgorod had extended these traditional powers in treaties with their local princes, carefully preserving the non-territorial status of their temporary rulers by forbidding them to possess land within their borders and by making them dependent on patrons or supporters living in Novgorod. At the same time Great Novgorod remained a part of the grand principality of all Russia, and the Novgorod boyars had for a long time steadfastly upheld the tradition acknowledging the bearer of the title of grand prince as their own prince. As a result of strong political and economic pressures, the uniting in one person of the grand princely rule of Vladimir and Great Novgorod had become a firmly established element in the "ancient traditions and rights," even in Novgorod's system of common law. The attempt by one of the Novgorod parties to transfer the princely power now to the Lithuanian grand prince was seen as a radical departure from this tradition. Under the terms of Great Russia's princely law, the "ancient traditions and rights" also meant the acknowledgment of Novgorod as the votchina of the grand prince of all Russia. This connection of Great Novgorod with the grand principality was subjected to severe trial when the grand principality became the votchina of the lords of Moscow. The reconstruction of the internal relations of the grand principality on new votchina principles had a fatal effect on the freedom of Novgorod.

In the treaty of 1471, Ivan, following the precedent of Iazhelbits, strengthened the unconditional attachment of Great Novgorod to the structure of the grand principality of all Russia. The Novgorod boyars were bound "not to forsake the Grand Prince for any other power," and henceforth were not to receive into their dependent towns any Lithuanian or Russian princes hostile to the Grand Prince. The Grand Prince and his deputies were to assume an active role as rulers of Novgorod, mainly in the work of the courts but also quite specifically in Novgorod's foreign relations. The freedom of the Novgorod church from the immediate jurisdiction of the metropolitan in Moscow was restored, in accordance with the "ancient tradition," by the consecration of Theophil as archbishop of Novgorod in December of the same year.

The Grand Prince's increased authority opened up new opportunities for interfering in Novgorod's domestic affairs, which had in fact become extremely strained. The heads of the boyar oligarchy had stirred up deep dissatisfaction in Novgorod's middle and lower classes, while the plans of the Lithuanian party had run afoul of the interests of the Novgorod merchants, who were seeking new commercial ties with northeastern Russia.

The Boretsky party apparently did not consider its cause hopeless. For some years after 1471 we see members of this party surrounding the senior posadnik, Vasili Ananin, and they were to make repeated efforts to rally the people of Novgorod against their opponents by acts of open terror. But the majority of persons having a voice in the veche were not on their side. A contemporary writing in the Pskov chronicle tells us that it was the inhabitants and younger citizens of Novgorod who invited Grand Prince Ivan to judge their cause: "The posadnik and great boyars are oppressing us and no one is able to bring them to trial. As these violent men have done, so the Grand Prince should do to them, judging their violence and giving them their just rewards."

In October, 1475, Ivan accepted this invitation and traveled to Novgorod with a large retinue for the purpose of holding court. The detailed account of his journey notes how even in the outlying districts, while he was still on the highroad, petitioners came out to meet him. The chief petitioners came before him in the city itself. These were the victims of the greatest pillage and loss, and they denounced those who stood accused before the Grand Prince—the boyars of the Boretsky party. The Grand Prince conducted the trial "in the Novgorod manner," i.e., in the presence of the Archbishop and posadnik and before an assembly of the city's council of boyars, but he set his own staff officials to investigate the matter instead of officials from Novgorod. The accused persons were found guilty and sentenced; the aged posadnik Ananin and the boyar Feodor Boretsky were ordered to be seized and their supporters were released on payment of fines. The charge of attempted desertion to the side of Lithuania had been introduced into this case, which gave a political character to what might otherwise have been a simple criminal proceeding. This gave Ivan a pretext for sending the two ringleaders to Moscow in chains. He ordered the rest of the guilty persons to pay "full damages" in proportion to the losses sustained by their victims, and "the fault-of-the-person charges" in accordance with the city's existing laws. As was the custom, the Grand Prince collected many rich gifts during this visit, not only from boyars, but also from merchants, ordinary citizens, and boyars' sons [36] who came to him with their petitions and "memorials." We are told that "no one was overlooked who came to him with a gift." The Grand Prince gave gifts in return "out of his supplies of rich clothing and damask and goblets and silver ladles and sable scarves and horses, to each according to his worth."

This impressive and triumphant reception in Novgorod evidently convinced Ivan that the ground had been prepared for the full establishment there of his powers of state. It was not by chance that this "peaceful expedition" was described so carefully and in such detail, obviously by the hand of one of the Grand Prince's secretaries. Petitioners and litigants pursued the Grand Prince even after his departure, and he began to send his officials from Moscow to investigate their charges and set times for the appearance of the accused in his court in Moscow. Thus a practice developed which was clearly detrimental to the old Novgorod tradition. Bringing citizens of Novgorod to trial in Moscow "was an unheard-of procedure, contrary to the established tradition of the land and to the Grand Prince's custom, but one that the grand princes now brought upon them." Novgorod's boyar leadership had lost the support of large segments of the population, which now turned to a new power to "redress their wrongs." At the same time the Grand Prince's deputies in Novgorod were accused by these boyars of unlawfully judging the posadnik's and archbishop's cases in Gorodishche, just as the Grand Prince himself was unlawfully transferring Novgorod cases to Moscow, in violation of the tradition that

36. The lowest and poorest rank of gentry (not literally the sons of boyars).—ED.

he judge only those cases that "could not be corrected" in the courts of the posadnik and grand princely deputy, and then only when he himself was present in Novgorod.

Such was the background of the famous incident of March, 1472, when Novgorod envoys did homage to Ivan as their sovereign. Here again was an action "without precedent, no other grand prince having been called 'sovereign' [*gosudar*], but only by the title 'master' [*gospodin*] of the Novgorod land." This step was almost certainly arranged in Moscow with the help of men from Novgorod who had come to seek the Grand Prince's favor. Obviously this was not just a matter of a form of address. According to the Muscovite chronicle, the Novgorod envoys came before Grand Prince Ivan III and his son Ivan "to do homage to them and to acknowledge them both as their sovereigns." This led to a return visit to Novgorod by envoys from the Grand Prince, for the purpose of "consolidating that form of state which was desired." The official representatives of Great Novgorod answered their demands by saying that "they would not negotiate the question," and a savage party conflict broke out in which the group hostile to Moscow took the upper hand. Those posadniks and boyars who were "in the Grand Prince's favor" were forced to flee. Ivan then launched a final expedition against Novgorod, and the leaders of the city were unable to organize any serious resistance. Their request for a settlement marked the beginning of an extremely interesting period of negotiation on the question of the relation of Great Novgorod to the grand principality. In these negotiations there was a clash of two radically different political viewpoints, and the parties involved had great difficulty finding a common language.

The Novgorod boyars began the negotiations with a request for the restoration of "the ancient tradition" as they understood it, and for the abolition of those departures from it that were so clearly evident in recent practice. Grand Prince Ivan insisted first of all that Novgorod declare its willingness to petition him as "sovereign" of Great Novgorod, and he backed up his demand by a tight blockade of the city. Only after a second demand on his part and a new consultation in Novgorod did envoys finally bring him Novgorod's acceptance of this condition. At last Grand Prince Ivan found the basis he sought for answer-

ing the question of how he intended to confer his otchina and
how his future state was to be understood. His answer was simple
enough, but still largely unintelligible to the men of Novgorod:
"We the grand princes wish to hold the powers of state in our
otchina of Great Novgorod just as we hold them in Moscow."

His envoys entered Novgorod for further consultations, as
the Grand Prince continued to move his army closer to the
city. They returned with a new proposal for a treaty dealing
with the terms and conditions of his princely rule. Without
really answering the substance of Novgorod's requests, Ivan
bluntly put the basic question: "I the Grand Prince have already
informed you that we wish to hold the powers of state in our
otchina of Great Novgorod as we do in the 'downstream land'
and in Moscow, and are you now informing me and giving me
instruction as to what the nature of our state should be, when
you are a part of that state?"

The reply of the Novgorod boyars was characteristic: they
were forced to renounce the principle of agreement by treaty
("We are not giving instructions regarding your state") and
to beg the Grand Prince to "make plain" to them the nature of
the "downstream tradition," so far unknown to them, that
tradition "by which our sovereigns the grand princes hold the
powers of state in the 'downstream land.'" The exercise of
sovereign power unlimited by any norm of established law or
ancient custom was not just unacceptable to Novgorod; it was
altogether incomprehensible.

In reply they received a clear definition in negative terms of
the new "tradition" to which they were being required to submit. There was to be no veche bell, no posadnik, and the Grand
Prince was "to hold all the powers of state in Novgorod."
The "downstream tradition" was further explained by the demand that there be organized within Great Novgorod a system
of landholding by court and state officials which would define
volosts and villages "in which the Grand Prince would be as
in his otchina," and that there be a surrender to the Grand
Prince's domain of those lands listed in the name of Novgorod's
prince and held at that time by the Novgorod clergy and boyars.
This harsh clarification of the new regime was softened a little
by Ivan's promise that in the disposition of his otchina, certain

Novgorod requests would be fulfilled. He would not carry out any "deportations" from the Novgorod land, would not violate the landholding rights of the Novgorod boyars, and would preserve the courts as they had been in the past and "as they stand in the land today." The men of Novgorod submitted to and accepted this "conferral" by Ivan of his otchina, as well as the basic principles of the new "tradition," but they still demanded a prohibition of summons to trial in Moscow and compulsory service in the "downstream" host.

Thinking they had won certain real even if limited assurances, they awaited their formal ratification. Again there was violent disagreement among the Novgorod boyars. Some began to say that the sovereign should "give them surety" by a kissing of the cross, but this request was refused. Next they demanded that the Grand Prince's boyars kiss the cross, and that his deputy in Novgorod should also be bound by such a vow. These requests also were denied. They were even denied a "charter" formally underwriting the assurances given, and were forced to rest content with the Grand Prince's verbal declaration of bestowal. Ivan evidently took this course because he regarded this declaration not as a formal obligation, but simply as a statement expressing his own arbitrary decision.

The Grand Prince immediately began organizing his landholding in Novgorod and the levy of a general household tax. The Novgorod democracy had been replaced in fact by the new state. On January 15, 1478, the Grand Prince's boyars made every resident of every suburb and department of Novgorod take an oath to the Grand Prince. The Novgorod boyars with their children and common people were "enjoined" to the Grand Prince, and his representatives were installed in the court of Iaroslavl.

A Polish historian has noted how this establishment of direct grand princely power in Novgorod alarmed the rulers of the Livonian order, Sweden, and Lithuania. No sooner had "the Grand Prince of Moscow taken Novgorod and despoiled its veche" than Muscovite officials appeared in Rzhev and its volosts, in the Veliki Luki country and in the Kholm region, forcing the local population to take an oath in the name of the Grand Prince and driving out the representatives of Lithuanian power.

The Lithuanian state now felt direct pressure from its persistent and stubborn neighbor to the east. At Moscow's request the forces of the Crimean khan began to make raids in the west Russian volosts. In 1478 the Lithuanian assembly was already urging the organization of a grand principality distinct from the power of the Polish throne, but Casimir decided to return to Vilna and become directly involved in Lithuania's eastern affairs. The ruling powers of the Livonian order considered the question as one of "returning Moscow to the position it once occupied," and sought agreements with Casimir and the king of Sweden. Moscow's enemies in the west now formed a coalition with the Golden Horde, but as we have already noted, this alliance never seriously threatened the Russian grand principality.

We have no direct information about how these attempts to resist Moscow affected the situation in Novgorod. We do know that in October, 1479, the Grand Prince made a visit to Novgorod, and while there took Archbishop Theophil into custody and sent him to Moscow. The Archbishop was accused of plotting to "turn Novgorod over to the King or to some other power." This sedition was not really settled until the Grand Prince quarreled with his brothers and the country was threatened by the invasion of Khan Akhmet. Moscow's need to stand more firmly on its western frontier and to eliminate completely the possibility of separate alliances by local powers was bound to be sharpened by these events. In the 1480's the Grand Prince liquidated the rest of the Lithuanian party in Novgorod by means of arrests and deportations, and these measures were then expanded into a broad "revision of persons and lands," which destroyed the boyar class in Novgorod and widely affected other social groups as well, especially its "free persons" and merchants. Other, more reliable elements from the center of the grand principality were settled in Novgorod in their place, and the foundation was laid for the whole system of service landholding and taxation which existed along the Novgorod frontier in later times.

The great task of organizing the Novgorod land led to a basic change in the position of other western regions in Great Russia. For a while Pskov preserved the external forms of its democracy under the direction of Muscovite deputies, whom Pskov received as its princes in accordance with its ancient tradition. We have seen how Vasili II placed Prince Vladimir of Rostov on the throne of Pskov as one of his serving princes, "neither at the request of that city nor in accordance with the ancient tradition." At the beginning of the independent reign of Ivan III, Vladimir was driven out of Pskov "in disgrace" by its leading men. Ivan was angered at this, but agreed to "give them a prince of their choice," and sent Prince Ivan of Zvenigorod, who "kissed the cross to Pskov and all its ancient traditions and rights." Prince Feodor Shuisky succeeded Ivan in 1467, again at the request of Pskov and after kissing the cross to its tradition. His authority as the Grand Prince's deputy was significantly increased, however, with the administration of Pskov's dependent towns and courts being transferred into his hands. Shuisky then began to "do violence" to the people of Pskov, and they petitioned for his replacement by Prince Ivan Obolensky. Instead, the Grand Prince sent Obolensky's brother Iaroslav, who in the presence of a veche assembly ascended the throne of Pskov as the Grand Prince's deputy in February, 1473. Once more there was a kissing of the cross to the Pskov charters and all the city's ancient traditions.

Under the Grand Prince's earlier deputies the men of Pskov had conducted their affairs in accordance with the age-old veche system, and waged war against the Germans with the aid of Muscovite troops. In the 1470's, as the whole national situation was becoming much more complicated and strained, Pskov was exposed to vigorous attack by the Germans and became an important Russian military outpost. Its princely deputies carried on their activities in cooperation with the Grand Prince's representatives in Novgorod, settling various questions of defense, truces, and treaties at meetings sometimes in Pskov and sometimes in Novgorod. This arrangement certainly met the local military needs of the Pskov boyars, but in the course of time Pskov's interests were swallowed up in the general policy of the grand principality. The deputy ruler of Pskov acquired special significance in the eyes of the grand princely power in Moscow, and a reexamination of his status became inevitable. In 1475 Prince Iaroslav set new demands before the men of

Pskov, and the city sent its posadniks to the Grand Prince with letters appealing for his support of its ancient tradition. They could present only the petitions of their local princes, however, which Ivan regarded as having little force, "since they were not the petitions of a grand prince."

Iaroslav had demanded a substantial increase in his revenues at the expense of the income of the Pskov treasury. Pskov was forced to abandon its attempt to defend its "tradition" on the principle of its ancient "charters" and seek refuge in the argument that Prince Iaroslav's demands were simply "unbearable." "We cannot live under them," they said. The whole issue was turned over to the Grand Prince for judgment. He then gave orders for a new allocation of Pskov's revenues and a further broadening of his deputy's judicial powers. This quickly touched off violent protests, and there was an outbreak of popular demonstrations against the deputy and his "courtiers." Ivan recalled Iaroslav and in answer to Pskov's petition sent another member of the Shuisky family to rule in his place. The new deputy turned out to be a very poor military commander and administrator, and Iaroslav soon returned. The city's ancient traditions gradually gave way in the face of these changes, and all military and civil questions, the courts and obligations of citizenship were made subject to control and regulation by the representatives of the grand principality. As in the case of Riazan, the formal incorporation of Pskov in the Muscovite state was to come later, by way of an elimination of the vestiges of power that had long since lost their force and meaning.

The closing decades of the fifteenth century marked another turning point in the history of eastern Europe. Across its length and breadth the old system of international relations was being destroyed and a new one formed in its place. A prominent feature of this process was the rise of the Muscovite state, which had now completed the long task of unifying Great Russia, and an important episode in this work of unification was the "seizure of Tver." The overthrow of the Tver principality was one of the determining factors in and consequences of the complicated situation on Russia's western frontier, and part of the broad plan that Ivan III developed as he sought new support for his struggle with Lithuania. During this period Grand Prince Ivan made a number of alliances with the enemies of the house of Jagiello, including agreements with Stefan, the *voevoda* [37] of Moldavia, whose daughter was married to Ivan's son in 1483; with Matthew Corvin, king of Hungary; with Emperor Frederick III; and with the Roman *curia*, counting on its influence on the policies of the Polish-Lithuanian Union. His closest and most important alliance was with the Crimean khan. It was obviously necessary for Ivan to destroy the support that the Lithuanian state had been finding in the Russian lands midway between Moscow and Lithuania, and to fix his western boundary definitely and with the greatest possible advantage to himself by bringing these wavering Russian powers under his own control.

At the beginning of his reign a treaty with the Grand Prince of Tver, Boris' eleven-year-old son Mikhail, was at least a formal confirmation of the relations that had been developed under Vasili the Blind. It provided for the solidarity of the two grand princes on the principles of equal brotherhood, forbade the Grand Prince of all Russia to interfere in Tver's internal affairs, and guaranteed the right of Grand Prince Mikhail and the Tver princes to have a "clear path" to the land of the Horde. In fact, however, Tver was in a position of real dependence on the ruler of Great Russia, and Tver regiments took part in both of Ivan's campaigns against Novgorod and in the massing of Great Russian armies against Khan Akhmet on the Ugra River. Moscow was in fact forcing Tver to do its will and had begun to swallow up its military and economic resources. In the 1470's a sizable section of Tver's boyar class went over to Moscow.

After 1480 Moscow's suppression of Tver increased noticeably. The fall of Novgorod, the Grand Prince's increasingly dictatorial administration of Pskov, the denial of all claims to the throne on the part of the Grand Prince's brothers, the new treaty with Riazan—all these signs of the growth and concentration of power in Moscow were bound to cause anxiety among those responsible for the political destiny of Tver, no less than Tver's helplessness before Moscow in their disputes over land lying along their borders. Mikhail once more tried to find support in Lithuania, and on the death of his first princess he began negotia-

37. *Voevoda:* a ruler of a district, who dealt with all matters except those pertaining to the church.—TRANS.

tions with Casimir looking to a protective alliance and a new marriage with one of the King's granddaughters. Their treaty reestablished the relations between Tver and Lithuania defined by the treaty of 1449 between Casimir and Grand Prince Boris. This alliance "against all adversaries, with no seizure of one another's land," was obviously aimed at Ivan.

The alarm in Tver echoed the alarm in Lithuania. Following the failure of his grand coalition, Casimir sought to strengthen his ties with Russian powers opposed to Moscow's expansion. At the time of his treaty with Tver he also renewed his pact with the "upland princes" of Vorotynsk, Odoevo, and Novosil, binding them to faithful service in his name. None of these efforts was successful. Ivan learned of these negotiations, and the rapid advance of his "border force" on Tver brought Mikhail to submission. A new treaty placed the grand principality of Tver definitely within the Muscovite political system. Mikhail kissed the cross "to his master [gospodin] and elder brother Grand Prince Ivan of all Russia and to his son Ivan also, as his elder brother." He acknowledged himself as equal to the Grand Prince's younger brother Andrei, laid aside his kissing of the cross to King Casimir, and bound himself not to have any dealings with him without Ivan's knowledge, nor to go over to his side, nor to "withdraw in any matter" from the grand princes of Moscow, and promised to send military forces in campaigns undertaken by the Grand Prince's army.

The grand principality of Tver still stood as a separate and distinct domain alongside the votchina of the grand princely family of Moscow (with its rule over the domains of Moscow, Novgorod, and Pskov), but it was obviously no longer able to maintain this separation. One after another the Tver princes withdrew and entered the service of Moscow—first Andrei of Mikulin, then Osip of Dorogobuzh, and then the Tver boyars. The ground was cut from under Mikhail's feet, and his attempt to renew relations with King Casimir led to his final and complete downfall. The Tver courier was intercepted. Refusing Mikhail's repeated requests for peace on the Grand Prince's terms, Ivan marched on Tver with a huge force. Abandoned by almost all his boyars, Prince Mikhail fled to Lithuania and Tver kissed the cross in submission to the Grand Prince of all Russia. Ivan decided not to abolish the grand princely throne in Tver completely, and gave it to his son Ivan. When Ivan III departed for Moscow, his son "came to live in the city of Tver," received the homage of the Tver boyars who had been in Mikhail's service, and issued them his own deeds of grant to their votchinas in the Tver land.

The Tver grand principality had become a votchina of the Muscovite sovereigns, and yet it remained distinct from their Muscovite state. Signs of this distinction were preserved even after the death of the younger Grand Prince Ivan—in the special office and title of the Tver chamberlain, in the enrollment of persons subject to state service "according to the Tver register," and finally in the actually fantastic yet formally instituted restoration of the Tver grand principality as the domain of the converted Tatar Semeon Bekbulatovich in the reign of Ivan the Terrible. At first the preservation of the old ruling and serving classes was a real convenience, simplifying the handling of Tver's resources and increasing Moscow's influence in border disputes with the Tver boyars.

The consolidation of Moscow's power in Tver naturally increased Muscovite influence also on the western frontier, and the undefined position of the Chernigov prince could not continue for long. Moscow's attack on Chernigov was hastened by the increasing confusion of relationships within the Russo-Lithuanian state. Its eastern districts were still ruled by minor hereditary princes serving both Lithuania and Moscow as the occasion offered. These minor princes ruled either their own inherited domains or lands granted to them as votchinas by the Lithuanian grand prince. Some of them were direct descendants of Rurik and native to the Chernigov land; some were Russified descendants of Gedymin; some were Muscovite exiles driven across the Lithuanian frontier as a result of disturbances in Great Russia. In accordance with the views of the time, the possession of a princely domain as a votchina led to the admission that such a prince had the right to move from the service of one grand prince to another, not only personally, but also with his votchina. In the fifteenth century the grand principality of Lithuania was trying to strengthen the ties of these lands to the Russo-Lithuanian state, and in its treaties with these votchina princes there was an agreement that they "would not separate their land from the Lithuanian grand principality," especially in the event of a throne left vacant. In Lithuania's treaties with Moscow, Tver, and Riazan it was stipulated that "service princes must not be received with their votchinas." The restored power of the Lithuanian grand prince and the union with Poland under Casimir threatened the minor west Russian princes no less than the growth of Moscow threatened the udel or votchina princes of Great Russia. The Russified Lithuanian princes were the first to rebel against this new oppression by King Casimir. Mikhail, the exiled hereditary prince of Kiev, together with Prince Feodor of Belaia and the Golshansky family, secretly sought support in Moscow and "thought to cut themselves off from the Grand Prince of Lithuania and settle along the river Berezina." Mikhail and Prince Golshansky were seized and executed in August of 1481, while Feodor escaped to Moscow.

This "conspiracy among the princes," about which our sources give so little information, prompted a whole series of defections to the side of Moscow in the 1480's and 1490's, involving both princes and their votchinas. Lithuania's internal troubles were thus compounded, with the result that Great Russia advanced to the southwest. One after another the princes of Vorotynsk turned to Moscow, knowing that they could get no strong protection from Casimir, and then, supported by Moscow, they joined the princes of Odoev in attacking their neighbors. Apparently many of these defections to Moscow occurred as a result of "grievances" stemming from border disputes, as in the case of the Tver boyars. The princes of Peremysl, Belev, Mesets, and Viazma transferred to Moscow, and Ivan received them "with their votchinas." He defended them against the forces of the Lithuanian grand prince, and in the peace treaty of 1494 won control not only over these princes, but also over others whose votchinas had been overrun in the course of his military operations. In 1500 Prince Semeon of Belaia came over to Moscow, and after him Prince Semeon of Mozhaisk, with the lands of Chernigov, Starodub, Gomel, and Liubek, as well as Prince Vasili (a descendant of Dmitri Shemiaka) with Rylsk and Novgorod Seversk. The peace treaty of 1503 secured these acquisitions also to Moscow. Although all these agreements were entered into on the basis of udel-votchina principles and concepts, the reference to the obsolete right of a prince's removal with votchina had degenerated into a diplomatic trick, and the whole struggle between Lithuania and Moscow for the Chernigov principalities can be viewed as an aspect of the new national policy of the Muscovite sovereign, skillfully constructed on a modified votchina theory and designed to lay the foundation for his claims to the entire inheritance of the princely house of Rurik from the earliest times. In the end this struggle will carry us beyond the limits of the formation of the Great Russian state, with the seizure of territories that had never been organically connected with the grand principality of Vladimir and Great Novgorod. This process had its beginning in the struggle, under Ivan III, for Smolensk.

The unification of the vast territory of Great Russia under the immediate rule of the grand prince of Moscow gave rise to a unique and complex theory regarding the nature of this sovereignty. The unification of the Moscow otchina with the lands of the grand principality of Vladimir (in the narrow sense) had led to the theory of their unity as a single hereditary state in the hands of the grand prince of all Russia. It must be said that the theory of the unity of Moscow with Novgorod and Pskov developed in a somewhat different way. Their inclusion within the grand princely domains complicated the whole notion of the grand principality. In his official documents Ivan III spoke of this principality as a threefold domain, including Moscow, Novgorod, and Pskov. But then the term "grand principality" still preserved its earlier meaning, indicating the Moscow-Vladimir region without Novgorod and Pskov, these latter being seen as special otchinas of the grand prince. When alongside Novgorod and Pskov another otchina was added, that of Tver, Ivan III began to speak of "all my grand principalities." In the light of the political theories of the time, what was in the foreground was not the unity of his territory, but the plenitude of grand princely sovereignty over all its various parts; not the gathering of territories, but the gathering of power. Just how Ivan III conceived of this plenitude of votchina (hereditary) power is reflected vividly in an episode involving the people of Pskov in 1499, following the death of his eldest son, Ivan, in Tver, at a time when he was still undecided on the question of his successor. In 1498 Ivan III had bestowed the grand princely rule of Vladimir, Moscow, and Novgorod on Prince Dmitri of Suzdal (his grandson). A year later he "made a conferral to his son Vasili, naming him grand prince and giving him Great Novgorod and the grand principality of Pskov." A special envoy from Moscow brought the news to the Pskov boyars. Their fears were immediately aroused, and a party of Pskov envoys came before the two grand princes, Ivan and Dmitri, with a petition "that they hold their otchina according to the tradition, and that whoever would be grand prince in Moscow would also be their sovereign." Ivan angrily replied: "Do you think that I am not free to choose between Dmitri and my son? I will give the principality to whichever one I wish." Ivan evidently understood the Pskov petition as an attempt to interfere in the struggle between the rival parties supporting Dmitri and Vasili in the grand princely court, and did not see its bearing on the question of the unity of power and state territory. He therefore asserted his votchina right to dispose of his grand principalities in any way he wished, either in part or as a whole.

This story is illuminating. Not even Tsar Ivan the Terrible could add anything to this as an expression of the idea of hereditary autocracy. This plenitude of sovereign power was not elevated as a general principle, however; it still bore the stamp of Ivan's personal character. He did not explicitly pass this absolute power on to his son. His riad established udel domains for Vasili's younger brothers (Iuri, Dmitri, Semeon, and Andrei); these udels were hereditary domains with their own independent administrative systems, and, most important, by the terms of their father's testament they were beyond the reach of the Grand Prince. Ivan also gave his sons shares in Moscow and Tver and fixed the amount of each one's payment "toward the Horde's outlay" and "the Tatar expenses." Thus in many ways the traditional manner of defining interprincely relations was retained.

The treaty between his sons Vasili and Iuri, which was composed at his command at the same time as his testament, defined Vasili as "the master and eldest brother" of the younger princes. Grand Prince Ivan had bestowed "all his grand principalities"

—Vladimir, Moscow, Novgorod, Pskov, and Tver—on his eldest son, Vasili. There was still no established term to describe these domains as a unit, but the victory of the principle of monarchy was reflected in the fact that there was no mention in Ivan's testament of a division into udels of the grand princely otchina itself. This was not the dividing up of a joint inheritance, but a distribution of bequests to the members of the grand princely family, a distribution determined not by the traditional rights of these princely sons, but by their father's personal wish. The ancient family law had lost its force. A vacant udel would now revert entirely to the Grand Prince. The udel princes had lost their character as participants in the Grand Prince's political power. They were forbidden to coin money in their own udels. Their judicial rights (at least in the villages around Moscow) were limited, since their clerks now had to make reports to the Grand Prince's deputies. There was no longer any mention of a possible termination of the Grand Prince's right to exact tribute from their domains. All traces of the udel-votchina system were obliterated by the demand that the younger princes "listen to" the Grand Prince "in all things." But the new system of absolute autocratic monarchy was not yet constructed in law; it had not yet developed to the point of abolishing the obsolete formulae of the father's riad. The text of Ivan's testament still made use of traditional phrases, but this terminology was inconsistent with the new order that had now come into being.

IV.

The unification of power over the whole of Great Russia in the hands of a single heir to all the grand principalities had elevated him to the position of "sovereign over all the sovereigns of the Russian land." This apt phrase of a contemporary scribe indicates the tendency to accept the will of the sovereign grand prince as taking precedence over all other ruling and administrative rights that had developed in the life of Great Russia during the udel-votchina period. Thus all princely rights were now regarded as subordinate to and originating in the will of the grand prince. This concentration of absolute power in the grand prince and

the new political self-determination of Great Russia were inseparably bound up with radical changes in the Russian metropolitan see. Its breakdown into two local churches had become inevitable; the church of Great Russia now existed alongside the church of West Russia. Equally inevitable was the final nationalization of the former as an ecclesiastical-political institution within the Muscovite state.

After the death of Metropolitan Photius, the ecclesiastical disorder in Moscow accompanying the consecration of the Greek prelate Isidore to the metropolitan see and then the whole matter of the Florentine Union had resulted in a fifteen-year period of strain and confusion in the Russian see. Isidore was deposed in the autumn of 1441, and Metropolitan Designate Jonas then became the church's administrative head. Even apart from the perplexing ecclesiastical questions raised by the Florentine Union, Great Russia's internal struggle and its complicated international relations had shown the need for a decisive attempt to secure the national character and political reliability of the metropolitan see. The authorities in Moscow decided to elect and consecrate a metropolitan in Russia, but from the outset efforts were made to take this action with the consent of the church in Constantinople.

The efforts to win the patriarch's approval of this action were unsuccessful, however, and not without hesitation and disagreement the Muscovite powers finally determined to consecrate their own metropolitan at a council of Russian bishops. Jonas' enthronement took place on December 15, 1448. The Muscovite character of the metropolitan see had been restored. Metropolitan Jonas now revived and continued the tradition of Metropolitans Peter and Alexei, and the tradition was given new life by the solemn and triumphant canonization of Alexei. Later Jonas himself became the third saint in the Russian see. In the memorials of its three saints Moscow has glorified and given sacred meaning to the great steps in the development of its ecclesiastical policy and to its final triumph. Beginning with Jonas the metropolitan see entered organically into the structure of the Muscovite state. The metropolitan now stood at the head of a national local church, at the price of a temporary break with the patriarch

ate in Constantinople. The Russian church survived as a lawful jurisdiction in the Greek church by maintaining ties with the patriarch of Jerusalem.

Metropolitan Jonas succeeded in keeping the West Russian dioceses under his jurisdiction at first. His consecration coincided with peace negotiations between the grand princes of Moscow and Lithuania. The question of the unity of the metropolitan see was raised in these meetings, and in the beginning of 1451 Jonas received Casimir's consent to occupy "the throne of the metropolitan of Kiev and all Russia." In 1458, however, the consecration of Grigori (a protégé of Isidore) by Pope Calixtus III as metropolitan of Russo-Lithuania marked the beginning of the final division of the see. Dominated by the power of the grand prince, the Great Russian see lost the support it once had in Constantinople as well as its other wide-ranging political connections, and began to live its own provincial "Great Russian" life. But it still dreamed of recovering its earlier significance as the church of all Russia, through the subjection to Moscow of the Russian regions included in the Polish-Lithuanian agreement. There was a merging of the destinies and interests of church and state in Great Russia. The fall of Constantinople ended the waning authority of the Greek church and transformed the Russian church into a truly autocephalous communion. In this same period Russia's independence from the Tatars had become increasingly effective, and this process was completed under Ivan III with the consolidation of what was in fact the autocratic Great Russian state.

Metropolitan Jonas was consecrated by Russian bishops on the nomination of the Grand Prince, who acted on the advice of his mother and brothers as well as all the Russian princes, clergy, and boyars. After Jonas, succession to the see was decided formally by the preceding metropolitan, but in fact by the grand prince. In the new political conditions of Great Russia the significance of the metropolitan see was not at all what it had been under Peter and Alexei. Regardless of the degree of his own personal influence, the Russian metropolitan was now definitely in the service of the secular power and an obedient instrument of its policies. All of Jonas' pastoral activity was closely bound up with the aims of the Grand Prince. In his own name

and in the name of the sacred council the Metropolitan issued
letters calling now for the repression of the rebellious Dmitri
Shemiaka, now for the subduing of the restless Viatka boyars,
now for greater submission on the part of the free city of Pskov
to its "patrimonial prince." The authority of his sacred office
gave the Metropolitan an exalted position in Muscovite society,
but since he had been chosen by the Grand Prince from a
subject class that lived at the mercy of the Grand Prince's
sovereign power, his position was without any firm legal guarantees. Just as elevation to the metropolitan see in accordance with
the canonical principles of conciliar action had been reduced
to the simple execution of a decision made by the secular power,
so this power could bring the metropolitan to a supposedly
voluntary resignation of his office or even deposition through its
control of a submissive episcopal council.

Metropolitan Geronti, the successor of Metropolitans The-
odosius and Philip, felt the full weight of his subservient position.
In a dispute over a procession with banners and crosses that had
been arranged in connection with the consecration of the newly
rebuilt Cathedral of the Assumption in Moscow (i.e., in a matter
that was purely ecclesiastical and liturgical), Ivan's personal
whims caused new churches to stand unconsecrated for over
two years after the Metropolitan was forced to flee with his
staff into a monastery. The affair ended in compromise, since,
although the Grand Prince did let the Metropolitan return to
Moscow in the face of support given to him by almost all the
Russian bishops, he still refused to allow any formal ecclesiastical
settlement of the disputed question.

Similar pressure was exerted in a dispute between Bishop
Vassian of Rostov and Metropolitan Geronti over the removal
of the St. Cyril Monastery in Beloozero from Vassian's jurisdiction. Ivan acted as a dictatorial head of the church's council, and
as in the case of Geronti's elevation to the metropolitan see, the
council's canonical authority in no way lessened the church's
dependence on the secular power. The Grand Prince "sanctioned" the convening of the council, provided it with a place
of meeting, entered imperiously into its proceedings, and gave
its decision legal force by his own ratification. In the 1480's
Ivan tried to take advantage of Geronti's temporary withdrawal

into a monastery due to illness as an occasion for replacing him with another man, and "refused to accept him" when he decided to return to his see. Geronti "did not abandon his see willingly," and was taken by force on the "many occasions" that he escaped the monastery. Only a refusal to pursue the undignified controversy on the part of the Grand Prince's candidate forced Ivan to restore Geronti to his see. These incidents were in themselves trivial, but they were characteristic of the time, and they shed light on the Grand Prince's intent to establish absolute patrimonial sovereignty even in the realm of the church's internal administration. The Grand Prince was not always successful in these tests of strength. There were occasions when he was made to yield to the sanctity of the metropolitan office or to canon law and tradition, and there were times when he had to assume the role of the church's defender and patron. Both Russian society and the Russian church faced a long process of reeducation before they were to enter fully into the new order.

The grand principality occupied a similar position in relation to the church in the all-important and long vexing question of ecclesiastical lands. Let us consider only certain basic aspects of this question, insofar as it was related to the general process of the gathering of power.

In the Great Russia of the udel period, as well as in the later Muscovite era, it is not quite accurate to speak of "church lands." A. S. Pavlov has said: "The custom of landholding developed in our church not by way of any canonical or formal decree, but following the national pattern of votchina law." Votchinas belonged not to the church, but to separate ecclesiastical institutions—to the metropolitan see, or to an episcopal see, or to monasteries or individual churches—and the superiors or governing bodies of these institutions were the fully competent rulers of such votchina domains. The great domains of the metropolitan see existed as a distinct, separate, and complex unit within the whole body of Great Russian land, alongside other similar domains. The spiritual heads of the episcopal and monastic votchinas had their own individual titles and deeds of ownership, and as great rulers of patrimonial domains they stood in a direct and immediate relationship to the secular power rather than to the metropolitan. Thus from the legal, sociological viewpoint there was a genuine similarity between the landholding of ecclesiastical institutions and that of the boyars, and this similarity had important consequences. Although the canonical regulations concerning church domains did not correspond either in principle or in practice to the provisions affecting boyar landholdings, nevertheless the "spiritual sovereigns" of these domains were treated in the same way as boyars and free men serving in the grand prince's court, and like them looked to the grand principality for aid and protection. In the period of the breakdown of power into local grand principalities, the bishops and abbots were drawn by common interest into local political and social groupings, and by this very fact into opposition to the center of grand princely power in Great Russia and to the metropolitan see—to the extent that the latter was allied with the grand prince. Like the secular votchinas of the boyars, their votchinas were "an institution having not only territorial but also administrative significance, and they were one of the fundamental elements in the state structure" of every principality in the Russian middle ages (N. P. Pavlov-Silvansky). What might be called ruling rights were an organic feature of both religious and secular landholdings in this era.

As early as 1857 K. A. Nevolin noted the special role played in the development of grand princely power by the princes' practice of issuing charters of grant designed to strengthen and define the ruling rights and domains of the great landholders. These charters did not create a new form of law, but simply confirmed an order of things that had come into being "spontaneously and in accordance with the common law." "The rights of immunity, for example, Pavlov-Silvansky wrote, "stemmed not from the individual charters of the princes, but from the common law." But as Nevolin has also noted, the acceptance of these charters carried an inevitable threat to the legal position of the large landhold.

The old order was bound to find itself in opposition to a new, well-established, and centralized princely power. It could not, however, be suddenly abolished. The way was opened for its abolition by *neposudnye* charters.[38] What had previously belonged to a votchina ruler by virtue of votchina law was now secured to the large landholder by a charter granting as it were a special privilege.

38. *Neposudnye charters:* charters issued and having force outside the jurisdiction of courts of law; the acts of a sovereign power.—TRANS.

The acceptance of such a charter not only confirmed the specific rights and privileges of its recipient (whether religious or secular), but also made these rights so dependent on the grand prince's arbitrary will that the votchina law of the great landholders was gradually converted into a law wholly determined by the grand principality. The grand princes developed their own version of the votchina law out of this practical dependence of votchina tradition on their own consent, first in the provision for revision of charters whenever they were renewed, and later by the institution of general decrees. This tendency gathered momentum when the Grand Prince of Moscow emerged as the hereditary sovereign of the whole of Great Russia and began to acknowledge only those charters that had been issued by the "grand princes" and reject those issued by "local princes," and when he began to assume absolute control over all the forces of the land in the difficult task of organizing them to serve the needs of his own expanding "sovereign rule." As these charters began to serve as the legal basis and proof of landhold rights, they led to a denial both of the independent status of such rights and of their power to restrict the right of the sovereign. This new concept of charter was obviously connected with the grand principality's desire to free itself from the limitations of the age-old common law and complete its task of building an absolute autocracy.

The chronicles have preserved the story of an incident that clearly shows the direction of Ivan's thought as well as the first sign of opposition to it on the part of the Muscovite boyars. This is the story of Prince Ivan Obolensky, the Grand Prince's deputy in the Veliki Luki region. The Grand Prince removed Obolensky from his position as deputy in 1470 after the people of the land petitioned him "concerning forced sales and other grievances." The Grand Prince judged Obolensky in the presence of the people, and where he was found guilty of the charges brought against him he was ordered to pay damages, and in fact did pay them. But the Grand Prince also "commanded the payment of additional sums" without trial. The chronicler explains this by saying that the people, relying on the Grand Prince's support, had exaggerated their claims for damages, "and where he had taken little, they made complaints about many things." Obolensky refused to bow to this injustice and left the Grand Prince to join the Grand Prince's brother, Prince Boris of Volok. Boris answered Ivan's demand that Obolensky be turned over to the Grand Prince by saying: "Whoever has some charge to make against him, let him bring his charges into court and let justice be done." This story is usually quoted as an illustration of the struggle to abolish the right of withdrawal, but it has another and more important meaning. Surely Prince Boris' protest against the subsequent seizure of Obolensky by the Grand Prince's men—"Now violence will be done to those who separate from the Grand Prince, and he will seize them without trial"—makes it clear that the whole incident took place in the context of a dispute not over the right of withdrawal, but over the demand that the case be decided in the courts and according to law rather than by the whim of the Grand Prince.

To my knowledge this is the earliest recorded instance of a protest against an arbitrary grand princely decision, as opposed to the traditional determination of a case in the grand prince's court "with the boyars of the accused present." Obolensky's withdrawal was only a way of escaping such arbitrary judgment and finding sanctuary with another prince. Both of these factors supporting the freedom of the boyars—the right of withdrawal and the existence of powerful princely rivals—disappeared with the unification of Great Russia under the monarchical authority of the Muscovite sovereign. Angrily punishing them for their rebelliousness and even their passive resistance, Ivan reduced his former free servants to the position of "born servants" or "state serfs."

The complete subjugation of the great landowners to the grand prince's hereditary sovereign power acquired a deeper significance when questions were raised concerning the control of those lands that constituted the inner core of the Muscovite state. Ivan III's struggle for these territories became more and more aggressive with the subjugation of each additional independent principality. As we have seen, the joining of these lands to his own votchina domains also raised doubts concerning the charters issued by local powers who no longer had authority to grant them. In short, it had shaken the accepted legal foundations of Russian life and had opened up the possibility of their revision. Behind the fragmentary evidence provided by our sources we can see the broad scope and intensive nature of the Grand Prince's program of "revision of lands and persons" and "deportation," in which whole segments of the population were uprooted from their homelands and flung into new regions, to be "settled" there in accordance with a decree of the state and as dependent servants of its sovereign.

A direct and consistent plan to seize votchina control of the whole of Great Russia might well have led to the immediate overthrow of the privileged landholding class at this time, such as happened in the terrible years of the Oprichnina. This did not happen, however. In the turbulent period of the formation of the Muscovite state, Ivan III stood too much in need of support from the strong boyar forces serving in his name to take such a step. A compromise was made between grand princely power and boyar privileges, a compromise that was arrived at to a large extent in the disputes over ecclesiastical lands. The Grand Prince's need to extend his power over the Great Russian territories led first not to a final breakdown of boyar land-holdings, but to a secularization of the vast domains of ecclesiastical institutions. Here the stumbling block was not the "waywardness" of a powerful and influential class, but the church's assignment of domains to its "spiritual sovereigns" and the deep-rooted independence of the episcopate. As it happened, however, the Grand Prince's seizure of episcopal and monastic lands in the Novgorod region did not provoke any fundamental objection at first. On the contrary, Metropolitan Jonas and his successors vigorously supported and carried out Moscow's policies in Novgorod. With the consent of Metropolitan Semeon, Ivan "seized the ecclesiastical votchinas in Novgorod [in 1500] and distributed these monastic and ecclesiastical lands to the sons of the boyars as their estates." We can see from the Novgorod court records that much more land was taken from the Novgorod monasteries at this time than in the earlier period of confiscation (1478), even from those that the Grand Prince had previously spared, "not taking land from them since they were poor and had little." A. S. Pavlov has noted that there are "developments in other regions that remind us of the fate of the ecclesiastical lands in Novgorod." On the basis of his study, Pavlov has con-

cluded that Ivan III had in mind a general revision of all ecclesiastical landholdings, with the same reason offered as had been given
to the men of Novgorod: that such lands were in fact the property of the sovereign grand prince and had only been "assigned"
to the ecclesiastical institutions.

Eventually the church's leaders protested the Grand Prince's
program of secularization, however, and Ivan had to yield here
too, just as he had retreated from the massive revision of boyar
landholdings. Instead of a radical and hasty overthrow of
established structures, we see a slower and more gradual process
of reorganization. But the questions of both ecclesiastical and
boyar landholdings had been raised sharply. In his correspondence
with Kurbsky, Tsar Ivan the Terrible will mention his grandfather's "decree," by which many votchinas were taken from
boyars permanently and without possibility of redistribution, and
the *Stoglav* (The Hundred Chapters) will refer to decrees made
by both Ivan III and Vasili III prohibiting the assignment of
votchinas to monasteries. Although there are only a few such
references to controversies over land in the fifteenth century,
they do give us some indication of the urgency of this issue
in the reign of Ivan III. Ecclesiastical and secular landholdings
were just as much a matter of dispute at that time as the question
of the grand prince's hereditary right to the grand principality
(in the controversy with Pskov) or the question of the absolute
nature of his power (in the negotiations with Novgorod).

The unification of Great Russia was accomplished by the
liquidation of all local independence in favor of a single grand
princely power in Moscow. Although destined to oblivion, these
local powers were still the bearers of the "ancient traditions and
rights" that were the foundations of Great Russian life. Their
fall shattered the deep-rooted traditions of the land. Faced with
the task of building a new order of life on the ruins of the old
regime, the grand princely power sought not only unity, but
complete freedom to dispose of the country's forces as it wished.
The Muscovite monarchy was the forerunner of the Muscovite
autocracy.

Conclusions

The two basic processes in the political evolution of Great Russia in the thirteenth to fifteenth centuries—the fragmentation of territory and power, and the simultaneous movement toward strengthening the political unity of the land—did not follow one another but ran parallel, held in constant tension and interacting so as to mold the structure of the grand principality of Vladimir as it passed through a series of historical crises.

II.

The formation of minor votchina principalities, through the breakdown of the hereditary domains within the various lines descending from Vsevolod III, was a rather late development, and it was directly connected with the loss of power experienced by the lesser ruling princes in the face of increasing grand princely sovereignty concentrated in the hands of the princes of Moscow.

III.

Originally an udel was a prince's share in a common votchina possessed jointly with his brothers, and received by him in accordance with the provisions of his father's testament. The basic features of an udel domain—its hereditary nature, the absence of the right to dispose of one by testament, the return of a vacant udel into the joint domain of the family and its subdivision then among the surviving brothers, the possibility of its partial redivision in order to preserve a balance in the size of shares held by surviving brothers—made it similar to peasant land-holding by shares, with which it also had in common the element of instability, the tendency to break away into a completely separate unit or votchina.

IV.

From the second half of the fourteenth century the term udel acquired a new meaning. It became simply a domain granted by the grand prince to a lesser prince "as his udel and votchina." The term "udel prince" is encountered only in the literature of the sixteenth century, and then only with the meaning of "a hereditary prince of a family estate."

V.

The renunciation of udels and votchina principalities in the testa-ments of princes appeared first in the period of decline in udel domain, as a way of consolidating land and power seized by the grand prince. Other forms of semivoluntary surrender of udels and votchina principalities—for example, *kupli* (purchases)—had the same significance, as violations of the law of udel domain and indications of its replacement by the grand prince's absolute sovereignty.

VI.

The territory of the Muscovite state was created by a merging of the Moscow votchina and the grand principality of Vladimir into a single votchina ruled by the Muscovite sovereign.

VII.

The unification of Great Russia under the dominion of the grand princes of Moscow was accomplished not by way of a gathering together of lands, but by a gathering of power, as a development and realization of the ancient patriarchal tradition regarding the grand prince's rule "in his father's place."

VIII.

The concentration of power in the hands of the Muscovite sovereign was achieved by way of the collapse in fact and the denial in principle of the ancient princely law in favor of the principle of hereditary autocracy.

Index